Studies on Entrepreneurship, Structural Change and Industrial Dynamics

The ‘Studies on Entrepreneurship, Structural Change and Industrial Dynamics’ series showcases exceptional scholarly work being developed on the still unexplored complex relationship between entrepreneurship, structural change and industrial dynamics, by addressing structural and technological determinants of the evolutionary pathway of innovative and entrepreneurial activity.

The series invites proposals based on sound research methodologies and approaches to the above topics. Volumes in the series may include research monographs and edited/contributed works.

More information about this series at http://www.springer.com/series/15330

José Manuel Saiz-Álvarez • João Leitão •
Jesús Manuel Palma-Ruiz
Editors

Entrepreneurship and Family Business Vitality

Surviving and Flourishing in the Long Term

Springer

Editors
José Manuel Saiz-Álvarez
EGADE Business School-Tecnologico
de Monterrey
Zapopan, Jalisco, Mexico

João Leitão
University of Beira Interior
Covilhã, Portugal

Jesús Manuel Palma-Ruiz
Universidad Autónoma de Chihuahua
Chihuahua, Mexico

ISSN 2511-2023 ISSN 2511-2031 (electronic)
Studies on Entrepreneurship, Structural Change and Industrial Dynamics
ISBN 978-3-030-15525-4 ISBN 978-3-030-15526-1 (eBook)
https://doi.org/10.1007/978-3-030-15526-1

This Springer imprint is published by the registered company Springer Nature Switzerland AG.
The registered company address is: Gewerbestrasse 11, 6330 Cham, Switzerland

Acknowledgments

To our families for their encouragement while preparing this book, and to all those who have made the publication of this book possible.

We extend this gratitude to the prestigious publishing house Springer Nature Switzerland AG, and especially to Prashanth Mahagaonkar—Senior Editor, Ruth Milewski—Senior Editorial Assistant Business/Economics, David Bull—Vice-President, and Eric Schmitt—Managing Director, and all the Springer Nature Development Team.

We thank all the 36 authors who have accepted to participate in this book for their excellent work and collaboration and are located in universities and research centers across America (Brazil, Chile, Colombia, Ecuador, and Mexico) and Europe (Austria, Belgium, Germany, Italy, Portugal, Spain, and the United Kingdom).

We acknowledge the commitment to research of our academic institutions, EGADE Business School-Tecnologico de Monterrey (Mexico), the Catholic University of Santiago de Guayaquil (Ecuador), Autonomous University of Manizales (Colombia), Universidad Autónoma de Chihuahua (Mexico), the University of Beira Interior (Portugal), and the University of Lisboa (Portugal), where we work or are visiting professors, as well as the support received from the National Council of Science and Technology (CONACYT) in Mexico, and the Mexican Academy of Sciences.

Finally, we also express our gratitude to all the authors whose works were submitted but not accepted for publication. We encourage them to persist in this captivating, and highly demanding, world of research and to strive for the diffusion of knowledge to benefit the global society.

José Manuel Saiz-Álvarez
Jesús Manuel Palma-Ruiz
João Leitão

Contents

Contributors

About the Editors

José Manuel Saiz-Álvarez is Ph.D. (Hons) in Economics and Business Administration, from the Autonomous University of Madrid (Spain), and Ph.D. (Hons.) in Sociology, from the Pontifical University of Salamanca (Spain). He is now a research professor at EGADE Business School-Tecnologico de Monterrey (Mexico) and visiting professor at the Catholic University of Santiago de Guayaquil (Ecuador), Autonomous University of Manizales (Colombia), and St Francis Xavier University of Chuquisaca (Bolivia). He was Director of the BA Doctoral Program, Nebrija University (Spain), and Director of the Master in Microcredits and Social Inclusion, Pontifical University of Salamanca (Spain and Guatemala). He is member of GEM Jalisco (Mexico) and Academic Leader at Tecnologico de Monterrey (Mexico); holds Diploma of recognition, the House of Representatives of the Capitol of Puerto Rico; and was Honorary Professor, Autonomous University of Madrid (Spain). He belongs to the National System of Researchers of the National Council for Science and Technology (CONACYT) (Mexico) and the Mexican Academy of Sciences, and is officially accredited in Spain by the National Agency for the Evaluation of Quality and Accreditation (ANECA). He has extensively published with prestigious international publishers on entrepreneurship, family business, labor market, innovation, economic integration, and outsourcing.

Jesús Manuel Palma-Ruiz is an Associate Professor at the Universidad Autónoma de Chihuahua (Mexico). He holds an International Ph.D. (Hons.) in Business and Entrepreneurial Management with application to SMEs, entrepreneurship, and family firms from the University of Cantabria (Spain). He belongs to the National System of Researchers of the National Council for Science and Technology (CONACYT) (Mexico). He is a former scholar for the Walton International Program (USA), Carolina Foundation (Spain), and CONACYT (Mexico and Spain). With more than 15 years of professional experience in both private and public sectors, he has been a professor of business for graduate and undergraduate levels at Tecnológico de Monterrey and Universidad Autónoma de Chihuahua (Mexico), collaborating in business incubation, family business, and technology parks programs. He has been visiting professor and Santander's Bank Chair of Family Business Coordinator at the University of Cantabria (Spain). He collaborates with research groups in Spain and Mexico, where he has been involved in the International Urban Cooperation region-to-region Program (EU), GEM and GUESSS projects, among others. He has published in scientific journals on topics related to entrepreneurship and family business and coedited books with Springer and IGI Global.

João Leitão holds a Habilitation in Technological Change and Entrepreneurship, University of Lisbon, Instituto Superior Técnico, and a Ph.D. in Economics, University of Beira Interior (Portugal). Since 1999, he is an Assistant Professor (tenured) in Economics and Entrepreneurship. He is an associate researcher of the CEG-IST, University of Lisbon (Portugal), and external research fellow of the Instituto Multidisciplinar de Empresa, University of Salamanca (Spain). He is author and coauthor of scientific books on benchmarking, clusters, cooperation networks, entrepreneurship, entrepreneurship education, innovation, competitiveness, public policies, and quality of life. He won the 2018 National Prize of Innovation based on Knowledge and the Best Paper Award of the Interdisciplinary European Conference in Entrepreneurial Research—IECER 2012. His research work has been published in several leading journals. He is member of distinguished editorial and reviewer boards of indexed international journals.

About the Authors

Sebastián Aparicio is an Assistant Professor of Entrepreneurship at Durham University Business School (UK). He is also a Researcher at the Centre for University Entrepreneurship (CIEU-UAB) (Spain). He has a Ph.D. (International Doctorate in Entrepreneurship and Management—IDEM) from the Department of Business at Universitat Autònoma de Barcelona (UAB—Spain). His research is focused on the link between entrepreneurship and economic development.

Unai Arzubiaga is an Assistant Professor and researcher in Business and Management at the University of the Basque Country (UPV/EHU). He received his International Ph.D. in Management from the University of the Basque Country in 2016 with a predoctoral research stay in Lancaster University (UK) in 2014. He has an MBA in Leadership Development by the University of Deusto (Spain). He performed consulting services between 2006 and 2009 in Deloitte. His current research is focused on the topics of entrepreneurship and innovation, family businesses, strategy, and corporate governance. He has published articles in journals such as *Journal of Business Venturing*, *International Entrepreneurship and Management Journal*, *Australian Journal of Management*, *International Business Review*, and *Review of Managerial Science*, among others, and is also a reviewer.

Danny C. Barbery-Montoya is B.Sc. in Economics (specialized in marketing) at the Escuela Superior Politécnica del Litoral (Ecuador), Master's in Business Administration of Escuela de Posgrados de Administración de Empresas (Ecuador), Master's in Creation and Business Management from Nebrija University (Spain), Ph.D. in Business Sciences from Nebrija University (Spain), and Professor at Universidad de Especialidades Espíritu Santo (Ecuador).

Ismael Barros-Contreras is a Senior Lecturer at the Austral University (Chile). He has been the School Director of Commercial Engineering and the Head of the Management Department of the Austral University (Chile). He has been a Visiting Scholar at the University of Valladolid (Spain) and Visiting Researcher of the Centre for Family Business at Lancaster University (UK). His research areas are strategic management and family business.

Jonathan Bauweraerts is an Assistant Professor in the Control, Accounting, Risk Management and Entrepreneurship Department at the University of Mons–Warocqué School of Business and Economics (Belgium). His main research fields are entrepreneurship and corporate governance in the family business context.

Jana Bövers is a Scientific Associate in the Faculty of Business Administration and Economics, endowed chair for business administration, in particular management of family business leadership at Bielefeld University (Germany).

John Eddson Burgos-Burgos is an Assistant Professor in the Academic Unit of Business Sciences at the Technical University of Machala (Ecuador). He is currently a candidate of Ph.D. in Economics, Business, and Legal Sciences from the University of Almeria (Spain). He holds a Master's in Business Administration, Diploma in University Teaching, and B.Sc. in Accounting and Auditing, and he is Public Accountant and Commercial Engineer.

Julen Castillo-Apraiz is a Lecturer in Management in the Economía Financiera II (Economía de la Empresa y Comercialización) Department, Faculty of Economics and Business (Sarriko) at the University of the Basque Country UPV/EHU (Spain), and International Ph.D. from the University of the Basque Country UPV/EHU (Spain). His current research interests include strategic management, quality management, corporate social responsibility, new trends in learning, and research methods (e.g., partial least squares, and structural equation modeling, PLS-SEM).

Francesca Maria Cesaroni is an Associate Professor of Business Administration in the Department of Economics, Society and Politics at the University of Urbino Carlo Bo (Italy). She is the director of the Research Center on Entrepreneurship and Small-Medium Firms—University of Urbino (Italy). She is also a member of the scientific board of Ipazia, the Italian Scientific Observatory on Gender Issues. Her main research interests include entrepreneurship, women entrepreneurs, small business, family business, and corporate financial communication.

Alicia Coduras-Martínez holds a Ph.D. in Political Sciences from Pompeu Fabra University (Spain) and a B.Sc. in Economics and Business Administration from the University of Barcelona (Spain). She has been a professor of Statistics and Econometrics at the University of Barcelona (1985–1991) and Pompeu Fabra University (1991–1999). In Spain, later she joined IE Business School (1999–2012), Nebrija University (2012–2014), and EDEM University (2013–2015). From 2016, she is the technical director of the GEM (Global Entrepreneurship Monitor) Saudi Arabia Team, member of the GEM Global Data Team, and senior statistical consultant at Opinometre Institute in Barcelona (Spain). She has written more than 200 reports and published in prestigious specialized journals.

Sofia I. F. Correia is Media planner in Caetsu advertising agency. She received her Master's in Economics from Faculdade de Economia do Porto (FEP), University of Porto (Portugal).

Serena Cubico is an Assistant Professor of Management in the Department of Business Administration at the University of Verona (Italy). She holds a Ph.D. in Organizational Psychology, and before entering academia, she was as consultant for small and medium-sized business (entrepreneurship, human resources management, training, career guidance) and Coordinator of the Youth Entrepreneurial Centre—University of Verona (Italy). Her main research areas are entrepreneurship (youth and female, education, start-up), organizational behavior in SMEs, family business, entrepreneurial competencies, and potential (identification, assessment, measurement).

Claudia Felix is the Director of the Tecnologico de Monterrey (Sonora Norte) (Mexico), where she works as an Associate Professor in Leadership and Business. She has a Ph.D. (International Doctorate in Entrepreneurship and Management—IDEM) from the Department of Business at Universitat Autònoma de Barcelona (UAB—Spain). Her research is focused on the link between leadership and entrepreneurship. She participates in several international research projects (e.g., GEM Mexico).

Gloria Charão Ferreira is a postdoctoral researcher in Regional Development, Research Line in Business Management at the Universidade Regional do Noroeste do Rio Grande do Sul (UNIJUÍ/Brazil); Ph.D. in Management from the University of Beira Interior (UBI/Portugal), recognized in Brazil by the University of Vale do Itajaí (UNIVALI / Brazil); Master's in Business Management and Strategy from Potiguar University (UnP / Brazil); and effective member of the *Associação Nacional de Estudos em Empreendedorismo e Gestão de Pequenas Empresas* (ANEGEPE/Brazil). Her research interests include absorption capacity, dynamic capabilities, entrepreneurial ecosystem, and family business management.

João M. Ferreira is an Associate Professor at the University of Beira Interior (UBI) (Portugal). He holds a Ph.D. in Entrepreneurship and Small Business Management from the Autonomous University of Barcelona (Spain). Currently, he is the Scientific Coordinator of NECE—Research Centre in Business Sciences. His research interests include strategy, competitiveness, and entrepreneurship. He is editor and reviewer board of some international journals, author of some books, and has published extensively in a variety of leading journals.

Remedios Hernández-Linares is an Associate Professor in the Department of Financial Economy and Accounting at the University of Extremadura (Spain). She received her Ph.D. from the University of Cantabria (Spain). Her primary research interests include family businesses, business strategy, entrepreneurship, and higher education learning. Her work has appeared in *Scientometrics, Family Business Review, Journal of Family Business Strategy, European Journal of Family Business,* and the book titled *The Routledge Companion to Family Business.*

Juan Hernangómez-Barahona is a Full Professor at the University of Valladolid (Spain), where he has been the Dean of the School of Business Administration and the Head of the Management and Marketing Department. He has been an academic coordinator of the UNESCO Chair in the management area for South American countries. Currently, he is the Director of the Chair of Family Business of the University of Valladolid (Spain). His research areas are the behavioral organization, family business, and strategy.

Christina Hoon started her career after completing her B.Sc. in Economics as a research associate and doctoral candidate at the Leibniz Universität Hannover (Germany). After completing her Ph.D., she became a Scientific Assistant (postdoc) and worked for the Institute for Personnel and Labor at the Leibniz Universität Hannover (Germany). Since September 2015, she is the holder of the endowed Chair for Business Administration, in particular the management of family business leadership at the University of Bielefeld (Germany). She manages the Chair, coordinates its research activities, and holds various lectures on various topics around the management of family businesses.

Julieth Paola Huffington-Smith holds an M.A. in Sustainable Development Projects from EAN University (Colombia) and a B.Sc. in Tourism and Hotel Management from the Autonomous University of the Caribbean (Colombia).

María Concepción López-Fernández is an Associate Professor of Strategy and holds the Santander Chair in Family Business at the University of Cantabria (Spain). Her main research interests include entrepreneurship, family business, strategy, innovation, flexibility, and tourism. Her articles have been published, among others, in *Family Business Review*, *Journal of Family Business Strategy*, *Journal of Small Business Management*, *International Journal of Production Research*, *R&D Management*, *Journal of Manufacturing Systems*, *Cornell Hospitality Quarterly*, and *Tourism Management*.

Natalia Martín-Cruz is an Associate Professor at the University of Valladolid (Spain). She has been Vice-President of the Strategy and Quality Department and Head of the Management and Marketing Department of the University of Valladolid (Spain). She has been a Visiting Scholar at the University of California at Berkeley (USA) and Stanford University (USA). He has lectured in international universities including the Copenhagen Business School (Denmark), Innsbruck University (Austria), or HEC Liège (Belgium). Her research areas are entrepreneurship, family business, and international cooperation.

Marta Pérez-Pérez is an Assistant Professor of Operations Management in the Business Administration Department at the University of Cantabria (Spain). Her main primary topics of research include strategic management of manufacturing and supply chain flexibilities, systematic reviews through bibliometric analysis, entrepreneurship and family firms, and information and communication technology within European Higher Education Area (EHEA). She has coauthored a significant number of national and international conference papers, books, and journal articles including those appearing in the *Journal of Manufacturing Systems, International Journal of Production Research*, *Journal of Small Business Management*, *Revista Española de Documentación Científica*, and *Estudios Gerenciales*.

Rafael Ignacio Pérez-Uribe is a Ph.D. in Business Sciences, Nebrija University (Spain); Diploma of Advanced Studies in Applied Economics, Nebrija University (Spain); M.Sc. in Organizational Management from EAN University (Colombia); M.Sc. from the Université du Québec à Chicoutimi (Canada); Specialist in Evaluation and Construction of Management Indicators for Higher Education, School of Business Administration; Associate Researcher (graduate studies as Kenkyusei) in Total Quality Control and Quality Circles, University of Fukushima (Japan); Business Administrator, Jorge Tadeo Lozano University (Colombia); Director of the research group in Management of large, medium, and small companies (G3pymes); and Professor in the Research and Knowledge Management Division, EAN University (Colombia).

Alicia Ramírez-Orellana is an Associate Professor at the University of Almeria (Spain) since 2009, holds a Ph.D. from the University of Almeria (Spain) since 2002, has professional practice as a professor at the University of Almeria (Spain) since October 1997-present, completed a research stay at the University of California-Los Angeles (UCLA) from October 2014 to February 2015, and is an Entrepreneur for the creation of a waste management company (Gestora de Residuos del Sur SL) that participates in an R&D project of the European Union (www.fertiplus.eu). Areas of research include family business; energy and economy; corporate social responsibility; international accounting regulations.

María del Pilar Ramírez-Salazar has a Ph.D. in Managerial Sciences, Nebrija University (Spain), and a Ph.D. in Management, EAN University (Colombia). She is Maître et Sciences Université du Québec à Chicoutimi (Canada); specialist in Evaluation and Creation of Managerial Indicators for Tertiary Education, Business Administration School, EAN University (Colombia); Professional in Pedagogy, Universidad Pedagógica Nacional (Colombia); member of the research group in Management of large, medium and small companies (G3pymes); and professor in the Online Education School at EAN University (Colombia).

Alfonso A. Rojo-Ramírez is a Full Professor of Accounting and Finance in the Department of Economics and Business at the University of Almeria (Spain). He also directs the Family Business Chair at this University since 2009. He is the recipient of the IFERA2017 Contribution to Practice Award. He has been the director of the Department of Business Administration at the University of Almeria (Spain).

Daniel Ruiz-Palomo holds a Ph.D. in Economic and Business Sciences from the University of Malaga (Spain) and holds a university degree specialized in international accounting from the Universitat Oberta of Catalunya (Spain). He is an Associate Professor in the Department of Finance and Accounting at the University of Malaga (Spain). His teaching focuses mainly on corporate finance, financial statement analysis, and intermediate or higher accounting. His research is strongly focused on the application of quantitative techniques to issues such as performance, innovation, capital structure, management control systems, or specific issues of family businesses, among others. He has published in international journals, such as the *Canadian Journal of Administrative Sciences*, *European Journal of Family Business*, *Universo Contábil*, *Revista Iberoamericana de Contabilidad de Gestión*, and *Revista de Contabilidad y Tributación*, among others.

Carlos Salcedo-Pérez is a Ph.D. in Business Sciences, Specialized in Family Business and Entrepreneurship, Nebrija University (Spain); Master's in Economic Development, the University of Southern Mississippi (USA); and B.Sc. in Business Administration, the University of Southern Mississippi (USA).

Annalisa Sentuti is a research fellow in Business Administration in the Department of Economics, Society, and Politics at the University of Urbino Carlo Bo (Italy). She teaches Business Administration and Accounting at the University of Urbino Carlo Bo (Italy). She is a member of the scientific board of Ipazia, the Italian Scientific Observatory on Gender Issues. Her main research interests include gender in management and organizations, family business, women entrepreneurs, and small and medium-sized businesses.

Ana M. Serrano-Bedia received her Ph.D. in Business Administration from the University of Cantabria (Spain), where she has been Associate Professor of Operations Management in the Department of Business Administration since 1996. She has coauthored more than 30 peer-reviewed articles in a variety of topics. Her primary research interests are in the fields of innovation management, manufacturing flexibility, entrepreneurship, and family firms.

Teresa Spiess is a lecturer in the Management, Communication & IT department at the Management Center Innsbruck (MCI) (Austria), where she has been a faculty member since 2012. She completed her Ph.D. in Management at the University of Innsbruck (Austria). Her research interests lie in the areas of organizational behavior and strategic management with a special focus on family business management. Since 2018, Teresa has been active as a postdoc researcher at the Family Business Center at the MCI, where she mainly focuses on the role of employees in family businesses. She is the author and coauthor of several publications and serves as a reviewer for some conferences and journals.

Aurora A. C. Teixeira is an Associate Professor at the University of Porto (Portugal), where she holds the chairs of Macroeconomics and Innovation Management. She received her Ph.D. from SPRU-Science Policy Research Unit (University of Sussex, UK). Her current research interests include technology commercialization, U-I linkages, economic growth, structural change, entrepreneurship, scientometrics, and academic ethics. She has published in journals such as *Cambridge Journal of Economics, China Economic Review, Ecological Economics, European Planning Studies, Industrial and Corporate Change, Journal of Evolutionary Economics, Portuguese Economic Journal, Regional Studies, Research Policy, Scientometrics, Social Indicators Research,* and *Structural Change and Economic Dynamics.*

Carlos L. Torres-Briones holds a Master's in Business Administration of Espiritu Santo University (Ecuador), Master's in Creation and Business Management of Nebrija University (Spain), and Ph.D. in Business Sciences, Nebrija University (Spain), and is a Professor at Universidad de Guayaquil (Ecuador).

Luis Arturo Torres-García Ph.D. (Hons) in Business and Entrepreneurial Management with application to SMEs, entrepreneurship, and family firms at the University of Cantabria (Spain), and former Associate Vice-President of Alumni Relations at Tecnologico de Monterrey (Mexico).

David Urbano is a Professor of Entrepreneurship at the Department of Business (Universitat Autònoma de Barcelona, UAB—Spain). His Ph.D. was in Entrepreneurship and Small Business Management (UAB and Växjö University—Sweden), and his research is focused on the conditioning factors of entrepreneurship in different contexts using an institutional approach. He has several scholarly international publications, and he is currently participating in various Spanish and international research projects (GEM, PSED, and GUESSS).

Anita Zehrer is Head of the Family Business Center at the Management Center Innsbruck (MCI) (Austria). She is an Adjunct Professor at the University of Notre Dame in Sydney (Australia). From 2007 to 2015, she was Deputy Head of the MCI Tourism Department; from 2012 to 2017, she was Deputy Head of the Academic Council; and from 2012 to 2016, she was an Adjunct Professor at the University of Canberra (Australia). From 2009 to 2018, she served as Vice-President of the German Association for Tourism Research DGT, from 2014 to 2017, she was a member of the Tourism Advisory Board of the Federal Ministry of Foreign Affairs and Energy (Germany), and from 2016 to 2017, she was a tourism expert at the Committee of Regions at the European Union. Her research interests are diverse and include entrepreneurship and leadership, family business management, consumer behavior, service experiences, and service design. She currently serves on several editorial boards, such as the *Journal of Travel Research, Journal of Vacation Marketing*, and *Tourism Analysis*, and is a reviewer for a range of tourism, entrepreneurship, and family business journals.

Introduction to Entrepreneurship and Family Business Vitality

José Manuel Saiz-Álvarez, Jesús Manuel Palma-Ruiz, and João Leitão

Abstract The economic globalization and increased competitive pressures for most firms demand innovative, efficient, and effective management strategies to comply with such dynamic, increasingly technological, and highly uncertain environments. Faced with this scenario, companies need to deploy critical strategies to survive and flourish in the long term, breaching challenges, seizing opportunities to hold a competitive position. The uniqueness of family firms means that they face a series of specific challenges, and whose analysis has eclipsed the study of other relevant aspects of change and development. Vital strategies require more than just focusing on the internal and external environment; those must also involve a constant search to integrate and coordinate the resources and actions that support competitive advantages and superior performance. The authors of this book review the different scenarios for entrepreneurship and family firms and propose strategies to tackle the challenges and seize the possibilities to grow in this competitive environment.

Keywords Competitive advantage · Critical strategies · Challenges · Innovation · Leadership · Entrepreneurship · Family firms · Socioemotional intelligence · Socioemotional wealth

This chapter aims to address the main topics and contents of the book Entrepreneurship and Family Business Vitality—Surviving and Flourishing in the Long Term.

J. M. Saiz-Álvarez
EGADE Business School-Tecnologico de Monterrey, Zapopan, Jalisco, Mexico

J. M. Palma-Ruiz (✉)
Universidad Autónoma de Chihuahua, Chihuahua, Mexico
e-mail: jmpalma@uach.mx

J. Leitão
University of Beira Interior, Covilhã, Portugal

J. M. Saiz-Álvarez et al. (eds.), *Entrepreneurship and Family Business Vitality*,
Studies on Entrepreneurship, Structural Change and Industrial Dynamics,
https://doi.org/10.1007/978-3-030-15526-1_1

1 Book Overview

Although, on average, more than 85% of the companies in the world are family microenterprises, and small and medium family businesses, the family business is barely analyzed. This book aims to contribute to a better understanding of the family business from a multidisciplinary perspective since specialists from universities located in the American and European continents participate in the book to give a transatlantic vision of this object of study. As a result, the vision and analysis of the topics studied and described are highly enriched.

This book is organized in four parts. Parts I to III are dedicated to different economic and psychological aspects related to family firms, and Part IV includes some case studies. Part I analyzes how socioemotional intelligence and socioemotional wealth determine proactive behavior to resolve conflicts in family firms. In the second chapter, entitled "Between Reason and Emotion: Socioemotional Intelligence as a Non-tangible Resource for Strategy, Operation, and Sustainability for Family Business" and written by Danny C. Barbery-Montoya from the Universidad de Especialidades Espíritu Santo (Ecuador), and Carlos Luis Torres-Briones from Universidad de Guayaquil (Ecuador), by applying the wealth of socioemotional intelligence matrix or SEIW matrix, these authors describe the financial and nonfinancial wealth in family business, and considering the management of emotional and social intelligence, innovation, and risk as crucial elements for taking decisions, they place family and profitability as the focus of their leaders' decisions. As a result, four types of family firms can be defined.

The analysis of social emotions is applied to family firms in the third chapter, entitled "Small Family Firms and Strategies Coping the Economic Crisis: The Influence of Socio-emotional Wealth," and written by Francesca Maria Cesaroni from the University of Urbino Carlo Bo (Italy), Annalisa Sentuti from the University of Urbino Carlo Bo (Italy), and Serena Cubico from the University of Verona (Italy), by means of the socioemotional wealth perspective is used to understand how, during phases of economic recession, family firms control their decision-making process by implementing ambidextrous strategies to limit the impact of a financial crisis.

This analysis on social emotions ends with the fourth chapter, entitled "Employees' Change-Oriented and Proactive Behaviors in Small- and Medium-Sized Family Businesses," and written by Teresa Spiess and Anita Zehrer, both from MCI Management Center Innsbruck-Internationale Hochschule GmbH (Austria), who shed light on how the socioemotional intelligence and wealth influence employees' change-oriented and proactive behaviors and the structural conditions they find to support or hinder these behaviors.

In addition to socioemotional intelligence and wealth, Part II analyzes how leadership is crucial for family firms to succeed. At this respect, the fifth chapter, entitled "Entrepreneurial Leadership Across Countries: The Role of Informal Institutions," written by Claudia Félix from Tecnologico de Monterrey, Sonora Campus (Mexico), Sebastián Aparicio from Durham University Business School (UK), and David Urbano from Universitat Autònoma de Barcelona (Spain), examines the influence of informal institutions on the probability of becoming an entrepreneurial leader. In this regard, institutional economics is used to frame the hypotheses that relate environmental factors and entrepreneurial leadership. These hypotheses are tested through logistic regression analysis using a sample of 67,268 individuals from the World Values Survey (WVS) for 50 countries. The main findings show that informal institutions such as independence, risk-taking, and networking increase the probability of becoming an entrepreneurial leader. Also, networking and religious faith moderate the relationship between autonomy and entrepreneurial leadership.

Moreover, leadership is also affected by generational diversity, especially in family firms, which can sustain senior entrepreneurship and shared leadership when conflicts and tensions appear. This relationship is analyzed from the sixth to ninth chapters. In the sixth chapter, entitled "Generational Diversity as a Moderator for the Relationship Between Absorptive Capacity and Innovation Performance at Family Firms," Gloria Charão Ferreira from the Universidade Regional do Noroeste do Rio Grande do Sul (UNIJUÍ) (Brazil), and João M. Ferreira from the University of Beira Interior (Portugal), study family firms' capacity to manage the generational diversity and external environments to maximize their innovation performance. This analysis is complemented in the seventh chapter, entitled "Shared Leadership at the Top of Family Firms: How Sibling Teams Engage in Successful Co-leadership," written by Christina Hoon and Jana Bövers, both from the Bielefeld University (Germany), where are explored shared leadership arrangements at the top of family firms where leadership is equally divided among a group of family members rather than focused on a designated leader. These authors affirm that shared leadership is positive in hybrid and flexible family firms, as the co-leaders integrate their shared leadership activities into concerted action and a shared entrepreneurial spirit while maintaining familiness.

The eighth chapter, entitled "Territorial Maps of Senior Entrepreneurship: A Multidimensional Analysis Based on GEM Data," written by Alicia Coduras Martínez from the Global Entrepreneurship Research Association, London Business School (UK), and José Manuel Saiz-Álvarez from EGADE Business School, Tecnologico de Monterrey (Mexico), applies APS GEM (Global Entrepreneurship Monitor) data. The authors use a multidimensional analysis based on a regression analysis of a nonlinear (cubic) polynomial equation between senior entrepreneurship and the United Nations' human development index. This analysis makes it possible to define territorial maps of senior entrepreneurship to recognize the strongest nations of the world on senior entrepreneurship to analyze the main factors affecting it. These authors suggest that senior entrepreneurship will increase in the coming years due to the aging of the population ("Papy Boom"), especially in Europe and a lesser extent to some regions of the United States and Japan. Finally, and related to senior entrepreneurship, four groups of countries are formed.

Finally, the ninth chapter, entitled "Relationship Conflicts in Family Firms: An Empirical Analysis," written by Ismael Barros-Contreras from the Universidad Austral de Chile (Chile), and Juan Hernangómez-Barahona and Natalia Martín-Cruz, both from the University of Valladolid (Spain), analyzes conflicts in Spanish family firms with the use of a partial least squares structural equation model. The results show that inserting family members as CEOs and in the board of directors enhances family values and culture into the firm, thus reducing conflicts.

Complementary to leadership, Part III analyzes how innovation plays a crucial role in firms. In the tenth chapter, entitled "Commitment to Learning, Knowledge and Strategic Renewal: Do Family Firms Manage Them Differently?," Marta Pérez Pérez from the University of Cantabria (Spain) and Remedios Hernández Linares from the University of Extremadura (Spain), apply structural equations modeling in the form of partial least squares by following a multi-group approach to show that knowledge management practices (mainly, generation, flow, and storage) are critical resources for developing sustainable competitive advantages to benefit family firms.

The eleventh chapter, entitled "The Moderating Effects of Family Farms Between Innovation, Information Systems and Training-Learning over Performance," written by Alfonso A. Rojo-Ramírez from the University of Almería (Spain), Alicia Ramírez-Orellana from the University of Almería (Spain), John Eddson Burgos-Burgos from the Technical University of Machala (Ecuador), and Daniel Ruiz-Palomo from the University of Malaga (Spain), analyzes the moderation effect with the help of a partial least squares structural equation model that being a family farm exerts on the information systems or productive processes' innovation performance relationship of the agricultural banana companies.

Part III ends with the twelfth chapter, entitled "The Effect of CEO Attributes on the Internationalization-Performance Relationship in Private Family Firms," written by Jonathan Bauweraerts from the University of Mons (Belgium), which explores the influence of CEO attributes on the internationalization-performance relationships of private family firms based on the upper echelon theory and the socioemotional wealth perspective. This author affirms that CEOs play a crucial role in the internationalization of private family firms and that some of their attributes have moderating effects on the internationalization-performance relationship.

One of the main strengths of this book is to complement these empirical chapters with cases from family firms in Colombia, Mexico, Portugal, and Spain. Cases are grouped in Part IV of this book. Regarding Spain and Mexico, in the thirteenth chapter, entitled "Is being Conservative at Home While Taking Risks Abroad a Suitable Competitive Strategy? The Case of Spanish Family Firms Internationalizing to Mexico," written by Julen Castillo-Apraiz and Unai Arzubiaga, both from the University of the Basque Country UPV/EHU (Spain), and Jesús Manuel Palma-Ruiz from the Universidad Autónoma de Chihuahua (Mexico), where partial least squares structural equation modeling is used, the authors analyze the impact of the competitive strategies of some Spanish family firms in their internationalization process to Mexico, both at exploitation (at a national level by better using firms' resources and knowledge) and exploration (at international level by exploring new ways of doing) levels. They conclude that family firms' exploitation strategy (at a national level) has a positive impact on firms' exploration strategy (at international level), so being more efficient and leveraging knowledge at a national level help to pursue opportunities internationally actively.

In the fourteenth chapter, entitled "Corporate Venturing Determinants in Mexican Family Firms," written by Luis Arturo Torres-García from Tecnologico de

Monterrey (Mexico), and M. Concepción López-Fernández and Ana M. Serrano-Bedia, both from the University of Cantabria (Spain), with the help of the resource-based and knowledge-based views and the upper-echelons theory, the authors explore by performing a binomial logistic regression analysis, which factors determine the decision to join corporate venturing in Mexican family firms.

These pages are complemented with the fifteenth chapter, related to Portugal, entitled "Determinants of the Economic Performance of Portuguese Family Firms: Is Innovation Relevant?," written by Aurora A.C. Teixeira and Sofia F. Correia, both from the University of Porto (Portugal). These authors assess the importance of innovation and technological capabilities in the performance of family firms in Portugal to show that internal factors are more relevant in explaining family firms' economic performance as a driver for economic growth.

The book ends with a chapter related to family firms in Colombia. In the sixteenth chapter, entitled "RISE Model: Its Application on Diving Enterprises Located in the San Andres Archipelago," written by María del Pilar Ramírez-Salazar, Rafael Ignacio Pérez-Uribe, Carlos Salcedo-Pérez, and Julieth Paola Huffington-Smith, all from EAN University (Colombia), these authors identify the level of fulfillment of the four sustainability dimensions (environmental, economic, social, and managerial) included in the 11-factor RISE Model, in 3 diving enterprises located in the Archipelago of San Andres (Colombia) to analyze the maturity level of each firm related to each dimension and factor for designing a path for innovation and corporate sustainability to foster economic development in the region.

Let us hope that this book contributes to understanding better the family business idiosyncrasy competing in a globalized economic world.

Part I
Family Firms: Socioemotional Intelligence and Wealth

Between Reason and Emotion: Socioemotional Intelligence as a Non-tangible Resource for Strategy, Operation, and Sustainability for the Family Business

Danny Christian Barbery-Montoya and Carlos Luis Torres-Briones

Abstract Financial and non-financial wealth in the family company has been a subject of discussion by several authors, placing family and profitability as the focus of their leaders' decisions. In this study, we explain how the relevant variables work together to defend this wealth while considering the management of emotional and social intelligence and considering innovation and risk factors as elements of the decisions taken by the leading members of the family business. Through theoretical review, the authors present the wealth of socioemotional intelligence matrix or SEIW matrix, and according to the use of this socioemotional intelligence, four types of enterprises can be defined, which in turn takes us to pose the three-dimensional model Dual-SEIW as a solution. This model establishes, for the stakeholders, a performance profile of the business where the priorities are money and family.

Keywords Family business · Risk · Innovation · Wealth · Stakeholders · SEIW matrix

1 Introduction

Financial performance is a variable present in all types of business including family businesses; it is based on the autonomy and the proactivity of those who make it (Kallmuenzer, Strobl, & Peters, 2018). This shows a clear need for independence which may lead to actions that generate income for the family. However, it is not

D. C. Barbery-Montoya (✉)
Universidad de Especialidades Espíritu Santo, Guayaquil, Ecuador
e-mail: dbarbery@uees.edu.ec

C. L. Torres-Briones
Universidad Santa Maria, Guayaquil, Ecuador
e-mail: ctorresr@usm.edu.ec

J. M. Saiz-Álvarez et al. (eds.), *Entrepreneurship and Family Business Vitality*, Studies on Entrepreneurship, Structural Change and Industrial Dynamics, https://doi.org/10.1007/978-3-030-15526-1_2

easy to measure the impact of family involvement when managing the profits (Ferramosca & Allegrini, 2018), whether the financial performance is the key to the sustainability of the family business is still to be defined. As a matter of fact, the establishment of non-financial objectives is also an issue discussed by scholars in this field, with cases where there are dominant shareholders who pursue this type of self-interest goals (Chua, Chrisman, De Massis, & Wang, 2018), which in turn are backed by socioemotional wealth, term which describes familiar elements such as control, belonging, emotional attachment (Drago, Ginesti, Pongelli, & Sciascia, 2018), and other variables which manifest themselves in the strategy and operation of the organization, in such a way that they may become a competitive advantage, helping create value with the economic agents of family businesses (Gallizo, Mar-Molinero, Moreno, & Salvador, 2017). The socioemotional wealth can be managed under a perspective of exchange, with actors in the supply chain of a family business, practicing emotional intelligence, creating resonance, and working in harmony with stakeholders (Boyatzis & Soler, 2012).

Also, the goals of the organization are also influenced by the degree of risk aversion displayed by those who make corporate governance. In many cases, irrational decisions are made about the risk, also influenced by emotions of a family nature (Hiebl, 2014), and based on the control of the business where information seems to be a determining factor (Terlaak, Kim, & Roh, 2018), the family harmony, inheritance and employment of family members (Molly, Uhlaner, De, & Laveren, 2018). Under this perspective, doubts arise about the direct relationship between risk and the future perception of a nonmonetary failure or a financial failure which is linked to a debt accumulation (Molly et al., 2018). In the first case: What is the perceived risk surrounding nonmonetary failures? What is the feared nonmonetary debt? Studies show that this family control is based on two dimensions: financial wealth and socioemotional wealth, which seek to establish a balance between money and reason (Gomez-Mejía & Zellweger, 2015).

It should also be noted that the strategy and operation of the company will be influenced by the style of leadership used by the owner to build trust and commitment (Allen, George, & Davis, 2018) which will ensure its sustainability in the long term. In this context, this leadership will impact on the innovation and performance levels displayed within the family organization (Meroño-Cerdán, López-Nicolás, & Molina-Castillo, 2018), i.e., showing its effects through the use of new technologies (Souder, Zaheer, Sapienza, & Ranucci, 2017).

In parallel, the socioemotional wealth also boosts innovation levels within the organization, taking into account the secure exchange of information between members (Filser, De Massis, Gast, Kraus, & Niemand, 2018), which again becomes a high value intangible for the organization, thereby ensuring business sustainability (Memili, Fang, Koç, Yildirim-Öktem, & Sonmez, 2018).

Considering these issues as highly relevant for the scientific study of how family businesses function, a deepening of this concept is called in order to understand the cause and effect of emotions. Thus, the objective of this study focuses on the theoretical foundation and exploratory research for handling these dimensions within the organization, establishing a model known as Dual-SEIW (based on the duality of emotional and monetary wealth sought by social-emotional intelligence) where the relevant variables at the time of making decisions for the sustainability of the family business are explained in terms of reason-emotion, levels of risk aversion, and search for innovation.

2 Background

Cisneros, Ramírez, and Hernández (2011) state that the idea of a family business evokes the need to establish a financial organization which is sustained by socially recognized affinity ties, such as the relationship between parents and children, siblings, or individuals with certain kinship. Its goal is to give generational continuity and control over property rights, either to ensure financial security for the family, preserve the heritage, or maintain the parental union.

Most businesses worldwide are family-owned. Statistics confirm over 90% in the United States, 88% in Switzerland, and 98% in Italy, thus being the essence of the market economy (Martínez Echezárraga, 2011) and replicating this pattern in other countries. Miller and Le Breton-Miller (2007) describe the essential economic influence of these organizations in the United States, representing 35% of the Fortune 500 companies, sources for 78% of new jobs, 59% of the workforce, and 50% of the GDP. Specialists attempt to classify the different types of family business based on several criteria, being the two most common: setting scales for the degree of family involvement within the business and the development of typologies (Tàpies, 2011). The most recognized model, for setting scales, is the F-PEC scale model, comprising three subscales: power, experience, and culture (Astrachan, Klein, & Smyrnios, 2002). It is noted that there is no single typology for family businesses, although there are first generation, second generation, and senior companies. According to 3i Europe, 61% of the companies in Spain are managed and controlled by the first generation and only 39% by other generations: 24% by the second generation, 9% by the third generation, and 6% for the fourth and subsequent generations (Amat, 2007).

2.1 Socioemotional Wealth

In family businesses, wealth is measured in two areas: family and business. The first one is emotional; the other is business or finance related. Therefore, when family businesses make their decisions, not only the economic and financial aspects of business come into play but also the socioemotional behavioral basis: the economic theory of the firm against or in conjunction with behavioral theory. In the first theory, the prime target for decision-making is the creation of wealth for the stakeholders.

Aspects such as profit, profitability, growth, cost, and competition are everyday magnitudes and should be considered for achieving the goal (Martínez & Rojo, 2015).

The share capital gives access to broader information sources and improves the quality, relevance, and timeliness of information (Adler & Kwon, 2002). The share capital also includes associativity, understood as the ability of participants to subordinate individual goals and actions to collective goals and actions. Associativity is generated, in part, by a high degree of interdependence among members or by the general understanding of the work organization, implicit regulations, and trust (Pearson, Carr, & Shaw, 2008).

Hollander and Elman (1988) tried to explain behaviors using three interactive elements: family, business, and environment. Behavior and transactions between the three components of the system respond to five elements: family culture, organizational culture, and three related cycles of life, the individual's, the family's, and the business. Thus, the propositions for managing family businesses are, to a greater or lesser degree, focused on the formalization and rationalization of activities. It is an attempt to reduce the apparent uncertainty resulting from family influence and its bureaucratization; short-term results are mainly favored. On the other hand, proposals seeking assimilation of the uncertainty caused by the market and family influence assume a multi-rational vision which finds strategic advantages in these companies. Through this lens, the continuity of the organization is accepted as a primary task, and therefore the road leads to long-term results (Cisneros et al., 2011).

It is therefore understood that family businesses present a constant interaction between family and environment; the management of strengths and weaknesses, through which the use of some techniques which facilitate and promote the development and implementation of chosen strategies, is noted. Pereira (2006) mentions the organizational model of the strategic process for the family business developed by Ussman, Jimenez, & Garcia (2001), which is shown in Fig. 1.

Thus, the socioemotional wealth is a topic of discussion in academia, referring to how family members identify themselves with the company, as well as the connection between them and the control and influence they have within the organization (Ferraro & Marrone, 2016). These elements create a framework for decision-making and become a contribution to the human capital of a company (Zachary, 2011).

In addition, socioemotional wealth seeks to perpetuate the family dynasty in the business and strengthen social ties in such a way that the family maintains control of the share capital of the company (Maloni, Hiatt, & Astrachan, 2017); this family wealth becomes a differential variable in relation to nonfamily businesses, contributing in their performance and sustainability, but it can also become an encumbrance which affects the life cycle of the company (Vassiliadis & Vassiliadis, 2014) since its leaders will seek to defend it although this may affect it financially (Allen et al., 2018). However, from a positive point of view, socioemotional wealth is seen as that non-financial wealth related to a family affection for ownership of a company (Casillas & Moreno-Menéndez, 2017).

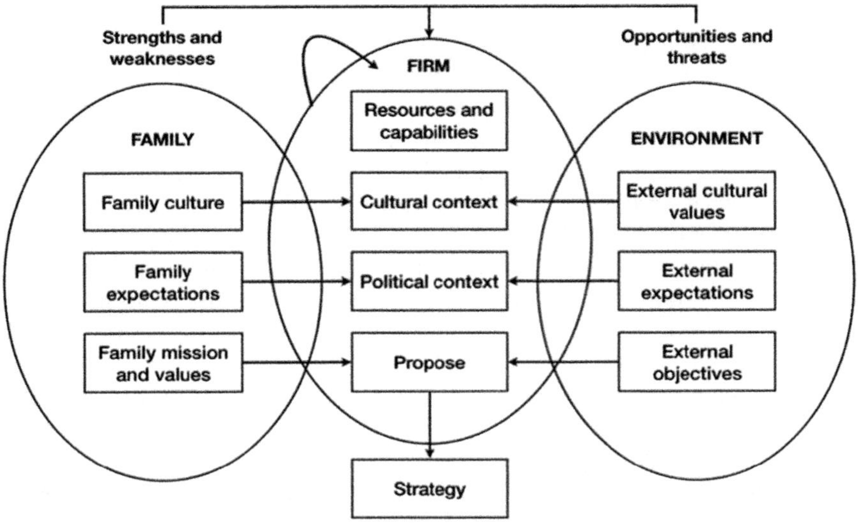

Fig. 1 Organizational model of the strategic process of family business. Source: Ussman et al. (2001) quoted by Pereira (2006)

2.2 *Risk Aversion*

Risk aversion is one of the variables influencing decisions within family businesses which are always trying to be consistent with sustainable and measured growth and never jeopardize the family welfare. Besides making decisions on issues which might affect them, family businesses, like all businesses, must be able to properly manage the enterprise-family relationship while evaluating the dynamics governing the behavior of the founders, next generations, family, shareholders, and company. Therefore, it is important to develop skills to identify and solve difficulties arising from these dynamics, adopt strategies to promote growth, transfer power and control, always seeking the generation of wealth for the company (San Martín Reyna & Durán Encalada, 2016). Businesses must coexist with four levels of uncertainty:

1. A bright future: forecasts with small margins of error; uncertainty is not a determining variable for decision-making.
2. Alternative scenarios: a few probable futures which eliminate each other are presented, and in the case one subsists, it will almost and entirely vary the strategy.
3. A range of potential futures: a series of possible not discrete futures are identified, which can be defined by a limited number of variables and whose outcome can be a wide range of possibilities.
4. Total confusion: a future virtually impossible to predict, unlimited variables and unlimited possibilities (Berger & Hannan, 1997).

Moreover, Santamaría and Oviedo (2016) based their study on two variables comprising several dimensions which are focused on analyzing the elements of uncertainty and risk, and they statistically demonstrate a significant evidence that a relation between risk aversion and market share exists in Ecuador, based on a three-dimensional risk aversion, uncertainty and risk, aversion and distrust within the family business, and risk type, while market share is based on expansion strategies and customer satisfaction, behavioral approach, and cultural approach.

In addition, it is noted within the study that 75% of participants in the sample said that they felt distrust within the family business, while 62.5% indicated that at some point while investing, they felt an aversion to debt, although this means there is fear to invest on improvements, it also emphasizes the confidence they have in their family business. Risk aversion becomes important in family businesses in order to avoid uncertainty in their investments. Whereas family businesses, like any other entity, seek profit, the degree of risk aversion can be mild or advanced, noting that if the risk is advanced, the losses can be momentary, but this possibility can also generate a higher profit.

According to St. Martín and Durán (San Martín Reyna & Durán Encalada, 2016), the effects of succession over the financial performance of these companies are different from the effect of this performance when the third generation takes over the company; therefore, second-generation family businesses are characterized by showing increased risk aversion in terms of debt, and an even more conservative approach when compared with third-generation family businesses, characterized by a higher preference for financing through debt, toward a greater wealth creation for the company. Some psychological and sociological studies regarding the factors underlying risk perception have revealed that a multiplicity of factors is affecting the way people perceive, assess, and manage risks. Current studies on risk perception ponder this aspect pointing to the importance of including multivariate analysis on the researches being conducted on this construct (Mikulic et al., 2012).

Likewise, García Berumen González, García Soto, and Domenge Muñoz (2012) mention that the size and age of the company, formality in the administrative and strategic planning, attitude toward family control, and age of the director influence decisions on the type of financing sources to be used. One of the most commonly used models to measure and assess risk, proposed and validated by Rohrmann (1994), on the perception of risk in different social groups, has been used in some countries, and it is giving good results. Regarding this model, Mikulic et al. (2012) propose the central variables for risk assessment: ecological attitude, adverse impacts, risk as a threat, benefits of technology, and acceptance of risk.

2.3 *Approach for Innovation*

Throughout history, the innovation process has been a factor which has made possible the creation of a modern, industrialized, and sophisticated society and has also become an influential source of power among nations in the world (Corma, 2013).

The needs of human beings are becoming more explicit and sophisticated; therefore, innovation has grown to become the precise element of growth and advancement in societies and entities. Family businesses are not far from this concept, a company which does not innovate is not progressing, and today, technology and advances in consumer behavior make innovation and continuous improvement something imperative to be sought.

Álvarez Venegas, Álvarez Venegas, García Santana, García García, and Sainz Zamora (2015) indicate that the innovation can be the result of an improvement process (continuous or incremental), but improvements do not necessarily lead organizations to generate innovation. However, improvement can give way to innovation and using a model of continuous improvement; innovation can become the only way to generate a change which allows organizations to adapt to the changing environment and become competitive (Fig. 2).

According to Aponte (2015), there are different studies with varied approaches on how to analyze innovation as a concept and process, as well as the relation between the different stages involved, specific elements, and their relations. It is essential to know the characteristics of innovation, which, according to Trott (2005), are based on the presence of two elements, novelty and commercial exploitation, novelty being an emphasis on generating new ideas that go through an invention and innovation process to ensure commercial success. Nevertheless, Sánchez (2003) notes that as far as the business sector is concerned, the presence of family PYMEs is more noticeable in mature and conventional technology sectors. This reality is in line with the lower investment in I + D carried out by these companies, risky business which, again, may be contrary to its objectives due to their lower risk appetite. Added funding difficulties presented by these types of activities and the reduced size and scale of the company do not facilitate these investments.

López, Serrano, Gómez, and García (2012) researched the innovation performance of family businesses and concluded (1) an exploratory strategy allows to obtain better results in terms of patents, incremental innovations, and internal effects (response period); (2) the CEO's level of education or training affects the qualitative

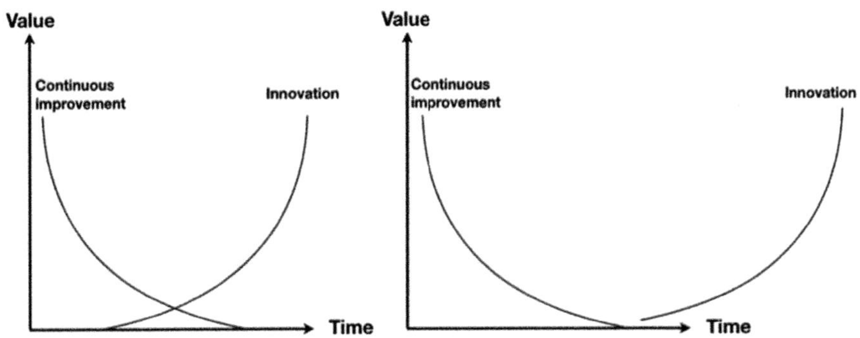

Fig. 2 Main differences between continuous improvement and innovation. Source: Álvarez Venegas et al. (2015)

impact of innovation; and (3) first-generation family businesses request more patents, creating the outline of the entrepreneurial founder character more clearly.

As such, innovation is a planned process, and related decisions are professional; here the owner or CEO of the family business carries them out in conjunction with family members; however, it is not excluded that in many cases the motivation to innovate is generated by intuition.

2.4 *Emotional Intelligence and Stakeholders*

There are different levels of authority within families, and this promotes the presence of a hierarchy which claims authority among its members, each with a different level of power for decision-making regarding different activities presented to the family business, which in turn are derived from the behavior of each member of the family, showing their interests, goals, and contribution to the organization. Although companies face such behavior due to the difficulty of access to resources which can be essential and vital as a contribution to the shaping of competitive advantages, a line of command which controls the company and the stakeholders is kept, and it is at this moment where socioemotional wealth is shown.

While socioemotional wealth is presented as a non-financial asset of family businesses, we have to know how to manage in order to exploit in a better way. Boyatzis and Soler (2012) refer to two particular issues which complement the concept of socioemotional wealth: emotional intelligence (EI) and social intelligence (SI), referring to the intelligent use of emotions in order to properly manage oneself and others. This intelligence is managed by the organizations' CEOs, influencing its performance with their leadership style (Goleman, Boyatzis, & Mckee, 2004). Others authors like Boyatzis (2009) come up with a third type of intelligence, cognitive intelligence, where the importance of managing emotions within the context of emotional wealth arises always considering the influence exerted by the owner or head of the family, on decisions to guarantee the sustained success of the company for the family and its stakeholders. There should be consistency among the interests of the company, family, and stakeholders to ensure the continuity of the organization, where the latter also have interests in stability, growth, and competitiveness (Luan, Chen, Huang, & Wang, 2015); therefore, the CEO should have the management of their needs among his solutions (Tucker, 2011).

2.5 *Sustainability for Monetary and Nonmonetary Wealth*

Family businesses are the longest-lived of all companies in the world, even in recessionary environments, such as wars, plagues, and pandemics (Miller & Le Breton-Miller, 2007).

The average proportion of long-term debt and the percentage of debt to credit institutions of family SMEs are also higher. These facts may reflect the preference for external financing rather than allowing new shareholders to enter the capital of the company, which could lead to a loss of control (Sánchez, 2003). Monetary or financial crises can be highly destructive, and apparently, they are not compatible with sustainability. Harder to see is how some mechanisms embedded in the present monetary system, when not in crisis, shape individual and collective behavior. Among the positive effects, we have to mention smart money, which triggers a burst of business and scientific innovation with no historical precedent (Lietaer, Arnsperger, Goerner, & Brunnhuber, 2012).

Not only the financial structure of the company is defended here but also the family within. Maintaining sustainability is also reflected in the continuity of the dynasty members in control and managing of the company (Maloni et al., 2017); however, we need to address the fact that this generational transmission can be significantly affected, when differences pop up in each generation (Marett, Marler, & Marett, 2018), which affect communications between members but most likely the socioemotional wealth (SEW) of the company. The intellectual capital working in an organization continually progresses up the organizational hierarchy of the company. It is also worth mentioning that intellectual capital tends to change its scale of values, giving a slightly lower level to money and trying to keep prestige and social recognition.

3 Issues and Controversies

According to OECD (2018), the PYMEs' population is highly heterogeneous, and financial difficulties vary greatly depending on the characteristics of the companies, such as the age, size, location, sector, or potential growth. The business owner's main characteristics, as can be gender or business experience, can also influence the access to financing. Although the need to adopt policies to the different needs of the business population is widely recognized, data collection efforts do not always capture detailed information on these parameters. The leadership is no longer an indispensable requirement for senior executives in organizations only. Today it is necessary for all hierarchical levels because leadership can support other human resources policies, for example, communications. For all members to feel motivated to work with enthusiasm and focus their efforts toward the same goal, somebody must enable the communication channels among the involved personnel, so that information flows smoothly and quickly (Santiago, 2008). Therefore, a leader must commit to being purely professional, either delegating, persuading the workgroup, commanding, or engaging in the tasks. The leader does not focus on one behavior only; he, as an enterprise, must analyze the situations arising, in order to make prompt decisions either through his emotions or through reason, which in the end will allow financial and emotional stability and confidence in his risk perception.

In the economic globalization, the importance of intellectual capital is growing against competing with ideas, knowledge, and procedures, rather than repeating processes, all this is synthesized in the "seven-Ks of knowledge" (know-how, know-what, know-when, know-who, know-whom, know-why, and know-whose); modern companies are increasingly characterized by their intangible values where fluency and quality of information are fundamentally important (Saiz Álvarez, 2009).

Meanwhile, Naredo (2002) indicates that the approaches by environmental economics, ecological economics, and institutional economics should be supplemented to have the economic speech cover issues involving the achievement of objectives by terms, scales, and different levels of aggregation. Socioeconomic sustainability is the concept of a social and solidary economy in a transition process; it accepts the path of apparent generalized financial "subsidies" (education, training, tax exemptions, health systems, etc.) from the principle of progressive redistribution of the public economy, as well as contributions of labor or other resources (voluntary work, mutual aid networks, use of housing for production, etc.) often based on relations of reciprocity and not accounted as costs. Entrepreneurship must be able to cover the cash expenses (no imputations) with the income obtained from the market and achieve the reproduction of its reference members or communities; whether such reproduction is simple or complex, that is another matter (Coraggio, 2008).

According to Fabio (2006), the rule of weak sustainability requires that wealth generation is maintained constant or rising, keeping the means of production such as the human-made capital, the natural capital, and the human capital in the equation. Therefore, it is required to know how much of the productive base should be used on each period; the environmentally adjusted net national product gives this measure. Briozzo, Vigier, Castillo, Pesce, and Speroni (2016) pointed, from a theoretical approach, the financing decisions and their associated variables. This helps to understand the decisions over the capital structure in PYMEs, including financial hierarchy, life cycle, legal form, sector, and professionalism of the entrepreneur, among others.

Meeting the goals is what every company looks for; that is why money and family end up just being day-to-day decisions, and if they are made considering measurable and parameterized factors, the achievement is a balance between emotion and reason. In this regard, Fabio (2006) mentions that strong sustainability is based on models expressing the equilibrium between the natural and human system, and to be measured, it requires the controversial definition of capital stock to keep.

4 Solutions and Recommendations

4.1 Interaction of Study Variables

The review of some literature shows the family business as a more human business; first, there is an introspective which defines its emotional side given by the SEW and its rational side (connected to emotional) given by EI and SI. Studies by Goleman et al. (2004) and Boyatzis and Soler (2012) establish the rational side as an essential element to handle the emotional side focusing on the CEOs of organizations as transmitters of their emotions and indicating that these are the influencers of their leadership style. Faced with this proposal, the inclusion of EI and SI into SEW is proposed, giving way to what we have called the socioemotional intelligence wealth or SEIW, which is defined as a non-financial wealth owned the family business through its leader, to have control over his own and other's emotions, and it goes together with decisions where reason and emotion play an important role in issues related to innovation or perception of risk.

The degree of innovation search and risk aversion influence the performance of organizations through decisions given by their CEO. In the family business, the decisions made by its leader are accompanied by high emotional doses, considering the presence and pressure of the closest family members, in addition to the role of stakeholders within the system of the organization. The emotional charge is associated with decision-making where risk and search for innovation are involved in order to maintain the business over time, which in turn results in four types of business models according to the SEIW they possess (Fig. 3).

Hound Firms (Intuitive SEIW) Innovation and emotion are presented as the engine for optimistic ventures which are followed on instinct. Decisions made by the highest authority of the family are taken in part due to the motivation that he receives from his closest collaborators together with his intuition. In this type of model, there is low-risk perception.

Archer Firms (Planned SEIW) Innovation and reason are presented in a planned manner. The decisions made have a more professional nature, and the use of EI and SI keeps intuitive emotions apart. The family plays a vital role as a consultant and not as a motivator; the model perceives a moderate risk.

Roller-Coaster Firms (Unpredictable SEIW) Risk perception is mixed with emotion and can lead to unpredictable decisions. In this model, the emotional pressure of the CEO is given by the family and the situation, in such a way that it can exhibit unexpected behavior where he can be very fearful or very bold in his decisions.

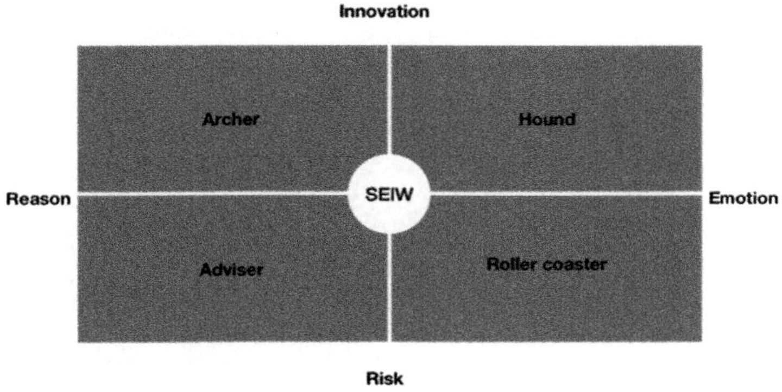

Fig. 3 Socioemotional Intelligence applied to innovation or wealth risk: matrix SEIW. Source: Authors' own figure

Advised Firms (Conservative SEIW) Risk perception and reason are mixed, and the decision-making becomes slow due to professional assistance and questioning by the family. The CEO seeks too much advice and perceives risk as an element affecting his financial wealth.

4.2 Profiles Based on Leadership

While companies can be classified according to their levels of innovation and risk, according to emotional or rational decision-making, it is also established that family businesses take care of their financial and non-financial wealth (Chua et al., 2018; Drago et al., 2018). This care for wealth shows a new classification from the initial classification, where a dual model focused on the wealth of the company, which is called Dual-SEIW or RIMF model (risk, innovation, money, and family) would be obtained.

Considering the duality based on wealth, this three-dimensional model shows eight types of leadership. It is noted that the model shows a trend in the care exercised by the family CEO over such wealth, that is, it shows the prioritization according to the approach for decision-making. Thus, the companies classified according to its SEIW give way to a dual questioning from the main member and leader of the organization, over his decisions: Is the company the main priority? Is the family the main priority?

This binary thinking can be understood as the trigger for a series of decisions and actions within the company, becoming the first criterion at the moment of establishing a strategic path. Thus, eight models of leadership, based on the duality of the raison d'etre of the company, are listed (Fig. 4):

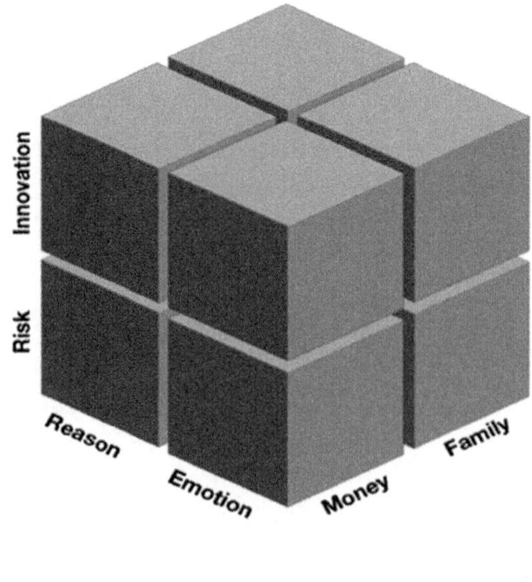

Fig. 4 The Dual-SEIW cube or RIMF model. Source: Authors' own figure

- Hound firms based on financial wealth: listed as companies where the CEO, using his intuition, seeks opportunities to improve profitability and financial indexes.
- Hound firms based on non-financial wealth: companies seeking opportunities to protect the owner family and their relatives through intuitive decision-making. The CEO uses his emotions focusing on the family rather than on financial issues.
- Archer firms based on financial wealth: companies focused on financial wealth, where the CEO makes rational decisions for the development of innovation.
- Archer firms based on non-financial wealth: companies where the search for innovation is made through rational decisions to benefit the family first.
- Roller-coaster firms based on financial wealth: companies where risk perception is handled emotionally and the impact on profitability is prioritized.
- Roller-coaster firms based on non-financial wealth: companies where risk perception is handled emotionally; family and relatives are prioritized.
- Advised firms based on financial wealth: companies where risk perception is rational and very focused on the impact of decisions over monetary assets and profitability.
- Advised firms based on non-financial wealth: companies where the rational perception of risk analyzes the impact on family members.

Theoretical studies, the base for the current proposal, define the links within the chain of decisions; however, authors believe that the dilemma "family or company" is the initial cause leading to a rational or emotional behavior which affects the strategies, actions, and even the control of the company. Sustainability, in the long run, given by the generational transmission of the company (Zachary, 2011), is a behavior where the family approach has a greater importance when compared with the interest on financial issues; however, long-term profitability can lead the family CEO to provide solutions which take isolated family interest to the side and instead establish family security solutions even outside the company.

4.3 About the Environment: Socioemotional Intelligence Connecting with Stakeholders

The company does not work isolated from the environment and even more so when there are stakeholders who can significantly affect its performance. The idea of showing the RIMF model is to establish the CEO's approach and exchange in the company with this environment, in such a way that the company generates a perception of his performance versus the system where he operates. Thus, family businesses can be classified as innovative, risky, serious, and friendly, where there is great growth in family or finances. While interaction with stakeholders does not establish a change in the company, we pretend to establish that they can better define their position against others and have a clearer idea of the projection as a corporate brand, connected to the objectives, values, and expectations of the stakeholders (Ussman et al., 2001), and where you can have a better and more precise idea of

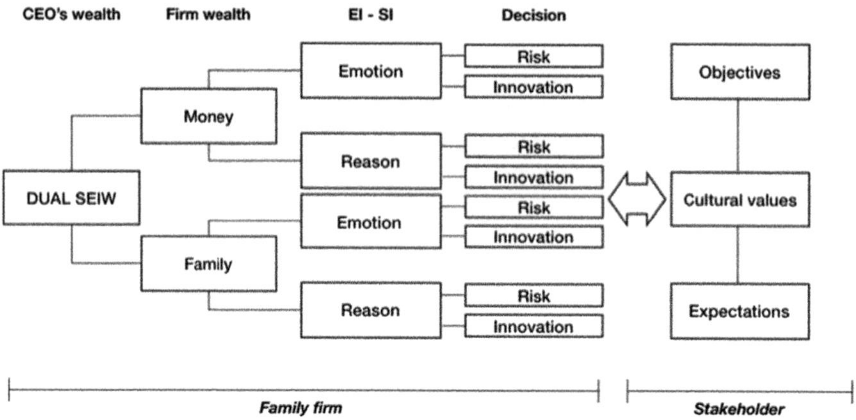

Fig. 5 The interaction between the family firm and stakeholder. Source: Authors' own figure

its performance in the supply chain (Maloni et al., 2017), related to the consumer (Allen et al., 2018) and to internal communications between members of the organization (Marett et al., 2018) (Fig. 5).

5 Conclusion and Future Research

Family businesses own financial wealth and non-financial wealth based mainly on the family. In this context, the reviewed literature shows that both are the engines of the company and, in turn, an influence for the head of the family group when taking decisions which affect some member of the company. The significance given by the CEO of an organization to decision-making will be complemented by the use of his emotional and social intelligence, carried away by his emotions or by his reasoning when making decisions that encourage innovation and seek to control or minimize risk. Therefore, we present two study models as a result: first, a matrix that expresses the use of reason and emotion according to innovation or risk; it has been called the matrix of socioemotional wealth or SEIW matrix, which allows to visualize and understand four types of companies, managed by the family or financial objectives of the CEO. Thus, it is proposed, under the context of the matrix of socioemotional wealth, the Dual-SEIW cube or the RIMF model which graphically shows the strategic movements that may be taken in order to lead a family business and also interact with stakeholders.

The authors make this proposal in a way for the CEOs of organizations to have a much clearer leadership style as well as to apply the model, so they understand the perception of the company from an external perspective. The matrix can also be applied to measure the study variables from an internal perspective, i.e., the personal vision of family members and company employees, regarding the type of company where they work, and the leadership style projected.

We propose three alternatives for future research: first, the development of a measurement system for these variables for the stakeholders, so that a more reliable result about the company is obtained; second, the development of a measurement system for the degrees of perceived risk or innovation levels in line with the goals, values, and expectations of stakeholders, so as to obtain a clear result in terms of a company response within its environment; and finally, the authors leave an open door for the investigative line of Dual-SEIW as an analysis of the leadership style of the CEOs of organizations, understanding their way of perceiving the world and conflict solving.

References

Adler, P., & Kwon, S. W. (2002). Social capital: Prospects for a new concept. *Academy of Management Review, 27*(1), 17–40.

Allen, M. R., George, B. A., & Davis, J. H. (2018). A model for the role of trust in firm-level performance: The case of family businesses. *Journal of Business Research, 84*, 34–45.

Álvarez Venegas, R., Álvarez Venegas, J., García Santana, T. L., García García, I. T., & Sainz Zamora, R. O. (2015). *Enfoques de innovación en las organizaciones. Universidad Internacional* (1st ed.). Cuernavaca: Universidad Internacional.

Amat, J. M. (2007). *La continuidad de la empresa familiar* (p. 2000). Madrid: Gestión.

Aponte, G. (2015). El proceso de gestión de innovación tecnológica: sus etapas e indicadores relacionados. *Revista Venezolana de Análisis de Coyuntura, 21*(1), 59–90.

Astrachan, J. H., Klein, S. B., & Smyrnios, K. X. (2002). The F-PEC scale of family influence: A proposal for solving the family business definition problem. *Family Business Review, 15*(1), 45–58.

Berger, A. N., & Hannan, T. H. (1997). Using efficiency measures to distinguish among alternative explanations of the structure-performance relationship in banking. *Managerial Finance, 23*(1), 6–31.

Boyatzis, R. E. (2009). Competencies as a behavioral approach to emotional intelligence. *Journal of Management Development, 28*(9), 749–770.

Boyatzis, R. E., & Soler, C. (2012). Vision, leadership and emotional intelligence transforming family business. *Journal of Family Business Management, 2*(1), 23–30.

Briozzo, A., Vigier, H., Castillo, N., Pesce, G., & Speroni, M. (2016). Decisiones de financiamiento en pymes: ¿existen diferencias en función del tamaño y la forma legal? *Estudios Gerenciales, 32* (138), 71–81.

Casillas, J. C., & Moreno-Menéndez, A. M. (2017). International business and family business: Potential dialogue between disciplines. *European Journal of Family Business, 7*(1–2), 25–40.

Chua, J. H., Chrisman, J. J., De Massis, A., & Wang, H. (2018). Reflections on family firm goals and the assessment of performance. *Journal of Family Business Strategy, 9*(2), 107–113.

Cisneros, L., Ramírez, G., & Hernández, A. (2011). Control en la empresa familiar control in family businesses. *AD-Minister, 18*, 49–76.

Coraggio, J. (2008). La sostenibilidad de los emprendimientos de la economía social y solidaria. *Otra Economía, 2*(3), 41–57.

Corma, F. (2013). *Innovación, innovadores y empresa innovadora*. Madrid: Ediciones Díaz de Santos.

Drago, C., Ginesti, G., Pongelli, C., & Sciascia, S. (2018). Reporting strategies: What makes family firms beat around the bush? Family-related antecedents of annual report readability. *Journal of Family Business Strategy, 9*(2), 142–150.

Fabio, A. (2006). Desarrollo sostenible y sus indicadores. *Revista Sociedad y Economía, 11*, 200–229.

Ferramosca, S., & Allegrini, M. (2018). The complex role of family involvement in earnings management. *Journal of Family Business Strategy, 9*(2), 128–141.

Ferraro, H., & Marrone, J. (2016). Examining employment relationship activities in family owned business research introduction. *Journal of Family Business Management, 6*(3), 210–224.

Filser, M., De Massis, A., Gast, J., Kraus, S., & Niemand, T. (2018). Tracing the roots of innovativeness in family SMEs: The effect of family functionality and socioemotional wealth. *Journal of Product Innovation Management, 35*(4), 609–628.

Gallizo, J. L., Mar-Molinero, C., Moreno, J., & Salvador, M. (2017). Family business and value-added distribution: A socioemotional wealth approach. *Academia Revista Latinoamericana de Administración, 30*(1), 2–22.

García Berumen González, J., García Soto, P., & Domenge Muñoz, R. (2012). Determinantes de la estructura de capital en la pequeña y mediana empresa familiar en México. *Contaduría y Administración, 57*(3), 67–96.

Goleman, D., Boyatzis, R., & Mckee, A. (2004). Primal leadership: The hidden driver of great performance. *Harvard Business Review, 94*(8), 46–48.

Gomez-Mejía, L., & Zellweger, T. (2015). In the horns of the dilemma: Socioemotional wealth, financial wealth, and acquisitions in family firms. *Journal of Management, 44*(4), 1369–1397.

Hiebl, M. R. W. (2014). Risk aversion in the family business: The dark side of caution. *Journal of Business Strategy, 35*(5), 38–42.

Hollander, B. S., & Elman, N. S. (1988). Family-owned business: An emerging field of inquiry. *Family Business Review, 1*(2), 145–164.

Kallmuenzer, A., Strobl, A., & Peters, M. (2018). Tweaking the entrepreneurial orientation-performance relationship in family firms: The effect of control mechanisms and family-related goals. *Review of Managerial Science, 12*(4), 855–883.

Lietaer, B., Arnsperger, C., Goerner, S., & Brunnhuber, S. (2012). *Money and sustainability – The missing link. Book review*. London: The Club of Rome.

López, M., Serrano, A., Gómez, R., & García, G. (2012). El efecto del familiness en la performance innovadora de las empresas familiares: un análisis exploratorio. *Revista de Empresa Familiar, 2* (2), 7–21.

Luan, C., Chen, Y., Huang, H., & Wang, K. (2015). CEO succession decision in family businesses – A corporate governance perspective. *Asia Pacific Management Review, 23*(2), 130–136.

Maloni, M. J., Hiatt, M. S., & Astrachan, J. H. (2017). Supply management and family business: A review and call for research. *Journal of Purchasing and Supply Management, 23*(2), 123–136.

Marett, E., Marler, L., & Marett, K. (2018). Socioemotional wealth importance within family firm internal communication. *Journal of Family Business Management, 8*(1), 22–37.

Martínez Echezárraga, J. (2011). *Empresas familiares, reto al destino: claves para perdurar con éxito*. Buenos Aires: Ediciones Granica.

Martínez, M. J., & Rojo, A. A. (2015). La riqueza socioemocional en la empresa familiar. *Balance. Revista de Economía, 1*(20), 12–14.

Memili, E., Fang, H. C., Koç, B., Yildirim-Öktem, Ö., & Sonmez, S. (2018). Sustainability practices of family firms: The interplay between family ownership and long-term orientation. *Journal of Sustainable Tourism, 26*(1), 9–28.

Meroño-Cerdán, A., López-Nicolás, C., & Molina-Castillo, F. (2018). Risk aversion, innovation and performance in family firms. *Economics of Innovation and New Technology, 27*(2), 189–203.

Mikulic, I., Cassullo, G., Crespi, M., Caruso, A., Elmasian, M., & Muiños, R. (2012). Evaluación de la Percepción de Riesgo en Diferentes Grupos Sociales: Propuesta de un Modelo de Ecuaciones Estructurales. *Anuario de Investigaciones, XIX*, 37–44.

Miller, D., & Le Breton-Miller, I. (2007). Kicking the habit: Broadening our horizons by studying family businesses. *Journal of Management Inquiry, 16*(1), 27–30.
Molly, V., Uhlaner, L., De, A., & Laveren, E. (2018). Family-centered goals, family board representation, and debt financing. *Small Business Economics, 51*, 1–18.
Naredo, J. (2002). Economía y sostenibilidad: la economía ecológica en perspectiva. *Polis Revista Latinoamericana, 1*(2), 1–28.
OCDE. (2018). *Financiamiento de PYMES y Emprendedores 2018*. Retrieved from https://www.oecd.org/cfe/smes/SPA-Highlights-Financing-SMEs-and-Entrepreneurs-2018.pdf
Pearson, A., Carr, J., & Shaw, J. (2008). Toward a theory of familiness: A social capital perspective. *Entrepreneurship: Theory and Practice, 32*(6), 949–969.
Pereira, B. (2006). *Empresas familiares vs. Empresas no familiares un análisis estático y dinámico de sus diferencias, a partir de características y elementos del proceso estratégico. El caso de las empresas de carpintería y mobiliario de Galicia*. Doctoral Theses, University of Vigo, Vigo, Spain.
Rohrmann, B. (1994). Risk perception of different societal groups: Australian findings and cross-national comparisons. *Australian Journal of Psychology, 46*(3), 150–163.
Saiz Álvarez, J. M. (2009). Capital intelectual, protocolo y empresa familiar. *Anuario Jurídico y Económico Escurialense, 62*, 377–388.
San Martín Reyna, J., & Durán Encalada, J. (2016). Sucesión y su relación con endeudamiento y desempeño en empresas familiares. *Contaduria y Administracion, 61*(1), 41–57.
Sánchez, N. (2003). Las Pyme Familiares en España: ¿Qué nos dicen los datos? *Investigaciones Europeas de Dirección y Economía de la Empresa, 9*(2), 115–128.
Santamaría, E., & Oviedo, A. M. (2016). Efectos de la Aversión al Riesgo en Estrategias de Expansión sobre la Participación de Mercado. *Sotavento MBA, 28*, 64–73.
Santiago, M. (2008). Factores determinantes en la gestión de recursos humanos en empresas de servicios que incorporan de manera sistemática nuevas tecnologías Un estudio de caso en la comunidad valenciana. *Revista científica Pensamiento y Gestión, 24*, 88–131.
Souder, D., Zaheer, A., Sapienza, H., & Ranucci, R. (2017). How family influence, socioemotional wealth, and competitive conditions shape new technology adoption. *Strategic Management Journal, 38*(9), 1774–1790.
Tàpies, J. (2011). Empresa familiar: un enfoque multidisciplinar. *Universia Business Review, 32*, 12–25.
Terlaak, A., Kim, S., & Roh, T. (2018). Not good, not bad: The effect of family control on environmental performance disclosure by business group firms. *Journal of Business Ethics, 0* (0), 1–20.
Trott, P. (2005). *Innovation management and new product development*. London: Pearson Education.
Tucker, J. (2011). Keeping the business in the family and the family in business: What is the legacy? *Journal of Family Business Management, 1*(1), 65–73.
Ussman, A., Jimenez, J. J., & Garcia, P. M. (2001). Una reflexión sobre el proceso de dirección estratégica de la empresa familiar: propuesta de un modelo. In *Actas del I Congreso Nacional de Investigación sobre la Empresa Familiar* (pp. 347–372). Valencia: OPVI.
Vassiliadis, S., & Vassiliadis, A. (2014). The Greek family businesses and the succession problem. *Procedia Economics and Finance, 9*, 242–247.
Zachary, R. K. (2011). The importance of the family system in the family business. *Journal of Family Business Management, 1*(1), 26–36.

Small Family Firms and Strategies Coping the Economic Crisis: The Influence of Socio-emotional Wealth

Francesca Maria Cesaroni, Annalisa Sentuti, and Serena Cubico

Abstract In this chapter, the socio-emotional wealth perspective is used to understand how, during phases of economic recession, a company's family nature can influence its decision-making processes and the implementation of an ambidextrous strategy, as well as its effectiveness. A qualitative analysis based on a case study is presented in this chapter. The analyzed case involves an Italian family-owned small business that faced the recent economic crisis adopting a mix of defensive and offensive strategies. Thanks to this balanced—ambidextrous—strategy, the company was able to limit the impact of the crisis and then to recover positive profit margins. This study contributes to the extant literature by shedding light on how the aim of preserving the socio-emotional wealth can influence small family firms' ability to adopt ambidextrous strategies in order to face an economic recession.

Keywords Family firms · SMEs · Decision-making · Strategies · Economic crisis · Defensive approach · Offensive approach · Ambidextrous strategies · Socio-emotional wealth

1 Introduction

The last few years were particularly difficult for the Italian economy, characterized by a deep and persistent recession that is not yet definitively overcome and puts a strain on Italian companies and their competitiveness.

F. M. Cesaroni (✉) · A. Sentuti
Department of Economics, Society, and Politics, University of Urbino Carlo Bo, Urbino, Italy
e-mail: francesca.cesaroni@uniurb.it; annalisa.sentuti@uniurb.it

S. Cubico
Department of Business Administration, University of Verona, Verona, Italy
e-mail: serena.cubico@univr.it

J. M. Saiz-Álvarez et al. (eds.), *Entrepreneurship and Family Business Vitality*,
Studies on Entrepreneurship, Structural Change and Industrial Dynamics,
https://doi.org/10.1007/978-3-030-15526-1_3

Data has shown that in Italy micro and small enterprises are those who suffered most from the crisis (Altobelli, 2014; Carnazza, 2014; Cerved, 2014; Istat, 2014). Significant reduction in turnover (Carnazza, 2014), liquidity crisis (Nicolai, 2014), and credit crunch (European Commission, 2013) affected most of the Italian small businesses in the period 2008–2013. Micro and small businesses' mortality rate and number of bankruptcies and non-bankruptcy insolvency proceedings significantly increased during the crisis (Altobelli, 2014; Cerved, 2014).

Several authors have analyzed the behavior adopted by companies in dealing with the economic recession, and it is widely recognized that strategies implemented by firms can be traced back to two main opposed approaches (Deans, 2009; Miles & Snow, 1978):

A *defensive approach*, short term oriented and aimed at maintaining efficiency and guaranteeing the survival of the business

An *offensive approach*, medium-long term oriented and based on new investments and innovation process to maintain and strengthen the company's competitive advantage

It is a matter of the fact that these two approaches force entrepreneurs to face a dilemma and to choose the best approach to adopt to deal with an economic recession. A solution to this dilemma may be an ambidextrous strategy (Kitching, Blackburn, Smallbone, & Dixon, 2009) that combines a defensive and an offensive approach (Chowdhury & Lang, 1996; Robbins & Pearce II, 1992; Sternad, 2012), in order to maintain a balance between retrenchment and investments and between short term and medium-long term. Several authors agree that an ambidextrous strategy is an ideal combination of effectively addressing economic downturns (Kitching et al., 2009; Pearce & Michael, 2006). However, these strategies have been mainly analyzed in relation to large companies (Pearce & Michael, 2006), while disregarding small businesses' characteristics, including their typically family nature. Family firms' characteristics should be duly considered, as Italy is a country with an unusually high number of family businesses. In fact, according to the European Family Businesses Federation, over 75% of Italian companies have a family nature, and this percentage is not very different from that of the leading European countries (Germany 75%, France 75%, the United Kingdom 65%, Spain 85%). The same data are also confirmed by the Italian statistics institute (ISTAT): according to the latest Census of Industry and Services, in fact, the Italian economic system is characterized by companies with a high concentration of ownership shares, with a predominantly family control and centralized company management. Although family firms are almost uniformly widespread in every economic macro-sector, their presence is unusually high among small companies.

It is widely recognized that the involvement of the family on businesses' ownership and management deeply affects their goals, behavior, and decision-making processes. In family business research, these concepts are at the basis of the socio-emotional wealth perspective (SEW) (Gomez-Mejia, Cruz, Berrone, & De Castro, 2011; Gomez-Mejia, Haynes, Nuñez-Nickel, Jacobson, & Moyano-Fuentes, 2007; Gomez-Mejia, Makri, & Larraza-Kintana, 2010). It aims to offer a specific model for the analysis of family firms' decision-making processes and strategic behaviors, taking in due consideration their uniqueness and distinctive characteristics (Berrone, Cruz, & Gomez-Mejia, 2012; Gomez-Mejia et al., 2011).

In this chapter, this theoretical approach is used to understand how, during phases of economic recession, the aim of preserving the socio-emotional wealth can influence small family firms' ability to adopt ambidextrous strategies in order to face an economic recession.

A qualitative analysis based on a case study is presented in this chapter. The selected firm is an Italian family-owned small business that faced the recent economic crisis adopting a mix of defensive and offensive strategies. Thanks to this balanced—ambidextrous—strategy, the company was able to limit the impact of the crisis and then to recover profit margins. Because of these characteristics, the selected company can be considered an emblematic case study, and it is particularly useful to analyze the influence of socio-emotional wealth in small family firm's decision-making, especially during a period of economic recession.

The chapter is structured as follows. The next two sections present the primary literature on the strategic response of companies to the economic crisis and, with regard to family firms, the socio-emotional wealth approach. Then, the research questions and the methodology employed in the empirical research are illustrated, and the description of the analyzed case is shown. Finally, the key results of the study are discussed, and the main conclusions are drawn.

2 Strategies to Deal with the Economic Crisis: Defensive Approach, Offensive Approach, or Both?

It is widely recognized that the economic crisis represents one of the most critical and difficult challenges that companies face during their life cycle (Latham, 2009; Latham & Braun, 2011). Nevertheless, in the literature on business strategy and management, little attention has been devoted to the strategies adopted by companies to deal with the economic recession (Kitching et al., 2009).

It is generally accepted that companies can adopt two types of strategies they have to face an economic downturn: the first is the adoption of measures aimed at maintaining efficiency through cost-cutting, selling of non-strategic assets, and reducing personnel costs; the second is based on new investments, organizational renewal, introduction of new products and processes, and research of new markets and new customers. The first choice is a defensive one, as it is intended to guarantee the survival of the business in the short term. On the contrary, the second is an offensive choice, aimed at creating opportunities for long-term value creation. According to the classification of Miles and Snow (1978), the so-called defenders adopt the first approach, while the second characterizes the behavior of firms labeled as prospectors.

From another perspective, firms may face an economic crisis by adopting *externally directed* or *internally directed* strategies. The former requires actions directed toward the market and aimed to change marketing strategies, pricing strategies, international orientation, etc. The latter involves actions directed toward the firm in order to change its structures, processes, systems, or resources (Chattopadhyay, Glick, & Huber, 2001; Sternad, 2012). In this wide range of possibilities, and combining both perspectives, four main strategies may be identified to explain how firms may respond to an economic crisis: restructuring strategies, resizing strategies, reorganization strategies, and innovation and development strategies (Kitching et al., 2009; Papaoikonomou, Segarra, & Li, 2012; Sternad, 2012).

Restructuring strategies are internally directed actions that involve cutting costs, reducing personnel costs, and reducing investments in order to improve efficiency. Such strategies relate to traditional product/market combinations and do not involve significant dimensional variations (Guatri, 1995). Firms try to increase efficiency by growing productivity and reducing expenses on a wide range of activities.

Resizing strategies are external-directed actions oriented to refocusing the core business and disinvesting non-core assets. The disinvestment of products/product lines, withdrawing from markets, selling parts of the business, and closure of plants or production sites are examples of resizing actions (Latham, 2009; Sternad, 2012).

Both restructuring and resizing strategies are defensive (Deans, 2009), and they are the most common approaches adopted by firms to deal with recession conditions (Latham, 2009; Michael & Robbins, 1998; Robbins & Pearce II, 1992), especially in the short term (Kitching et al., 2009). Even in Italy, data confirmed that defensive strategies were the most frequently used by small businesses to deal with the crisis (Cesaroni & Sentuti, 2014; Istat, 2014; Pencarelli, Savelli, & Splendiani, 2008).

About the effectiveness of such strategies in times of economic crisis, opposing assessments can be made (Kitching et al., 2009). Looking at the problem in a positive perspective, in fact, an economic crisis can be an incentive to improve and rationalize the company, through a critical review of its product portfolio and focusing on its core business. The crisis also leads firms to act to improve efficiency and reduce operating costs by optimizing the asset utilization and divesting marginal and less profitable activities. However, there are negative aspects. Cutting costs and activities is often a knee-jerk reaction to adverse market conditions, which, however, did not involve any strategic repositioning of the company. As a consequence, cost- and asset-cutting can weaken the business's competitiveness and reduce its ability to face the later stages of economic recovery successfully.

Even if defensive strategies are prevalent for firms in times of crisis, other studies suggest alternative strategies to cope with the recession. They require countercyclical investments and processes of technological and organizational innovation, aimed at strengthening the company and allow it to better tackle the economic crisis and become more competitive and better prepared for the post-recession. These strategic responses seem inspired by the idea, put forward by Penrose, according to which "depression is sometimes looked on as a good time to expand: costs are low, the plant can be constructed, and equipment bought cheaply" (Penrose, 1995, p. 244).

Reorganization strategies and innovation and development strategies belong to this second group.

In particular, *reorganization strategies* are internally directed actions focused on renovation and improving organizational aspects, for instance, by redefining responsibilities, enhancing information system controls, investing in human resources, and so on. Such strategies aim to redevelop the firm and improve its organizational structure. According to some authors (Papaoikonomou et al., 2012; Pearce & Michael, 2006), investments in human resources are especially useful during the economic crisis. Programs designed for training employees in specific skills and employee benefits are useful in maintaining high motivation and commitment during times of recession (Brenner, 2009). Furthermore, by retaining skilled employees, the firm is prepared to meet rising demands when conditions change (Pearce & Michael, 2006).

Innovation and development strategies are external-directed actions concerned with the competitive position of businesses and aimed to counteract demand decrease. Such strategies adopt an offensive approach (Deans, 2009), and examples include investment into new markets, new product development, business diversification, and increased marketing costs (Kitching et al., 2009; Papaoikonomou et al., 2012; Sternad, 2012). These strategies require entrepreneurs' ability to perceive economic crisis as "opportunities to invest, innovate and expand into a new market in order to achieve or extend a competitive advantage during the recession and beyond" (Kitching et al., 2009). These strategies, however, are risky and not easy to implement, not only because they imply the ability of firms to look beyond and not to dwell on the difficulties of the moment but also because they often require large amounts of resources concerning finance, managerial, and technical expertise.

Indeed, during the economic crisis, business owners and managers have to face a dilemma: to favor a short-term perspective and thus protect the current financial performance of the company or to look at the long term and make new investments. The latter causes an immediate absorption of resources, but they can enhance the competitive position of the company and thus allow it to gain an advantage in the long term, even in the post-recession. The two alternatives cause opposing risks: the emphasis on short-term performance is likely to weaken the company's long-term competitiveness, and its performance can deteriorate in the post-recession; on the contrary, focusing on long-term goals, the company could be involved in initiatives that absorb resources and thus cause a further deterioration of the immediate performance, further threatening its survival. Some studies show that too much emphasis on downsizing and cost-cutting strategies can lead to adverse effects in the long term (DeDee & Vorhies, 1998), while anti-cyclical actions can facilitate achieving high performance in the phase of economic recovery (Roberts, 2003; Wan & Yiu, 2009). Pearce and Michael (1997), through the analysis of a sample of start-up manufacturing firms, show that firms that had made marketing investments (e.g., advertising) achieve the highest earnings compared to companies that had cut costs during the recession.

According to some authors, the most effective solution to dealing with economic downturns is the adoption of the so-called "balanced" or "ambidextrous" strategies

(Kitching et al., 2009). The latter combine an offensive and a defensive approach, pursuing both efficiency improvements and strategic investments (Chowdhury & Lang, 1996; Robbins & Pearce II, 1992; Sternad, 2012).

The concept of ambidexterity has been used in the literature on business strategy and management to identify a successful way to face an economic recession. When adopting this strategy, companies can be able to combine retrenchment and investment (Kitching et al., 2009; Pearce & Michael, 2006; Rhodes & Stelter, 2009). In particular, companies can face the first phase of a recession with actions aimed at reducing costs and ensuring the short-term survival of the company, in order to avoid incurring excessive losses; in the second phase, companies can shift attention to the long term, through investments that can enable the firm to successfully address the post-recession and pursuing growth and/or development.

The validity of this kind of approach toward economic crisis is confirmed by several famous case studies, such as Dell Computer, Southwest Airlines, and Black and Decker (Pearce & Michael, 2006). In particular, Pearce and Michael (2006) warn firms of risk arising from excessive reducing of personnel costs (e.g., job training, hiring, and education) during recessions. Investing in human capital and retaining skilled employees allow companies to implement changes imposed by recession thanks to qualified and motivated collaborators. Moreover, with this approach, firms are prepared for the economic recovery even when it may be more difficult to find and recruit people with skills needed for the company.

Studies focused on ambidextrous strategies for addressing economic crisis are very few and often lack empirical evidence (Kitching et al., 2009; Rhodes & Stelter, 2009). At the same time, existing empirical investigations are focused on large companies (Pearce & Michael, 2006) and significantly ignore small businesses' peculiarity and characteristics, including their typical family nature.

It is well known that, compared to larger firms, small businesses are characterized by a more limited amount of resources—particularly knowledge, skills, finance, managerial competences, systems, and organizational structures. For instance, in a large firm, strategic activities (analysis, choice, and implementation) are often carried out by different teams and by specific organizational units. On the contrary, in a small business, a single person—the entrepreneur—is very often responsible for all strategic activities (Curran, 1996; O'Gorman, 2006). As a consequence, small businesses may have more difficulties in implementing ambidextrous strategies. These strategies require the ability to steadily scan and analyze the environment and quickly respond to significant changes with appropriate and differentiated actions, aligned with evolving external conditions. This behavior is documented in several empirical studies, which show that, during the recent economic recession, Italian small businesses mainly adopted defensive strategies (Cesaroni & Sentuti, 2014; Istat, 2014; Pencarelli et al., 2008). The organizational characteristics of small businesses and their limited resource endowment raise doubts about their ability to effectively adopt ambidextrous strategies. These limitations may have even more significant influence during periods of economic recession since the crisis can further reduce available resources.

The ability of small firms to adopt ambidextrous strategies to face periods of the economic crisis has not yet been the subject of neither theoretical nor empirical analysis, and this despite the widespread presence of small businesses in many countries, including Italy. This is why in this chapter we present a case study, concerning a small family business that has successfully managed to adopt an ambidextrous strategy during the recent economic crisis. The results from the analysis of this case are useful for understanding (1) whether theoretical literature recommendations regarding large companies are consistent with small firms' characteristics and (2) what factors can allow small firms to effectively combine defensive and offensive strategies in a situation of economic recession.

3 The Influence of the Socio-emotional Wealth

If the characteristics of small businesses raise doubts about their ability to adopt ambidextrous strategies to face periods of economic crisis, we must take into account that a very high percentage of small businesses have a family nature, especially in Italy. So, we need to ask how the distinctive factors of small family businesses can affect the adoption and implementation of ambidextrous strategies.

Indeed, literature on family firms shows that they "are highly dependent on a single decision-maker, the owner" (Feltham, Feltham, & Barnett, 2005, p. 13) and the composition of the board in such firms is very often a mirror of family characteristics and objectives (Corbetta & Salvato, 2004; Voordeckers, Van Gils, & Van den Heuvel, 2007). Values and interests of the dominant group shape companies' decision-making (March, 1962). As a consequence, in small family firms, the owner family's values and expectations play an essential role (Andrews, 1987; Pant & Lachman, 1998), and the will of the family members strongly influences strategic choices, more than what happens in large companies (Cubico et al., 2017; Miller, 1987). Moreover, in small family firms, the lack of necessary resources can affect their ability to perceive and effectively respond to external change (Smallbone, Cumbers, Syrett, & Leigh, 1999).

Especially in recent years, several scholars have tried to analyze family firms' objectives, behaviors, and strategies, in order to understand whether, and how, the involvement of the family in companies' ownership, governance, and management can affect firms' performance and their ability to overcome periods of economic crisis (Allouche, Amann, Jaussaud, & Kurashina, 2008; Amann & Jaussaud, 2012; Basco, 2013; Gallo, Tápies, & Cappuyns, 2004; Mazzi, 2012; Minichilli, Brogi, & Calabrò, 2015). Several theoretical perspectives have been adopted in such analyses—agency theory, stewardship theory, and resource-based view—without ever reaching univocal results (O'Boyle Jr, Pollack, & Rutherford, 2012). According to some authors (Sciascia, Mazzola, & Kellermans, 2014), one of the main reasons for the lack of unambiguous data is that these theories have been developed in other contexts and only later adopted in family business studies. Adaptations of the original theories have therefore been necessary, and this explains why these theories have not been able to explain the behavior of family businesses fully. This is why more recently, in family business studies, a new theoretical perspective was born. It is based on the concept of socio-emotional wealth (SEW) and aims to analyze the behaviors and distinctive characteristics of family businesses (Gomez-Mejia et al., 2011).

SEW perspective is an all-encompassing approach that captures the "affective endowments" of family owners, including the family's desire to exercise authority, the enjoyment of family influence over the business, the will to maintain clan membership within the firm, the desire to appoint trusted family members to prominent roles, the retention of a strong family identity, and the will to ensure the continuation of the family dynasty (Berrone et al., 2012; Gomez-Mejia et al., 2007). According to this perspective, the primary distinguishing characteristic of family firms is the great importance attached to noneconomic objectives (emotional and social needs of the family) and their central role in influencing their decision-making processes and strategic choices (Gomez-Mejia et al., 2011). The fundamental priority of the family business is to maintain family control over the company, acting conservatively and avoiding business decisions that can jeopardize business continuity, even if it means accepting an increase in the risk of poor performance (Gomez-Mejia et al., 2007). In family firms, decision-making processes are therefore conditioned by the noneconomic purpose of preserving their SEW.

This is particularly true for the first-generation family businesses as they present a stronger emotional attachment to the firm than multigenerational family businesses: the former is more oriented to nonfinancial goals and less interested in economic and financial performance (Sciascia et al., 2014). First-generation leaders prioritize ensuring the survival of the firm to pass it on to next generations, especially during an economic downturn (Arrondo-Garcia, Fernandez-Mendez, & Menendez-Requejo, 2016).

In first-generation firms, trans-generational sustainability is one of the most critical nonfinancial goals. It has significant implications for the decision-making time frame (Astrachan & Jaskiewicz, 2008; Zellweger, Eddleston, & Kellermanns, 2010). The founder generation tries to ensure the longevity of the company as much as possible, to guarantee its long-term continuity (Le Breton-Miller & Miller, 2009). Control, influence, sense of dynasty, and emotional attachment have a stronger weight in the first generations, given these companies' founder-centric orientation (Berrone et al., 2012). Moreover, the objectives, values, and feelings that characterize the first-generation members create a solid cohesion in company leadership. It also reduces the likelihood of conflicts and facilitates decision-making processes. Finally, these characteristics can prove particularly beneficial in periods of economic stress when the unity of the family leadership can be decisive for the company's survival, even if it is severely threatened (Essen, Strike, Carney, & Sapp, 2015).

From the socio-emotional wealth perspective, the preservation of "affective endowments" (Berrone et al., 2012) can be threatened by low performance which can put at risk the survival of the firm and the maintenance of SEW. According to Berrone et al. (2012), the threat of poor performance is twofold, as family members can suffer financial distress, primarily if they have invested most of their money in a single organization, and they can lose their SEW because they might have to sell or close the company. During phases of economic growth and stability, the company does not need to make drastic decisions, and therefore the likelihood of conflicts between financial and nonfinancial goals is low. On the contrary, during periods of economic downturn and when the company faces poor performance, radical and extreme decisions could be necessary, and first-generation family firms could be more oriented toward SEW preservation than toward financial performance recovery.

Thus, the benefits deriving from a first-generation leadership with solid cohesion regarding shared goals, values, and feelings may be stronger in family businesses with low performance than those with high performance. As suggested by Gomez-Mejia et al. (2007), family-owned businesses may be inclined to expose themselves to greater performance risk, if it is necessary to preserve their socio-emotional wealth. Consequently, they are opposed to losing regarding a threat to their socio-emotional wealth even if it means taking on a higher performance risk.

In conclusion, the SEW perspective leads us to believe that the will to preserve the socio-emotional wealth can play a dominant role in affecting the decision of family businesses to implement ambidextrous strategies. Moreover, in small family businesses, the "affective endowments" (Berrone et al., 2012) and the strong attachment of family members to the business may counterbalance for the limitations resulting from the small size of the company, thus making possible the effective implementation of ambidextrous strategies.

4 The Case Study

4.1 The Research Questions and Methodology

This work aims to analyze how a small family firm may adopt ambidextrous strategies. In particular, concerning periods of economic recession, this study seeks to answer the following questions:

1. What conditions can favor the implementation of these strategies in small family firms?
2. How can socio-emotional wealth influence family firms' ability to adopt ambidextrous strategies?

The empirical survey is based on the qualitative analysis of an in-depth case study. This methodology promotes the understanding of a holistic phenomenon, complex and that evolving (Eisenhardt, 1989; Wolcott, 1994), such as that of the present study. Moreover, as suggested by Yin (1994), a single case study can be useful for exploratory purposes, if it is used as a "prelude case" or pilot case. In this sense, the present study can be considered the first phase of a broader exploratory survey, which may subsequently be realized when starting with the information gathered by the current investigation.

The case analyzed was selected with the logic of a predetermined criterion of importance (Patton, 1990), namely, because it meets some essential requirements that are consistent with the object of the search. The purpose is to select an information-rich case whose study allows a better understanding of the questions under examination.

The selected firm is an Italian manufacturing family-owned small business that, as it will be explained in the next section, faced the economic crisis by adopting a mix of defensive and offensive strategies. This approach runs counter to the prevalent approach of small businesses that—as already mentioned above—have mainly adopted defensive strategies aimed at reducing costs to deal with the economic downturn. However, thanks to its balanced or ambidextrous strategy, the selected company has initially contained the impact of the crisis and has more recently recovered profit margins. For these reasons, it is considered that this company represents the ideal starting point in analyzing modes and dynamics that can facilitate the adoption of ambidextrous strategies in small businesses.

Before starting primary data gathering, secondary data was collected (company reports and websites) to familiarize with the company history and activities. However, the key data source was represented by in-depth, semi-structured, face-to-face interviews. Guided by a checklist, interviews were carried out in the company and had involved the founder (JS), a minority shareholder (BG), and the founder's daughter (HS). The questions were aimed to collect information regarding:

- The founder and his stockholders (age, history, education, professional profile, role in the company, etc.)
- The composition of the new generation (younger members of the family owners involved or not in the business, education, training, role in the company when applicable, etc.)
- The company (history, evolution, products, and markets, internationalization, etc.)
- The impact of the crisis and the strategic actions taken to deal with it; modes followed and conditions that have favored implementing different strategies

Interviews have been recorded and transcribed verbatim. Data thus gathered has been integrated with secondary data acquired during the company visit at engineering and design office, production department, showroom, research, and development office. Further data was collected through field notes taken during the interviews, financial statements from 2007 to 2013 (necessary in acquiring business performance during the crisis), and some sessions of informal dialogues that have affected the subjects interviewed and other interlocutors (i.e., members of the new generation already involved in the company or still undergoing training).

Data and information have been synthesized into an extensive case report and then analyzed to gradually achieve, with an inductive approach, the first draft of primary results. In particular, we have tried to comprehend how strategies have evolved and how they were implemented during the crisis. We have also analyzed what the conditions that have guided this process are and what has been the trend of business performance in the period 2007–2013.

Results that emerged were compared and integrated with the literature on this topic, in order to answer the research questions and outline a first descriptive framework on the adoption of ambidextrous strategies in small businesses.

4.2 The Research Context: An Italian Small Family-Owned Business

Shoes[1] Spa was founded in 1969 by JS and his brother. It operates in the footwear industry and produces molds for soles and cutting dies and technical tools for uppers processing. The roles of the two brothers have been clear and well-defined from the beginning: JS handles sales, while his brother manages the production process. In its early stages, the company focused on the local market, and it mainly supplied the thriving regional footwear district. In the 1980s, the enterprise began to internationalize. Its main exports went mainly to North African countries, and—in a few years—it reached a stable level of 20–30% in exports. In 2002, the company reached a peak of 68 employees. Even members of the new generation started to work in the family business. The first to enter was JS's eldest daughter, in 1997, after taking a degree in law. She began to support her father and then became an accounting manager. In 2000, the entrepreneur understood the necessity to significantly invest in staff training, in order to facilitate the increased use of technology-driven CAD/CAM. So, he decided to diversify and, together with an existing company in the same industry, create a new business, specialized in technical training and prototyping. The new company overgrew. So, he decided to open a branch in Campania and implemented essential projects, with great satisfaction for the entrepreneur. He recalls: "We had ten outstanding years, we invested, we grew enormously."

The year of 2003 was crucial for the company and the entrepreneur: his brother decided to leave for a personal reason, and JS had to find the money to pay off his brother share: "I took over my brother's shares with a concrete goal. I thought that the company is not only for a single generation, but for several generations, both for the owners' families and also for all the collaborators. Thinking about selling or worse close a company with a 40-year history did not feel right." At the same time, two minority stakeholders were involved in the ownership. They work with JS since 1976: "When I took over my brother's shares, they joined the ownership. I did not need to ask them, because it was implied, and they bought the shares."

Meanwhile, the footwear industry began to show an evident crisis—"*a general change*," "*a transformation*," as JS says. Competition from China, Spain, and Turkey became more and more intense, especially on the low-quality target. Also, many local businesses decided to decentralize their production abroad. Thanks to two banks and the entry of two stockholders, JS's brother is now paid off. The two

[1]For privacy reasons we use a fantasy name.

new stockholders do not belong to the founder's family, but they are his loyal collaborators, who have worked in the company for years. They have become a production manager and sales manager. From the strategic point of view, in the national market, the company faced the crisis by trying to penetrate the luxury market, taking advantage of the high quality of its products. In the foreign market, it grew throughout Eastern Europe countries.

In 2005, JS's second daughter joined the company, after a degree in international diplomatic science and a postgraduate in footwear technology and model design. She began working in the commercial office and is currently responsible for the foreign market. In the same period, the third member's son joined the firms, working alongside his father in the technical department. Everything was going well when in "2007–2008 the world collapsed" as JS says. The "slow down" in the footwear industry turned into a dramatic collapse: company's performance worsened very quickly, turnover dropped, 2008 ends with a net profit of almost half compared to 2007 and in 2009 the company recorded a significant loss. Two thousand ten was a year of tough but necessary choices to "save the company."

The first plan was to focus all resources and energies on the firms' core business by selling the training company. The entrepreneur says: "We had to devote precious time to understanding, managing, conserving, reorganizing, starting again... I had some thoughts and shareholders shared it: let's leave the training company behind and concentrate on this company. And so, we did." And BG confirms: "JS was CEO here and there, I was production manager here and there ... we had to choose because we had to be full-time here. So, we sold it, and we focused all our resources on the personal and financial issues here. This decision was crucial because it gave us the resources to move forward."

The second plan was to review processes to cut costs and gain efficiency. The crisis brings up many inefficiencies that they could no longer tolerate, because of company's low profits. Therefore, they began a long and painful reorganizational process, with a team of consultants who helped them identify areas that needed to be more efficient. JS initially took a position against the staff cuts (9 out of 55, with a cut of over 16% of the workforce). He is concerned about his employees ("they have grown up with me") and the negative image return ("I could not pretend to solve my problem by putting laying people off"). So, he asked employees to take a 10% voluntary reduction of salary, and at the same time, he thought to reset his CEO salary. But not everyone accepted this proposal, and the idea was put aside. "In any case, my salary was brought to zero, I reset it then, and I have not yet resumed it." After a few weeks, JS recognized the need—now imperative—to reduce staff. JS says: "I had to accept this thing and it was helpful, I must admit. This reorganization immediately started giving results, but not just because we reduced costs. We realized that we were reducing costs and producing more." In order to keep costs down, in this first phase, the company made only necessary investments, as they are considered necessary to keep the business competitive. Then, they carefully analyzed the main suppliers, in order to improve the raw material supply. These strategies allowed the company to recover efficiency and free up financial and managerial resources needed to continue investing and innovating quickly

"Investing 'headlong to death,' so we could move forward and do things we had never done before. We invested in machinery, technology, training, software, hardware, in everything at 360° !", said BG—"There is a crisis, but we cannot cry over it. We have to roll up our sleeves and not give up. We had to invent ourselves to do new things, better things, to be better equipped: we had always done so."

Throughout the second phase of the crisis (from 2012 to 2014), the firm has since engaged in the development and innovation of product and process, to recover and maintain its competitive advantage. JS says: "innovation and research are essential. The company has made major investments in recent years, including 2014 and 2015. We are not out of the crisis; however, despite the necessity, it is essential to innovate and pursue investments through innovation, because it does not come so easily, just because one thinks of it throughout the night. It requires facilities and training staff. However, for small and medium-sized businesses, and therefore also for us, it is tough because it requires many investments. So, even though we know innovation is essential, we must seek to modulate investments and distribute them over time." The right financial structure—a result of the self-financing policy always pursued by the company—allows it to obtain the necessary credit from banks to complete investments. The new projects, therefore, are financed half by the company's resources and half by capital credit.

The most important investments are intended to acquire new technologies (e.g., the latest generation 3D prototyping system, three new work centers, new testing facilities). They enable the company to offer its customers innovative and quality products and a design and prototyping service. Other investments have been designed to make processing more efficient (e.g., a photovoltaic system, new software to automate some processing, etc.) and to train staff, so that they can follow the company's technological evolution and shift toward the high-quality and luxury segment. At the same time, the company seeks to grow along various lines: penetrating new markets, particularly the United States and Latin American countries; looking for new customers, ready to pay a higher price for products of higher quality; and occupying market niches left "free" by competitors who failed because of the crisis. The company also started some important partnerships. The first, with a machinery manufacturer, in order to develop product and process innovations to produce soles, and the second with the local university, in order to develop a new marketing project. Marketing, in fact, and particular unconventional marketing strategies, is another area that the company intends to develop. A project has been launched to use social media marketing strategies. Now the company has 48 employees and around a four million EUR turnover, with a net income of 95,000 EUR. The "hard choices" and "the enormous financial effort" have allowed it to limit the impact of the crisis, to recover profitability and to continue its competitiveness over time. The decision-making process was crucial: "Sharing, confrontation is essential, even animatedly. However, we must not waste time when choices are to be made. You have to be fast. If you do not quickly make the choices penalizes the company. Now when I have to decide I close my eyes and go on." In this context, the desire to leave a healthy company for the next generations has counted a lot: "Over the years the desire to leave a thriving company to my children inspired me. I did it for myself, of course, but especially for my children. And for co-owner families. But also, for all the staff. I want to be honest; it is not that I say it for goodness, I have it in my blood. If I did this little that I did, it was thanks to all my collaborators, because we have exceptional people, who give the soul for the business. So, the desire to have and leave a healthy company is for a general context, both for offspring, for families who own the property, but also for all the staff, and the whole community."

Today, the JS's strategic goal is to continue to improve management processes in order to increase efficiency. At the same time, the company is trying to grow again, above all by improving the management of sales.

4.3 Results and Discussion

The analyzed case allowed us to identify the actions taken to implement an ambidextrous strategy. The company has consciously carried out some very different strategic actions, overall consistent with the concept of ambidexterity.

In the first phase, focused on the short term, the company has adopted a defensive approach in responding to the crisis and "protecting itself" from the recession, safeguarding its economic performance. This approach has been outward oriented, with a downsizing strategy aimed at redefining the core business and divesting non-core activities (e.g., the training company). Furthermore, this approach has been inward-oriented. A restructuring strategy has been carried out through a thorough review of the business processes, in order to cut costs, reduce workforce, and limit investments to a minimum in order to maintain competitiveness (Fig. 1).

Financial resources (including time and managerial resources), retrieved with downsizing and restructuring strategies, gave new strength to the company that has started investing and innovating again. Defensive strategies, therefore, have not only been necessary in order to preserve the company from the crisis but have also proved

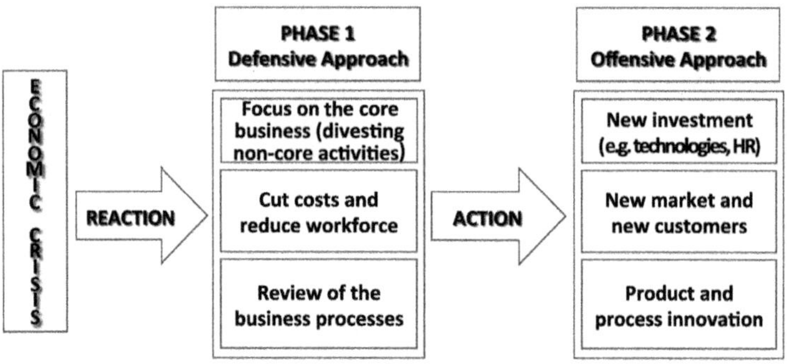

Fig. 1 Strategic actions and implementation of the ambidextrous strategy. Source: Authors' own figure

fundamental to quickly returning to invest. Thus, the second phase started (Fig. 1). It was no longer a reaction phase but an active one. It was characterized by an offensive approach, preparing the ground for a lasting medium to long-term relaunch. The enterprise has adopted strategies of profound internal reorganization in order to improve and renew production and management processes. This result has been achieved through investments in new technologies and staff training projects. The offensive strategy was also outward oriented, with innovation and development strategies aimed at innovating products, penetrating new markets, reaching new customers, and adopting more effective marketing initiatives. The path taken was particularly virtuous, as it allowed the company to offer its customers not only a product but also some high-value services.

This behavior, aimed first at reducing the economic downturn impact and then at maintaining and strengthening the company's competitive position, is in line with results reported by Pearce and Michael (2006)—referred to large-size enterprises—and with theoretical model suggested by Kitching et al. (2009) and by Rhodes and Stelter (2009). The ambidextrous strategy was implemented with an incremental logic and subsequent phases. The approach followed by the firm was not planned. However, it was based on the entrepreneur's ability to steadily monitor the environment, capturing the right signals and readily and adequately responding to change. In this perspective, defensive strategies have preceded and prepared the following offensive strategies. The crisis may lead to a collapse of economic performance, which, in turn, highlights the company's inefficiencies and makes it necessary to recover efficiency in the short term. It is very important that the company does not lose its innovative propensity. To this end, the role of the entrepreneur seems to be crucial.

Several financial and managerial resources were used to implement the ambidextrous strategy overcoming typical liability of smallness (Fig. 2). In particular, financial resources were retrieved with phase 1 and thanks to an excellent financial structure. Managerial resources came partially from internal factors (entrepreneur, new generation's skills, knowledge and competences, top management team) and partly from external factors (consultants, network). In this sense, the system of relations helped the firm's path to survival and development.

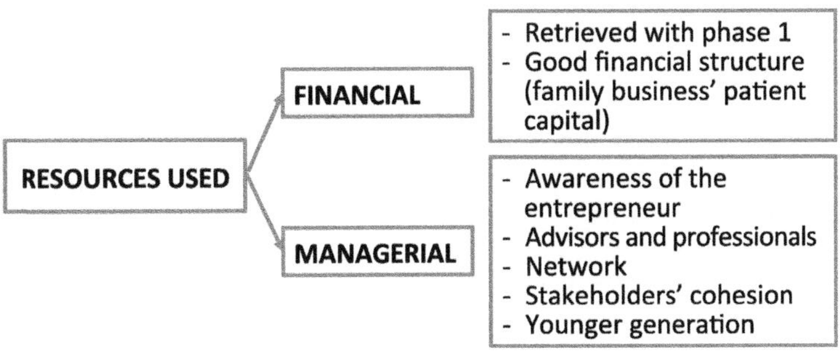

Fig. 2 Resources used to implement the ambidextrous strategy. Source: Authors' own figure

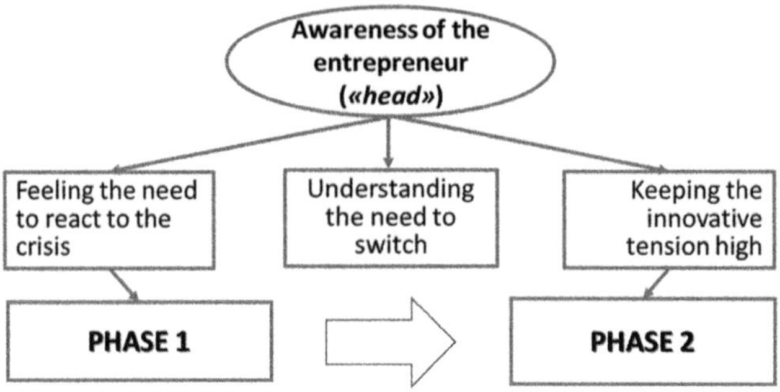

Fig. 3 The role of the entrepreneur's awareness. Source: Authors' own figure

Coming to our first research question, we focused on conditions that can favor the implementation of these strategies in small family firms enabling the company to overcome the limitations of resources that generally hamper this approach.

From results, two groups of conditions arise necessary conditions, indispensable in implementing an ambidextrous strategy and facilitating conditions, which can facilitate this strategy without being indispensable.

The necessary conditions include, above all, the awareness of the entrepreneur (Fig. 3). According to Feltham et al. (2005), a single decision-maker usually leads family businesses. For this reason, the entrepreneur's behaviors and competences are crucial in an entrepreneurial firm. In our study, the entrepreneur was the "head," who conceived the ambidextrous strategic. Entrepreneur's awareness can take many forms, and it is crucial in order to design and implement both phases of the ambidextrous strategy. In particular, in phase 1, awareness of the need to immediately react to the crisis by cutting costs and non-core activities was indispensable in order to trigger the initial defensive phase. The entrepreneur also needed to be aware that some "hard choices" (e.g., layoff) can be essential in ensuring the survival of the company over time. This step was anything but easy, especially for a small family business owner, as he usually prefers a low turnover (Chrisman, Chua, & Steier, 2005). The entrepreneur lives in close contact with his employees and for this reason can be put in the position to make unpleasant decisions from a personal point of view, although vital to an economic plan. This attitude is likely to slow the decision-making processes. However, during a crisis, they should be very quick. To successfully implement an ambidextrous strategy, some tough choices need to be made. They can save the company and give employees the opportunity to continue working for the company in the future. At the same time, the entrepreneur must know that defensive choices are needed not only to stem the recession's effects but also to create the essential resources to finance phase 2. Here the entrepreneur must be aware of the need to move from Step 1 to Step 2.

Moreover, the firm must start innovating again and investing in human resources, to keep the innovative tension high. Constant training of the staff has been not only a goal per se but also a necessary condition in allowing the company to acquire the skills needed to realize innovation strategies and exploit new technologies' full potential. As Pearce and Michael (2006) argue, human resources' collaboration is indispensable even during an economic downturn. The company cuts personnel costs by mostly laying off employees with obsolete skills and less orientation toward change. At the same time, however, it invested in the training of human resources, which remained (characterized by an average age that, in some businesses, stood at 30, with a greater attitude toward new technologies and less resistance to change).

The entrepreneur's awareness must be accompanied by two other essential conditions, always related his central role in the company. The first is the entrepreneur's openness. This implies his ability to build long-term networks with a variety of people (non-family members, consultants, universities, other companies, etc.). They can help the company to gain timely access to information and knowledge, which are useful in leading its strategic behavior, to maintain a high innovative tension and compensate for its limited internal resources.

In an ever more complex and rapidly changing context, the ability to activate partnerships, alliances, and networks is crucial for small businesses' survival, development, and growth (Street & Cameron, 2007). Such relationships stimulate the process of knowledge development and growth management, which can be vital for small businesses. The second essential condition concerns the entrepreneur's willingness to accept suggestions, the external help, in particular, from external consultants, who can help the entrepreneur gain a more objective view of the company, as well as offer new knowledge and managerial skills.

Finally, a good relationship between non-family stockholders is a crucial priority. In a situation of crisis, it may not be easy to agree on the firm's vision and strategic goals. However, it is essential to be united in strategic choices since it makes decision-making and strategies implementation faster.

Among *conditions facilitating the adoption of ambidextrous strategies*, it is important to point out the family nature of the business. This is strictly connected to our second research question, which questioned how the socio-emotional wealth could influence family firms' ability to adopt ambidextrous strategies. We think that the analyzed small family firm was more prone to adopt an ambidextrous strategy because by doing so it was able to counteract the low performance which was putting at risk the survival of the firm and the maintenance of SEW, preserving and enhancing its "affective endowments" (Berrone et al., 2012). In doing this, the entrepreneur has been greatly stimulated by the idea of being able to leave a healthy company to his children, to the co-owner families, and the whole staff. This is consistent with the sense of dynasty and the family control orientation typical of the founder generation, who tries to ensure the stability of the company as much as possible, in order to safeguard its continuity (Le Breton-Miller & Miller, 2009). Furthermore, the great attention toward the non-family employees, which are conceived "as part of the family," can be considered a dimension of the "binding social ties" which characterized family firms with a high level of SEW (Berrone et al., 2012). Also, the unwillingness for layoff and the related concern for corporate reputation can be interpreted in this perspective.

Moreover, according to literature (Le Breton-Miller & Miller, 2006), family businesses define their goals with a medium- to long-term perspective. Their main concern is to create conditions that allow the company to continue over time, from generation to generation. Some studies also have highlighted that family business, even during economic downturns, tend to invest more than non-family businesses, because they are more likely to "prepare for the future" (Amann & Jaussaud, 2012). The SEW related to the family nature of the business, therefore, can support the entrepreneur's awareness about the need not only to preserve the company in the short term but also ensure its continuity in the medium to long term. A medium-long-term perspective also relates to the concept of patient capital (Sirmon & Hitt, 2003), often associated with family businesses. This factor has enabled the company to achieve a solid financial structure over the years, thanks to a self-financing policy; have a good relationship with banks, that is, to continue to receive the money needed to finance investments; and continue to invest over the medium to long term, without expecting an immediate return on investment, all that has made the company better able to address difficulties caused by the crisis and to return to invest in phase 2.

Finally, the involvement of some new generation family members was another critical factor. They have brought new essential skills, particularly useful during phase 2. Compared to seniors, new-generation family members (thanks to their higher education level) are more familiar with managerial techniques and are more adept with new technologies, and they speak foreign languages. These skills are essential for a company that aims for development and growth, also in international markets (Cesaroni & Sentuti, 2010). For these reasons, younger family members can facilitate phase 2, since they can compensate for the lack of managerial resources that generally characterizes small businesses. However, so that their contribution becomes concrete, the attachment of family members to the business and the will to offer a perspective of continuity to the company seem to be essential.

To sum up, it seems clear that some of the primary conditions which favored the adoption and implementation of an ambidextrous strategy stemmed from the desire to maintain and enhance the family business's SEW. These factors in the crisis period have played a decisive role in guiding the decision-making processes and the strategic choices of the company.

5 Conclusions

Literature and empirical research agree that ambidextrous strategies are particularly useful in limiting crisis impact and preserving the company's competitiveness. Available studies, however, have mainly been focused on large companies. The literature has devoted little attention to small businesses also ignoring their universal family nature. The general idea is that small businesses should face more significant difficulties in successfully pursuing an ambidextrous strategy and in overcoming its implicit trade-off, because of their limited financial and managerial resources.

This paper examined the characteristics of a family small business's strategic behavior in a crisis context, in order to understand how they can adopt an ambidextrous strategy. This study also goes beyond the recognition of small businesses' limits. It individualizes necessary and facilitating conditions used to activate financial and managerial resources functional in order to implement an ambidextrous strategy. Finally, the crucial role of SEW in influencing the family firms' ability to adopt ambidextrous strategies was underlined. These results provide useful insights both on theoretical and practical level.

Concerning implication for research, our study contributes to the literature on small business, by analyzing conditions that can favor the implementation of ambidextrous strategies enabling the company to overcome the limitations of resources that generally hinder this approach. At the same time, our research offers new insights into the crucial role of SEW within family firms, by suggesting that it can improve the family firms' strategic behavior during periods of economic crisis, favoring the first-generation family business attitude toward the adoption of ambidextrous strategies.

At the practical level, results underline how to manage a firm during an economic downturn. In a period like that, small businesses have to continue looking at the medium to long term and maintaining a high propensity to innovate. Also, firms have to protect and develop their competitiveness thanks to relationships with some external subjects, such as consultants, universities, suppliers, customers, etc. These subjects can facilitate timely access to useful knowledge, in order to integrate internal skills and competences with new managerial skills form external help.

It should be recognized that there are some limitations to this research, many of which suggest further opportunities for empirical research. One of the main limitations is its generalization, as the study is derived from the analysis of only one case. It may be considered a pilot case, and it is hoped that it will be followed by more empirical studies focusing on small businesses' ambidextrous strategies to deal with the economic crisis with particular attention to the role of the family nature of the company.

Acknowledgments This study received financial support from ESU Verona-Italy (Regional Agency for the Right to Study).

References

Allouche, J., Amann, B., Jaussaud, J., & Kurashina, T. (2008). The impact of family control on the performance and financial characteristics of family versus nonfamily businesses in Japan: A matched-pair investigation. *Family Business Review, 21*(4), 315–329.

Altobelli, C. (2014). La piccola impresa sfinita dalla crisi rivive tra fallimenti, metamorfosi e piccoli successi. *Microimpresa – Imprese tra crisi e fiducia, 35*(1), 17–52.

Amann, B., & Jaussaud, J. (2012). Family and non-family business resilience in an economic downturn. *Asia Pacific Business Review, 18*(2), 203–223.

Andrews, K. R. (1987). *The concept of corporate strategy*. Homewood, IL: Irvwin.

Arrondo-Garcia, R., Fernandez-Mendez, C., & Menendez-Requejo, S. (2016). The growth and performance of family businesses during the global financial crisis: The role of the generation in control. *Journal of Family Business Strategy, 7*(4), 227–237.

Astrachan, J. H., & Jaskiewicz, P. (2008). Emotional returns and emotional costs in privately held family businesses: Advancing traditional business valuation. *Family Business Review, 21*(2), 139–149.

Basco, R. (2013). The family's effect on family firm performance: A model testing the demographic and essence approaches. *Journal of Family Business Strategy, 4*(1), 42–66.

Berrone, P., Cruz, C., & Gomez-Mejia, L. R. (2012). Socioemotional wealth in family firms: Theoretical dimensions, assessment approaches, and agenda for future research. *Family Business Review, 25*(3), 258–279.

Brenner, B. (2009). The value of increasing investment in employee benefits during an economic downturn. *Journal of Financial Service Professionals, 63*(1), 29–31.

Carnazza, P. (2014). La performance congiunturale delle imprese artigiane e i principali fattori di competitività: i principali risultati di un'indagine ad hoc. *Microimpresa – Imprese tra crisi e fiducia, 35*(1), 85–102.

Cerved. (2014). *Osservatorio su fallimenti, procedure e chiusure di imprese.* http://www.cervedgroup.com/documents/10156/105548/OsservatorioFallimentiProcedureChiusureImpreseDic2014_it.pdf

Cesaroni, F. M., & Sentuti, A. (2010). Nuove generazioni ed evoluzione dell'impresa familiare: la sfida della successione imprenditoriale. Analisi di alcuni casi di successo. *Piccola Impresa/Small Business, 2*, 63–89.

Cesaroni, F. M., & Sentuti, A. (2014). *Imprese femminili e crisi economica. Credito, competitività e conciliazione in una prospettiva di genere*. Milano: FrancoAngeli.

Chattopadhyay, P., Glick, W. H., & Huber, G. P. (2001). Organizational actions in response to threats and opportunities. *Academy of Management Journal, 44*(5), 937–955.

Chowdhury, S. D., & Lang, J. R. (1996). Turnaround in small firms: An assessment of efficiency strategies. *Journal of Business Research, 36*(2), 169–179.

Chrisman, J. J., Chua, J. H., & Steier, L. (2005). Sources and consequences of distinctive Familiness: An introduction. *Entrepreneurship: Theory and Practice, 29*(3), 237–247.

Corbetta, G., & Salvato, C. A. (2004). The board of directors in family firms: One size fits all? *Family Business Review, 17*(2), 119–134.

Cubico, S., Favretto, G., Ardolino, P., Noventa, S., Bellini, D., Gianesini, G., & Leitão, J. (2017). Family business and entrepreneurship: Competences and organizational behavior. In T. Devezas, J. Leitão, & A. Sarygulov (Eds.), *Industry 4.0 entrepreneurship and structural change in the new digital landscape* (pp. 333–347). Cham: Springer.

Curran, J. (1996). Small business strategy. In M. Warner (Ed.), *International encyclopedia of business and management*. London: International Thompson Press-Routledge.

Deans, G. K. (2009). Making a key decision in a downturn: Go on the offensive or be defensive? *Strategic Direction, 25*(8), 3–13.

DeDee, J. K., & Vorhies, D. W. (1998). Retrenchment activities of small firms during economic downturn: An empirical investigation. *Journal of Small Business Management, 36*(3), 46–61.

Eisenhardt, K. M. (1989). Building theories from case study research. *Academy of Management Review, 14*(4), 532–550.

Essen, M., Strike, V. M., Carney, M., & Sapp, S. (2015). The resilient family firm: Stakeholder outcomes and institutional effects. *Corporate Governance: An International Review, 23*(3), 167–183.

European Commission. (2013, November). *2013 SMEs' access to finance survey*. Analytical Report. http://ec.europa.eu/enterprise/policies/finance/files/2013-safe-analytical-report_en.pdf

Feltham, T. S., Feltham, G., & Barnett, J. J. (2005). The dependence of family business on a single decision-maker. *Journal of Small Business Management, 43*(1), 1–15.

Gallo, M. A., Tápies, J., & Cappuyns, K. (2004). Comparison of family and nonfamily business: Financial logic and personal preferences. *Family Business Review, 17*(4), 303–318.

Gomez-Mejia, L. R., Cruz, C., Berrone, P., & De Castro, J. (2011). The bind that ties: Socioemotional wealth preservation in family firms. *Academy of Management Annals, 5*(1), 653–707.

Gomez-Mejia, L. R., Haynes, K., Nuñez-Nickel, M., Jacobson, K. J. L., & Moyano-Fuentes, J. (2007). Socioemotional wealth and business risks in family-controlled firms: Evidence from Spanish olive oil mills. *Administrative Science Quarterly, 52*(1), 106–137.

Gomez-Mejia, L. R., Makri, M., & Larraza-Kintana, M. (2010). Diversification decisions in family-controlled firms. *Journal of Management Studies, 47*(2), 223–252.

Guatri, L. (1995). *Turnaround. Declino, crisi e ritorno al valore*. Milano: EGEA.

Istat. (2014). *Rapporto sulla competitività dei settori produttivi*. https://www.istat.it/it/files/2014/02/Rapporto-Competitivit%C3%A0-2014.pdf

Kitching, J., Blackburn, R., Smallbone, D., & Dixon, S. (2009). *Business strategies and performance during difficult economic conditions*, URN 09/1031, Kingston University and Bath University, Project Report. http://eprints.kingston.ac.uk/5852/1/Kitching-J-5852.pdf

Latham, S. (2009). Contrasting strategic response to economic recession in start-up versus established software firms. *Journal of Small Business Management, 47*(2), 180–201.

Latham, S., & Braun, M. (2011). Economic recession, strategy, and performance: A synthesis. *Journal of Strategy and Management, 4*(2), 96–115.

Le Breton-Miller, I., & Miller, D. (2006). Why do some family businesses out-compete? Governance, long-term orientations, and sustainable capability. *Entrepreneurship Theory and Practice, 30*(6), 731–746.

Le Breton-Miller, I., & Miller, D. (2009). Agency vs. stewardship in public family firms: A social embeddedness reconciliation. *Entrepreneurship: Theory and Practice, 33*(6), 1169–1191.

March, J. G. (1962). The business firm as a political coalition. *Journal of Politics, 24*(4), 662–678.

Mazzi, C. (2012). Family business and financial performance. Current state of knowledge and future research challenges. *Journal of Family Business Strategy, 2*(3), 166–181.

Michael, S. C., & Robbins, D. K. (1998). Retrenchment among small manufacturing firms during recession. *Journal of Small Business Management, 36*(3), 35–45.

Miles, R. E., & Snow, C. C. (1978). *Organizational strategy, structure, and process*. New York: McGraw Hill.

Miller, D. (1987). Strategy making and structure: Analysis and implications for performance. *Academy of Management Journal, 30*(1), 7–32.

Minichilli, A., Brogi, M., & Calabrò, A. (2015). Weathering the storm: Family ownership, governance, and performance through the financial and economic crisis. *Corporate Governance: An International Review, 24*(6), 552–568.

Nicolai, D. (2014). Le difficoltà di liquidità delle piccole imprese. *Microimpresa – Imprese tra crisi e fiducia, 35*(1), 103–116.

O'Boyle, E. H., Jr., Pollack, J. M., & Rutherford, M. W. (2012). Exploring the relation between family involvement and firms' financial performance: A meta-analysis of main and moderator effects. *Journal of Business Venturing, 27*(1), 1–18.

O'Gorman, C. (2006). Strategy and the small business. In S. Carter & D. Jones-Evans (Eds.), *Enterprise and small business* (2nd ed.). Harlow: Financial Times/Prentice Hall.

Pant, P. N., & Lachman, R. (1998). Value incongruity and strategic choice. *Journal of Management Studies, 35*(2), 195–212.

Papaoikonomou, E., Segarra, P., & Li, X. (2012). Entrepreneurship in the context of crisis: Identifying barriers and proposing strategies. *International Advances in Economic Research, 18*(1), 111–119.

Patton, M. Q. (1990). *Qualitative evaluation and research methods* (3rd ed.). London: Sage.

Pearce, J. A., & Michael, S. C. (1997). Marketing strategies that make entrepreneurial firms' recession-resistant. *Journal of Business Venturing, 12*(4), 301–314.

Pearce, J. A., & Michael, S. C. (2006). Strategies to prevent economic recessions from causing business failure. *Business Horizons, 49*, 201–209.

Pencarelli, T., Savelli, E., & Splendiani, S. (2008). *Strategic awareness and growth strategies in small-sized enterprises (SE)*. In 8th Global Conference on Business & Economics, October 18–19, Florence, Italy.

Penrose, E. (1995). *The theory of the growth of the firm* (3rd ed.). Oxford: Oxford University Press.

Rhodes, D., & Stelter, D. (2009). Seize advantage in a downturn. *Harvard Business Review, 87*(2), 50–58.

Robbins, D. K., & Pearce, J. A., II. (1992). Turnaround: Recovery and retrenchment. *Strategic Management Journal, 13*(4), 287–309.

Roberts, K. (2003). What strategic investments should you make during a recession to gain competitive advantage in the recovery? *Strategy & Leadership, 31*(4), 31–39.

Sciascia, S., Mazzola, P., & Kellermans, F. W. (2014). Family management and profitability in private family-owned firms: Introducing generational stage and the socioemotional wealth perspective. *Journal of Family Business Strategy, 5*(2), 131–137.

Sirmon, D. G., & Hitt, M. A. (2003). Managing resources: Linking unique resources, management, and wealth creation in family firms. *Entrepreneurship Theory and Practice, 27*(4), 339–358.

Smallbone, D., Cumbers, A., Syrett, S., & Leigh, R. (1999). The single European market and SMEs: A comparison of its effects in the food and clothing sector in the UK and Portugal. *Regional Studies, 33*(1), 51–62.

Sternad, D. (2012). Adaptive strategies in response to the economic crisis: A cross-cultural study in Austria and Slovenia. *Managing Global Transitions: International Research Journal, 10*(3), 257–282.

Street, C. T., & Cameron, A. F. (2007). External relationships and the small business: A review of small business alliance and network research. *Journal of Small Business Management, 45*(2), 239–266.

Voordeckers, W., Van Gils, A., & Van den Heuvel, J. (2007). Board composition in small and medium-sized family firms. *Journal of Small Business Management, 45*(1), 137–156.

Wan, W. P., & Yiu, D. W. (2009). From crisis to opportunity: Environmental jolt, corporate acquisitions, and firm performance. *Strategic Management Journal, 30*, 791–801.

Wolcott, H. F. (1994). *Transforming qualitative data: Description, analysis, and interpretation*. Thousand Oaks, CA: Sage.

Yin, R. K. (1994). *Case study research: Design and methods*. London: Sage.

Zellweger, T., Eddleston, K. A., & Kellermanns, F. W. (2010). Exploring the concept of familiness: Introducing family firm identity. *Journal of Family Business Strategy, 1*(1), 54–63.

Employees' Change-Oriented and Proactive Behaviors in Small- and Medium-Sized Family Businesses

Teresa Spiess and Anita Zehrer

Abstract This chapter sheds light on family business employees' change-oriented and proactive behaviors and the structural conditions they find to support or hinder these behaviors. A study consisting of 20 semi-structured interviews with family business owners and employees is reported. The results give the first idea for linkages to existing theory in family business research and can be seen as a basis for additional theoretical considerations as well as empirical studies.

Keywords Work behavior · Family business · Employee · Competitive advantage · Collective intelligence · Creativity · Social skills

1 Introduction

Understanding how to gain and maintain a competitive advantage over competitors is, and for the last few decades has been, a driving force for a multitude of practitioners as well as researchers and is equally important for the family as well as non-family businesses. Especially against the background of changing business environments (e.g., through drivers like technology, globalization, power structures, digitization), an organization's potential to adapt to those changing conditions can be seen as a possible source of competitive advantage (Reeves & Deimler, 2011). In order to enhance this adaptive potential, instead of relying solely on the resources of owners and top management, increasing complexity might require the involvement of various sources of competencies and knowledge inside a company. Also within emerging new paradigms like open strategy (Gegenhuber & Dobusch, 2016; Matzler, Füller, Koch, Hautz, & Hutter, 2014; Whittington, Cailluet, & Yakis-Douglas, 2011), opening processes formerly reserved for management to larger

T. Spiess (✉) · A. Zehrer
MCI Management Center Innsbruck—Internationale Hochschule GmbH, Innsbruck, Austria
e-mail: teresa.spiess@mci.edu; anita.zehrer@mci.edu

J. M. Saiz-Álvarez et al. (eds.), *Entrepreneurship and Family Business Vitality*, Studies on Entrepreneurship, Structural Change and Industrial Dynamics,
https://doi.org/10.1007/978-3-030-15526-1_4

collectives (e.g., within the organization) comes into consideration. Using the collective intelligence of an organization can lead to more unconventional thoughts and diverse solutions (Matzler, Strobl, & Bailom, 2016) and can, therefore, contribute to maximizing potential opportunities. Also, Potočnik and Anderson (2016) report a proliferation of studies related to change and innovation-related concepts in the Social Science Citation Index starting from the 1980s, with a tripling of the studies from 1999 to 2014 alone. With a recent and ongoing focus on the future of jobs in the era of digitization, the increased interest in these topics is unlikely to stop. Frey and Osborne (2016), for example, found that jobs demanding creative or social intelligence are less susceptible to computerization. The Future of Jobs Report published by the World Economic Forum (2016) comes to a similar conclusion. Social skills, complex problem-solving, creativity, and innovation are expected to be the skills most required for more than a third of the jobs by 2020. As an organization, being able to identify, recruit, and manage talented workers who possess these skills will become increasingly important regarding organizational effectiveness (World Economic Forum, 2016).

While the importance of internal resources as sources of sustained competitive advantage is a central notion throughout classical business literature (e.g., Janssen, 2000; MacKenzie, Podsakoff, & Podsakoff, 2011; Podsakoff, MacKenzie, Paine, & Bachrach, 2000; Wright, 2001), employees' active participation to the long-term survival of an organization is a topic neglected by family business literature so far. Especially agency theory (Jensen & Meckling, 1976; Schulze, Lubatkin, Dino, & Buchholtz, 2001), as well as stewardship theory (Davis, Schoorman, & Donaldson, 1997) and structural differences resulting from the respective conditions and attitudes, would, however, offer interesting aspects and potential antecedents for employees change-oriented and proactive behaviors. Whether and under which conditions stewardship effects like the lifelong commitment of family CEOs to the businesses or long investment horizons (Miller & Le Breton-Miller, 2006) negatively influence psychological climates for innovation or proactivity could be one of many questions in this regard. Another question could be whether and under which conditions high family involvement in management could enable more change-oriented and proactive behaviors by employees. Besides agency and stewardship theory, also the paradigm of socioemotional wealth (Gómez-Mejía, Haynes, Núñez-Nickel, Jacobson, & Moyano-Fuentes, 2007) could offer a perspective for analyzing employees' change-oriented and proactive behaviors in family businesses. A possible question resulting from such a perspective could be whether change-oriented and proactive behaviors of family business employees are more likely to be accepted when they target on maintaining or even increasing the socioemotional wealth of the family business.

So while in general, today employees' change-oriented and proactive behaviors are no longer "seen as inappropriate, disrespectful or even subversive, [but] have become increasingly sought by organizations" (Anderson, de Dreu, & Nijstad, 2004, p. 149), the special conditions and differences of family businesses in this regard have not been looked at. Katz (1964) very early on stated that an "organization which depends solely upon its blueprints of prescribed behavior is a very fragile social system" (p. 132). The importance of this statement is also evident for family businesses.

Thus, the study described in the paper at hand follows the overall question of how family business employees' change-oriented and proactive behaviors are supported and hindered. A qualitative study consisting of 20 semi-structured interviews is reported. The findings are a first step on the way to a more holistic view on the topic and can be the basis for additional theoretical considerations and empirical studies.

2 Literature Review

Overall, family businesses are acknowledged to be the prevalent form of the business organization all over the world (e.g., Sharma, Chrisman, & Gersick, 2012). These businesses account for 85% of all organizations within highly developed OECD countries (Van den Berghe & Carchon, 2003; de Massis, Frattini, Pizzurno, & Cassia, 2015) and represent the majority of organizations in Central Europe (e.g., Mandl, 2008). This demographic situation is quite similar in Tirol. Approximately 80% of the entire resident organizations are family-owned, and most of them can be categorized as small- and medium-sized organizations (Mandl, 2008). However, this predominance of small and medium-sized organizations displays disadvantages, especially regarding innovation. Small businesses have to deal with restricted access to capital markets, limited potentials for diversification, and lacking economies of scale (Pechlaner, Raich, Zehrer, & Peters, 2004), which can also impact their potentials for innovation. Extant research tackling the issue of innovation in family businesses deals with factors influencing the innovation process in regard to inputs (e.g., Matzler, Veider, Hautz, & Stadler, 2015) or outputs (e.g., Classen, van Gils, Bammens, & Carree, 2012). While the role of employees' change-oriented and proactive behaviors in this regard is a topic of growing interest in literature on small- and medium-sized enterprises in general, the interplay with the structural specifics of family businesses seems to be a topic neglected by research so far.

Over 50 years ago, Katz (1964) described types of employee behavior necessary for the functioning of an organization. He specified that employees not only need to be brought into an organization but also need to show constant physical as well as psychological attendance. Although holding people in a system is important for low turnover and therefore organizational effectiveness, they also need to actively show certain behaviors in order to contribute to effectiveness. This can be through two broad classes of behavior: (1) dependable role performance, which means the carrying out of the assigned roles and tasks, and (2) innovative and spontaneous behavior, meaning actions beneficial for organizational effectiveness although not specified by role prescriptions. Planning can never be accurate enough to anticipate every possible environmental change or every aspect that can go wrong in an organization. Innovation, spontaneous cooperation, and protective and creative behaviors are therefore essential for organizational effectiveness (Katz, 1964). Starting from these considerations on innovative and spontaneous behaviors, a plethora of different concepts in the area of change-oriented and proactive behaviors was developed. These include, for example, organizational spontaneity (George & Brief, 1992), personal initiative (Frese, Kring, Soose, & Zempel, 1996), taking charge (Morrison & Phelps, 1999), voice (Van Dyne & LePine, 1998), employee creativity (Amabile, 1988; Oldham & Cummings, 1996; Zhou & Shalley, 2003), intrapreneurship (Hisrich, 1990; Pinchot, 1985), issue selling (Dutton & Ashford, 1993), innovative work behavior (Farr & Ford, 1990; Scott & Bruce, 1994), proactive behavior (Crant, 2000), as well as contextual performance (Borman & Motowidlo, 1997).

Criticizing this phenomenon-driven approach, Parker and Collins (2010) look at various separate constructs related to change and proactivity in the workplace and try to analyze their distinctiveness empirically. They theorize, for example, that individual innovation (i.e., innovative work behavior), voice, taking charge, and problem prevention (i.e., personal initiative) contribute to a higher-order factor of proactive work behavior and also theorize two other higher-order factors, namely, proactive PE-fit behaviors and proactive strategic behaviors. Although their results show that these constructs have many similarities, they do not completely overlap. This is also in line with research on change-oriented Organizational Citizenship Behavior (Chiaburu & Baker, 2006), which is another umbrella term for such behaviors. It can generally be defined as "constructive efforts by individuals to identify and implement changes concerning work methods, policies, and procedures to improve the situation and performance" (Choi, 2007, p. 469). Also, similar to the research by Parker and Collins (2010), research on change-oriented Organizational Citizenship Behavior considers constructs like taking charge, personal initiative, voice, as well as creative and innovative performance to share important similarities (Chiaburu & Baker, 2006). Although different antecedents could influence theoretically certain aspects of these narrower behaviors, or result in different outcomes, adopting a broader view of change-oriented and proactive behaviors subsuming more narrow concepts seems applicable for this stage of the project.

Overall, the research on what triggers change-oriented and proactive behaviors is well advanced. So, on an individual level, various antecedents are well established, such as intrinsic motivation (Amabile, 1988), openness to experience (George & Zhou, 2001; Wu, Parker, & de Jong, 2014), proactive personality (Seibert, Crant, & Kraimer, 1999; Seibert, Kraimer, & Crant, 2001), organizational commitment (Ng, Feldman, & Lam, 2010), or self-efficacy (Ng & Lucianetti, 2016). Regarding employees' perceptions of organizational factors, perceived organizational support (Eisenberger, Fasolo, & Davis-LaMastro, 1990), psychological contract fulfillment (Ramamoorthy, Flood, Slattery, & Sardessai, 2005), as well as a psychological climate for innovation (Scott & Bruce, 1994) seem to influence change-oriented and proactive behaviors positively.

The person-situation debate has very early roots, for example, in Lewin's (1935) popular equation $B = f(P, E)$, which states that behavior (B) is a function of the person (P) as well as the environment (E). Both elements have subsequently been the subject of research. In the late 1960s, Mischel (1973), for example, criticized the core of direct effect personality research by stating that the importance of personality is generally overstated and emphasizing the importance of the situation in this regard. Later he admitted that these considerations might have been taken too seriously by some authors advocating a strict situationist view. So while, on the one hand, this critique led to a stream of research emphasizing cognitive variables in the formation of behavior within the context of socio-cognitive theory (Bandura, 1988; Mischel, 1973), it also led on the other hand to a crisis of especially personality research, with the number of publications only increasing again in the early 1980s (Swann & Seyle, 2005). However, the critique also spurred the person-situation debate and considerations about person-situation interaction that is based on it, which overtook considerations on the debate during the 1990s (Webster, 2009). Contemporary perspectives try to "put the person back together" (Barenbaum & Winter, 2008, p. 18) and acknowledge human nature in its complexity, as well as tending to adopt interactionist perspectives (also see, e.g., Fleeson & Noftle, 2009; Funder, 2001, 2006, 2008, 2009 for reviews).

Thus, after a long ongoing debate about whether the person or the situation is a better predictor of future behavior, research seems to have concluded that both the person and the situation have an important influence on behavior. Snyder and Ickes (1985) summarize that "historically, the interactional approach to the study of personality and social behavior emerged as the attempted synthesis of a dialectical tension between the dispositional approach (the original thesis) and the situationist movement that developed in reaction to it (the antithesis)" (p. 896). Funder (2001) also concludes that "the long-standing and controversy generating dichotomy between the effect of the situation versus the effect of the person on behavior, ... is and always was a false dichotomy (p. 200)." Funder (2008) states that even within the extreme positions, valuable knowledge can be produced. On the person-side, research can deal with either the development of traits regarding nature versus nurture or the influence of traits associated with various criteria. Adopting such a position could lead to some fruitful results. The ignorance of the respective other position will however always lead to an incomplete picture of the complete personality triad of persons, situations, and behaviors (Funder, 2006, 2008, 2009). Alternatively, as Funder (2008) summarizes: "What people do depends both on who they are—their dispositions such as personality traits—and the situation they are in. The obviousness of this statement only highlights how odd it is that each side of this equation has fans" (p. 568).

In summary and applied to the study at hand, from an interactionist perspective, the reasons for work behavior not only lie within the employees themselves but are also influenced by the conditions (i.e., task level, social level, organizational cues) they are confronted with (e.g., Funder, 2008; Mischel, 1977; Tett & Burnett, 2003). When looking at the phenomenon of change-oriented and proactive behaviors in family businesses, in general, it is an obstacle that studies on organizational behavior neglect family firms as an influence in this regard. This is because, firstly, it is obvious that employees as resources for competitive advantages are a topic equally important for the family as well as non-family businesses and secondly because there are various findings on how such conditions might differ in family businesses compared to other organizations: the altruistic culture of family firms (Dyer,

2009), the social responsibility of family firms (Dyer & Whetten, 2006), the higher climate of job security reported for family firms (Lee, 2006), different (also participative) leadership styles in family firms (Dörflinger et al., 2013), and family entrepreneurial orientation (Zellweger, Nason, & Nordqvist, 2012) just to name a few.

Since we strongly believe that these different conditions employees are faced with in family businesses also influence their change-oriented and proactive work behaviors, the study at hand will shed first insights.

3 Methodology and Study Design

To gain a better understanding of the possible differences, employees in small- or medium-sized family businesses face in regard to their change-oriented and proactive behaviors, and we conducted 20 semi-structured interviews lasting between 24 and 72 min.[1] Qualitative interviews are considered an adequate approach for this stage of the project, as the aim is to gain a broader overview of the topic of how structural differences inherent to family businesses influence or moderate employees' change-oriented and proactive behaviors. As this approach can be classified as theory-building, qualitative research design is considered suitable (Bryman & Bell, 2015; Creswell, 2014). Understanding different subjective views and different reasons for individual behavior can be a first step in gaining a broader understanding of the topic and can also be a source for subsequent hypothesis generation and future theory testing (Rost, 2005).

Table 1 gives an overview of the interview partners' position and gender, as well as the respective organizations concerning the business sector and the number of employees. The interviewees consisted of 13 employees and 7 owners of different Tirolean small- or medium-sized businesses. They were directly contacted via telephone and given a short description of the research topic. In order to ensure being able to gain a broad overview of different views on the topic and also to be able to talk about different structural conditions, employees as well as owners of small or medium-sized family businesses from different business sectors, with a different number of employees, were asked and invited to join the interviews. In order to ensure a comfortable atmosphere, the interviews were held in the employees' and owner's free time and a neutral environment outside the respective companies. The interviews were recorded and transcribed. All interview partners were older than 18 years and signed a form to consent their participation in the study.

To specifically analyze and interpret the collected material, the qualitative content analysis is a suitable method. Typing is the qualitative counterpart to quantitative generalization. Thus, theoretical statements regarding found regularities are also possible within qualitative research (Lamnek & Krell, 2016). In particular, we

[1]Interviews were conducted with the help of Julia Gschwentner and Johanna Herzog.

Table 1 Overview of interview partners

Person	Position	Gender	Number of employees in the organization	Business sector of the organization
IP01	Employee	Female	<49	Trade
IP02	Employee	Female	<249	Tourism
IP03	Employee	Female	<49	Tourism
IP04	Employee	Female	<49	Tourism
IP05	Employee	Female	<249	Information
IP06	Employee	Female	<249	Information
IP07	Employee	Female	<249	Industry
IP08	Employee	Female	<249	Tourism
IP09	Employee	Male	<249	Industry
IP10	Employee	Female	<249	Tourism
IP11	Owner	Male	<49	Trade
IP12	Employee	Female	<49	Information
IP13	Owner	Male	<49	Tourism
IP14	Owner	Male	<49	Industry
IP15	Owner	Male	<49	Industry
IP16	Owner	Male	<49	Industry
IP17	Owner	Male	<249	Tourism
IP18	Employee	Female	<249	Trade
IP19	Employee	Female	<49	Information
IP20	Owner	Female	<49	Tourism

Source: Authors' own table

applied the summarizing content analysis following the steps by Mayring (2016) for the study at hand.

Thus, first, the irrelevant parts of the interviews (such as elongated explanations, repetitive and clarifying phrases) were eliminated. In a second step, paraphrases were formulated for the remaining material about the research question. Then equivalent paraphrases were eliminated. This can also be summarized as the first reduction according to Mayring (2016). The second reduction then consisted of summarizing and integrating similar paraphrases in order to derive a category system (Mayring, 2016). Following this method, this category system is then applied to the source material, which we also applied in a next step. This process was supported by multiple iterations as well as frequent discussions within the coding team, which also supported interrater reliability.

4 Results

Regarding the results, we could find two different patterns mainly related to the family, which were linked to different phenomena within the organization and led to different forms of change-oriented and proactive behaviors. These patterns are outlined in Table 2.

The first underlying family pattern related to change-oriented and proactive behaviors we could identify can be called "bureaucratic deciders reluctant to change." The family itself is less addressed by interviewees talking about these organizations. The organization seems to revolve around the owner. Owners, who are described as bureaucratic deciders, are also described as reluctant to change with a few carefully selected agents at most. These agents are either family members or long-term employees that seem to have almost been accepted as extended family members and are fully trusted. The owner's idea of "we have always done it that way" is fully transported to the employees. Therefore, they do not see a potential or a reason to engage in change-oriented or proactive behaviors. Nepotism or also long-term agents occupying higher positions and thus hindering promotions are topics discussed for the same cases. These structures do not only seem to support the overall climate of rather maintaining the status quo but also seem to negatively impact job satisfaction and motivate self-interest as well as counterproductive work behaviors. One interviewee, for example, stated that the inability to change procedures through their actions, as well as the fact that positive actions or engagement would not lead to any changes or a promotion, in the end, results in performing as low as possible. Change-oriented and proactive behaviors in this regard are rarely reported, and if so only for self-serving reasons. Example excerpts are: "I rarely

Table 2 Patterns related to change-oriented and proactive behaviors

Bureaucratic deciders reluctant to change	Non-bureaucratic accessible gatekeepers
– Bureaucratic communication and decision structures	– Non-bureaucratic communication and decision processes
– Nepotism	– Owners are personally present and involved in most of the organization's processes
– Almost no direct contact to owner or family members for most of the employees	– High family involvement with employees
– Low levels of trust "[The successor] is mainly interested in his bank account. However, he does not know how things work, and he does not understand that people put much effort into their work and how the processes are"	– Higher levels of trust "What is special is that the entrepreneurial family is very close to the employees and always gives an ear to them"
– Change-oriented and proactive behaviors rarely happen and if so mostly for self-serving reasons	– Change-oriented and proactive behaviors happen, but are rarely autonomous (i.e., only restricted to narrow areas, reserved for long-term employees, the final decision lies with the owner)

Source: Authors' own table

apply such behaviors, but sometimes of course I do. In the end, I want to make it as easy as possible for myself and do not want to have to fix errors afterward," or "I do work proactively in my job. However, my main aim is to look after myself and to come forward. I do not mean it in an egoistic way, but I want to make the best of the situation for me," or "Honestly, I do not have the opportunity to work proactively. Processes are either clearly defined, or I will have to ask my supervisor for permission. Some of the rules do not make much sense or could be improved, but I have the impression that they just want to leave everything the way it is and don't want to make changes."

The second underlying family pattern related to change-oriented and proactive behaviors we could identify can be called "non-bureaucratic accessible gatekeepers." The family itself is more often addressed by interviewees talking about these organizations. For the pattern of non-bureaucratic accessible gatekeepers, or in other words owners and families who are open to change, the non-bureaucratic decision process is emphasized as an advantage of family businesses and facilitation of change-oriented and proactive behaviors. Either the owners themselves are consistently personally present and involved in most of the organization's processes, or this task is shared between a small number of close family members. In contrast to the first group of owners, these owners are described as always having an open door and being interested in employees' ideas and suggestions. Although in these cases change-oriented and proactive behaviors were more frequent or more likely to be accepted and sometimes even encouraged, the owners and families are still described as gatekeepers regarding innovation. The final decision on whether an idea or behavior is accepted seems to be taken by the owners and family. The reasons for these decisions are however not always transparent or comprehensible for the employees. Example excerpts are "We are highly desired to think along and not to bother our boss with minor decisions," or "In a way, I think I can work proactively. For certain work steps and decisions, I need a higher authority. For other work steps I can certainly work proactively," or "Processes are not exactly specified in our company, which makes proactive behaviors necessary. The family, however, makes most decisions and even if they are not directly involved, decisions are at least influenced by the family in a way."

5 Discussion

The main finding of the study at hand is that differences in change-oriented and proactive behaviors are connected to two different patterns mainly related to the family, which are linked to different phenomena within the organization and lead to these different forms of change-oriented and proactive behaviors.

When looking for several explanations of our results in family business literature, a link can be drawn to the concept of *family entrepreneurial orientation* (Zellweger et al., 2012) or more precisely aspects thereof. Family entrepreneurial orientation (FEO) can be defined as "... The attitudes and mindsets of families to engage in entrepreneurial activity" (Zellweger et al., 2012, p. 143). The concept goes back to first considerations on *family orientation*, which was developed as the counterpart to *entrepreneurial orientation* for family businesses (Lumpkin, Martin, & Vaughn, 2003, 2008). While the concept of entrepreneurial orientation is described with dimensions such as risk-taking, proactiveness, competitive aggressiveness, autonomy, and innovativeness (Lumpkin & Dess, 1996; Miller, 1983), family orientation is described with dimensions such as loyalty, interdependency, security, stability, and tradition (Lumpkin et al., 2003, 2008). Proponents of the concept of family orientation usually see it in opposition to entrepreneurial orientation and postulate that both cannot exist at the same time; another line of argumentation is that both can coexist, but the dimensions of competitive aggressiveness and risk-taking are less important in family businesses (Lumpkin, Brigham, & Moss, 2010; Zellweger & Sieger, 2012).

Zellweger et al. (2012) take up on this and argue that in order to be able to describe the entrepreneurial behavior of family businesses, dimensions of entrepreneurial orientation, as well as family orientation, have to be considered and that they can well exist simultaneously. They thus suggest the concept FEO and argue for two broad dimensions of the transgenerational lookout and change orientation (subsuming narrower dimensions such as preservation orientation, transgenerational lookout, and change orientation) as well as risk and innovation orientation (subsuming narrower dimensions such as risk orientation, resources focus, proactiveness, and innovativeness).

Having a closer look at the results of the study at hand, especially the dimensions of the transgenerational lookout and change orientation, can be applied to differentiate between the two patterns found. Low levels of the transgenerational lookout and change orientation are, for example, connected to the family striving to preserve existing businesses, making decisions primarily with the success of the current generation in mind, and being resistant to change (Zellweger et al., 2012). Elements can also be found in the descriptions of the "bureaucratic deciders reluctant to change," for example, within the frequent mentions of nepotism and unwillingness to change, just to name a few. High levels of the transgenerational lookout and change orientation are, for example, connected to the family striving to create new businesses, making decisions primarily with the success of future generations in mind, and being very willing to change (Zellweger et al., 2012). Elements can also be found in the descriptions of the "non-bureaucratic accessible gatekeepers," for example, within the frequent mentions of the families' openness to change and interest in employees' ideas, as well as the description of the family as constantly personally present and engaged.

6 Conclusion, Limitations, and Further Research

To summarize the results of the study at hand, it seems as if FEO indirectly influences employees' change-oriented and proactive behaviors and is thus indirectly accountable for spurring or hindering internal opportunities for innovation in the long run. The results show that low levels of the transgenerational lookout and change orientation lead to low levels or only self-serving forms of change-oriented and proactive employee behaviors. High levels of the transgenerational lookout and change orientation lead to higher levels of change-oriented and proactive employee behaviors. These behaviors are however rarely completely autonomous. The final decision on whether an idea or behavior is accepted seems to be taken by the owners and family. It thus seems as if the structural conditions employees find in family businesses have an impact on their change-oriented and proactive behaviors, and therefore these employee behaviors should be further analyzed with a special focus on family businesses. Following this line of reasoning and developing it further might be an interesting endeavor for future research.

Along with FEO another concept, which might be interesting in this regard, is socioemotional wealth (Gómez-Mejía et al., 2007). Our results show that the family businesses analyzed are not automatically avoiding their employees' change-oriented and proactive behaviors. The climate for change seems to be highly dependent on FEO. The businesses allowing for more of these behaviors seem to have less bureaucratic structures, more family involvement in the actual processes, and also more personal involvement of the family with the employees. Although in these cases families seem to be more open to change, they also seem to be very careful in sorting out which ideas or suggestions are worth following or and which are not. Autonomous behaviors are rarely accepted. Retaining family control and thus securing socioemotional wealth (Gómez-Mejía et al., 2007) could be one explanation for these results and might be a perspective worth following for further research in this regard.

Another interesting aspect found in the interviews is that it seemed as if the described structures spur such behaviors although, for example, promotion is not an option in the long run. Which mechanisms motivate employees to perform such behaviors in these environments might also be an interesting endeavor for further research and could be analyzed against the background of stewardship theory (Davis et al., 1997; Miller & Le Breton-Miller, 2006). On the other hand, bureaucratic structures with less direct contact with the owner or close family members seem to result in less interest for or involvement in change-oriented or proactive behaviors. This could be explained drawing on or extending considerations on agency theory (Jensen & Meckling, 1976; Miller & Le Breton-Miller, 2006) and could also be an interesting topic for further research.

Madison, Kellermanns, and Munyon (2017) found that agency as well as stewardship mechanisms coexist in family businesses and have different influences on various outcomes. While agency governance mechanisms are, for example, more closely related to counterproductive agent behaviors, stewardship governance mechanisms increase pro-organizational behaviors. The results of this study point in a similar direction also for employee behaviors. So how organizational structures and family involvement, as well as agentic or stewardship aspects and their coexistence in family businesses, influence change-oriented and proactive employee behaviors might be a final interesting question to be tackled within further research projects.

The study at hand does not come without limitations. While a somewhat open qualitative study can offer various opportunities to understand the reasons for individual behavior better and thus support theory building, it is less focused and leads to results, which are non-generalizable. Future studies could, for example, focus on narrowing down the research setting and, for example, concentrate on interview partners with a background in similar organizations concerning FEO. The broader quantitative setting in order to be able to compare family businesses regarding FEO would also be an option. Another strategy could be to apply a case study-based approach in order to get more profound insights into a specific family business and thus be able to gain a better understanding of employees' change-oriented and proactive behaviors in a particular setting.

Another aspect needed to be discussed is the qualitative self-report of behavior applied in the study at hand. The general notion within research on change-oriented and proactive behaviors is that self-ratings, as well as supervisor ratings of these behaviors, come with pros and cons. While self-ratings are described to be better suited to capture the behavioral notion of change-oriented and proactive behaviors and are argued to be more subtle (Janssen, 2000; Madrid, Patterson, Birdi, Leiva, & Kausel, 2014), supervisor ratings are sometimes considered more objective (Ng & Feldman, 2012). In previous quantitative research, moderate correlations between the two ratings are reported (Abstein, Heidenreich, & Spieth, 2014; Janssen, 2000). When applying supervisor ratings, there is a chance that these will not be able to capture unfinished attempts such as generating or promoting ideas that encounter resistance and are stopped or postponed. In the case of small role innovations, supervisor ratings might not be able to capture these behaviors at all. Thus, in quantitative research, it is common to apply self-ratings of change-oriented and proactive behaviors in order not to miss relevant information (Madrid et al., 2014). Another strategy or opportunity for further research—may be in combination with a case study approach—could thus be to focus on experiments in order to determine employees' change-oriented and proactive behaviors.

References

Abstein, A., Heidenreich, S., & Spieth, P. (2014). Innovative work behaviour: The impact of comprehensive HR system perceptions and the role of work-life conflict. *Industry & Innovation, 21*, 91–116.

Amabile, T. M. (1988). A model of creativity and innovation in organizations. In B. M. Staw & L. L. Cummings (Eds.), *Research in organizational behavior* (10th ed.). Greenwich, CT: JAI Press.

Anderson, N. R., de Dreu, C. K. W., & Nijstad, B. A. (2004). The routinization of innovation research: A constructively critical review of the state-of-the-science. *Journal of Organizational Behavior, 25*, 147–173.

Bandura, A. (1988). Organizational applications of social cognitive theory. *Australian Journal of Management, 13*, 275–302.

Barenbaum, N. B., & Winter, D. G. (2008). History of modern personality theory and research. In O. P. John, R. W. Robins, & L. A. Pervin (Eds.), *Handbook of personality: Theory and research* (pp. 3–26). New York: Guilford Press.

Borman, W. C., & Motowidlo, S. J. (1997). Task performance and contextual performance: The meaning for personnel selection research. *Human Performance, 10*, 99–109.

Bryman, A., & Bell, E. (2015). *Business research methods*. Cambridge: Oxford University Press.

Chiaburu, D. S., & Baker, V. L. (2006). Extra-role behaviors challenging the status-quo. *Journal of Managerial Psychology, 21*, 620–637.

Choi, J. N. (2007). Change-oriented organizational citizenship behavior: Effects of work environment characteristics and intervening psychological processes. *Journal of Organizational Behavior, 28*, 467–484.

Classen, N., van Gils, A., Bammens, Y., & Carree, M. (2012). Accessing resources from innovation partners: The search breadth of family SMEs. *Journal of Small Business Management, 50*, 191–215.

Crant, M. J. (2000). Proactive behavior in organizations. *Journal of Management, 26*, 435–462.

Creswell, J. W. (2014). *Research design: Qualitative, quantitative, and mixed methods approaches* (4th ed.). Los Angeles: Sage.

Davis, J. H., Schoorman, F. D., & Donaldson, L. (1997). Toward a stewardship theory of management. *The Academy of Management Review, 22*, 20–47.

de Massis, A., Frattini, F., Pizzurno, E., & Cassia, L. (2015). Product innovation in family versus nonfamily firms: An exploratory analysis. *Journal of Small Business Management, 53*, 1–36.

Dörflinger, C., Dörflinger, A., Gavac, K., & Vogl, B. (2013). *Familienunternehmen in Österreich: Status Quo 2013*. Wien: Austrian Institute for SME Research.

Dutton, J. E., & Ashford, S. J. (1993). Selling issues to top-management. *Academy of Management Review, 18*, 397–428.

Dyer, W. G. (2009). *Cultural change in family firms: Anticipating and managing business and family transitions* (Jossey-Bass social and behavioral science series) (1st ed.). San Francisco, CA: Jossey-Bass.

Dyer, W. G., & Whetten, D. A. (2006). Family firms and social responsibility: Preliminary evidence from the S&P 500. *Entrepreneurship: Theory and Practice, 30*, 785–802.

Eisenberger, R., Fasolo, P., & Davis-LaMastro, V. (1990). Perceived organizational support and employee diligence, commitment, and innovation. *Journal of Applied Psychology, 75*, 51–59.

Farr, J. L., & Ford, C. M. (1990). Individual innovation. In M. A. West & J. L. Farr (Eds.), *Innovation and creativity at work* (pp. 63–80). Chichester: Wiley.

Fleeson, W., & Noftle, E. E. (2009). In favor of the synthetic resolution to the person-situation debate. *Journal of Research in Personality, 43*, 150–154.

Frese, M., Kring, W., Soose, A., & Zempel, J. (1996). Personal initiative at work: Differences between East and West Germany. *Academy of Management Journal, 39*, 37–63.

Frey, C. B., & Osborne, M. A. (2016). The future of employment: How susceptible are jobs to computerization? *Technological Forecasting and Social Change, 114*, 254–280.

Funder, D. C. (2001). Personality. *Annual Review of Psychology, 52*, 197–221.

Funder, D. C. (2006). Towards a resolution of the personality triad: Persons, situations, and behaviors. *Journal of Research in Personality, 40*, 21–34.

Funder, D. C. (2008). Persons, situations, and person-situation interactions. In O. P. John, R. W. Robins, & L. A. Pervin (Eds.), *Handbook of personality: Theory and research* (pp. 568–582). New York: Guilford Press.

Funder, D. C. (2009). Persons, behaviors, and situations: An agenda for personality psychology in the postwar era. *Journal of Research in Personality, 43*, 120–126.

Gegenhuber, T., & Dobusch, L. (2016). Making an impression through openness: How open strategy-making practices change in the evolution of new ventures. *Long Range Planning, 50* (3), 337–354.

George, J. M., & Brief, A. P. (1992). Feeling good-doing good: A conceptual analysis of the mood at work-organizational spontaneity relationship. *Psychological Bulletin, 112*, 310–329.

George, J. M., & Zhou, J. (2001). When openness to experience and conscientiousness are related to creative behavior: An interactional approach. *Journal of Applied Psychology, 86*, 513–524.

Gómez-Mejía, L. R., Haynes, K. T., Núñez-Nickel, M., Jacobson, K. J. L., & Moyano-Fuentes, J. (2007). Socioemotional wealth and business risks in family-controlled firms: Evidence from Spanish olive oil mills. *Administrative Science Quarterly, 52*, 106–137.

Hisrich, R. D. (1990). Entrepreneurship/intrapreneurship. *American Psychologist, 45*, 209–222.

Janssen, O. (2000). Job demands, perceptions of effort-reward fairness and innovative work behavior. *Journal of Occupational and Organizational Psychology, 73*, 287–302.

Jensen, M. C., & Meckling, W. H. (1976). Theory of the firm: Managerial behavior, agency costs, and ownership structure. *Journal of Financial Economics, 3*, 305–360.

Katz, D. (1964). The motivational basis of organizational behavior. *Behavioral Science, 9*, 131–146.

Lamnek, S., & Krell, C. (2016). *Qualitative Sozialforschung: Mit Online-Materialien* (6th ed.). Weinheim: Beltz.

Lee, J. (2006). Family firm performance: Further evidence. *Family Business Review, 19*, 103–114.

Lewin, K. (1935). *A dynamic theory of personality: Selected papers*. New York: McGraw Hill.

Lumpkin, G. T., Brigham, K. H., & Moss, T. W. (2010). Long-term orientation: Implications for the entrepreneurial orientation and performance of family businesses. *Entrepreneurship & Regional Development, 22*, 241–264.

Lumpkin, G. T., & Dess, G. G. (1996). Clarifying the entrepreneurial orientation construct and linking it to performance. *The Academy of Management Review, 21*, 135.

Lumpkin, G. T., Martin, W., & Vaughn, M. (2003). *From entrepreneurial orientation to "family orientation": Generational differences in the management of family businesses*. Paper presented at the 22nd Babson College Entrepreneurship Research Conference, Wellesley, MA.

Lumpkin, G. T., Martin, W., & Vaughn, M. (2008). Family orientation: Individual-level influences on family firm outcomes. *Family Business Review, 21*, 127–138.

MacKenzie, S. B., Podsakoff, P. M., & Podsakoff, N. P. (2011). Challenge-oriented organizational citizenship behaviors and organizational effectiveness: Do challenge-oriented behaviors really have an impact on the organization's bottom line? *Personnel Psychology, 64*, 559–592.

Madison, K., Kellermanns, F. W., & Munyon, T. P. (2017). Coexisting agency and stewardship governance in family firms: An empirical investigation of individual-level and firm-level effects. *Family Business Review, 30*, 347–368.

Madrid, H. P., Patterson, M. G., Birdi, K. S., Leiva, P. I., & Kausel, E. E. (2014). The role of weekly high-activated positive mood, context, and personality in innovative work behavior: A multilevel and interactional model. *Journal of Organizational Behavior, 35*, 234–256.

Mandl, I. (2008). *Overview of family business relevant issues*. Final report, project on behalf of the European Commission, Austrian Institute for SME Research, Vienna.

Matzler, K., Füller, J., Koch, B., Hautz, J., & Hutter, K. (2014). Open strategy – A new strategy paradigm? In K. Matzler, H. Pechlaner, & B. Renzl (Eds.), *Strategie und Leadership* (pp. 37–55). Wiesbaden: Springer Fachmedien.

Matzler, K., Strobl, A., & Bailom, F. (2016). Leadership and the wisdom of crowds: How to tap into the collective intelligence of an organization. *Strategy & Leadership, 44*, 30–35.

Matzler, K., Veider, V., Hautz, J., & Stadler, C. (2015). The impact of family ownership, management, and governance on innovation. *Journal of Product Innovation Management, 32*, 319–333.

Mayring, P. (2016). *Einführung in die qualitative Sozialforschung: Eine Anleitung zu qualitativem Denken* (6th ed., Pädagogik). Weinheim: Beltz Verlag.

Miller, D. (1983). The correlates of entrepreneurship in three types of firms. *Management Science, 29*, 770–791.

Miller, D., & Le Breton-Miller, I. (2006). Family governance and firm performance: Agency, stewardship, and capabilities. *Family Business Review, 19*, 73–87.

Mischel, W. (1973). Toward a cognitive social learning reconceptualization of personality. *Psychological Review, 80*(4), 252–283.

Mischel, W. (1977). The interaction of person and situation. In D. Magnusson & N. S. Endler (Eds.), *Personality at the crossroads: Current issues in interactional psychology.* Symposium held in Stockholm, June 22–27, 1975 (pp. 333–352). Hillsdale, NJ: Erlbaum.

Morrison, E. W., & Phelps, C. C. (1999). Taking charge at work: Extra role efforts to initiate workplace change. *Academy of Management Journal, 42*, 403–419.

Ng, T. W. H., & Feldman, D. C. (2012). A comparison of self-ratings and non-self-report measures of employee creativity. *Human Relations, 65*, 1021–1047.

Ng, T. W. H., Feldman, D. C., & Lam, S. S. K. (2010). Psychological contract breaches, organizational commitment, and innovation-related behaviors: A latent growth modeling approach. *Journal of Applied Psychology, 95*, 744–751.

Ng, T. W. H., & Lucianetti, L. (2016). Within-individual increases in innovative behavior and creative, persuasion, and change self-efficacy over time: A social-cognitive theory perspective. *The Journal of Applied Psychology, 101*, 14–34.

Oldham, G. R., & Cummings, A. (1996). Employee creativity: Personal and contextual factors at work. *Academy of Management Journal, 39*, 607–634.

Parker, S. K., & Collins, C. G. (2010). Taking stock: Integrating and differentiating multiple proactive behaviors. *Journal of Management, 36*, 633–662.

Pechlaner, H., Raich, F., Zehrer, A., & Peters, M. (2004). Growth perceptions of small and medium-sized enterprises (SME's)—The case of South Tyrol. *Tourism Review, 59*, 7–13.

Pinchot, G. (1985). *Intrapreneuring: Why you do not have to leave the corporation to become an entrepreneur* (2nd ed.). New York: Harper & Row.

Podsakoff, P. M., MacKenzie, S. B., Paine, J. B., & Bachrach, D. G. (2000). Organizational citizenship behaviors: A critical review of the theoretical and empirical literature and suggestions for future research. *Journal of Management, 26*, 513–563.

Potočnik, K., & Anderson, N. R. (2016). A constructively critical review of change and innovation-related concepts: Towards conceptual and operational clarity. *European Journal of Work and Organizational Psychology, 25*, 481–494.

Ramamoorthy, N., Flood, P. C., Slattery, T., & Sardessai, R. (2005). Determinants of innovative work behaviour: Development and test of an integrated model. *Creativity and Innovation Management, 14*(2), 142–150.

Reeves, M., & Deimler, M. (2011, July–August). Adaptability: The new competitive advantage. *Harvard Business Review*, 134–141.

Rost, J. (2005) 'Differentielle Indikation und gemeinsame Qualitätskriterien als Probleme der Integration von qualitativen und quantitativen Methoden. Symposium: Qualitative und quantitative Methoden in der Sozialforschung: Differenz und/oder Einheit?', 1. Berliner Methodentreffen Qualitative Forschung, 24.–25. Juni 2005.

Schulze, W. S., Lubatkin, M. H., Dino, R. N., & Buchholtz, A. K. (2001). Agency relationships in family firms: Theory and evidence. *Organization Science, 12*, 99–116.

Scott, S. G., & Bruce, R. A. (1994). Determinants of innovative behavior: A path model of innovation in the workplace. *Academy of Management Journal, 37*, 580–607.

Seibert, S. E., Crant, M. J., & Kraimer, M. L. (1999). Proactive personality and career success. *Journal of Applied Psychology, 84*, 416–427.

Seibert, S. E., Kraimer, M. L., & Crant, M. J. (2001). What do proactive people do? A longitudinal model linking proactive personality and career success. *Personnel Psychology, 54*, 845–874.

Sharma, P., Chrisman, J. J., & Gersick, K. E. (2012). 25 Years of family business review. *Family Business Review, 25*, 5–15.

Snyder, M., & Ickes, W. (1985). Personality and social behavior. In G. Lindzey & E. Aronson (Eds.), *Handbook of social psychology* (3rd ed., pp. 883–947). New York: Random House.

Swann, W. B., & Seyle, C. (2005). Personality psychology's comeback and its emerging symbiosis with social psychology. *Personality & Social Psychology Bulletin, 31*, 155–165.

Tett, R. P., & Burnett, D. D. (2003). A personality trait-based interactionist model of job performance. *Journal of Applied Psychology, 88*, 500–517.

Van Dyne, L., & LePine, J. A. (1998). Helping and voice extra-role behaviors: Evidence of construct and predictive validity. *Academy of Management Journal, 41*, 108–119.

Van den Berghe, L. A. A., & Carchon, S. (2003). Agency relations within the family business system: An exploratory approach. *Corporate Governance, 11*, 171–179.

Webster, G. D. (2009). The person-situation interaction is increasingly outpacing the person-situation debate in the scientific literature: A 30-year analysis of publication trends, 1978–2007. *Journal of Research in Personality, 43*, 278–279.

Whittington, R., Cailluet, L., & Yakis-Douglas, B. (2011). Opening strategy: Evolution of a precarious profession. *British Journal of Management, 22*, 531–544.

Wright, P. M. (2001). Human resources and the resource-based view of the firm. *Journal of Management, 27*, 701–721.

World Economic Forum. (2016). *The future of jobs employment, skills and workforce strategy for the fourth industrial revolution*. Retrieved from http://reports.weforum.org/future-of-jobs-2016/.

Wu, C.-H., Parker, S. K., & de Jong, J. P. J. (2014). Need for cognition as an antecedent of individual innovation behavior. *Journal of Management, 40*, 1511–1534.

Zellweger, T. M., Nason, R. S., & Nordqvist, M. (2012). From longevity of firms to transgenerational entrepreneurship of families. *Family Business Review, 25*, 136–155.

Zellweger, T., & Sieger, P. (2012). Entrepreneurial orientation in long-lived family firms. *Small Business Economics, 38*, 67–84.

Zhou, J., & Shalley, C. E. (2003). Research on employee creativity: A critical review and directions for future research. In J. Martocchio (Ed.), *Research in personnel and human resources management* (Vol. 22, pp. 165–217). Oxford: Elsevier.

Part II
Family Firms: Leadership

Entrepreneurial Leadership Across Countries: The Role of Informal Institutions

Claudia Felix, Sebastian Aparicio, and David Urbano

Abstract This chapter examines the influence of informal institutions on the probability of becoming an entrepreneurial leader. In this regard, institutional economics is used to frame the hypotheses that relate to environmental factors and entrepreneurial leadership. These hypotheses are tested through logistic regression analysis, using a sample of 67,268 individuals from the World Values Survey (WVS) for 50 countries. The main findings show that informal institutions such as independence, risk-taking, and networking increase the probability of becoming an entrepreneurial leader. Also, networking and religious faith moderate the relationship between independence and entrepreneurial leadership. The contributions of this chapter are both conceptual, regarding development in the field of leadership and entrepreneurship and practices concerning business and education.

Keywords Entrepreneurship · Leadership · Culture · Institutional economics

1 Introduction

The fields of leadership and entrepreneurship have undergone similar development in many ways (Cogliser & Brigham, 2004). Much of the initial research in the field of entrepreneurship has focused on identifying characteristics that differentiate

---

C. Felix
Tecnológico de Monterrey, Hermosillo, Sonora, Mexico
e-mail: c.felix@tec.mx

S. Aparicio
Durham University Business School, Durham, UK
e-mail: sebastian.aparicio@durham.ac.uk

D. Urbano (✉)
Department of Business, Universitat Autònoma de Barcelona, Barcelona, Spain
e-mail: david.urbano@uab.cat

J. M. Saiz-Álvarez et al. (eds.), *Entrepreneurship and Family Business Vitality*, Studies on Entrepreneurship, Structural Change and Industrial Dynamics, https://doi.org/10.1007/978-3-030-15526-1_5

entrepreneurs from non-entrepreneurs (McClelland, 1961). In this sense, it is suggested that the extant literature mostly analyzes leadership and entrepreneurship separately (Harrison, Leitch, & McAdam, 2015), though, there are few authors who specifically deal with the relationship between leadership and entrepreneurship (Ensley, Pearson, & Pearce, 2003; Felix, Aparicio, & Urbano, 2018; Koryak et al., 2015). This scarcity of studies is surprising considering the coincidences between the traits of leaders and entrepreneurs, who are affected by the environment where they interact (Van Hemmen, Alvarez, Peris-Ortiz, & Urbano, 2015). Hence, scholars suggest that informal institutions are relevant for leadership and entrepreneurship, considering that values, norms, and beliefs can determine the social desirability of being a leader and entrepreneur as a career option (Gong, Huang, & Farh, 2009).

Addressing the phenomenon of entrepreneurial leadership from an institutional perspective, existing research highlights the importance of informal institutions for leadership and entrepreneurship (Thornton, Ribeiro-Soriano, & Urbano, 2011; Urbano, Aparicio, & Audretsch, 2019). By using these lenses, it might be possible to direct the attention to the rules, norms, and beliefs that influence organizations and their members, which can vary widely across countries and cultures (Aparicio, Felix, & Urbano, 2018; Fang, 2010). In this approach, informal institutions become relevant when daily interactions with others are considered, especially taking into consideration that these interactions depend on the codes of conduct and norms of behavior existing in a given society (North, 1990). Although prior research has indicated that leadership and entrepreneurship are influenced according to personal traits and characteristics, few empirical studies have provided concrete connections between sociocultural context and entrepreneurial leadership, and even fewer have studied this relationship from an institutional perspective (cf. Jennings, Greenwood, Lounsbury, & Suddaby, 2013; Van Hemmen, Alvarez, Peris-Ortiz, & Urbano, 2015).

Thus, by using an institutional approach, this chapter seeks to address this gap by specifically investigating the role of informal institutions on the probability of becoming an entrepreneurial leader. Using a sample of 67,268 individuals from 50 countries, it is statistically demonstrated through logistic regression analysis that informal institutions increase the probability of becoming an entrepreneurial leader. Notably, our findings reveal that variables such as independence, risk-taking, religious faith, and networking are related to entrepreneurial leadership. This article suggests implications for the fields of business, education, and public policy.

The chapter follows a conventional structure. We initially reviewed the literature on entrepreneurial leadership from the institutional perspective and proposed the hypotheses. Then we outlined the methodology. In the next section, we present the main results. Finally, the chapter concludes with the discussion and conclusions.

2 Theoretical Background

2.1 Entrepreneurial Leadership

It is claimed that entrepreneurial leadership is an emerging field that remains theoretical and lacks definitional clarity and appropriate tools to assess its characteristics and behaviors (Harrison et al., 2015). Gupta, MacMillan, and Surie (2004, p. 242) defined the concept as "leadership that creates visionary scenarios that are used to assemble and mobilize a 'supporting cast' of participants who become committed by the vision to the discovery and exploitation of strategic value creation." By contrast, Kuratko (2007) presented entrepreneurial leadership as "a unique concept combining the identification of opportunities, risk-taking beyond security and being resolute enough to follow through" (Harrison et al., 2015, p. 695). Gupta et al. (2004) proposed that the concept of entrepreneurial leadership involves fusing the concepts of "entrepreneurship" (derived from Schumpeter, 1934), "entrepreneurial orientation" (from Covin & Slevin, 1988), and "entrepreneurial management" (analyzed by Stevenson & Jarillo, 1990) with leadership. It is recognized that entrepreneurial leadership embraces three important aspects: first, entrepreneurial behaviors and attitudes (Gupta et al., 2004); second, the distinctions or similarities between leaders and entrepreneurs (Baumol, 1968); and third, new business owners who adopt leadership roles in order to grow (Ensley, Hmieleski, & Pearce, 2006; Gupta et al., 2004). Since one of the main purposes of any firm is to grow, this study adopts an approach involving the last aspect. In particular, we are interested in analyzing how informal institutions explain the decision of adopting an entrepreneurial leadership role across countries.

2.2 Entrepreneurial Leadership from an Institutional Perspective

North (1990) develops a broad concept of an institution, who defines them as those "rules of the game in a society [...] that shape human interaction" (North, 1990, p. 3). This author distinguishes between formal (political rules, economic rules, contracts, etc.) and informal institutions (codes of conduct, attitudes, values, norms of behavior) that impact different organizations and organizational actors. Because societies are endowed by nature with different environments, members of society must adopt models of behavior to achieve success.

Although there are scholars linking explicitly institutional economics and entrepreneurial activity (Jennings et al., 2013; Thornton et al., 2011; Urbano, Aparicio, & Audretsch, 2018; among others), few works have linked the institutional perspective and entrepreneurial leadership (Van Hemmen et al., 2015; Yousafzai, Saeed, & Muffatto, 2015). A typology based on both the cognitive approach and sociocultural factors has proven useful for entrepreneurial research (Liñán, Moriano, & Jaén, 2016).

The role of beliefs, perceptual variables, and cultural contexts involves the set of meanings required to interpret actions such as entrepreneurial activity and leadership (Wolfgang, 2008). The principles of social order (e.g., laws and traditions) do not determine organizational structure but rather establish parameters as to which organizational forces are conceivable and which alternative forms impossible (Antonacopoulou et al., 2001). The emergence of leadership roles represents an additional stage of institutionalization (Smircich & Morgan, 1982). Most recent findings suggest small but significant relationships between informal institutions such as cognitive ability, values, attitudes, leadership emergence and effectiveness (Felfe & Schyns, 2014), as well as with organizational strategies (Koryak et al., 2015). Similarly, there is an approach suggesting that informal institutions affect entrepreneurial leadership, where independence, risk-taking, religious faith, and networking were used as examples of these types of institutions (Felix et al., 2018; Swiercz & Lydon, 2002). These variables are in line with the Schwartz Theory of Basic Values (Schwartz, 2012), which have also often been associated with leadership (Van Hemmen et al., 2015) and entrepreneurship (Liñán et al., 2016).

2.3 Independence

Independence is defined as a preference for decision-making control, to serve one's objectives, to choose one's path, and to be confident in one's abilities (Douglas & Shepherd, 1999). Independence describes an individual's desire for freedom, control, and flexibility in the use of time (Carter, Gartner, Shaver, & Gatewood, 2003). Some authors use independence and autonomy as similar concepts (House, Hanges, Javidan, Dorfman, & Gupta, 2004; Lumpkin, Cogliser, & Schneider, 2009). Here, the need for autonomy refers to the experience of having choices and of initiating action oneself (Ryan & Deci, 2002). Entrepreneurs value independence, individualism, and freedom (Van Hemmen et al., 2015). In this regard, independence was found to be an important reason when an entrepreneur chooses to start a new business (Carter et al., 2003). Independence has also been associated with leadership. In this sense, Bass and Bass (2008) point out that independence is a personal attribute of leadership approached through subjective experience (i.e., being one's boss). An important contribution to this topic was made by House et al. (2004), who created a new dimension that refers to independent and individualistic leadership attributes. This dimension is measured by a single subscale of autonomous leadership, consisting of individualistic, independence, and autonomous behaviors. In education, there is a strong consensus that autonomy or independence is related to performance and leadership (Keddie, 2016). In business, autonomy moderates the relationship between the quality of leader-member exchange and innovative service behavior, such that the relationship is stronger for persons with greater job autonomy (Dhar, 2016). Leaders need autonomy to take the initiative, be creative, learn from mistakes, assume responsibilities, and handle difficult situations in their way (Chiniara & Bentein, 2016). In summary, we expect that the greater the preference for independence, the greater the incentive to be an entrepreneurial leader. It is therefore hypothesized:

Hypothesis 1 *A high preference for independence increases the probability of becoming an entrepreneurial leader.*

2.4 Risk-Taking

The debate about the role of an individual's attitude to risk in the decision to become an entrepreneur and in entrepreneurial success is largely studied. In the definition of entrepreneurship and everyday observation, entrepreneurs are perceived as more risk-prone than other people. According to Wärneryd (1988, p. 407), "...there seems to be general agreement that risk bearing is a necessary [...] prerequisite for being called an entrepreneur." Since most individuals are risk-averse, and since the perceived fear of failure is an important component of the risk attached to starting a new business, reduced perception of the likelihood of failure should increase the probability that a company will start a new business (Boermans, 2010). What matters is not the respondent's fear of failure, but the degree to which the fear of failure affects the behavior of individuals (Radu & Redien-Collot, 2008). In this regard, risk-taking is also associated with leadership behavior (Clark & Waldron, 2016) and leader performance (Frost, Fiedler, & Anderson, 1983). Founder managers are more likely to invest considerable time and effort in building their firms and are therefore more willing to accept the risks (Mousa & Wales, 2012). Risk-taking requires tolerance of ambiguity and the ability to make decisions with some uncertainty (Isaksen & Lauer, 2002). Being the leader of a group often involves making risky decisions. In general, entrepreneurs and leaders of organizations also, as would be expected, have higher risk-taking propensities and tolerance for ambiguity than do managers in general (Van Hemmen et al., 2015). The following hypothesis is thus derived:

Hypothesis 2 *Favorable attitudes toward taking risk increase the probability of becoming an entrepreneurial leader.*

2.5 Religious Faith

Religion can be defined as a particular institutionalized or personal system of beliefs, values, and practices relating to the divine—a level of reality or power that is regarded as the "source" or "ultimate," transcending yet immanent in the realm of human experience (Worden, 2005). Religiosity is the acceptance of a particular set of organized beliefs, rituals, and practices having to do with God, morality, the origins of life, and an afterlife (Bass & Bass, 2008). People with dissimilar cultural beliefs and religious values have looked at entrepreneurship with varying degrees of legitimacy. Woodrum (1985) found participation in religious activities to be a predictor of entrepreneurial success. Religion has also been found to have a significant effect on leadership behavior (Hage & Posner, 2015; Hofstede, 1980). Religious affiliation and values associated with particular faith traditions necessarily affect the way that people think and behave and also play a major role in shaping individual traits (McCleary & Barro, 2006). Fernando and Jackson (2006) reported that religion had a significant effect on the critical thinking and decision-making processes of business leaders. In summary, religions are depositories of wisdom and of values, related at the same time to leadership positions. This leads to the following hypothesis:

Hypothesis 3 *Religious faith increases the probability of becoming an entrepreneurial leader.*

2.6 Networking

In general terms, social networks are defined by a set of actors (individuals and organizations) and a set of connections between those actors (Brass, 1992). Granovetter's (1985) account of the role of personal relationships includes strong ties and weak ties (Shaw, 1997). People connected by strong ties trust each other and are likely to share contacts and information, so reliance on strong ties militates against the generation of new information and fresh perspectives to create and exploit business opportunities for growth and development (Chell & Baines, 2000). Networks are increasingly perceived as a key element of entrepreneurship (Stuart & Sorenson, 2007). Davidsson and Honig (2003) found that networking was a robust and consistent predictor of nascent entrepreneurs. Entrepreneurs are often those with a wide range of casual contacts, suggesting that a variety of trusted social connections is an important prerequisite for discovering an entrepreneurial idea (Shane, 2000) and for garnering the resources to start a new business (Shane & Cable, 2002). Scholars recognize leadership as a property of the collective, implying that networks matter for those who want to become leaders (Cullen-Lester & Yammarino, 2016). The empirical support for this idea is strong, since previous findings have shown how social networks contribute to the strategic influence of managers, helping them to leverage organizational resources for innovation (Kelley, Peters, & O'Connor, 2009), increasing or decreasing new venture performance (though this depends on the context they are embedded) (Stam & Elfring, 2008), and strengthen the effects of entrepreneurial orientation on creative performance (Chen, Chang, & Chang, 2015). The following hypothesis is thus formulated:

Hypothesis 4 *Networking increases the probability of becoming an entrepreneurial leader.*

3 Method

3.1 Data and Variables

We rely on World Values Survey (WVS), which is a database that has been widely used by researchers to analyze different topics such as values and cultural change (Inglehart & Baker, 2000) and social capital and innovation (Dakhli & De Clercq, 2004), among others. We used data from the 2005–2008 wave because this database contains the most suitable proxy for our dependent variable. The final sample was composed of 67,268 individuals from 50 countries.[1]

3.2 Dependent Variable

From these possible explanations of professional/occupational status, we created our dependent variable: entrepreneurial leadership, taking a value of 1 if the individual is the employer/management of an establishment with employees and 0 in other cases. This variable was seen as a proxy for entrepreneurial leadership, and it allows us to empirically understand the concept of entrepreneurial leadership to represent those who are entrepreneurs and, at the same time, become leaders by having subordinates. This proxy uses the definition of entrepreneurial leadership as the leadership role performed in entrepreneurial ventures (Renko, Tarabishy, Carsrud, & Brännback, 2015). In the same approach, Swiercz and Lydon (2002) define "career entrepreneurial leaders" as individuals who not only create new organizations but go on to lead these organizations to sustainable success. This is also in line with Cogliser and Brigham (2004), who suggests that in practice, successful entrepreneurs are often managers coincidentally combining these two functions in one person.

3.3 Independent Variables

In this chapter, we present informal institutions as a set of perceptual, cognitive, and social variables. The mental models created by individuals represent the cumulative experience, learning, feelings, and meanings about how the physical and social worlds work (Gaglio, 1997). These are also a distinctive set of perceptual and

[1]Andorra, Argentina, Australia, Brazil, Bulgaria, Burkina Faso, Canada, Chile, China, Cyprus, Egypt, Ethiopia, Finland, France, Georgia, Germany, Ghana, Guatemala, India, Indonesia, Japan, Jordan, Korea, Malaysia, Mali, Mexico, Moldova, Morocco, Netherlands, Norway, Peru, Poland, Romania, Rwanda, Serbia, Slovenia, South Africa, Spain, Sweden, Switzerland, Taiwan Province of China, Thailand, Trinidad and Tobago, Turkey, Ukraine, United Kingdom, United States, Uruguay, Vietnam, Zambia.

cognitive processing skills related to entrepreneurship (Gaglio & Katz, 2001). A Likert scale was used to indicate the extent to which informal institutions matter for entrepreneurial leadership. To test our proposed hypotheses, we have used a set of variables contained within the WVS. Thus, independence considers those respondents that were asked how much independence they have in performing tasks at work (1 = no independence at all to 10 = complete independence). With regard to risk-taking, we look at those respondents asked about the importance of adventure, taking risks and having an exciting life (1 = not at all important to 6 = very important). Religious faith considers the respondents that were asked the following question: "do you consider it is especially important that religious faith is a quality that children can be encouraged to learn at home?" (1 = not at all important to 6 = very important). Finally, to capture networking, we have taken respondents that were asked whether they were active members of a voluntary professional organization (1 = yes, 0 = no).

3.4 Control Variables

We controlled for gender (at the individual level) and gross domestic product (GDP) based on purchasing power parity (PPP) per capita (at country level). Previous research has indicated that independent of culture, there are differences in the profiles of male and female entrepreneurs (Fernald & Solomon, 1987). The decision to start a business is far more complex for women than it is for men (Bird & Brush, 2002). Women participation rates in entrepreneurship are significantly lower than rates for men (Langowitz & Minniti, 2007). Hence, a dummy for gender was included (0 = female, 1 = male). Additionally, we included the GDP PPP per capita as a control variable given that the level of development of countries is a key factor in explaining entrepreneurial activity (Urbano, Aparicio, & Querol, 2016). The data source used for the GDP-PPP variable is the International Monetary Fund World Economic Outlook database and the average of the years 2005–2007 was used.

3.5 Model and Statistical Technique

Given the binary nature of the dependent variable, we analyzed the effect of informal dimensions on entrepreneurial activity through a binomial logistic model, as follows:

$$P(\mathrm{EL}_i) = f(\mathrm{II}_i, \mathrm{CV}_i) \tag{1}$$

where EL_i is entrepreneurial leadership, II_i represents the set of informal institutions, and CV_i, the control variables for each individual i in our sample.

4 Results

Descriptive statistics and the correlation matrix of the variables used in this analysis are reported in Table 1. As can be seen, all variables considered are significantly correlated with entrepreneurial leadership, as expected. Given the correlations among independent and control variables, a test for the problem of multicollinearity was employed, showing that multicollinearity is not a major problem in the models. The variance inflation factors (VIF) are lower than 3 which is far from 5.

Table 2 presents five logit models testing the informal factors that determine entrepreneurial leadership. Model 1 presents the logistic regression results with only control variables. Model 2 introduces only informal factors. Model 3 presents all informal dimensions and control variables. Finally, we include an interaction term in Models 4 and 5. Consistent with existing literature, the results suggest that sociodemographic characteristics are quite crucial for understanding the likelihood of becoming an entrepreneurial leader (Davidsson & Honig, 2003). In Model 1, the overall model is significant, all coefficients are significant with a p value of ≤ 0.001, and they have the expected sign. According to the gender coefficient, being male increases the probability of becoming an entrepreneurial leader by 3.6%, which is a result consistent with the extant literature (cf. Carter et al., 2003). On the other hand, the coefficient of GDP PPP indicates that higher income increases the probability of entrepreneurial leadership.

Regarding Model 2, we found that the overall model is highly significant. In this sense, and despite religious faith was not significant, independence, risk-taking, and networking coefficients are significant, with a p value ≤ 0.001, showing the expected sign. Similarly, Model 3 was found significant. All coefficients of variables were statistically significant ($p \leq 0.001$). In this case, pseudo R-squared increases concerning Model 1 and Model 2, and the Akaike information criterion (AIC) is lower (and preferable) than the previous model.

Contrasting these results with the hypotheses proposed, hypothesis 1 predicts a positive relationship between independence and the likelihood of becoming an entrepreneurial leadership. In Model 3, the results show that hypothesis 1 is supported and in line with the previous literature we have found (Carter et al., 2003). Hypothesis 2 predicts a positive relationship between risk-taking and the likelihood of becoming an entrepreneurial leader. The results also supported hypothesis 2. As Douglas and Shepherd (Douglas & Shepherd, 1999) predicted, these entrepreneurial characteristics are found on those individuals that are considered leaders. Hypothesis 3 predicts a positive relationship between religious faith and the likelihood of becoming an entrepreneurial leader, which is similar to Hage and Posner (2015).

On the other hand, hypothesis 4 predicts a positive relationship between networking and the likelihood of becoming an entrepreneurial leader. Our data supported this hypothesis. Some studies tend to support this positive statistical relationship between networking and new business activity (Urbano et al., 2016).

Table 1 Descriptive statistics and the correlation matrix

Variable	Mean	Std. dev.	1	2	3	4	5	6
1. Entrepreneurial leadership	0.0511	0.2202	1					
2. Independence	6.5787	2.8316	0.1417***	1				
3. Risk-taking	3.1372	1.5889	0.018***	0.0076	1			
4. Religious faith	0.4055	0.4910	−0.0387***	−0.0523***	0.0281***	1		
5. Networking	0.0683	0.2523	0.0453***	0.0752***	0.0591***	−0.01***	1	
6. Gender	0.4786	0.4995	0.0836***	0.0296***	0.1299***	−0.0466***	0.0468***	1
7. GDP PPP	14,732	13,653	0.0945***	0.1075***	−0.0954***	−0.2952***	0.0358***	−0.0119***

***$p < 0.01$

Source: Authors' own table

Table 2 Logit results predicting entrepreneurial leadership

	Model 1		Model 2		Model 3		Model 4		Model 5	
	d*F*/d*x*	Std. err	d*F*/d*x*	Std. err	d*F*/d*x*	Std. err	d*F*/d*x*	Std. err	d*F*/d*x*	Std. err
Informal institutions										
Independence (INDEPE)			0.0141***	0.0004	0.0132***	0.0004	0.0151***	0.0006	0.0132***	0.0004
Risk-taking			0.0034***	0.0007	0.0028***	0.0007				
Religious faith			−0.0034	0.0024	0.0059**	0.0026	0.0573***	0.0103		
Networking			0.0156***	0.0042	0.0119***	0.0039			0.0611***	0.0222
INDEPE X religious faith						−0.0055***	0.0009			
INDEPE X networking									−0.0041***	0.0015
Control variables										
Gender	0.0353***	0.0016			0.0296***	0.0022	0.0310***	0.0022	0.0309	0.0022
GDP PPP	0.0000***	0.0000			0.0000***	0.0000	0.0000***	0.0000	0.0000***	0.0000
Number of observations	67,222		42,484		42,463		43,488		43,488	
LR Chi-square statistic	1041.63		1012.7		1339.42		1371.34		1350.28	
Pseudo R-squared	0.0384		0.0438		0.0579		0.0582		0.0573	
Log pseudolikelihood	−13043.444		−11064.49		−10896.961		−11097.299		−11107.829	
Percent correctly predicted	94.89%		92.26%		92.26%		92.32%		92.32%	
AIC	26092.89		22138.98		21807.92		22206.61		22227.66	

***$p < 0.01$; **$p < 0.05$; *$p < 0.10$

Source: Authors' own table

Finally, Models 4 and 5 explored the effect of informal institutions, showing changes depending on the presence of other informal institutions. In Model 4 the interaction between independence and religious faith was included. Overall Model 4 was significant. The interaction term is negative and statistically significant. In Model 5 the interaction term between independence and networking were included. The results show that the relationship between the level of independence and entrepreneurial leadership is stronger for lower rather than higher levels of networking. This model is negative and significant, and all coefficients are statistically significant ($p \leq 0.001$). The negative interaction term between independence and networking indicates that the relationship between independence and entrepreneurial leadership is weaker for those people with networks versus those who do not.

5 Discussion and Conclusions

This article aimed to investigate the role of informal institutions on the probability of becoming an entrepreneurial leader. Studies of entrepreneurship and leadership are receiving increasing attention because of leaders as the core element of the entrepreneurial process (Gupta et al., 2004). The study of entrepreneurs as leaders is a gap in both bodies of knowledge (Cogliser & Brigham, 2004) and even more so from an institutional perspective.

As mentioned above, entrepreneurial leadership exists at the nexus of entrepreneurship and leadership (Harrison et al., 2015). This research has explored informal institutions, such as cognitive abilities, attitudes, and values. These factors prove essential for the development of entrepreneurial leadership (Renko et al., 2015). This article provided evidence that informal institutions increase the probability of being an entrepreneurial leader. Specifically, informal institutions such as independence, risk-taking, and networking facilitate the emergence of new entrepreneurial leaders, who might be related to new processes, products, or services (Jia, Chen, Mei, & Wu, 2018). The results also show that religious faith is significantly related to entrepreneurial leaders, and this might be associated with a transcendent purpose in life. We also found that interaction between the informal institutions may be relevant for entrepreneurial leadership. In this case, the relationship between independence and entrepreneurial leadership is moderated by social, cognitive, and normative dimensions as networking and religious faith.

In this study, the negative interaction term between independence and religious may indicate that the relationship between independence and entrepreneurial leadership is stronger when there is less religious faith rather than higher. The institutional profiles of some religions restrict self-employment, but others encourage self-employment activities. These findings underline the obvious fact that religious traditions differ in their beliefs about human behavior and, therefore, in their effect on the decision to be a leader or entrepreneur (Hage & Posner, 2015). Along the same lines, the negative interaction term between independence and networking can be understood through the influence of social identity and personal identity (Day & Harrison, 2007).

Also, the findings indicate that the informal factors seem to have a direct and moderate effect on leadership and entrepreneurship. In this sense, informal institutions such as independence, networking, and religious faith appear to exert complementarily, rather than substitutive, influence on entrepreneurial leadership. Support was found for the beneficial effect of informal dimensions on entrepreneurial leadership, as well as the substitution effect between cultural-cognitive dimensions such as independence and normative burdens such as networking.

Several implications are arising from this study. Regarding business, managers can benefit from this chapter by adopting and developing informal institutions to revitalize organizations and energize followers especially encouraging the development of cognitive and normative dimensions. This study also responds to the call of economic and societal challenges for more entrepreneurial attitudes and behaviors (Urbano et al., 2019), even in areas previously thought of as anti-entrepreneurial, such as government, the military, and education (Renko et al., 2015). This study adds elements and suggests that policymakers, managers, and teachers should deliberately work in training programs that encourage the skills of leaders such as the degree of independence, ability to make decisions, capacity to pursue primary purposes by faith or beliefs, skill to relational capital, and risk-taking.

There is much more to learn in the area of entrepreneurship and leadership. The present chapter provides insights into the understanding of entrepreneurship and leadership, linking these two concepts by providing an institutional approach. In doing so, we contribute to the dialogue around the need for alignment. The future looks more challenging, and future leaders will need to be more involved and able to flexibly move from one mental schema to another (Zhang, Waldman, Han, & Li, 2015). Leadership perceptions, social perceptions, and social context in general are part of this process (Stam, Lord, van Knippenberg, & Wisse, 2014). Athanasopoulou and Selsky (2015) point out that they will need to understand how their environment (external, organizational, or interpersonal) and the perspective by which it is analyzed (institutional, cultural, cognitive, or other) shape their decisions and actions.

For this reason, the identification of informal factors might strengthen leadership and entrepreneurial profiles. This study has made a preliminary step in initiating further research to contribute to ongoing efforts to integrate the fields of social behaviors, strategy, leadership, and entrepreneurship. In doing so, this study contributes to the dialogue around the need to create individual and collective factors that fortify entrepreneurial leadership.

We acknowledge that our findings are subject to various limitations that suggest avenues for additional research. Our entrepreneurial leadership variable may not capture the broader concept of leadership and entrepreneurship (Gupta et al., 2004). On the other hand, the moderating effect presented in this study raises challenges for future research. We also encourage future studies to examine leadership as a multilevel process where the first level is the leader; the second considers relationships with followers, peers, and superiors; and the third constitutes the organizational climate and culture (Day & Harrison, 2007). There is an increasing need to understand how leadership might be constructed more collectively and integrated (Day & Harrison, 2007). Additional research could explore which dimensions can most effectively substitute for (or complement) unfavorable institutional conditions. Entrepreneurial leadership is becoming a global requirement and the more we can understand the elements that reinforce this concept, the more we can advance the concept itself.

Acknowledgments Claudia Felix acknowledges financial support for Ph.D. studies from Tecnológico de Monterrey. Sebastian Aparicio acknowledges financial support for Ph.D. studies from COLCIENCIAS Ph.D. Program Chapter 3 (617/2013), Enlaza Mundos Municipio de Medellín (2013), and Fundación ECSIM. Also, David Urbano acknowledges the financial support from the Spanish Ministry of Economy & Competitiveness [project ECO2017-87885-P], the Economy & Knowledge Department—Catalan Government [project 2017-SGR-1056], and ICREA under the ICREA Academia Programme.

References

Antonacopoulou, E., Bresnen, M., Burrell, G., Collinson, D. L., Corbett, M., Dale, K., & Swan, J. (2001). *Organizational studies: Critical perspectives on business and management: Vol 1 (of 4 vols), modes of management*. London and New York: Routledge.

Aparicio, S., Felix, C., & Urbano, D. (2018). Informal institutions and leadership behavior: A cross-country analysis. In S. Göker (Ed.), *Leadership* (pp. 41–60). London, UK: IntechOpen.

Athanasopoulou, A., & Selsky, J. W. (2015). The social context of corporate social responsibility: Enriching research with multiple perspectives and multiple levels. *Business & Society, 54*(3), 322–364.

Bass, B. M., & Bass, R. (2008). *The Bass handbook of leadership: Theory, research, and managerial applications* (4th ed.). New York: Free Press.

Baumol, W. J. (1968). Entrepreneurship in economic theory. *The American Economic Review, 58* (2), 64–71.

Bird, B., & Brush, C. (2002). A gendered perspective on organizational creation. *Entrepreneurship: Theory and Practice, 26*(3), 41–65.

Boermans, M. A. (2010). The entrepreneurial society. *International Entrepreneurship and Management Journal, 6*(4), 523–526.

Brass, D. J. (1992). Power in organizations: A social network perspective. *Research in Political Sociology, 4*(1), 295–323.

Carter, N. M., Gartner, W. B., Shaver, K. G., & Gatewood, E. J. (2003). The career reasons of nascent entrepreneurs. *Journal of Business Venturing, 18*(1), 13–39.

Chell, E., & Baines, S. (2000). Networking, entrepreneurship and microbusiness behavior. *Entrepreneurship and Regional Development, 12*(3), 195–215.

Chen, M.-H., Chang, Y.-Y., & Chang, Y.-C. (2015). Entrepreneurial orientations, social networks, and creative performance: Middle managers as corporate entrepreneurs. *Creativity and Innovation Management, 24*(3), 493–507.

Chiniara, M., & Bentein, K. (2016). Linking servant leadership to individual performance: Differentiating the mediating role of autonomy, competence and relatedness need satisfaction. *The Leadership Quarterly, 27*(1), 124–141.

Clark, K. D., & Waldron, T. (2016). Predictors of leadership behavior in early career white-collar professionals: The roles of personal characteristics and career context. *Journal of Leadership and Organizational Studies, 23*(1), 27–38.

Cogliser, C. C., & Brigham, K. (2004). The intersection of leadership and entrepreneurship: Lessons to be learned. *The Leadership Quarterly, 15*(6), 771–799.
Covin, J. G., & Slevin, D. P. (1988). The influence of organizational structure on the utility of an entrepreneurial top management style. *Journal of Management Studies, 25*(3), 217–259.
Cullen-Lester, K., & Yammarino, F. (2016). Collective and network approaches to leadership: Special issue introduction. *The Leadership Quarterly, 27*(2), 173–180.
Dakhli, M., & De Clercq, D. (2004). Human capital, social capital, and innovation: A multicountry study. *Entrepreneurship and Regional Development, 16*(2), 107–128.
Davidsson, P., & Honig, B. (2003). The role of social and human capital among nascent entrepreneurs. *Journal of Business Venturing, 18*(3), 301–331.
Day, D. V., & Harrison, M. M. (2007). A multilevel, identity-based approach to leadership development. *Human Resource Management Review, 17*(4), 360–373.
Dhar, R. L. (2016). Ethical leadership and its impact on service innovative behavior: The role of LMX and job autonomy. *Tourism Management, 57*, 139–148.
Douglas, E., & Shepherd, D. A. (1999). Entrepreneurship as a utility maximizing response. *Journal of Business Venturing, 15*(3), 231–251.
Ensley, M. D., Hmieleski, K. M., & Pearce, C. L. (2006). The importance of vertical and shared leadership within new venture top management teams: Implications for the performance of startups. *The Leadership Quarterly, 17*(3), 217–231.
Ensley, M. D., Pearson, A., & Pearce, C. L. (2003). Top management team process, shared leadership, and new venture performance: A theoretical model and research agenda. *Human Resource Management Review, 13*(2), 329–346.
Fang, T. (2010). Asian management research needs more self-confidence: Reflection on Hofstede (2007) and beyond. *Asia Pacific Journal of Management, 27*(1), 155–170.
Felfe, J., & Schyns, B. (2014). Romance of leadership and motivation to lead. *Journal of Managerial Psychology, 29*(7), 850–865.
Felix, C., Aparicio, S., & Urbano, D. (2018). Leadership as a driver of entrepreneurship: An international exploratory study. *Journal of Small Business and Enterprise Developments*. https://doi.org/10.1108/JSBED-03-2018-0106.
Fernald, L. W., & Solomon, G. T. (1987). Value profiles of male and female entrepreneurs. *Journal of Creative Behavior, 21*(3), 235–247.
Fernando, M., & Jackson, B. (2006). The influence of religion-based workplace spirituality on business leaders' decision-making: An inter-faith study. *Journal of Management and Organization, 12*(1), 23–39.
Frost, D. E., Fiedler, F. E., & Anderson, J. W. (1983). The role of personal risk-taking ineffective leadership. *Human Relations, 36*(2), 185–202.
Gaglio, C. M. (1997). Opportunity identification: Review, critique, and suggested research directions. In J. A. Katz (Ed.), *Advances in entrepreneurship, firm emergence and growth* (Vol. 3, pp. 119–138). Greenwich, CA: JAI Press.
Gaglio, C. M., & Katz, J. A. (2001). The psychological basis of opportunity identification: Entrepreneurial alertness. *Small Business Economics, 16*(2), 95–111.
Gong, Y., Huang, J. C., & Farh, J. L. (2009). Employee learning orientation, transformational leadership, and employee creativity: The mediating role of employee creative self-efficacy. *Academy of Management Journal, 52*(4), 765–778.
Granovetter, M. (1985). Economic action and social structure: The problem of embeddedness. *American Journal of Sociology, 91*(3), 481–510.
Gupta, V., MacMillan, I., & Surie, G. (2004). Entrepreneurial leadership: Developing and measuring a cross-cultural construct. *Journal of Business Venturing, 19*(2), 241–260.
Hage, J., & Posner, B. Z. (2015). Religion, religiosity, and leadership practices. *Leadership and Organization Development Journal, 36*(4), 396–412.
Harrison, R., Leitch, C., & McAdam, M. (2015). Breaking glass: Toward a gendered analysis of entrepreneurial leadership. *Journal of Small Business Management, 53*(3), 693–713.

Hofstede, G. (1980). *Culture's consequences: International differences in work-related values*. Thousand Oaks, CA: Sage.

House, R. J., Hanges, P. J., Javidan, M., Dorfman, P. W., & Gupta, V. (2004). *Culture, leadership, and organizations: The GLOBE Study of 62 societies*. Thousand Oaks, CA: Sage.

Inglehart, R., & Baker, W. (2000). Modernization, cultural change and the persistence of traditional values. *American Sociological Review, 65*(1), 19–51.

Isaksen, S. G., & Lauer, K. J. (2002). The climate for creativity and change in teams. *Creativity and Innovation Management, 11*(1), 74–86.

Jennings, P. D., Greenwood, R., Lounsbury, M. D., & Suddaby, R. (2013). Institutions, entrepreneurs, and communities: A special issue on entrepreneurship. *Journal of Business Venturing, 28* (1), 1–9.

Jia, X., Chen, J., Mei, L., & Wu, Q. (2018). How leadership matters in organizational innovation: A perspective of openness. *Management Decision, 56*(1), 6–25.

Keddie, A. (2016). School autonomy as 'the way of the future': Issues of equity, public purpose, and moral leadership. *Educational Management Administration and Leadership, 44*(5), 713–727.

Kelley, D. J., Peters, L., & O'Connor, C. G. (2009). Intra-organizational networking for innovation-based corporate entrepreneurship. *Journal of Business Venturing, 24*(3), 221–235.

Koryak, O., Mole, K., Lockett, A., Hayton, J., Ucbasaran, D., & Hodgkinson, G. (2015). Entrepreneurial leadership, capabilities and firm growth. *International Small Business Journal, 33*(1), 89–105.

Kuratko, D. F. (2007). Entrepreneurial leadership in the 21st century: Guest editor's perspective. *Journal of Leadership and Organizational Studies, 13*(4), 1–11.

Langowitz, N., & Minniti, M. (2007). The entrepreneurial propensity of women. *Entrepreneurship Theory and Practice, 31*(3), 341–364.

Liñán, F., Moriano, J. A., & Jaén, I. (2016). Individualism and entrepreneurship: Does the pattern depend on the social context. *International Small Business Journal, 34*(4), 760–776.

Lumpkin, G. T., Cogliser, C. C., & Schneider, D. R. (2009). Understanding and measuring autonomy: An entrepreneurial orientation perspective. *Entrepreneurship: Theory and Practice, 33*(1), 47–69.

McCleary, R. M., & Barro, R. J. (2006). Religion and economy. *Journal of Economic Perspectives, 20*(2), 49–72.

McClelland, D. (1961). *The achieving society*. Princeton, NJ: Van Nostrand.

Mousa, F. T., & Wales, W. (2012). Founder effectiveness in leveraging entrepreneurial orientation. *Management Decision, 50*(1–2), 305–324.

North, D. (1990). *Institutions, institutional change, and economic performance*. Cambridge University Press.

Radu, M., & Redien-Collot, R. (2008). The social representation of entrepreneurs in the French Press. Desirable and feasible models? *International Small Business Journal, 26*(3), 259–298.

Renko, M., Tarabishy, A., Carsrud, A., & Brännback, M. (2015). Understanding and measuring entrepreneurial leadership style. *Journal of Small Business Management, 53*(1), 54–74.

Ryan, R. M., & Deci, E. L. (2002). Overview of self-determination theory: An organismic-dialectical perspective. In E. L. Deci & R. M. Ryan (Eds.), *Handbook of self-determination research* (pp. 3–33). Rochester, NY: University of Rochester Press.

Schumpeter, J. (1934). *The theory of economic development*. New Brunswick, NJ: Transaction Publishes.

Schwartz, S. H. (2012). An overview of the Schwartz theory of basic values. *Online Readings in Psychology and Culture, 2*(1), 1–20.

Shane, S. (2000). Prior knowledge and the discovery of entrepreneurial opportunities. *Organization Science, 25*(1), 448–469.

Shane, S., & Cable, D. (2002). Network ties, reputation, and the financing of new ventures. *Management Science, 48*(3), 364–381.

Shaw, E. (1997). The 'real' networks of small firms. In D. Deakins, P. Jennings, & G. Mason (Eds.), *Small firms: Entrepreneurship in the nineties* (pp. 7–17). London: Paul Chapman.

Smircich, L., & Morgan, G. (1982). Leadership: The management of meaning. *The Journal of Applied Behavioral Science, 18*(3), 257–273.

Stam, W., & Elfring, T. (2008). Entrepreneurial orientation and new venture performance: The moderating role of intra- and extra-industry social capital. *Academy of Management Journal, 51* (1), 97–111.

Stam, D., Lord, R. G., van Knippenberg, D., & Wisse, B. (2014). An image of who we might become: Vision communication, possible selves, and vision pursuit. *Organizational Science, 25* (4), 1172–1194.

Stevenson, H., & Jarillo, J. C. (1990). A paradigm of entrepreneurship: Entrepreneurial management. *Strategic Management Journal, 11*(5), 17–27.

Stuart, T. E., & Sorenson, O. (2007). Strategic networks and entrepreneurial ventures. *Strategic Entrepreneurship Journal, 1*(3–4), 211–227.

Swiercz, P. M., & Lydon, S. R. (2002). Entrepreneurial leadership in high-tech firms: a field study. *Leadership and Organization Development Journal, 23*(7), 380–389.

Thornton, P., Ribeiro-Soriano, D., & Urbano, D. (2011). Socio-cultural factors and entrepreneurial activity: An overview. *International Small Business Journal, 29*(2), 105–118.

Urbano, D., Aparicio, S., & Audretsch, D. (2018). Twenty-five years of research on institutions, entrepreneurship, and economic growth: What has been learned? *Small Business Economics*. https://doi.org/10.1007/s11187-018-0038-0.

Urbano, D., Aparicio, S., & Audretsch, D. B. (2019). *Institutions, entrepreneurship, and economic performance*. Cham: Springer.

Urbano, D., Aparicio, S., & Querol, V. (2016). Social progress orientation and innovative entrepreneurship: An international analysis. *Journal of Evolutionary Economics, 26*(5), 1033–1066.

Van Hemmen, S., Alvarez, C., Peris-Ortiz, M., & Urbano, D. (2015). Leadership styles and innovative entrepreneurship: An international study. *Cybernetics and Systems: An International Journal, 46*(3–4), 271–286.

Wärneryd, K. E. (1988). The psychology of innovative entrepreneurship. In W. F. van Raaij, G. M. van Veldhoven, & K. E. Wärneryd (Eds.), *Handbook of economic psychology* (pp. 404–447). Dordrecht, The Netherlands: Kluwer Academic.

Wolfgang, D. (2008). *The international encyclopedia of communication*. Hoboken, NJ: Wiley-Blackwell.

Woodrum, E. M. (1985). Religion and economics among Japanese Americans: A Weberian study. *Social Forces, 64*(1), 191–204.

Worden, S. (2005). Religion in strategic leadership: A positivistic, normative/theological, and strategic analysis. *Journal of Business Ethics, 57*(3), 221–239.

Yousafzai, S. Y., Saeed, S., & Muffatto, M. (2015). Institutional theory and contextual embeddedness of women's entrepreneurial leadership: Evidence from 92 countries. *Journal of Small Business Management, 53*(3), 587–604.

Zhang, Y., Waldman, D. A., Han, Y. L., & Li, X. B. (2015). Paradoxical leader behaviors in people management: Antecedents and consequences. *Academy of Management Journal, 58*(2), 538–566.

Generational Diversity as a Moderator for the Relationship Between Absorptive Capacity and Innovation Performance at Family Firms

Gloria Charão Ferreira and João M. Ferreira

Abstract The objective of this research study involves analyzing the capacities of family firms to absorb relevant information about the external environment and to incorporate this into their innovation-focused activities before then consequently analyzing the repercussions for innovation performance. This furthermore seeks to grasp whether, and to what extent, the generational diversity in the firm's management represents a valuable resource. In order to obtain these objectives, we opted for a quantitative study with the data collected by a questionnaire sent out by email to the managers of Brazilian firms, specifically those with their headquarters in the state of Rio Grande do Sul and registered with the Rio Grande do Sul Industrial Federation. The results of this study provide recognition of ACAP as an important predictor of FF innovation performance. In particular, the findings suggest that the potential absorptive capacity (PACAP) generates a positive and significant effect on the realized absorptive capacity (RACAP). We may also report the positive and significant effect of PACAP on the incremental innovation performance and, similarly, for the RACAP influence on the radical innovation performance. Contrary to that expected, however, the results point to generational diversity in the management of the FF which is not a significant moderator between ACAP and innovation performance.

Keywords Absorptive capacity · Innovation performance · Generational diversity · Family firm

G. C. Ferreira (✉)
Regional University of Northwestern Rio Grande do Sul (UNIJUÍ), Ijuí, Brazil

J. M. Ferreira
University of Beira Interior (UBI), Covilhã, Portugal
e-mail: jjmf@ubi.pt

J. M. Saiz-Álvarez et al. (eds.), *Entrepreneurship and Family Business Vitality*, Studies on Entrepreneurship, Structural Change and Industrial Dynamics, https://doi.org/10.1007/978-3-030-15526-1_6

1 Introduction

Against a backdrop characterized by accelerated change, driven in large part by the ongoing technological and information revolution, innovation performance has thus become a rising priority for firms. However, simultaneous to this challenge to innovate, they also encounter their inherent limitations, a situation that thus requires the search for and then the incorporation of external knowledge.

Meanwhile, no innovation process comes without its respective costs to the extent this necessarily requires the allocation of resources and capacities in order to ensure the success of external knowledge transfers. Hence, one fundamental facet to the process of knowledge creation and innovation stems from the capacity of firms to absorb external knowledge, a factor denominated the absorptive capacity (ACAP).

However, despite the clear relevance of this theme, only a few studies have explored the relationship between ACAP and family firms (FF) (Andersen, 2015; Zahra, Neubaum, & Larrañeta, 2007). Furthermore, Leone (2005), for example, is among those emphasizing the economic importance of such firms that this author states not only account for the ownership structure of approximately 90% of all Brazilian firms, directly generating over 2 million jobs, but also represents the fastest-growing business segment. Similarly, the *European Family Businesses* (2014) study estimates that 65–80% of European Union firms are FF and providing 40–50% of all private sector employment.

In addition to this leading role played in economic development, some research findings identify how these firms display particular characteristics of a strategic, managerial, and organizational nature that render them distinct to nonfamily firms (NFF) (Machado, Grzybovski, Teixeira, & Silva, 2013; Vries, Carlock, & Florent-Treacy, 2009) with the literature containing empirical evidence that reflect negative associations (Block, 2012; Cennamo, Berrone, Cruz, & Gomez-Mejia, 2012; Choi, Zahra, Yoshikawa, & Han, 2015; Chrisman & Patel, 2011; Classen, Van Gils, Bammens, & Carree, 2012; Gómez-Mejía, Takács Haynes, Núñez-Nickel, Jacobson, & Moyano-Fuentes, 2007; Gómez-Mejía et al., 2014; König, Kammerlander, & Enders, 2013) and positive (Carnes & Ireland, 2013; Cennamo et al., 2012; Gómez-Mejía et al., 2007; Kellermanns, Eddleston, & Zellweger, 2012), such as those between innovation and FF, for example.

In this sense, what distinguishes FF from NFF extends beyond the firm capital structure to incorporate the roles families play in the organization. Family interactions and involvement nurture a set of resources and capacities exclusive to FF and able to positively contribute to value creation processes (Chrisman, Chua, & Steier, 2005; Habbershon & Williams, 1999). Furthermore, family members frequently grow up closely bound up with the running of the firm, which may lead to a profound understanding and specific forms of tacit knowledge potentially generating competitive advantage for FF (Chirico & Salvato, 2016). Correspondingly, family involvement in management has emerged as a key factor distinguishing FF from NFF. Additionally, family members constitute a valuable source of human, financial, and social capital (Kim & Gao, 2013; Sciascia, Mazzola, & Chirico, 2013).

Hence, the objectives of this research involve analyzing the capacities of FF to absorb relevant information from the external environment and incorporate this into their innovation activities before subsequently analyzing the repercussions regarding the respective innovation performance. This also seeks to understand whether, and to just what extent, generational diversity in firm management represents an essential resource for firms portrayed here.

Therefore, taking into consideration these particularities and contradictions, this approaches the study of ACAP within the FF context as fertile research terrain, of relevance to thinking on the development of skills and capacities, as well as the adoption of strategies able to foster the growth, competitiveness, and longevity of these firms within the scope of boosting the creation of value.

2 Theoretical Framework and Hypothesis Development

2.1 *Absorptive Capacity (ACAP)*

Ever since the 1990s, the debate around ACAP has developed and attracted the attention of various researchers (Burcharth, Lettl, & Ulhøi, 2015; Camisón & Forés, 2010; Cohen & Levinthal, 1990; Flatten, Engelen, Zahra, & Brettel, 2011; Jones, 2006; Lane, Koka, & Pathak, 2006; Vega-Jurado, Gutiérrez-Gracia, & Fernándes-De-Lucio, 2008; Zahra & George, 2002). Initially, Cohen and Levinthal (1989, 1990) identify ACAP as conveying the ability of firms not only to recognize the value of new information and knowledge but also to assimilate and to exploit it for commercial purposes. Their studies provided a significant contribution and deemed as benchmark references in this field despite having restricted the concept to firms internally developing research and development (R&D) activities.

Meanwhile, the studies by Zahra and George (2002, p. 186) approach the ACAP concept more broadly in considering this as "a group of organizational routines and processes by which firms acquire, assimilate, transform and exploitation of knowledge to produce dynamic organizational capacities." Hence, the model put forward by these authors includes two antecedents (sources of complementary knowledge and employee experience), three moderating factors (activation triggers, social integration mechanisms, and the regimes of appropriability), as well as proposing a distinction between the two components, specifically between the potential absorptive capacity (PACAP), which includes the capacities for acquisition and assimilation, and the realized absorptive capacity (RACAP), which reflects the capacities for transformation and exploitation. These authors maintain that ACAP generates competitive advantage to the firm concerning strategic flexibility, innovation, and performance.

From the perspective of Zahra and George (2002), PACAP has received little attention from the research community when compared with RACAP. Meanwhile, they also argue that PACAP provides firms with the strategic flexibility necessary to be able to adapt in dynamic contexts. Hence, PACAP becomes perceived as a necessary condition for leveraging competitive advantages through innovation even while firms also need to develop their RACAP in order to fully benefit from the gains returned by ACAP (Fosfuri & Tribó, 2008; Zahra & George, 2002).

Within this scope, studying the PACAP of any organization helps identify and understand the extent to which it is receptive to external knowledge in the same way that measuring RACAP enables an understanding of whether the organization can apply new knowledge and develop it for commercial goals (Fosfuri & Tribó, 2008; Zahra & George, 2002). According to these authors, while PACAP acts on the interface between the firm and its surrounding environment, RACAP acts within the organization and is responsible for generating higher levels of firm performance. Correspondingly, PACAP emerges as a condition necessary to leveraging competitive advantage through innovation even while firms also need to develop RACAP to fully capitalize on the benefits of ACAP (Fosfuri & Tribó, 2008; Zahra & George, 2002). Given this, we may present the following research hypothesis:

Hypothesis 1 *The potential absorptive capacity (PACAP) of the firm has a positive and significant effect on the realized absorptive capacity (RACAP).*

There is a broad consensus that ACAP influences different results in organizations. Ever since the seminal works by Cohen and Levinthal (1989, 1990), there has been an association between ACAP and the results of innovation, and this has been subject to various studies over the course of time (Ebers & Maurer, 2014; Forés & Camisón, 2015; Jansen, Van Den Bosch, & Volberda, 2005; Kostopoulos, Papalexandris, Papachroni, & Ioannou, 2011; Murovec & Prodan, 2009; Tsai, 2001).

Murovec and Prodan (2009), for example, approach the effects of ACAP on different types of innovation, and the findings of their work point to a positive relationship with both product innovation and process innovation (greater production flexibility, increased productive capacity, reduction in labor costs per unit produced, and the reduction in materials and energy consumed per unit produced). Other studies identify innovation in a more general fashion (Cohen & Levinthal, 1990), while still others approach the impact of ACAP on innovation performance (Fosfuri & Tribó, 2008; Kostopoulos et al., 2011; Vinding, 2006), just as other authors emphasize the research interest in the specific typologies of innovation (Forés & Camisón, 2015). The latter recognizes the importance of the ACAP components to performance regarding both radical and incremental innovations.

Such considerations lead our understanding of innovation away from more linear and sequential logic to the extent that innovation involves interactive processes, thus stemming from the ongoing interactions between the firm and its surrounding environment (Ferreira, Raposo, & Fernandes, 2013; Ferreira, Fernandes, Alves, & Raposo, 2015). Such interactions provide for access to the information that in some way enables firms to boost their capacities to generate innovations (Chesbrough, 2010). Furthermore, it would be imprudent to perceive the existence of an environment rich in innovation opportunities as then any firm would have the capacity to detect and apply them effectively.

To this end, some firms are not able to grasp the need for change or may also lack the conditions and infrastructures necessary to managing such change. Such situations also reflect those firms that recognize the need to change, to seek out new knowledge, but that lack the capacity to identify the core sources of external information. Others may also lack any clear perception as to their own needs or be able to identify the opportunities but remain incapable of capturing the value of the acquired and assimilated knowledge (Tidd & Bessant, 2015).

A wide-reaching literature review carried out by Lane et al. (2006) details the recognition of innovation as a result of organizational learning and, consequently, deemed to be a result of the firm's respective ACAP. The literature also refers to the existence of a recursive relationship among the constructs, hence, to the extent that ACAP performs a vital role in innovation, firms getting involved in such processes receive boosts to their stocks of knowledge. Therefore, we may correspondingly formulate the following research hypothesis:

Hypothesis 2 *The absorptive capacity (ACAP) of the firm has a positive and significant effect on innovation performance.*

2.2 The Relationship Between the Absorptive Capacity Components and the Performance of Incremental and Radical Innovation

Within the various typologies deployed in empirical research on innovation, one leading approach considers the level of novelty and refers to "radical innovation" whenever this encapsulates the development and launch of a new product, process, or an entirely new way of organizing production. This type of innovation might lead to a fundamental rupture with the previously prevailing technological standard, bringing forth new industries, sectors, markets, and means of generating cost reductions and boosting the quality of already existing products. In turn, "incremental innovation" spans improvements to the organization of production within a firm without any alteration to its industrial structure (Freeman, 1988).

Another typology applied in empirical studies of product or process innovations stems from the studies by Kaufmann and Tödtling (2001) that classifies innovation as "new for the firm" versus "new to the market." The "new for the firm" category deals with innovations in which there are modifications and improvements to already existing products as well as products that are new to the firm and also known and classified as incremental innovation. The "new to the market" category is associated with radical innovations requiring more than incremental development and having no competitor in the market.

Hence, one crucial aspect requiring consideration encapsulates the level of newness involved in the innovation and ranging from incremental improvements to radical changes that transform prior perceptions of products or services. More specifically, authors highlight the need for research to be able to grasp the ongoing relationship between ACAP and the full extent of innovation in keeping with how radical innovation may feasibly require a firm to deploy an already deepened knowledge base (Lane et al., 2006; Van Den Bosch, Volberda, & Boer, 1999).

Some studies have referenced how ACAP may boost the incidence of incremental innovations taking into consideration how such innovations primarily arise out of the already existing knowledge base in the organization (Lane et al., 2006). Furthermore, the same authors mention how few works seek to understand the relationship between ACAP and radical innovation perhaps because this innovation type involves new combinations of existing technologies and know-how. According to Ritala and Hurmelinna-Laukkanen (2013), one restrictive factor on the development of radical innovation derives from a lack of diversification in the knowledge base given that the knowledge necessary for innovations of such magnitude very commonly stems from areas never before explored by the firm.

One of the empirical works that did seek to analyze this shortcoming was by Jansen et al. (2005) who took up the objective of studying how ACAP might influence two types of innovation: "exploratory" innovation and "exploitative" innovation associated with radical and incremental innovations, respectively. Their results convey how firms that search for incremental innovation present higher levels of RACAP to the extent that the firms striving for radical innovation also concentrate their efforts in developing their capacities for acquisition and assimilation, that is, their PACAP.

Adopting another perspective, Tidd and Bessant (2015) explain how, despite many firms being able to implement new projects and benefit from their capacities to search and acquire, implement, and refine new knowledge, they nevertheless still lack the capacity for radical innovation. They justify this position by pointing to the difficulties that firms display in grasping just where and how they might acquire new knowledge outside of their boundaries. Therefore, incremental innovation ends up providing firms with a constant and safe flow of advantages deriving from the perspective "doing what we know but doing it better," thus getting involved in activities that leverage the knowledge already existing in the firm.

Nevertheless, there is furthermore another question that we should not overlook given how this reflects an environment of uncertainties in which the search for competitive positions depends on their capacities to expand their frontiers and acquire the knowledge outside of their domains that then enables them to "do something different," or, expressed alternatively, to innovate radically. Such decisions may open up opportunities, but they also challenge the firm's capacity to reconfigure itself (Tidd & Bessant, 2015). Within this scope, we may grasp the importance of identifying the effects of the ACAP components on innovation performances, especially incremental and radical innovations. Hence, we arrive at the following research hypotheses:

Hypothesis 3 *The potential absorptive capacity (PACAP) has a positive and significant effect on the performance of incremental innovation.*

Hypothesis 4 *The realized absorptive capacity (RACAP) has a positive and significant effect on the performance of radical innovation.*

Based on the above, we may understand that innovation performance gets measured by the firm capacity to attain the results desired from a particular set of activities. In this research study approach, family firms (FFs) and their specific characteristics provide the scope for insights into the relationship ongoing among ACAP, the involvement of different generations of families in firm management, and the innovation performance.

2.3 *Family Involvement in the Management of Family Firms: The Moderating Role of Generational Diversity*

One essential characteristic of the FF context stems from how their survival interconnects with a theme that has been the subject of recurrent research: succession (Leone, 2005; Ussman, 2004), which renders the dispersion of ownership as a complex phenomenon that may have positive and negative effects on FF. The level of family influence stands out as a core factor in guiding the management practices of family organizations. Accordingly, the continuity of generations depends on their business capacities to enter into a new market as well as their capacity for revitalization. Studies by authors including Sciascia et al. (2013) and Filser, Brem, Gast, Kraus, and Calabrò (2016) refer to how the role played by the founder undergoes alterations to the extent that the subsequent generations participate in the business, deploying new knowledge and with different points of view arising out of this diversity.

While on the one hand, this generational diversity displays a cognitive nature to the extent it endows FF with different knowledge and perspectives, this may also emerge as a hindrance, eventually choking off these potential advantages. In this context, some studies suggest that second generation and longer FF may encounter difficulties of a relational nature among family members from different generations, which may then render dialogue more difficult alongside hindering the identification and exploration of new business opportunities (Barkema & Shvyrkov, 2007; Kellermanns & Eddleston, 2004; Kellermanns, Eddleston, Sarathy, & Murphy, 2012; Pérez-González, 2006).

According to Carney (2005), family control imposes capital restrictions that may hold back corporate growth. Similarly, FF tend to value continuity overgrowth and correspondingly prioritize the desire to maintain the status quo (Gersick, Davis, Hampton, & Lansberg, 2006; Salvato, 2004). Hence, Kellermanns and Eddleston (2006), on studying generational involvement, strategic planning, and corporate entrepreneurship, return results demonstrating a positive effect among the constructs only in the first-generation FF and not encountering the same effect in multigenerational FF.

On the contrary, studies carried out by Salvato (2004) and Ling and Kellermanns (2010) point to how having a single generation leading a firm may result in the perception of innovation as a difficult to develop activity with the diversified knowledge and experience of several generations potentially leading the firm to adopt other perspectives on this process. Some authors maintain that whenever FF engage different generations in strategic decision-making, they become better positioned to achieve their innovation objectives as well as to appropriately review past events (Salvato, 2004; Zahra, 2005).

According to Zahra (2005), in a study of 209 American FF, the higher the number of generations participating in the firm's management, the higher the focus on innovation. According to this author, the interpretation of this finding suggests that the engagement of various generations in managing the family business fosters insights and experiences and, therefore, new knowledge that may make the promotion of innovation possible. Similarly, Sciascia et al. (2013, p. 5) refer to how the diversified knowledge of various generations may lead to the "effective identification and evaluation of opportunities, as well as creative approaches to exploring them." This position receives corroboration from Kellermanns, Eddleston, Sarathy, et al. (2012) who affirm that multigenerational involvement in decision-making processes enable innovative actions to become more assertive and higher quality.

Clercq and Belausteguigoitia (2015) express a similar position in keeping with the results of their study by identifying how multigenerational involvement in the firm strategy may result in the development of a diversified repertoire of knowledge that enables FF to identify a broader set of alternatives for managing the results of innovation. Therefore, they propose that generational diversity in the management of FF acts to provide them with the capacity for accruing the benefits arising from ACAP and we may thus formulate the following research hypothesis:

Hypothesis 5 *Generational diversity moderates the relationship between the absorptive capacity (ACAP) of the firm and its innovation performance.*

With the objective of summarizing the theoretical relationships among the study constructs, specifically, the absorptive capacity, innovation performance, and generational diversity, Fig. 1 presents the conceptual model that depicts the relationship described in the hypotheses.

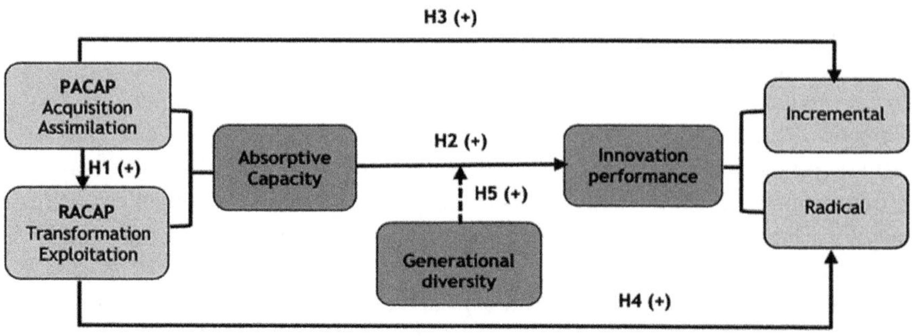

Fig. 1 Conceptual model. Source: Authors' own figure

3 Sample and Data Sources

This study adopts the ownership/management criteria and thus considers FF as entities in which a family owns more than 50% and is also responsible for its management (Astrachan & Kolenko, 1994). In order to carry out this study, we opted for a probabilistic sampling method that implements a random selection process (Marôco, 2014). The study population consists of Brazilian firms with their headquarters in the Rio Grande do Sul State and registered with the Rio Grande do Sul Industrial Federation (FIERGS, 2015), which has 10,980 registered members. We then verified that 2975 firms did not have any email contact address, a necessary condition for data collection participation. Thus, we reached a total number of 8005 firms. In order to obtain greater accuracy in estimating the minimum sample size, we evaluated the statistical power of the sample size, a priori in type, through recourse to the G*Power 3.1.9.2 software program (Faul, Erdfelder, Lang, & Buchner, 2007). The minimum recommended sample size was 55 cases but with the suggestion of doubling or tripling this number to better ensure a more consistent model (Ringle, Silva, & Bido, 2014). Therefore, the sample size ($n = 241$) holds the statistical capability for detecting any supposed relationship when this does exist. The instrument applied for the collection of data was the *Google Forms* platform that we made available to respondents. The link to the access to the research instrument was sent to the managers of the firms on the grounds of how resources and capacities get evaluated, acquired, constructed, allocated and explored which are susceptible to the decisions taken by the management of the firms in question. Data collection took place between October 2015 and January 2016.

3.1 Measures

3.1.1 Predictive Variable

In order to capture ACAP, we applied the structured questionnaire developed by Flatten et al. (2011), with a 7-point Likert-type scale (1 = totally disagree 7 = totally agree). This instrument has already undergone validation for the Brazilian context (Vicentin, 2015), with its utilization and justification characterized by its solid theoretical-conceptual grounding.

3.1.2 Dependent Variable

This study considers innovation performance from the perspective of the level of novelty and attributing the denomination of "radical innovation" whenever referring to the development and introduction of a new product and "incremental innovation" whenever dealing with the introduction of some improvement to a product inside a firm without any alteration to its industrial structure (Freeman, 1988; Kaufmann & Tödtling, 2001; Tödtling, Lehner, & Kaufmann, 2009; Vega-Jurado, Gutiérrez-Gracia, Fernández-De-Lucio, & Manjarrés-Henríquez, 2008). In order to measure innovation performance levels, as a benchmark reference, we applied the survey entitled Research into Innovation (PINTEC). This variable considers the response "No" = 0, thus reflecting no innovation, and "Yes" = to the absolute number corresponding to the innovation introduced by the firm and expressed in a natural logarithm (NL).

3.1.3 Moderator Variable

For the operationalization of this variable, we developed three questions and subsequently jointly analyzed them with the first stage, a dichotomist configuration, in which respondent indicates whether the firm contains different generations in its management. There then followed two multiple choice questions that seek to identify which generation holds responsibility for managing the firm. Thus, we here understand generational diversity as the number of generations that coexist in the firm at the time of the study. This adopts the "0" value when respondents refer to but one generation of the family participating in the management and "1" when replying two or more generations (Miller, Le Breton-Miller, & Lester, 2012).

3.1.4 Control Variables

We selected the control variables according to their potential for influencing the dependent and independent variables. The literature describes the size and age of firms as internal factors able to influence ACAP (Forés & Camisón, 2015; Kraiczy, Hack, & Kellermanns, 2014; Sørensen & Stuart, 2000; Zahra, 2005; Zahra et al., 2007). Due to the major variations in the number of members of staff of sample firms, we opted to transform this variable. Hence, the NL of the number of employees serves to measure the size of sample firms (Kraiczy et al., 2014; Zahra, 2003; Zahra, Hayton, & Salvato, 2004; Zahra et al., 2007). In the same way, as regards the firm age variable, we again opted for transformation given that the sample ages ranged from 1 year to 105 years. Therefore, through the application of the quartile results, we established four discrete categories (less than 15 years, from 16 to 24 years, from 25 to 36 years, over 37 years), a procedure also adopted by other authors (Zahra, Hayton, Neubaum, Dibrell, & Craig, 2008).

4 Analysis

The processing and analysis of the data took place according to the SPSS version 22.0 statistical software for descriptive analysis and SmartPLS 2.0.M3 program (Ringle, Wende, & Will, 2005) for analysis of both the measurement model and the structural model following the structural equation modeling technique. In order to achieve the aforementioned research objectives, we estimated two reflective models: the first contemplating the second-order latent variables (LVs) and then modeled in accordance with the hierarchical components approach in which all indicators measuring the first-order variable also interconnect with the higher-order variable (Hair, Hult, Ringle, & Sarstedt, 2014; Wetzels, Odekerken-Schröder, & Oppen, 2009). This model also presents the control and moderation variables and thereby seeks to confirm hypotheses H2 and H5.

The second estimated model spans the first-order LV with the objective of analyzing the relationships proposed in hypotheses H1, H3, and H4. This division arises from the unviability of establishing relational hypotheses among the indicators, and despite the hypotheses mentioned above reflecting the relationships between LVs, they require interpretation as indicators whenever applied to measure the second-order LV (Garver & Mentzer, 1999). We would here highlight that measuring ACAP as the reflective model is in keeping with previous studies (Flatten et al., 2011; Hernández-Perlines, Moreno-Garcia, & Yáñez-Araque, 2016; Leal-Rodríguez, Roldán, Ariza-Montes, & Leal-Millán, 2014; Wang, Senaratne, & Rafiq, 2015).

5 Empirical Results and Discussion

5.1 Sample Profile

A total of 273 firms took part in this study and, according to the criteria of ownership/management, we obtained two groups, specifically the FF and the NFF. The former group contains 241 (88.3%) firms and the latter group having 32 (11.7%) firms. Considering the context chosen for this study, only the first group of firms was subject to analysis.

As regards the academic level of respondents, 107 (44.4%) report undergraduate education, 85 (35.3%) hold a higher-level/MBA specialization, followed by 31 (12.9%) who finished school with a medium-level qualification. In terms of the position occupied by respondents, 76 (31.5%) describe themselves as holding the position of "one of the managers," the second largest percentage was "top management" accounting for 60 (24.9%) managers followed by the position "CEO/general director" identified by 48 (19.9%) respondents. In turn, the average number of years of employment in the firm totals 2.38 years with a standard deviation of 0.807 as well as respondents presenting an average period of leadership of 2.12 years with a standard deviation of 0.889, and, finally, there were previous working periods in other firms amounting to 1.85 years with standard deviation of 0.813.

The average number of active employees in sample firms comes in at 59.10 but again with a broad spectrum of answers to this question with FF ranging from a minimum of one employee to a maximum number of 829 members of staff. We may also report that 66 (27.4%) FF had been in business for less than 15 years, followed by 61 (25.3%) firms with between 25 and 36 years in operation. There are also a total of 59 FF (24.5%) with over 37 years in business while the 16–24 category accounts for 55 (22.8%) of the sample.

In the case of the firm area of activity, the industrial transformation sector holds the greatest weighting with a total of 224 (92.9%) firms, among which food product manufacturing firms prevail (on 16.1%), followed by beverage sector firms (11.2%) and with the furniture manufacturing sector in third place (10.3%).

As regards the question focusing on the founder of the firm, 80 (33.2%) respondents affirmed their "father/mother," followed by 61 (25.3%) who state that this had been "themselves" with a further 59 (24.5%) respondents opting for "others" (e.g., partnerships among cousins, uncles, parent-in-law, great-great-grandfather, etc.). The next most numerous answers received identified "Sibling/Siblings founded the particular firm" and "Grandfather/Grandmother," respectively, 22 (9.1%) and 19 (7.9%).

As regards the generational diversity variable, we may state that 126 FF (52.3%) had two or more generations responsible for firm's management and that in the remainder 115 firms (47.7%) a single generation of the family was holding such a position. With the objective of more specifically characterizing the generational diversity present in the FF management structures, we need to discriminate which generations coexist in the firm. Thus, we find that the first generation of the family manages 88 (36.51%) of these FFs, while in 84 (34.85%) there is the simultaneous involvement of the first and second generations in the management structure. This sample of FF displays a distribution from first-generation firms to firms being run by members of the fourth generation of the family while recording the lowest level of incidence (0.83%). As regards the generational presence on the board of directors, 87 (36.10%) of these FF report that the first generation of the family is present on the board, while 84 (34.85%) firms have representatives of the first and second generations on their boards. We would note that 15 (6.22%) of the FF report not having any such management body.

5.2 *Models Estimated*

5.2.1 Measurement Model: First Model Estimated (H2 and H5)

The actions were taken as regards the weightings of the indicators follow the recommendations handed down by Hair et al. (2014, p. 104). Thus, in this validation process, we may observe the coefficients of the factorial weightings of each first-order and second-order LV indicator from which we withdrew those with values of greater than 0.6 given that very low factorial weightings may affect subsequent analytical phases. This first analytical stage verified that the Aq1 (0.5694) and Ex1 (0.5930) indicators for the second-order ACAP LV and the Aq1 (0.5999) indicator for the first-order PACAP LV verged on the critical value of 0.6. Nevertheless, when testing following the elimination of these indicators, there was no increase in composite reliability and, taking into consideration the recommendation from Hair et al. (2014), we then maintained them in the correspondingly unaltered composition. Similarly, DeVellis (2012) points to the importance of maintaining replicability of the instrument in addition to providing yet another similar factor for future studies with this also guaranteeing that they do not overfit the study sample.

We evaluated convergent validity and reliability according to the average variance extracted (AVE) and the composite reliability (CR) of the LV. According to Becker, Klein, and Wetzels (2012), in order to verify the AVE and CR of second-order LV, researchers should deploy the coefficients of the paths that connect with the respective first-order LV. Hence, we made the calculations separately on an electronic worksheet according to the criteria of Garver and Mentzer (1999) and Hair, Tatham, Anderson, and Black (2005). All of the AVE and CR results are above 0.50 and 0.70, respectively, which enables us to affirm that the measurement model displays convergent validity and reliability.

In the continuity of this analysis, we evaluated the discriminant validity of the model. We verified that all of the first-order LV indicators return higher values in comparison with the corresponding cross loadings, which thus ensures their discriminant validity. This result suggests that the questions under study are indicators of the research constructs proposed here. We also adopted a second, more conservative, criterion in order to verify the discriminant analysis, proposed by Fornell and Larcker (1981), in which the core diagonal values (square roots of the average variance extracted) need to attain greater values than those of the respective lines and columns (correlations), thereby confirming the presence of discriminant validity (Hair et al., 2014). The LV correlations were lower than the AVE square roots and thus confirming discriminant validity. One exception was the correlation between RACAP and PACAP, which returned a higher result than the AVE squared root, suggesting the lack of discriminant validity among them even while, as we apply both LVs as reflective indicators for the same construct (ACAP) in this model, this does not represent a problem.

5.2.2 Structural Model: First Estimated Model (H2 and H5)

In order to evaluate the explanatory power of the structural model, we deploy the explained variance (R^2) of all the model's endogenous variables. For the field of the social and behavioral sciences, Cohen (1977, pp. 413–414) proposes that $R^2 = 2\%$ be classified as a small effect, $R^2 = 13\%$ as the average effect, and $R^2 = 26\%$ as a large effect. The R^2 of LV PACAP came in at 0.839. Thus, this accounts for 83.9% of the variation in this ACAP component in the model studied. Furthermore, we may also rank as high the R^2 results for RACAP (89.7%), InInc (73.7%), and InRad (70.8%). Applying the same criteria, it becomes clear that the R^2 of ACAP (1.7%) represents a coefficient with a low level of determination while the R^2 for DIn (16.3%) returns a medium effect.

5.2.3 Measuring Model: Second Estimated Model (H1, H3, and H4)

The second estimated model considers the first-order LV with the objective of analyzing the relationships set out in the hypotheses H1, H3, and H4. This second estimated model maintains size as the control dimension in keeping with the evidence of its influence over the innovation performances of this sample of FF ($t = 2.1256$). The evaluation of the outer loadings reports that the betas for the paths between the LV and the variables return values more than 0.6 and with no variable requiring exclusion. Hence, as in the first estimated model, we evaluated the convergent validity and reliability by the AVE and the CR of the LV, with all the results above 0.50 and 0.70, respectively, which enables us to ensure that the measurement model displays both convergent validity and reliability. Continuing our analysis, we then evaluated the cross loadings of the model, which resulted in the verification that all LV indicators attain values greater than those of the corresponding cross loadings, which ensures its discriminant validity. In relation to the Fornell and Larcker (1981) criterion, we were able to verify that the correlations among the LV were lower than the square root of AVE, again confirming discriminant validity in a situation that did not occur between the RACAP and PACAP LVs but, as explained above, both serve as reflective indicators of the same construct, and, therefore, this situation does not represent an impediment.

5.2.4 Structural Model: Second Estimated Model (H1, H3, and H4)

With the objective of evaluating the explanatory power of the second estimated model, we may report that the R^2 of LV RACAP is 0.555. Hence the model studied explains 55.5% of its variation. In turn, the R^2 results of LV InInc (15.3%) and InRad (4.4%) return an average level of the coefficient determinant (Cohen, 1977, pp. 413–414).

5.2.5 Estimated Model Predictive Relevance and Size Effects

Finally, we carried out an analysis of the adjustment quality indicators of the models, both obtained by recourse to the *Blindfolding* module: relevance or predictive validity (Q^2) or the Stone-Geisser indicator, applied with the criteria of results greater than zero, and size effect (f^2) or the Cohen indicator with its reference values of 0.02, 0.15, and 0.35 ranking as small, average, and large, respectively (Hair et al., 2014). The simulation with an omission distance of 7 found that the Q^2 results are greater than zero in both models and correspondingly confirming that the models presented attain predictive validity. The f^2 adjustment quality indicator reported a similar situation in which all LV values are greater than 0.35, which indicates that all the constructs are important to the general adjustment of the models estimated in this study.

5.3 *Discussion*

Following the analysis of Table 1, we may understand that of the five hypotheses tested in this study, four receive support. However, the hypothesis (H5) that advocated generational diversity in the management of family firms (FF) as a moderator for the relationship between the absorptive capacity (ACAP) and innovation performance did not gain sufficient empirical support.

The relationships revealed and supported by the employee analysis are in keeping with the results of Zahra and George (2002) across various aspects. Primarily, these revolve around the argument that the potential absorptive capacity (PACAP), thus, the firm capacity to acquire and assimilate external information, provides a necessary condition to leveraging competitive advantage through innovation all the while firms also need to develop their RACAP, hence, the capacity to transform and exploit knowledge (H1). The study by Zahra and George (2002), as well as those by other authors (Camisón & Forés, 2010; Ebers & Maurer, 2014; Flatten et al., 2011; Fosfuri & Tribó, 2008; Leal-Rodríguez et al., 2014), highlights how the firm capacity to transform and exploit information directly links with its capacity to acquire and assimilate knowledge that comes from beyond the organization's frontiers.

The authors had already drawn attention to how these two components of ACAP (PACAP and RACAP) coexist in firms, hence, firms cannot exploit external knowledge without first acquiring it. However, firms can possess the capacity to acquire and assimilate external knowledge and not be able to transform and exploit it successfully. Hence, we may affirm that both components contain different but complementary roles as proposed by Zahra and George (2002).

Table 1 Validation of the research hypothesis results

Hypotheses	Structural relationship	Structural coefficient	Standard error	*t*-Student	Results
H1	PACAP → RACAP	0.7453	0.0297	25.1240***	Supported
H2	ACAP → DIn	0.3359	0.0544	6.1784***	Supported
H3	PACAP → InInc	0.3101	0.0587	5.2829***	Supported
H4	RACAP → InRad	0.1903	0.0635	2.9969***	Supported
H5	ACAP * DivGer → DIn	0.0887	0.0897	0.9883	Not supported

Note: ***Level of significance 1% (≥2.58); **Level of significance 5% (≥1.96)
Source: Authors' own table

Innovation being a complex activity, and with firms facing ever more dynamic environments, there is the belief that efforts made to foster the development of PACAP end up enabling FF to explore new opportunities and adapt to changes in addition to how the continuous reformulation of their knowledge bases consequently influences their RACAP. The confirmation of this hypothesis also aligns with the results returned by other studies (Jansen et al., 2005; Zahra et al., 2007), which point to how an effective RACAP, with positive impacts on the firm's results, depends on continuous efforts focused on the acquisition and assimilation of new and external knowledge. On the other hand, this result runs counter to the positioning of Todorova and Durisin (2007) who question the need for the distinction between the respective components and, whenever supporting this distinction, indicating that both dimensions contribute to the formation of the ACAP construct.

One factor deemed of importance to shrinking the gap between PACAP and RACAP, identified by Zahra and George (2002), derives from social integration mechanisms. In this sense, this approaches whether the ambiances prevailing in FF are favorable to knowledge sharing practices (Habbershon & Williams, 1999; Habbershon, Williams, & Macmillan, 2003). In such environments, informal discussions may contribute to accelerating the transfer of experiences and knowledge (Miller, Wright, Le Breton-Miller, & Scholes, 2015). The organizational cultures and contexts characterizing these firms are determinant to processes of transforming and exploiting new knowledge. Given the results analyzed here, we may infer that the practices prevailing within FF contexts contribute to developing the components making up ACAP, which then enable better innovation performance standards.

We would highlight that approximately 94% of these FF declare they have boards of directors, a fact identified as one means of reducing the negative potential of the effects of family involvement in innovation and a finding in alignment with the studies by Carney (2005), Kellermanns, Eddleston, Sarathy, et al. (2012), and Machado et al. (2013). This behavior holds relevance to the introduction of formal knowledge sharing practices that incorporate means such as the scheduled and regulated exchange of information and that may boost the capacity of these firms to recognize and explore the business opportunities prevailing.

In turn, on analyzing Table 1, we may state that ACAP constitutes an essential predictor of innovation performance with this finding suggesting a recursive relationship between the constructs (H2). Expressed otherwise, innovation produces knowledge that becomes part of the ACAP of firms and the higher the frequency of innovating in a particular area, the higher the level of ACAP in this area and thereby creating what various authors refer to as a self-strengthening circle (Kostopoulos et al., 2011; Lane et al., 2006; Van Den Bosch et al., 1999).

These results contradict studies that research the innovative behaviors of FF in how they report a negative relationship between family involvement and the results of innovation with some such studies especially considering R&D investments (Chen & Huang, 2009; Chrisman & Patel, 2011; Gómez-Mejía et al., 2014; Nieto, Santamaria, & Fernandez, 2015). However, there is empirical evidence that FF generates entrance and exit rates of innovation that are different to NFF given that these firms benefit from the accumulation of social capital as well as establishing efficient routines for this conversion and pointed to as those "who do more with less" (Duran, Kammerlander, Van Essen, & Zellweger, 2016).

Furthermore, these results may be interpreted in keeping with the studies that report how FF, for example, in situations that fail to meet business performance expectations, or still furthermore, encounter economically difficult positions, remain particularly prepared to assume risks, and deepen their innovation-focused activities (Chrisman, Steier, & Chua, 2008; Chrisman et al., 2005). Under this perspective, we may consider the period Brazil is currently experiencing, when the performance of the local industrial base has gone through a contraction (FIERGS, 2015), as a trigger activating innovation (Zahra & George, 2002).

These triggers may be internal or external and, despite the negative context, may intensify the firm's efforts to learn new abilities and develop new knowledge that enables them to raise their ACAP. This comes in addition to how this Brazilian state is highly dependent on climatic factors and international markets (a significant grain exporter—soya, rice, wheat, and maize).

These positions may underpin the results returned by this study as regards ACAP and innovation performance to the extent that the authors identify how firms commonly perceive crises and recessions as investment opportunities (Winter, 2000; Zahra et al., 2007). Hence, the need for information and the will to learn would seem to interlink with crises in performance or competitiveness, which serve to intensify firm's efforts to seek out information and develop new competences (Zahra & George, 2002).

In turn, the relationship demonstrated between the potential absorptive capacity (PACAP) and the incremental innovation performance (H3) suggests that for this level of innovation, there is a trend toward applying the already existing knowledge in the firm given that the typology of inputs necessary to improve on a product are already incorporated into the firm's routines. We would importantly emphasize here that incremental innovation, despite only seeking to improve on that already existing, performs a fundamental role to firms maintaining their levels of competitiveness (Kaufmann & Tödtling, 2001; Pittino, Visintin, Bau, & Mazzurna, 2013; Tidd & Bessant, 2015).

Within this framework, Zahra and George (2002) and Zahra et al. (2007) have already identified the fact that firms face relatively few difficulties whenever seeking out incremental innovations to the extent that this type of innovation requires decision-making coherent with its respective trajectory. Such innovations, therefore, involve lower levels of risk when compared with radical innovations and are very common in response to the needs and specific problems of clients and suppliers. Hence, firms drawing upon their proximity to this type of information source introduce improvements to their already existing products and services (Freeman, 1988; Kaufmann & Tödtling, 2001; Pittino et al., 2013).

Similarly, in confirming the relationship between the realized absorptive capacity (RACAP) and the radical innovation performance (H4), this suggests that this typology receives more significant support from an ACAP based on a broad spectrum of knowledge. Indeed, when getting involved in innovations of this magnitude, firms encounter needs to seek out information that they may not find within their current knowledge base. Thus, this confirms that radical innovation performances may inherently need the search for new sources of external information that aid in expanding the prevailing scope of knowledge (Cruz & Nordqvist, 2012; Lane et al., 2006; Pittino et al., 2013; Van Den Bosch et al., 1999).

This result also indicates that the development of radical innovations incorporates a more complex pattern of organizational arrangements to the extent that to obtain higher performance standards, firms also need to develop their capacities to acquire and assimilate relevant information from the external environment. Zahra et al. (2007) approach this component as highly complex given that the capacity for information is one of the most critical and complicated facets of ACAP. This requires the capacity to integrate, summarize, and interpret different types of knowledge, which in turn needs complex organizational and cognitive abilities and skills.

The profile of the FF in this study contradicts the results presented by Zellweger and Sieger (2012) that consider it unlikely that FF innovate in any radical way, instead of involving themselves in innovations that these authors denominate as "invisible," hence, implemented incrementally. One possible relationship would be with the studies by Zahra et al. (2007) as they refer to how firms when in initial phases of their life cycle tend to concentrate more on those ACAP aspects related to the commercial exploration of externally acquired knowledge. For the authors, this type of approach reflects the urgent need for firms to take new products to the market, with the objective of survival, a fact that can justify the observed result in relation to the RACAP component and radical innovation in the case of family firms which, for the most part, are in the 1st generation.

We would also draw attention to how these results point to the FF in this sample investing their efforts in developing both incremental and radical innovations, which suggests a possible alignment with the studies of Le Breton-Miller and Miller (2011). These authors state that FFs hold a multi-temporal advantage, that is, the capacity to attain long-lasting success that endures due to a balance between their short-term and long-term orientations. They add that FF demonstrate an ambidextrous capacity, enabling their involvement in activities focused both on "exploratory" innovation and "exploitative" innovation, respectively associated with radical innovation and incremental innovation. Similarly, this finding corroborates what Sharma and Salvato (2011) conclude from their study when affirming that involvement in the simultaneous search for different levels of innovation might guarantee long-term survival, as well as the performance advantages of FF. Subsequently, a study was undertaken by Dolz, Iborra, and Safón (2015), of a sample of FF located in Spain, and reports similar results.

Contrary to expectations, the hypothesis suggests that the simultaneous involvement of several generations in the management would represent a significant moderator between firm's ACAP and its innovation performance (H5), did not receive any empirical support in this study. This result contradicts earlier studies that emphasized the importance of the involvement of different generations as a driving force for change and innovation, bestowing competitive advantage on FF (Cruz & Nordqvist, 2012; Kellermanns, Eddleston, Barnett, & Pearson, 2008; Litz & Kleysen, 2001; Zahra, 2005; Zahra et al., 2007). This similarly runs counter to the studies by Salvato (2004) and Chirico, Sirmon, Sciascia, and Mazzola (2011) that refer to how generational diversity constitutes a fertile environment for the exchange of knowledge, bringing about the recombination and development of new resources and capacities.

Another feasible explanation for this result may derive from how in both groups, thus FF with generational diversity versus FF without generational diversity, strategic decision-making remains heavily under the influence of the founder. This profile echoed in our sample here to the extent that firms with various generations of the family in the management concentrate in the first and second generations (34.85%) and, in turn, firms without any generational diversity are in the first generation (36.51%), and hence the differentiation between these groups did not receive support from the evidence. This explanation makes it possible to consider what Kellermanns, Eddleston, Sarathy, et al. (2012) denominate as the "founder effect," whenever the decisions of the founding generation (or the founder) achieve more significant results than the innovations ongoing at multigenerational firms.

6 Conclusion

Throughout this research, we were able to grasp the complexity surrounding absorptive capacity (ACAP) processes. Firms need to know where to seek out information and need to develop routines and processes that enable them to analyze, process, interpret, and understand the information in the meanwhile acquired before subjecting it to transformation and adaptation to the internally existing knowledge. Finally, that may transform the knowledge into something tangible and generate competitive advantage.

Hence, given this complexity, this study's objectives involved studying how family firms (FF) absorb relevant information on the external environment and incorporate it into their innovative activities and, furthermore, analyzing the repercussions returned for their innovation performance. This also sought to grasp how and to what extent did generational diversity in FF management establish an essential resource to these firms.

The study results recognize ACAP as an important predictor of FF innovation performance. In particular, the results suggest that the potential absorptive capacity (PACAP) holds a significant effect on the realized absorptive capacity (RACAP). Similarly, the PACAP and RACAP components return a positive and significant effect when analyzed concerning the performance of incremental and radical innovation, respectively. These relationships emerge due to PACAP being the dimension that enables firms to continually renew their stock of knowledge even while they can transform and apply it that may drive the development of innovative products incorporating radical levels of innovation. In turn, the involvement of various generations in the management of the FF did not configure as a significant moderator between ACAP and innovation performance.

Given this, we would raise some considerations. Firstly, this result seems to clearly convey the heterogeneous character of these firms and correspondingly demonstrate that not all FF are equally capable of exploring their resources and capacities, in this case, those stemming from the interactions between family generations (Ling & Kellermanns, 2010; Sharma & Salvato, 2011). In fact, FFs represent a unique scenario to the extent that they incorporate overlapping and complex systems—family, property, and management—with one of the main explanations for the sustainability of these firms potentially deriving from their search for a balance between tradition and renovation (Kellermanns, Eddleston, Sarathy, et al., 2012; Mahmoud-Jouini & Mignon, 2009).

Finding this equilibrium is no easy task for FF in particular as many may display the trend to make recourse to already well known and trodden search routines, which may eliminate the scope for perceiving other opportunities. The problem emerges when such routines perhaps fall short of dealing with a surrounding environment undertaking constant changes. According to this perspective, it would seem essential for FF to develop capacities that enable the strengthening of the factors existing in the firm as well as recognizing when and how to modify them in order to thereby enable the creation of new capacities, with this constituting an essential factor within the context of radical innovation. Hence, we may grasp how ACAP, alongside CD, performs an important role in achieving this equilibrium given how this facilitates firms accessing new knowledge, engaging in new partnerships and the perceptions of new market niches.

In turn, there is encouragement from the research results also demonstrating that the FF in this sample, despite the recession Brazil is currently experiencing, manage to convert their efforts and invest in their incremental and radical innovation performance levels, a fact that represents a significant contribution to the FF field of study given that perceptions about these firms generally identify them as adverse to innovation in keeping with their low levels of R&D investment.

At the beginning of this study, we identified three main shortcomings in the research literature, in particular (1) the shortage of studies relating the ACAP components to incremental and radical innovation performance, (2) the absence or lack of comprehension about the ways in which FF absorb external information and explore this in their innovation activities, and (3) the lack of approaches considering the family involved as a resource capable of enabling the relationship between ACAP and innovation performance. There thus emerge the main contributions of this work. Firstly, this study contributes to the evolution and consolidation of ACAP, strengthening this concept as an essential research input as well as its relevance to innovation processes (H2). In the same way, this perceives that the debate on the relevance of the distinctions between the ACAP dimensions has been more theoretical than empirical and, within this same perspective, this study makes an essential contribution in the sense of clarifying the role of the PACAP and RACAP components in incremental and radical innovation performance levels (H3 and H4, respectively). The analytical studies carried out in this work also return a contribution to the field of organizational capacities in empirically demonstrating a positive relationship between PACAP and RACAP (H1).

Another contribution made by this study stems from the fact that it fills an essential gap in the research on FF to the extent that it considers generational diversity in the management of these firms; the study deepens the discussion about the essential characteristics of a family firms and analyzes innovation from the perspective of generational diversity (H5). Therefore, in examining the influence of family involvement in ACAP, this research contributes to the debate on FF innovation. This furthermore maintains that these results strengthen what some authors identify when warning how resources in themselves do not generate competitive advantages as they also need to be efficiently and effectively managed so as to ensure their potential in terms of the creation of value (Carnes & Ireland, 2013; Habbershon et al., 2003; Zahra, 2016; Zahra, Sapienza, & Davidsson, 2006).

From the practical point of view, there is the expectation that this study aids managers of these FF within the scope of better understanding how to maximize the results of their innovation performance in ways that foster synergies among the generations. Such efforts would enable family members to interact intensively, and, based on this, they may deploy their complementary knowledge to develop new products. This research clarifies the essential factors for transforming ACAP and rendering organizations more innovative and sustainable. It would, therefore, be important for the managers of these firms to deploy social integration mechanisms that facilitate and stimulate, on a continuous basis, a favorable learning environment. It is equally recommendable that the firm's culture stimulates the family environment to the extent that family proximity to the business may elicit new perspectives about the conflicts existing in its dynamics. This change in perspective opens the path to the development of capacities fundamental to the firm's growth and longevity such as, the absorptive capacity.

In summary, we hope this study aids the managers of these FF within the framework of better understanding how to maximize their innovation performance results through nurturing synergies among the generations. This effort would enable members of the family to engage intensely and, based on such interactions, apply their complementary knowledge to developing new products. This research clarifies some of the essential factors susceptible to transforming ACAP and making organizations both more innovative and more sustainable.

Research processes span many stages and including that which the researcher dedicates to the choice of theme. Correspondingly, in defining the path of choice, we inevitably impose limitations on the study. Hence, we would assume the limitation arising from the utilization of but a single source of the informant. Meanwhile, according to Huber and Power (1985), organizations, due to factors of time and costs, tend to decline invitations to participate in studies in contrast with requests to donate the time of multiple informants. Thus, given the relevance of this study object, as well as the context of the application, the loss of organizations and their information were both critical and taken into consideration.

Nevertheless, in order to maximize the precision and reliability of the data, we took into due consideration the directives suggested by Huber and Power (1985) in order to obtain data on the quality of isolated informants, with these research instruments serving to focus on explicit and essential changes and tending to be subject to more reliable portrayal; the key informant, as the senior manager, in keeping with their position, tends to get involved or, when not possible, somebody close to the important event(s) and process(es) on which the researcher is gathering information.

This study deploys a sample of Brazilian FF, from the Rio Grande do Sul State, in addition to adopting a transversal structure. Thus, its results require interpretation with care; firstly, as they may not apply to FF from other countries/states and, secondly, due to their transversal nature, they reflect the situations of the firm respondent at the time of completing the research questionnaire. Future research may overcome such limitations through carrying out longitudinal studies that might produce different ideas about the nature and the strengths of the relationships examined here. Concerning the sample size, we would recommend the application of larger samples even while the results here did attain significance.

As another suggestion for future research, other researchers might consider how the multigenerational interactions require FF to develop capacities able to combine the knowledge bases held by different generations. Hence, longitudinal studies might also help in clarifying the changes in the cycle of development and how these impact on innovation and even on performance. The literature would also emerge richer should future studies examine the social integration mechanisms that FF deploy for the conversion of knowledge (formal and informal) as well as the effects of the generational involvement across different industrial contexts.

Finally, we would hope that the results set out here encourage recourse to innovation methodologies for the identification of potentially modifying variables with significant effects on the relationship between ACAP and the innovation performance of FF, such as entrepreneurial orientations, international strategies, and the dynamics of the owner families.

Acknowledgments This study was financed in part by the *Coordenação de Aperfeiçoamento de Pessoal de Nível Superior-Brasil* (CAPES) Finance Code 001, and NECE—Research Unit in Business Sciences funded by the Multiannual Funding Programme of R&D Centres of *Fundação para a Ciência e a Tecnologia* (FCT), under the project "UID/GES/04630/2013."

References

Andersen, J. (2015). The absorptive capacity of family firms. *Journal of Family Business Management, 5*(1), 73–89.

Astrachan, J. H., & Kolenko, T. A. (1994). A neglected factor explaining family business success: Human resource practices. *Family Business Review, 7*, 251–262.

Barkema, H. G., & Shvyrkov, O. (2007). Does top management team diversity promote or hamper foreign expansion? *Strategic Management Journal, 28*, 663–680.

Becker, J., Klein, K., & Wetzels, M. (2012). Hierarchical latent variable models in PLS-SEM: Guidelines for using reflective-formative type models. *Long Range Planning, 45*, 359–394.

Block, J. H. (2012). R&D investments in family and founder firms: An agency perspective. *Journal of Business Venturing, 27*(2), 248–265.

Burcharth, A. L. L. d. A., Lettl, C., & Ulhøi, J. P. (2015). Extending organizational antecedents of absorptive capacity: Organizational characteristics that encourage experimentation. *Technological Forecasting and Social Change, 90*, 269–284.

Camisón, C., & Forés, B. (2010). Knowledge absorptive capacity: New insights for its conceptualization and measurement. *Journal of Business Research, 63*(7), 707–715.

Carnes, C. M., & Ireland, R. D. (2013). Familiness and innovation: Resource bundling as the missing link. *Entrepreneurship: Theory and Practice, 37*(6), 1399–1419.

Carney, M. (2005). Corporate governance and competitive advantage in family-controlled firms. *Entrepreneurship: Theory and Practice, 29*(3), 249–265.

Cennamo, C., Berrone, P., Cruz, C., & Gomez-Mejia, L. R. (2012). Socioemotional wealth and proactive stakeholder engagement: Why family-controlled firms care more about their stakeholders. *Entrepreneurship: Theory and Practice, 36*(6), 1153–1173.

Chen, C., & Huang, J. (2009). Strategic human resource practices and innovation performance – The mediating role of knowledge management capacity. *Journal of Business Research, 62*, 104–114.

Chesbrough, H. (2010). Business model innovation: Opportunities and barriers. *Long Range Planning, 43*, 354–363.

Chirico, F., & Salvato, C. (2016). Knowledge internalization and product development in family firms: When relational and affective factors matter. *Entrepreneurship: Theory and Practice, 40*, 201–229.

Chirico, F., Sirmon, D. G., Sciascia, S., & Mazzola, P. (2011). Resource orchestration in family firms: Investigating how entrepreneurial orientation, generational involvement, and participative strategy affect performance. *Strategic Entrepreneurship Journal, 5*(4), 307–326.

Choi, Y. R., Zahra, S. A., Yoshikawa, T., & Han, B. H. (2015). Family ownership and R&D investment: The role of growth opportunities and business group membership. *Journal of Business Research, 68*, 1053–1061.

Chrisman, J. J., Chua, J. H., & Steier, L. P. (2005). Sources and consequences of distinctive familiness: An introduction. *Entrepreneurship: Theory and Practice, 29*(3), 237–247.

Chrisman, J., & Patel, P. (2011). Variations in R&D investments of family and non-family firms: Behavioral agency and myopic loss aversion perspectives. *Academy of Management Journal, 55* (4), 976–997.

Chrisman, J. J., Steier, L. P., & Chua, J. H. (2008). Toward a theoretical basis for understanding the dynamics of strategic performance in family firms. *Entrepreneurship: Theory and Practice, 32* (6), 935–947.

Classen, N., Van Gils, A., Bammens, Y., & Carree, M. (2012). Accessing resources from innovation partners: The search breadth of family SMEs. *Journal of Small Business Management, 50* (2), 191–215.

Clercq, D., & Belausteguigoitia, I. (2015). Intergenerational strategy involvement and family firms' innovation pursuits: The critical roles of conflict management and social capital. *Journal of Family Business Strategy, 6*(3), 178–189.

Cohen, J. (1977). *Statistical power analysis for the behavioral sciences* (Revised Ed.). New York: Academic Press.

Cohen, W. M., & Levinthal, D. A. (1989). Innovation and learning: The two faces of R&D. *Economic Journal, 99*, 569–596.

Cohen, W. M., & Levinthal, D. A. (1990). Absorptive-capacity – A new perspective on learning and innovation. *Administrative Science Quarterly, 35*(1), 128–152.

Cruz, C., & Nordqvist, M. (2012). Entrepreneurial orientation in family firms: A generational perspective. *Small Business Economics, 38*(1), 33–49.

DeVellis, R. F. (2012). *Scale development: Theory and applications* (3rd ed.). Thousand Oaks, CA: Sage.

Dolz, C., Iborra, M., & Safón, V. (2015). Empresa familiar, equipos directivos, diversidad y ambidiestría en las PYMES. *RAE-Revista de Administração de Empresas, 55*(6), 673–687.

Duran, P., Kammerlander, N., Van Essen, M., & Zellweger, T. (2016). Doing more with less: Innovation input and output in family firms. *Academy of Management Journal, 59*(4), 1224–1264.

Ebers, M., & Maurer, I. (2014). Connections count: How relational embeddedness and relational empowerment foster absorptive capacity. *Research Policy, 43*, 318–332.

European Family Businesses. (2014). *Families in business for the long term*. Retrieved from http://europeanfamilybusinesses.eu

Faul, F., Erdfelder, E., Lang, A.-G., & Buchner, A. (2007). G*Power 3: A flexible statistical power analysis program for the social, behavioral, and biomedical sciences. *Behavior Research Methods, 39*, 175–191.

Federação das Indústrias do estado do Rio Grande do Sul – FIERGS. (2015). *Cadastro das Indústrias, Fornecedores and Serviços do Rio Grande do Sul [CD]*. Porto Alegre: Unidade de Estudos Técnicos, Sistema FIERGS.

Ferreira, J., Fernandes, C., Alves, H., & Raposo, M. (2015). Drivers of innovation strategies: Testing the Tidd and Bessant (2009) model. *Journal of Business Research, 68*(7), 1395–1403.

Ferreira, J., Raposo, M., & Fernandes, C. (2013). Does innovativeness of knowledge-intensive business services differ from other industries? *The Service Industries Journal, 33*(7–8), 734–748.

Filser, M., Brem, A., Gast, J., Kraus, S., & Calabrò, A. (2016). Innovation in family firms: Examining the inventory and mapping the path. *International Journal of Innovation Management, 20*(6), 1–39.

Flatten, T. C., Engelen, A., Zahra, S. A., & Brettel, M. (2011). A measure of absorptive capacity: Scale development and validation. *European Management Journal, 29*(2), 98–116.

Forés, B., & Camisón, C. (2015). Does incremental and radical innovation performance depend on different types of knowledge accumulation capabilities and organizational size? *Journal of Business Research, 69*(2), 831–848.

Fornell, C., & Larcker, D. F. (1981). Evaluating structural equation models with unobservable variables and measurement error. *Journal of Marketing Research, 18*(1), 39–50.

Fosfuri, A., & Tribó, J. (2008). Exploring the antecedents of potential absorptive capacity and its impact on innovation performance. *Omega, 36*(2), 173–187.

Freeman, C. (1988). Japan: A new national system of innovation? In G. Dosi, C. Freeman, R. Nelson, G. Silverberg, & L. Soete (Eds.), *Technical change and economic theory*. London: Pinter Publishers.

Garver, M. S., & Mentzer, J. T. (1999). Logistics research methods: Employing structural equation modeling to test for construct validity. *Journal of Business Logistics, 20*, 33–57.

Gersick, K., Davis, J. A., Hampton, M. M., & Lansberg, I. (2006). *De geração para geração: ciclos de vida das empresas familiares*. Rio de Janeiro: Elsevier.

Gómez-Mejía, L. R., Campbell, J. T., Martin, G., Hoskisson, R. E., Makri, M., & Sirmon, D. G. (2014). Socioemotional wealth as a mixed gamble: Revisiting family firm R&D investments with the behavioral agency model. *Entrepreneurship: Theory and Practice, 38*(6), 1351–1374.

Gómez-Mejía, L. R., Takács Haynes, K., Núñez-Nickel, M., Jacobson, K. J. L., & Moyano-Fuentes, J. (2007). Socioemotional wealth and business risks in family-controlled firms: Evidence from Spanish olive oil mills. *Administrative Science Quarterly, 52*, 106–137.

Habbershon, T. G., & Williams, M. L. (1999). A resource-based framework for assessing the strategic advantages of family firms. *Family Business Review, 12*, 1–25.

Habbershon, T. G., Williams, M. L., & Macmillan, I. C. (2003). A unified systems theory of family firm performance. *Journal of Business Venturing, 18*(4), 451–465.

Hair, J. F., Hult, G. T. M., Ringle, C. M., & Sarstedt, M. (2014). *A primer on partial least squares structural equation modeling (PLS-SEM)*. Thousand Oaks, CA: Sage.

Hair, J. F., Tatham, R. L., Anderson, R. E., & Black, W. (2005). *Análise multivariada de dados* (5a ed.). Porto Alegre: Bookman.

Hernández-Perlines, F., Moreno-Garcia, J., & Yáñez-Araque, B. (2016). Using fuzzy-set qualitative comparative analysis to develop an absorptive capacity-based view of training. *Journal of Business Research, 69*, 1510–1515.

Huber, G. P., & Power, D. J. (1985). Retrospective reports of strategic managers: Guidelines for increasing their accuracy. *Strategic Management Journal, 6*, 171–180.

Jansen, J. J. P., Van Den Bosch, F. A. J., & Volberda, H. W. (2005). Managing potential and realized absorptive capacity: How do organizational antecedents matter. *Academy of Management Journal, 48*(6), 999–1015.

Jones, O. (2006). Developing absorptive capacity in mature organizations: The change agent's role. *Management Learning, 37*(3), 355–376.

Kaufmann, A., & Tödtling, F. (2001). Science-industry interaction in the process of innovation: The importance of boundary-crossing between systems. *Research Policy, 30*, 791–804.

Kellermanns, F. W., & Eddleston, K. A. (2004). Feuding families: When conflict does a family firm good. *Entrepreneurship Theory and Practice, 28*(3), 209–228.

Kellermanns, F. W., & Eddleston, K. A. (2006). Corporate entrepreneurship in family firms: A family perspective. *Entrepreneurship Theory and Practice, 30*(6), 809–830.

Kellermanns, F. W., Eddleston, K. A., Barnett, T., & Pearson, A. (2008). An exploratory study of family member characteristics and involvement: Effects on entrepreneurial behavior in the family firm. *Family Business Review, 21*(1), 1–14.

Kellermanns, F. W., Eddleston, K. A., Sarathy, R., & Murphy, F. (2012). Innovativeness in family firms: A family influence perspective. *Small Business Economics, 38*(1), 85–101.

Kellermanns, F. W., Eddleston, K. A., & Zellweger, T. (2012). Extending the socioemotional wealth perspective: A look at the dark side. *Entrepreneurship: Theory and Practice, 36*(6), 1175–1182.

Kim, Y., & Gao, F. Y. (2013). Does family involvement increase business performance? Family-longevity goals' moderating role in Chinese family firms. *Journal of Business Research, 66*(2), 265–274.

König, A., Kammerlander, N., & Enders, A. (2013). The family innovator's dilemma: How family influence affects the adoption of discontinuous technologies by incumbent firms. *Academy of Management Review, 38*(3), 418–441.

Kostopoulos, K., Papalexandris, A., Papachroni, M., & Ioannou, G. (2011). Absorptive capacity, innovation, and financial performance. *Journal of Business Research, 64*, 1335–1343.

Kraiczy, N., Hack, A., & Kellermanns, F. (2014). New product portfolio performance in family firms. *Journal of Business Research, 67*(6), 1065–1073.

Lane, P. J., Koka, B., & Pathak, S. (2006). The reification of absorptive capacity: A critical review and rejuvenation of the construct. *Academy of Management Review, 31*(4), 833–863.

Le Breton-Miller, I., & Miller, D. (2011). Commentary: Family firms and the advantage of multi-temporality. *Entrepreneurship: Theory and Practice, 35*(6), 1171–1177.

Leal-Rodríguez, A. L., Roldán, J. L., Ariza-Montes, J. A., & Leal-Millán, A. (2014). From potential absorptive capacity to innovation outcomes in project teams: The conditional mediating role of the realized absorptive capacity in a relational learning context. *International Journal of Project Management, 32*, 894–907.

Leone, N. (2005). *Sucessão na empresa familiar: preparando as mudanças para garantir sobrevivência no mercado globalizado*. São Paulo: Atlas.

Ling, Y., & Kellermanns, F. (2010). The effects of family firm-specific sources of TMT diversity: The moderating role of information exchange frequency. *Journal of Management Studies, 47* (2), 322–344.

Litz, R. A., & Kleysen, R. F. (2001). Your old men shall dream dreams, your young men shall see visions: Toward a theory of family firm innovation with help from the Brubeck family. *Family Business Review, 14*, 335–351.

Machado, R., Grzybovski, D., Teixeira, E., & Silva, M. (2013). Governança de pequenas empresas familiares brasileiras: Aspectos a considerar no modelo adotado. *Revista de Ciências da Administração, 1*(1), 198–210.

Mahmoud-Jouini, S. B., & Mignon, S. (2009). Entrepreneuriat familial et stratégies de pérennité: Contribution au concept d'innovation prudentielle. *Management international/International Management/Gestión Internacional, 14*(1), 25–41.

Marôco, J. (2014). *Análise Estatística com o SPSS Statistics*. Lisbon: ReportNumber.

Miller, D., Le Breton-Miller, I., & Lester, R. H. (2012). Family firm governance, strategic conformity, and performance: Institutional vs strategic perspectives. *Organization Science, 24* (1), 189–209.

Miller, D., Wright, M., Le Breton-Miller, I., & Scholes, L. (2015). Resources and innovation in family businesses. *California Management Review, 58*(1), 20–40.

Murovec, N., & Prodan, I. (2009). Absorptive capacity, its determinants, and influence on innovation output: Cross-cultural validation of the structural model. *Technovation, 29*, 859–872.

Nieto, M. J., Santamaria, L., & Fernandez, Z. (2015). Understanding the innovation behavior of family firms. *Journal of Small Business Management, 53*(2), 382–399.

Pérez-González, F. (2006). Inherited control and firm performance. *The American Economic Review, 96*(5), 1559–1588.

Pittino, D., Visintin, F., Bau, M., & Mazzurna, P. (2013). Collaborative technology strategies and innovation in family firms. *International Journal for Entrepreneurship and Innovation Management, 17*(1–3), 8–27.

Ringle, C. M., Silva, D., & Bido, D. (2014). Modelagem de Equações Estruturais com utilização do SMARTPLS. *Revista Brasileira de Marketing – ReMark, 13*(2), 56–73.

Ringle, C. M., Wende, S., & Will, A. (2005). *SmartPLS 2.0.M3*. Hamburg: SmartPLS. Retrieved from http://www.smartpls.de

Ritala, P., & Hurmelinna-Laukkanen, P. (2013). Incremental and radical innovation in coopetition—The role of absorptive capacity and appropriability. *Journal of Product Innovation Management, 30*, 154–169.

Salvato, C. (2004). Predictors of entrepreneurship in family firms. *Journal of Private Equity, 7*(3), 68–76.

Sciascia, S., Mazzola, P., & Chirico, F. (2013). Generational involvement in the top management team of family firms: Exploring nonlinear effects on entrepreneurial orientation. *Entrepreneurship Theory and Practice, 37*(1), 69–85.

Sharma, P., & Salvato, C. (2011). Commentary: Exploiting and exploring new opportunities over life cycle stages of family firms. *Entrepreneurship Theory and Practice, 35*, 1199–1205.

Sørensen, J. B., & Stuart, T. E. (2000). Aging, obsolescence and organizational innovation. *Administrative Science Quarterly, 45*(1), 81–112.

Tidd, J., & Bessant, J. (2015). *Gestão da Inovação [F. Nonnenmacher, Trad.]* (5a ed.). Porto Alegre: Bookman.

Todorova, G., & Durisin, B. (2007). Absorptive capacity: Valuing a reconceptualization. *Academy Management Review, 32*(3), 774–786.

Tödtling, F., Lehner, P., & Kaufmann, A. (2009). Do different types of innovation rely on specific kinds of knowledge interactions? *Technovation, 29*, 59–71.

Tsai, W. (2001). Knowledge transfers in intra-organizational networks: Effects of network position and absorptive capacity on business unit innovation and performance. *Academy of Management Journal, 44*(5), 996–1004.

Ussman, A. M. (2004). *Empresas familiares*. Lisbon: Edições Sílabo, Lda.

Van Den Bosch, F. A., Volberda, H. W., & Boer, M. D. (1999). Coevolution of firm absorptive capacity and knowledge environment: Organizational forms and combinative capabilities. *Organization Science, 10*(5), 551–568.

Vega-Jurado, J., Gutiérrez-Gracia, A., & Fernándes-De-Lucio, I. (2008). Analyzing the determinants of firm's absorptive capacity: Beyond R&D. *R&D Management, 38*(4), 392–405.

Vega-Jurado, J., Gutiérrez-Gracia, A., Fernández-De-Lucio, I., & Manjarrés-Henríquez, L. (2008). The effect of external and internal factors on firms' product innovation. *Research Policy, 37*(4), 616–632.

Vicentin, F. O. P. (2015). *Alianças and a sua contribuição no desenvolvimento da capacidade de absorção and no desempenho inovador das empesas dedicadas à biotecnologia*. Doctoral degree thesis, Faculdade de Economia, Administração and Contabilidade de Ribeirão Preto da Universidade de São Paulo, São Paulo, Brasil. Retrieved from http://www.teses.usp.br/teses/disponiveis/96/96132/tde-20072015-144106/pt-br.php

Vinding, A. L. (2006). Absorptive capacity and innovative performance: A human capital approach. *Economics of Innovation and New Technology, 15*, 507–517.

Vries, M., Carlock, R. S., & Florent-Treacy, E. (2009). *A Empresa Familiar no divã: uma perspectiva psicológica*. Porto Alegre, Brazil: Bookman.

Wang, C. L., Senaratne, C., & Rafiq, M. (2015). Success traps, dynamic capabilities and firm performance. *British Journal of Management, 26*, 26–44.

Wetzels, M., Odekerken-Schröder, G., & Oppen, C. V. (2009). Using PLS path modeling for assessing hierarchical construct models: Guidelines and empirical illustration. *MIS Quarterly, 33*(1), 177–195.

Winter, S. G. (2000). The satisfying principle in capability learning. *Strategic Management Journal, 21*, 981–996.

Zahra, S. A. (2003). International expansion of U.S. manufacturing family businesses: The effect of ownership and involvement. *Journal of Business Venturing, 18*(4), 495–512.

Zahra, S. A. (2005). Entrepreneurial risk-taking in family firms. *Family Business Review, 18*, 23–40.

Zahra, S. A. (2016). Developing theory-grounded family business research: Some suggestions. *Journal of Family Business Strategy, 7*, 3–7.

Zahra, S. A., & George, G. (2002). Absorptive capacity: A review, reconceptualization, and extension. *Academy of Management Review, 27*(2), 185–203.

Zahra, S. A., Hayton, J. C., Neubaum, D. O., Dibrell, C., & Craig, J. (2008). Culture of family commitment and strategic flexibility: The moderating effect of stewardship. *Entrepreneurship Theory and Practice, 32*, 1035–1054.

Zahra, S. A., Hayton, J. C., & Salvato, C. (2004). Entrepreneurship in family vs. nonfamily firms: A resource-based analysis of the effect of organizational culture. *Entrepreneurship Theory and Practice, 28*, 363–381.

Zahra, S. A., Neubaum, D. O., & Larrañeta, B. (2007). Knowledge sharing and technological capabilities: The moderating role of family involvement. *Journal of Business Research, 60*, 1070–1079.

Zahra, S. A., Sapienza, H. J., & Davidsson, P. (2006). Entrepreneurship and dynamic capabilities: A review, model and research agenda. *Journal of Management Studies, 43*(4), 917–955.

Zellweger, T. M., & Sieger, P. (2012). Entrepreneurial orientation in long-lived family firms. *Small Business Economics, 38*(1), 67–84.

Shared Leadership at the Top of Family Firms: How Sibling Teams Engage in Successful Co-leadership

Jana Bövers and Christina Hoon

Abstract This paper explores shared leadership arrangements at the top of a family firm where leadership is equally shared among a group of family members rather than focused on a designated leader. Pairing different capabilities, characteristics and leadership strategies is viewed as being of benefit in hybrid family firms which face the different sets of logic inherent in maintaining their familiness while also enabling flexibility. We build on the shared leadership approach and recent work on succession and sibling teams to examine the following research question: *How do sibling teams succeed in synchronizing their leadership efforts into a successful leadership team?* In this research, we draw upon a qualitative, inductive case study to explore two siblings who jointly hold the responsibility at the top of a family firm. Findings indicate that the co-leaders integrate their shared leadership activities into concerted action by considering their reciprocated affirmation, by drawing upon their shared entrepreneurial spirit, and by acknowledging their complementarity. By discovering the integrating mechanisms of shared leadership practices at the top of family firms, we contribute to both the family business literature and research on shared leadership.

Keywords Leadership · Family business · Sibling team · Intergenerational obligation · Succession

1 Introduction

Leadership is one of the most significant concerns in family firms. Scholars address family firm leaders, in particular in terms of succession and identify the factors that hinder family members in successfully overtaking leadership responsibility

J. Bövers (✉) · C. Hoon
Faculty of Business Administration and Economics, Bielefeld University, Bielefeld, Germany
e-mail: jana.boevers@uni-bielefeld.de; christina.hoon@uni-bielefeld.de

J. M. Saiz-Álvarez et al. (eds.), *Entrepreneurship and Family Business Vitality*,
Studies on Entrepreneurship, Structural Change and Industrial Dynamics,
https://doi.org/10.1007/978-3-030-15526-1_7

(Chrisman, Chua, & Sharma, 2003; Salvato & Corbetta, 2013; Sorenson, 2000). Specifically, through subsequent generational involvement, family firm leadership becomes increasingly dispersed (Gersick, Davis, Hampton, & Lansberg, 1997). In a founder-controlled firm, leadership is overly concentrated on a single founder with a focus on a heroic leadership style and entrepreneurial success (Anderson & Reeb, 2003). Since more and more parents promote multiple of their children as equal successors to the business it becomes increasingly likely that there is more than one person in charge. In these couplings, managing and owning the family firm comes along with sharing the responsibility for leadership between close family members equally. This is evident not only in a sibling partnership but also in a cousin consortium or a family dynasty where successors jointly run the family business, thereby constituting a co-leadership constellation at the top.

We are interested in a constellation of shared leadership and, more specifically, in sibling teams as one special form of successor teams, engaging in shared leadership at the top of family firms. Sibling teams are said to be especially challenging (Cater & Justis, 2010) and as such are of special importance for research on family business leadership and succession. More generally, shared leadership at the top of a firm is a practice in which individuals share the responsibility for and fully participate in the tasks of leadership such as goal setting and motivating task behaviors (Carson, Tesluk, & Marrone, 2007; Yukl, 1989).

In the family business literature, scholars have claimed a movement toward equally sharing leadership among family members (Gersick et al., 1997; Lansberg, 1999). As opposed to the popular notion that only a single powerful leader can run a family business, family firms increasingly move toward models in which more than one person holds leadership responsibility at the top. More specifically, by referring to the American family business survey, Alvarez and Svejenova (2005) demonstrate the growing number of family firms in which two or more family members serve as co-CEO in the succeeding generation.

Little research into sharing leadership roles traditionally occupied by one family member has been undertaken so far, partly due to difficulties in getting access to the inner sanctum of family corporations. However, gaining better insight into shared leadership at the top of family firms is of importance given that leadership is especially critical in family businesses where top management positions are transferred to the next generation. On the one hand, the employment of two or more family members in the top leadership is widely acknowledged as beneficial to making better use of the family's human resources (Cater & Justis, 2010; Rau, 2014). On the other hand, however, scholars claim that taking over leadership responsibility as equal partners calls for an uncommon amount of cooperation between the family members (Gersick et al., 1997; Lansberg, 1999). More critically, studies indicate conflicts stemming from rivalry and conflicting family relations (e.g., Grote, 2003; Nicholson & Björnberg, 2006). These rival top leadership relations face the risk of a rift between the family leaders that may impede the developement and survival of the family business in the long term. Thus, it is essential to understand what a family leadership team needs to cooperate successfully. This leads us to the following research question: *How do sibling teams succeed in synchronizing their leadership efforts into a successful leadership team?*

2 Theoretical Background

To provide insights into shared leadership in family firms as a popular and promising solution for succession in family businesses, we draw upon the current work on succession, with a special focus on intergenerational obligation, on sibling team research (Aronoff, Astrachan, Mendoza, & Ward, 1997; Farrington, Venter, & Boshoff, 2012) and on the shared leadership approach (Carson et al., 2007; Yukl, 1989).

2.1 Succession in Family Businesses

Succession has been the primary topic since the early stages of family business research (Sharma, 2004). Succession means the passing of authority and responsibility in the family business from one generation to the next (Steier & Miller, 2010). It is viewed as a success when the performance of the firm is positive and the stakeholders are continuously satisfied after the change in leadership (Le Breton-Miller, Miller, & Steier, 2004). However, research shows that many successions fail. Only 30% of family businesses make it into the second generation, 10–15% into the third, and 3–5% into the fourth (Aronoff, 1999).

Most research focuses on the perspective of the predecessors as the most critical factor during the succession process (Cabrera-Suárez, De Saá-Pérez, & García-Almeida, 2001; Dyer, 1986), neglecting the importance of the successor's readiness, interest, and capability to take over authority and responsibility of the family business (Birley, 2002; Brun de Pontet, Wrosch, & Gagne, 2007). Through the socialization process both in the family home and in the family business, a sense of obligation to pursue a career in the family firm is created (García-Álvarez, López-Sintas, & Saldaña Gonzalvo, 2002). It is described as a filial loyalty, an obligation the children feel towards their parents to accommodate themselves to their legacies (Lumpkin, Martin, & Vaughan, 2008)—in this case, the family business. Based on the intergenerational obligation which the successor generation feels and upon which the parental generation counts, a family succession is often the natural consequence (De Massis, Chua, & Chrisman, 2008). Accordingly, it is necessary to understand how the successor generation fulfills its generational obligation successfully and leads the family business into a successful future.

2.2 Sibling Teams

Adding to the difficulties of the succession process is the possibility that family business predecessors have multiple successors, for example, through siblings or cousins who are equally capable and willing to take over the business. What seems promising and beneficial to the family business on the one side (Cater & Justis, 2010) also poses a challenge to the team which has to function as an entity for the sake of the survival of the family business (Farrington et al., 2012). It is a common practice for predecessors to choose a leadership team as their replacement (MassMutual, Kennesaw State, & Family Firm Institute, 2007). So far, however, there is surprisingly little research on multiple successors sharing the authority and responsibility for a family business.

Cater and Justis (2010) found eight factors affecting shared leadership in multigenerational family firms. It can be enhanced by long-term orientation, close communication, shared understanding of appropriate succession planning, and higher decision quality. On the other hand, resistance to change, failure to release control by incumbent leaders, reporting relationship confusion, and increased decision time can inhibit the implementation and development of shared leadership in family firms. Cater and Kidwell (2014) found that excessive competition among successor group members hinders group effectiveness while cooperation, unified implementation of decisions, agreement to share power and authority, and the development of trust will enhance successor leadership group effectiveness. Cater, Kidwell, and Camp (2016) extended research on successor teams by identifying factors influencing the entry of members of successor teams into the family business, the team formation, as well as the performance of the successor team. They revealed two possible outcomes, a positive pathway leading to team commitment and a negative pathway potentially resulting in team and business dissolution. To consider the special family influence on this successor team, it is important to consider the apparent relationship between the successors. Siblings have a special form of relationship and preliminary research in this area has been undertaken.

Aronoff et al. (1997) conducted pioneer research on sibling teams in family businesses. In their conceptual work based on their experiences in family business consultancy, they considered different dimensions for the success of sibling teams, such as the characteristics of the team itself, the predecessor, the environment, and in-laws. Farrington et al. (2012) examined the basic factors needed for a team to function. They found empirical evidence for the influence of physical resources, skill diversity, and strategic leadership on sibling team success. No support was found for the idea that a team needs role clarity and competence to function. Cisneros and Deschamps (2015) examined the role of advisors in sibling team succession. They found three levels, namely, business, family, and individual, through which both family and nonfamily advisors influence the sibling team succession during the different stages of the succession process.

So, it is known that siblings constitute a special form of successor teams and a first basic understanding of their functioning has been derived. Our research should further clarify the understanding of the functioning of the sibling successor team and especially how this team is successful after the succession. Shared leadership serves as an additional theoretical base to fill this research gap.

2.3 Shared Leadership in Family Businesses

Shared leadership refers to "the distribution of leadership influence across multiple team members" (Carson et al., 2007, p. 1218). Applied at the top management level, shared leadership is a practice in which individuals share the responsibility for and fully participate in the tasks of leadership at the top of an organization, such as setting goals and motivating task behaviors (Carson et al., 2007; Yukl, 1989). Following the core definitions offered in this area of research (e.g., Avolio, Walumbwa, & Weber, 2009; Carson et al., 2007; Gronn, 2002), we conceptualize shared leadership as a group of actors fully sharing the responsibility for leadership. Empirical studies have explored how shared leadership relationships impact a variety of key organizational outcomes. For example, in their study, Mehra, Dixon, Brass, and Robertson (2006) demonstrate that teams with distributed-coordinated leadership exhibited higher levels of team performance than teams with one centralized leader. Further studies suggest that shared leadership practices improve team effectiveness (i.e., Carson et al., 2007; Taggar, Hackew, & Saha, 1999), enhance employees' job satisfaction, increase employee involvement, and lead to professional empowerment (Burke et al., 2006; Upenieks, 2000; Varkey, Karlapudi, & Hensrud, 2008; Wells, Ward, Feinberg, & Alexander, 2008). While shared leadership has initially been explored within groups or at lower hierarchical levels (Carson et al., 2007; Pearce & Sims, 2002; Perry, Pearce, & Sims, 1999), scholars propose the corporate apex as a promising setting for shared leadership, as well (Denis, Lamothe, & Langley, 2001; Ensley, Hmieleski, & Pearce, 2006). In traditional leadership literature, scholars merely have the view on leadership in which one CEO is mainly responsible for leadership effects that influence lower-level organizational members (Hambrick & Canella, 2004). Recent research, however, has suggested an alternative perspective on the role of leadership and identified that shared leadership might also flow laterally at the top of an organization (Mihalache, Jansen, Van den Bosch, & Volberda, 2014). In this view, the leadership task is shared among a group of top managers instead of being the duty of solely one person, i.e., the CEO. It is a "team process where leadership is carried out by the team as a whole, rather than solely by a single designated individual" (Ensley et al., 2006, p. 220). Hence, shared leadership implies that top executives share the tasks of deciding on the organizational goals and priorities, motivating each other, and influencing group maintenance (Ensley, Pearson, & Pearce, 2003; Perry et al., 1999). Whereas the traditional view of leadership—vertical leadership—involves the downward projection of influence from a single CEO, shared leadership entails the exertion of lateral influence among a pair of CEOs (Cox, Pearce, & Perry, 2003; Ensley et al., 2006; Pearce & Sims, 2002). To this end, vertical leadership is dependent upon the wisdom of an individual top executive, whereas shared leadership draws upon the knowledge of a collective of executives at the top of an organization, where every team member finds their role according to their knowledge, skills, and capabilities (Ensley et al., 2006). Hence, shared leadership in top management teams is viewed as enabling organizations to pursue exploratory and exploitative activities better, thereby stimulating organizational ambidexterity (Mihalache et al., 2014).

Based upon the positive effects that studies ascribe to sharing leadership responsibility between a group of leaders, scholars increasingly focus their attention on the mechanisms that enable the integration of these shared leadership efforts into concerted action (Gronn, 2002; Ulhoi & Müller, 2014). The demand for binding shared leadership efforts into concerted action is emphasized in Ensley and Pearce's (2001) study. They indicate that shared leadership actors need to think and act as a unit rather than as individuals with different views and agendas. Similarly, Mehra et al. (2006) propose that shared leadership processes only emerge when the information and knowledge that the shared leadership team conveys to the followers represent the actions of all team members. Only under these conditions can a team with shared leadership be successful.

In this paper, we argue that the shared leadership approach holds the potential to understand better how family members jointly share leadership responsibility. Family businesses face the tensions of moving between the tight alignment with their familiness and the need to remain flexible. While the maintenance of familiness provides a unique resource from which family firms might generate competitive advantages (Habbershon, Williams, & MacMillan, 2003; Rau, 2014), flexibility entails the potential for the strategic adaption of the business to dynamic environments.

3 Methodology

3.1 Research Design

In this chapter, we seek to provide insight into a shared leadership unit by exploring the underlying mechanisms that enable integration among interdependent individuals who share leadership responsibility. More precisely we are trying to answer the following research question: *How do sibling teams succeed in synchronizing their leadership efforts into a successful leadership team?* Given the underexplored and procedural nature of our research focus, we opted for a revelatory inductive single case study (Ketokivi & Mantere, 2010; Stake, 2005). A revelatory case study discusses a phenomenon previously inaccessible to science (Yin, 2018), generates a new or extended conceptual understanding (Hall & Nordqvist, 2008), and allows for elaborating a theory from a rich set of qualitative data (Patton, 2002). We chose a single case approach to ensure a sufficient depth of research and to benefit from the access to the inner sanctum of leadership in the family business. The single case was useful, as the phenomenon of interest was "transparently observable" (Eisenhardt, 1989).

3.1.1 The Case: Shared Leadership at the Top of a Family Hotel

Our case refers to a small hotel-restaurant that was taken over by a married couple in 1980. It was founded as a rural restaurant around 1900 by relatives of the wife. Today, the hotel is in its third generation as a family business, run by two siblings, both of whom are equally in charge of the hotel business. The siblings—son and daughter—officially took over the business in 2008 from their mother, after the father passed away a year earlier. They equally share leadership responsibility, while their spouses do not participate in the business. The parental generation, the mother, is still working in the hotel and restaurant. Although she has officially passed ownership and management entirely on to her children, she still has some discretionary power and functions as a consultant for the management team. The owning family seeks not only special support from the rural community but is also strongly engaged in sponsoring the local soccer team and in donating goods or money for events in the village.

The hotel has 19 long-term employees and is based upon a solid, long-term guest base. This long-term guest base is characterized, for example, by couples celebrating their marriage in the hotel and the subsequent celebration of their children's baptism or confirmations as well as their silver wedding anniversaries. There are special events, such as the traditional buffet on Wednesdays or the Christmas buffet, which have been offered for decades and still attract a large group of guests on a regular basis.

Given an ever more competitive gastronomy industry, the hotel is not only engaged in maintaining its traditional services but is also constantly offering new experiences and attractions to their guests. For example, the hotel is joining a network of hotels and restaurants that offer business consultancy and has become pioneers in cloud-based hotel reservation and registration programs. Further money has been invested in the constant renewal of facilities, both in the hotel and in the restaurant as well as in the introduction of a courtyard garden. Additionally, the hotel is keen on granting individual guest wishes, e.g., by preparing a barbecue at a celebration or by offering the hotel garden for a wedding ceremony. A new strategy they also pursue is making more offers with the aim of attracting large companies to hold their congresses, meetings, and workshops at their venue.

Since taking over ownership and management from their mother, the siblings have a formalized power-sharing arrangement that makes them equal partners in running the hotel. The siblings did divide up responsibilities and subject areas. Whereas the sister is in charge of the hotel and the service area of the restaurant, the brother manages the kitchen. Nevertheless, larger strategic decisions regarding their subject areas are made jointly. When their father died in 2007, the then 32-year-old daughter and 36-year-old son were already deeply involved in the business. Hence, no planned succession took place, but the siblings had to enter the business hastily as both parents got sick in 2005. At that time the brother, who had finished his apprenticeship as a cook and confectioner, led a kitchen abroad. As the cook in his parents' business got sick as well, he quit his old job with the intention of joining the family business permanently. At that time, his sister had already returned from her apprenticeship as a hotel manager and a few years of working experience in other organizations, and after that, she accepted her role in the organization. As such, the siblings officially took over the business in 2008, although the actual succession had already taken place.

Even though the parental generation had already made a lot of investments, e.g., the decision to add a hotel to the restaurant in 1994, the business changed dramatically following the transfer to the next generation. Not only were new investments made, such as the rebuilding of the restaurant and the hall, but the strategy was also changed. In this period, the business developed from a rural restaurant to a reputable and national boutique hotel and restaurant. The siblings reached these goals, for example, by reorganizing the menu, abolishing the bowling alley, and modernizing the kitchen. Additionally, the type of employment was changed. Before the siblings took over, only temporary staff and family members had been employed, except for a single chef. Now, all workers are permanently employed, and the siblings started an apprenticeship program to train their cooks and hotel managers. When the business grew bigger, the siblings also hired an office employee to take some work off the siblings' hands. Finally, the siblings introduced training for their employees, including workshops, regular meetings, and service quality training.

3.2 Data Collection

We relied on both primary and secondary sources of data. This included (1) semi-structured interviews with those individuals who would help us to enrich our understanding of the leadership in the family business, (2) archival data about the business under study and its environment, and (3) notes from attendances in key events and more informal meetings.

Overall, our case database comprised observations of meetings and workshops spanning a total of 8 years (2007–2015), interviews with all employees and the management team, as well as field-written documents of various genres (e.g., external press articles, proposals, internal documents, balance sheets). The second author collected real-time data over 20 months. The selection of the data sources was informed by our focus of inquiry, namely, to capture relevant and indicative data that allowed us to explore a shared leadership arrangement over time as well as the mechanisms that drive the integration of shared leadership efforts into a successful leadership team. In this respect, we followed Glaser and Strauss's (1967) suggestion to triangulate findings from diverse sources of data to obtain multiple vantage points into the phenomenon of inquiry.

Interviews and Field Observations In our study, 15 semi-structured interviews were conducted from June 2015 to September 2015 (181 pages; 70 min on average; transcribed verbatim). In order to identify relevant informants with insight into the organization's structure, strategy, and leadership actions (Kumar, Stern, & Anderson, 1993), we referred to the Three-Circle Model of Family Business (Tagiuri & Davis, 1996). Respondents included members of the owning family as well as all employees under a long-term employment contract. We excluded five employees from the interviews due to their contract being fixed for less than 1 year. Since we interviewed 13 employees as well as the 2 siblings, our sample included all relevant participants. All interviews took place in the informants' offices or a meeting room and lasted between 60 and 90 min. We tape-recorded the interviews and took notes during each conversation, thereby closely paraphrasing respondents and often abbreviating words to keep up. We recorded quotes verbatim and underlined them for future reference. In our study, the interviews served as a primary source to contextualize and sharpen our hermeneutic apparatus and provided an important supplementary triangulation source for understanding events from various perspectives (Duriau, Reger, & Pfarrer, 2007; Strauss & Corbin, 1990).

In addition to the interviews, the second author observed the interactions of the sibling management team in the family firm starting after the father died and the siblings took over responsibility from their mother. Further, the second author attended and observed several workshops and meetings related to leadership issues and captured these on-site observations in field notes. Field notes and notes based on informal conversations complemented the taped interviews.

Documents We asked the members of the management team to supply available company documents and family information. We also requested newspaper articles, advertisements, company catalogs, and other documents about the history of the hotel. Additionally, we tried, when we felt it was necessary, to gather this information independently. These documents form a secondary data source in our case and provide a running history of how the shared leadership arrangement developed over time.

3.3 Data Coding and Data Analysis

Data analysis drew upon established approaches for qualitative studies (Miles, Huberman, & Saldaña, 2014; Patton, 2002; Strauss & Corbin, 1990). To explore the integrating mechanisms, we began to identify all statements on these leadership issues via open coding—a procedure that breaks data down into pieces for comparison (first-order codes) and reassembles the data in new ways (second-order themes) (Strauss & Corbin, 1990). To enhance the validity of the emerging codes (Miles et al., 2014), the codes were labeled, and categories were constructed. After that, we reviewed the data again to see which, if any, fitted into a category (aggregated second-order dimensions). We began the open coding by reviewing all our data sources carefully and by identifying lines or passages that were fundamental

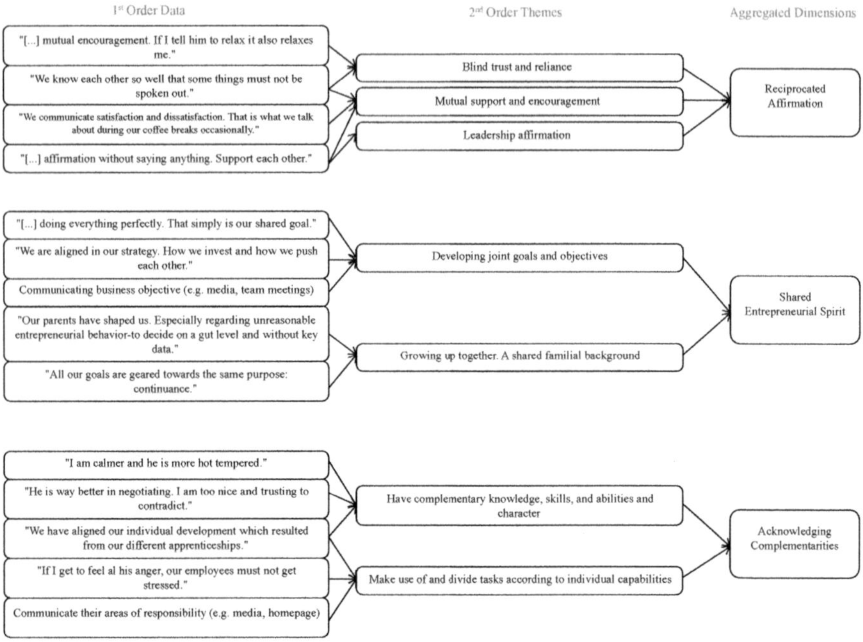

Fig. 1 Data structure. Source: Authors' own figure

exploration of the mechanisms of integrating shared leadership. This first-order data was the foundation for the next step. The second-order analysis involved synthesizing and clustering first-order data into second-order themes. These themes are of a higher level of abstraction and consist mainly of in vivo codes to preserve informant-level meanings. In the final step, we searched for overarching dimensions which linked the themes to each other. The whole process of open coding is iterative and follows the method of constant comparison (Glaser, 1978), meaning going back and forth in the different steps which are distinct but not sequential. For example, new units, which were found through first-order coding, are compared with previously identified codes and either categorized under existing or new codes. To draw theoretical conclusions from our data, we started by identifying conceptual categories and relationships emerging from the coding and analysis of our findings. Figure 1 displays the structure of our data, starting from first-order data in the form of representative quotes and getting to more general second-order themes and finally to the aggregated third-order dimensions (Gioia, Corley, & Hamilton, 2013). The display of the data structure is not a causal model but an illustration of the key elements and their relationships which serve as a base for the new integrating mechanism (Cisneros & Deschamps, 2015). We found the three integrating mechanisms of reciprocated affirmation, a shared an entrepreneurial spirit, and acknowledged complementarity.

To arrive at the best explanation for our data regarding a contextualization strategy (Ketokivi & Mantere, 2010), we drew on prior literature on sibling teams and shared leadership and returned to the data to perform further rounds of coding and comparisons. By iterating between theory and data, we further clarified and focused our findings and theoretical arguments.

4 Findings

From our longitudinal study, three mechanisms evolved that allowed the members of the sibling team synchronize their shared leadership qualities. In particular, we indicate that taking reciprocated affirmation into consideration, drawing upon a shared entrepreneurial spirit, and acknowledging complementarities enable co-leaders to integrate their shared leadership activities into well-functioning sibling team leadership. We present each of these three mechanisms in turn.

4.1 Reciprocated Affirmation

Both of the siblings operate in their sphere, making smaller, everyday decisions. However, when questions become broader or long term, joint decisions are made and communicated. Talking about how the integration of different viewpoints and agendas unfolds into concerted action, the siblings emphasized the role of affirmative considerations. More specifically, the sister reported: "For sure, we have our different perspectives. But, no matter how much we disagree concerning certain issues, I always take into consideration that we are more than professional partners. I remember discussing the new kitchen with him. When being confronted with the restaurant and especially cooking, my brother can be emotional and enthusiastic. My stance was that if we are going to invest in a new kitchen, there won't be money left to improve the hotel booking software. He insisted on the kitchen. In these situations, I always remind myself of the fact that dismissing him is not an option. I cannot throw him out of the hotel so I remind myself that a solution must be found" (Field note 1). So, resulting from that the siblings derived a leadership affirmation.

The brother also referred to the notion of their family bonds and highlighted the fact that their mother was still present in the hotel. "Our mother is still working at the hotel. Not on a day-to-day basis, but whenever we have a whole bunch of work, she is helping out. Seeing her on a regular basis always reminds me of what she has been doing for both, the hotel and family. The family is our primary driver and is always under consideration" (Int. 1, par 55). The strong background in the family results in blind trust and reliance.

Another important point resulting from the sibling relationship is a close and established communication. "We communicate satisfaction and dissatisfaction. That is what we talk about during our coffee breaks occasionally." (Int. 1, par 76). On the other hand, they also clearly express: "We know each other so well that some things must not be said" (Int. 2, par 88). This shows mutual support and encouragement between the siblings is very important to the siblings and helps them in synchronizing their individual views.

Taken together, leadership affirmation, mutual support, and encouragement as well as blind trust and reliance function as a reciprocated affirmation for the sibling leadership team.

4.2 *Shared Entrepreneurial Spirit*

The sister stated that many people understand their sibling relationship as having a mysterious, irrational basis, related to the fraternity. More specifically, she reported: "Whatever it is, I do not know. But what I know is that our shared childhood has strengthened our relationship with one of strong affection and trust. The same home influenced us" (Int. 1, par. 45). One of the employees stated: "It is so obvious that they are siblings. For sure, they are different and don't look much alike. But what I mean is that you feel they can talk honestly and frankly with each other" (Int. 15, par. 25). Similarly, another employee described this binding relationship in terms of "at least, they can communicate without speaking. You feel that they have already had years and years of practicing the way of how to deal best with each other" (Int. 11, par. 115). A shared familial background best describes this.

Further, each of the siblings reported that they know exactly where they come from, what they have, and what they are trying to achieve in the future. They share the same vision and have a shared understanding of what their hotel is likely to be in the future. Both of them show deep appreciation toward the entrepreneurial efforts of their mother. Concerning the latter, one of the siblings stated: "Our mother is still trying to influence the kinds of decisions we need to make. But today, she is not fully informed anymore and, in some points, not up to date. But, she did an excellent job when she was running the hotel. She always had a good spirit for what is necessary and what our guests will like and what not. This is why our hotel is still alive and is still so successful. I admire their spirit and we, my sister and me, still try to be as good as they have been in the past" (Int. 1, par. 10). Shared leadership comes along with individuals pursuing their work with their particular type of interest and effort.

With regard to what makes their shared leadership practices a successful team, the siblings both stated the importance of them being highly motivated and suited for the job, the hotel, and their family. One of the siblings stated: "Family, and our responsibility for what our parents have been building in the past, this is what is the most important thing—and we both completely agree on this principle. This is what we owe our mother. We owe our mother hard work and sympathy" (Int. 1, par. 4). In a similar vein, the other sibling stated: "We both want the business to do well, and we both are working hard to achieve this" (Int. 2, par. 65). So, the siblings are developing joint goals and objectives.

The sister also stated that most leadership issues are affected by their similar entrepreneurial spirit. In this vein, the sister reported in one of the interviews: "He is as passionate as I am about our hotel and restaurant, and as energized by any challenges that our hotel is facing. He always considers how ordinary things can be made better or improved, and so do I. He always has suggestions and ideas on how existing products or services offered in our hotel could be improved and refined. He is trying to make the same point as me" (Field note 2). Further, she reported that they are both continually questioning why things are done the way they are and that they are not afraid to make changes.

Taken together, by developing joint goals and objectives and having a shared familial background, the siblings show a shared entrepreneurial spirit, which enables them to integrate their shared leadership toward their employees.

4.3 Acknowledging Complementarity

Finally, the siblings' leadership is enabled by both individuals continuously acknowledging and valuing their complementary skills and expertise. In our case, both of the siblings were educated in the hotel industry. However, they each brought their individual leadership style and expertise into their co-leadership arrangement. While one brought visionary leadership and an aggressive sales approach, the other contributed by mentoring employees and imposing organizational discipline with a "coaching" approach. During our interviews, when asked about accounting or performance, this became evident as the brother replied to several of our questions in terms of: "I do not have a clue about those issues. The best thing is, you go and ask my sister, she is better than me in remembering those things." Afterward, he explained that his sister is best at remembering figures, charts, and numbers and that he always relies on her financial expertise. So, the data showed that they have complementary knowledge, skills and abilities of which they are aware and also use.

Neither of the siblings and none of the employees reported incidents of rivalry or competitiveness between the siblings. When asked about what makes them work as unique partners, the sister stated: "Over time, we increasingly acknowledged our different areas of expertise, without letting sibling rivalries or jealousies evolve." And: "I can say things to my brother that I cannot say to anyone else" (Int 1, par. 71). The siblings are opposites who understood and respected each other's strengths and weaknesses, namely, her financial and business acumen and his cooking capabilities. Neither of the siblings tried to trump the other or gain power at the expense of the other. The sister is the one who formally calls the shots, but she always makes decisions in consultation with her brother. She reported: "During discussions or critical problem solving with my brother, I often realize how significant our differences are for coming to a good decision. Somehow, we balance the skills of the one with the complementary abilities of the other. In this way, each of us plays out his or her unique strengths, such as leadership, cooking, or operations, while rallying around our hotel's goals" (Field note 5). By considering complementarities, they can downplay issues of power and status and demonstrate a united position toward their employees.

Overall, our analysis reveals that the siblings are well aware of their complementarity, thereby acknowledging their different skills that, when combined, become more useful than each of their individual skill sets in accomplishing their shared leadership efforts.

5 Discussion

Overall, our study provides insight into the mechanisms that enable a group of leaders to integrate their shared leadership efforts into a cohesive unity. More specifically, our study reveals that the co-leaders draw upon three integrative mechanisms, namely, taking reciprocated affirmation, sharing an entrepreneurial spirit, and acknowledging complementarity.

With regard to the mechanisms and processes that enable the integration of shared leadership practices, Ulhoi and Müller (2014) propose that a sense of co-responsibility within the group of leaders facilitates the development of a unified action program. Further, leadership can be emergent and continuously shared when a group of leaders has a joint vision, trusts each other, and has a sense of self-selection (Ulhoi & Müller, 2014). Finally, a shared sense of social order and interpersonal skills are viewed as supporting a shared leadership culture, since these create a mutual understanding about each other and reciprocity of exchange during leadership processes.

Our case also revealed that the application of these integrating mechanisms to the management of the family business led to a prosperous future for the business. Balancing familiarity and flexibility through the benefits of the leadership team, the siblings were able to preserve traditions on the one side but also introduce innovations and new business ideas on the other side. Thus, the integrating mechanisms are necessary for a team to manage the business successfully. In the context of family businesses, shared leadership arrangements are beneficial if a pair or a group of talented leaders can be selected from the family pool (Cater & Justis, 2010; Salvato & Corbetta, 2013). Pairing different capabilities, characteristics, and leadership styles might turn out as especially beneficial in hybrid family firms facing the different logics inherent in maintaining their familiness while enabling flexibility. This way, successors can handle pressure resulting from the intergenerational obligation they feel toward the predecessors and the family firm (Lumpkin et al., 2008).

Finally, our study adds to the findings of successful shared leadership teams in providing a strong emphasis on the positive aspect of shared leadership. Given that our case entails a co-leadership unit based upon a siblings' relationship, we demonstrate that shared leadership arrangements benefit from familiarity and partnership. More specifically, the leadership duo in our study has been built on the ground of an existing affective relationship. Co-leadership between a child and a parent, siblings, or other close family members is more likely to establish a strong working bond of mutual respect and collaboration (Cater & Justis, 2010). Hence, our study illustrates family co-leadership as prone to developing a strong attachment to the relationship, which acts as a barrier to the exit of one of the members of the duo. In family business research, scholars devote increasing attention to how family ties affect leadership relations (Gomez-Mejia, Nunez-Nickel, & Gutierrez, 2001; Handler, 1994). When exchange among members has started at an early age, a strong basis of insight on respective abilities and characters exists and, in turn, facilitates the entry into and the success of a co-leadership. Consequently, the state of being near in space and time has been considered as important factors in building co-leadership or in building stable leadership coalitions. In the literature, professional duos are understood as arising at work, usually through work proximity or repeated task-based interactions (Alvarez & Svejenova, 2005). In task-based interactions, actors may interact in work through role-specified surface encounters. As opposed to a task-based interaction, however, in our study, we indicate a co-leadership in which the individuals initially share a strong and binding social relationship and use it as a foundation on which to shape their professional working relationship. In our case, the bond between the individual members of the duo is not only a professional relationship but is multiplex in that both family ties and professional collaboration exist.

5.1 Contribution

Overall, we contribute to recent studies examining the importance of co-leadership in family firms. We offer a rich understanding of the integrating mechanisms of shared leadership practiced at the top of family firms. Thus far, family businesses have been viewed as being confronted with the challenge of governing and balancing the dual demands stemming from maintaining the consistency of familiness while seeking flexibility (Fitzsimons, James, & Denyer, 2011). Since sharing power and responsibility within a group of top executives is critical for balancing these dual needs, we sought to explore sharing leadership responsibility among some family members as being beneficial both to the long-term survival of the family firm and also helping the offspring of family business owners to manage their intergenerational obligation. Accordingly, we add to studies indicating the positive impact of shared leadership when facing family firm succession (Cater & Kidwell, 2014; Salvato & Corbetta, 2013) by providing insights into three integrating mechanisms that allow for synchronizing the shared leadership practices into a successful team.

Further, we extend the conceptual work on sibling teams by Aronoff et al. (1997), survey study on sibling team design elements by Farrington et al. (2012), and the case studies on advisors in sibling team succession by Cisneros and Deschamps (2015) by offering rich qualitative evidence on the functioning of a sibling leadership team. We could show the siblings can benefit from their special relationship in making use of their shared familial background and complementarity but also how the commitment of their special bond forces them to rearrange their relationship if necessary.

Also, our study contributes to the literature by refining and extending the shared leadership approach. First, since shared leadership is overly explored at the team level or lower management levels (Carson et al., 2007; Mihalache et al., 2014), our study provides a better understanding for how executives are likely to share leadership at the top of an organization. This is of relevance given that shared leadership studies demonstrate that the level of complexity and variability of team tasks may result in a greater need for shared leadership (Ulhoi & Müller, 2014). Given that top management teams face tasks with a high level of complexity and variability, our study provides better insight into how shared leadership evolves at the top of organizations. Second, we contribute to the shared leadership approach proposing that familiarity or liking among team members determines an important understanding for shared leadership processes. More specifically, in the shared leadership literature, studies emphasize the effect of familiarity (e.g., Bligh, Pearce, & Kohles, 2006) concerning a high-level connection between the thought and processes of two or more individuals. By researching shared leadership teams in which team members are family, we reaffirm the importance of this factor. Our study offers a shared leadership arrangement with individuals initially sharing a strong and binding social relationship. They use it as a foundation upon which they shape their professional partnership, thereby enabling unitarity in leadership. Hence, in our study, we emphasize the importance of familiarity on the emergence of shared leadership.

5.2 *Limitations and Future Research*

Our study is subject to the following limitations. First, a single case study comes with limitations for generalizability, hence our claim to a moderate level of generalization from our case into the theoretical model (Payne & Williams, 2005). Also, our choice of a small hotel organization comes with the potential oversampling into the familiness realm; whereas bigger and less family-controlled organizations might have further integrating mechanisms in use that provide the micro-foundations of the shared leadership practices. While our data set is rich regarding the leadership process, we have not covered the effect of concrete action for the followers as well as the effect on subsequent leadership processes.

In turn, these limitations also provide useful guidance for a future research agenda on co-leadership in family businesses. A multi-case study tracking co-leadership in different empirical contexts will allow scholars to elaborate on nuances, and, if needed, to refine our framework. Such studies would be in a position to compare and contrast the nature and process of sharing leadership responsibility and the role of integrating mechanisms. On a related note, future studies should explore whether shared leadership arrangements can be differentiated in terms of the number of leaders included as well as the involvement of family members and nonfamily members at the top. Further, we would welcome studies that cover co-leadership processes not only of a professional duo but also of triads or quartets of leaders being equally responsible at the top. Finally, it will sharpen the conceptual frame if we achieve an understanding of the conditions for breakdowns in co-leadership arrangements such as family members not being included, not being fully accepted, or not having equality in the shared leadership unit.

6 Conclusion and Practical Implications

This study provides a significant contribution by highlighting the importance of shared leadership at the top of family firms and suggests that shared leadership is a critical factor that can provide a unique competitive advantage.

Further, this study adds to the growing body of evidence indicating that a family firm does well when it relies on sharing leadership positions rather than looking to a single individual assigned to it. More specifically, we propose that involving more family members in active management is likely to reduce family conflicts that stem from next-generation family members being only owners of the firm—but not managers—and their increasing emotional attachment to the firm. However, the demand for leadership does not necessarily disappear or become less straightforward because it changes from an individual to a collective phenomenon (Barry, 1991). In this vein, family firms seek to systematically screen and select family members with the potential to gel as co-leaders at the top and provide them with systematic and joint training programs. Thus, we propose that a well-selected and well-trained family top co-leadership duo can be a source of sustained competitive advantage in family firms.

Our results also offer valuable insights for practitioners. By identifying the integrating mechanisms of shared leadership practices at the top of family firms, we advance the practice of sibling teams in three different ways. First, decision-makers in family businesses get insights into possible succession strategies, thereby learning more about how siblings can equally take over responsibility for leading the family firm. Second, we offer insights into how family teams can consolidate and strengthen their functioning. Finally, our study can be used by practitioners to learn more about how failing sibling teams can engage in improving their approach, thereby turning into a well-functioning co-leadership team.

References

Alvarez, J. L., & Svejenova, S. (2005). *Sharing executive power: Roles and relationships at the top*. Cambridge: Cambridge University Press.

Anderson, R. C., & Reeb, D. M. (2003). Founding-family ownership and firm performance: Evidence from the S&P 500. *The Journal of Finance, 58*(3), 1301–1328.

Aronoff, C. E. (1999). Family business survival: Understanding the statistics. *Family Business Advisor, 8*(7), 1–3.

Aronoff, C. E., Astrachan, J. H., Mendoza, D. S., & Ward, J. L. (1997). *Making sibling teams work*. Marietta, GA: Family Enterprise.

Avolio, B. J., Walumbwa, F. O., & Weber, T. J. (2009). Leadership: Current theories, research, and future directions. *Annual Review of Psychology, 60*, 421–449.

Barry, D. (1991). Managing the bossless team: Lessons in distributed leadership. *Organizational Dynamics, 20*(1), 31–47.

Birley, S. (2002). Attitudes of owner-managers' children towards family and business issues. *Entrepreneurship Theory and Practice, 26*(3), 5–19.

Bligh, M. C., Pearce, C. L., & Kohles, J. C. (2006). The importance of self- and shared leadership in team-based knowledge work. A meso-level model of leadership dynamics. *Journal of Managerial Psychology, 21*(4), 296–318.

Brun de Pontet, S., Wrosch, C., & Gagne, M. (2007). An exploration of the generational differences in levels of control held among family businesses approaching succession. *Family Business Review, 20*(4), 337–354.

Burke, C. S., Stagl, K. C., Klein, C., Goodwin, G. F., Salas, E., & Halpin, S. M. (2006). What type of leadership behaviors are functional in teams? A meta-analysis. *Leadership Quarterly, 17*(3), 288–307.

Cabrera-Suárez, K., De Saá-Pérez, P., & García-Almeida, D. (2001). The succession process from a resource- and knowledge-based view of the family firm. *Family Business Review, 14*(1), 37–48.

Carson, J. B., Tesluk, P. E., & Marrone, J. A. (2007). Shared leadership in teams: An investigation of antecedent conditions and performance. *Academy of Management Journal, 50*(5), 1217–1234.

Cater, J. J., III, & Justis, R. T. (2010). The development and implementation of shared leadership in multi-generational family firms. *Management Research Review, 33*(6), 563–585.

Cater, J. J., III, & Kidwell, R. E. (2014). Function, governance, and trust in successor leadership groups in family firms. *Journal of Family Business Strategy, 5*(3), 217–228.

Cater, J. J., III, Kidwell, R. E., & Camp, K. M. (2016). Successor team dynamics in family firms. *Family Business Review, 29*(3), 301–326.

Chrisman, J. J., Chua, J. H., & Sharma, P. (2003). Current trends and future directions in family business management studies: Toward a theory of the family firm. *Coleman White Paper Series, 4*, 1–63.

Cisneros, L., & Deschamps, B. (2015). The role of advisors and the sequence of their actions in sibling team succession. *Management, 18*(4), 282–308.

Cox, J. F., Pearce, C. L., & Perry, M. L. (2003). Toward a model of shared leadership and distributed influence in the innovation process: How shared leadership can enhance new product development team dynamics and effectiveness. In C. L. Pearce & J. A. Conger (Eds.), *Shared leadership: Reframing the hows and whys of leadership* (pp. 48–76). Thousand Oaks, CA: Sage.

De Massis, A., Chua, J. H., & Chrisman, J. J. (2008). Factors preventing intra-family succession. *Family Business Review, 21*(2), 183–199.

Denis, J. L., Lamothe, L., & Langley, A. (2001). The dynamics of collective leadership and strategic change in pluralistic organizations. *Academy of Management Journal, 44*(4), 809–837.

Duriau, V. J., Reger, R. K., & Pfarrer, M. D. (2007). A content analysis of the content analysis literature in organization studies: Research themes, data sources, and methodological refinements. *Organizational Research Methods, 10*(1), 5–34.

Dyer, W. G. (1986). *Cultural change in family firms*. San Francisco, CA: Jossey-Bass.

Eisenhardt, K. M. (1989). Building theories from case study research. *Academy of Management Review, 14*(4), 532–550.

Ensley, M. D., Hmieleski, K. M., & Pearce, C. L. (2006). The importance of vertical and shared leadership within new venture top management teams: Implications for the performance of startups. *The Leadership Quarterly, 17*(3), 217–231.

Ensley, M. D., & Pearce, C. L. (2001). Shared cognition in top management teams: Implications for new venture performance. *Journal of Organizational Behavior, 22*(2), 145–160.

Ensley, M. D., Pearson, A., & Pearce, C. L. (2003). Top management team process, shared leadership, and new venture performance: A theoretical model and research agenda. *Human Resource Management Review, 13*(2), 329–346.

Farrington, S. M., Venter, E., & Boshoff, C. (2012). The role of selected team design elements in successful sibling teams. *Family Business Review, 25*(2), 191–205.

Fitzsimons, D., James, K. T., & Denyer, D. (2011). Alternative approaches for studying shared and distributed leadership. *International Journal of Management Reviews, 13*(3), 313–328.

García-Álvarez, E., López-Sintas, J., & Saldaña Gonzalvo, P. (2002). Socialization patterns of successors in first- to second-generation family businesses. *Family Business Review, 15*(3), 189–203.

Gersick, K. E., Davis, J. A., Hampton, M. M., & Lansberg, I. (1997). *Generation to generation: Life cycles of the family business*. Boston, MA: Harvard Business School Press.

Gioia, D. A., Corley, K. G., & Hamilton, A. L. (2013). Seeking qualitative rigor in inductive research: Notes on the Gioia methodology. *Organizational Research Methods, 16*(1), 15–31.

Glaser, B. (1978). *Theoretical sensitivity: Advances in the methodology of grounded theory*. Mill Valley, CA: Sociology Press.

Glaser, B. G., & Strauss, A. L. (1967). *The discovery of grounded theory: Strategies for qualitative research*. Chicago: Aldire.

Gomez-Mejia, L. R., Nunez-Nickel, M., & Gutierrez, I. (2001). The role of family ties in agency contracts. *Academy of Management Journal, 44*(1), 81–95.

Gronn, P. (2002). Distributed leadership as a unit of analysis. *The Leadership Quarterly, 13*(4), 423–451.

Grote, J. (2003). Conflicting generations: A new theory of family business rivalry. *Family Business Review, 16*(2), 113–124.

Habbershon, T. G., Williams, M., & MacMillan, I. C. (2003). A unified systems perspective of family firm performance. *Journal of Business Venturing, 18*(4), 451–465.

Hall, A., & Nordqvist, M. (2008). Professional management in family businesses: Toward an extended understanding. *Family Business Review, 21*(1), 51–69.

Hambrick, D. C., & Canella, A. A. (2004). CEOs who have COOs: Contingency analysis of an unexplored structural. *Strategic Management Journal, 25*(10), 959–979.

Handler, W. C. (1994). Succession in family business: A review of the research. *Family Business Review, 7*(2), 133–157.

Ketokivi, M., & Mantere, S. (2010). Two strategies for inductive reasoning in organizational research. *Academy of Management Review, 35*(2), 315–333.

Kumar, N., Stern, L. W., & Anderson, J. C. (1993). Conducting inter-organizational research using key informants. *Academy of Management Journal, 36*(6), 1633–1651.

Lansberg, I. (1999). *Succeeding generations: Realizing the dream of families in business*. Boston, MA: Harvard Business Press.

Le Breton-Miller, I., Miller, D., & Steier, L. P. (2004). Toward an integrative model of effective FOB succession. *Entrepreneurship Theory and Practice, 28*(4), 305–328.

Lumpkin, G. T., Martin, W., & Vaughan, M. (2008). Family orientation: Individual-level influences on family firm outcomes. *Family Business Review, 21*(2), 127–138.

MassMutual, Kennesaw State University, & Family Firm Institute. (2007). *American family business survey*. Springfield, MA: Massachusetts Mutual Life Insurance Company and Affiliates.

Mehra, A., Dixon, A. L., Brass, D. J., & Robertson, B. (2006). The social network ties of group leaders. Implications for group performance and leader reputation. *Organization Science, 17*(1), 64–79.

Mihalache, O. R., Jansen, J. J. P., Van den Bosch, F. A. J., & Volberda, H. W. (2014). Top management team shared leadership and organizational ambidexterity: A moderated mediation framework. *Strategic Entrepreneurship Journal, 8*(2), 128–148.

Miles, M. B., Huberman, A. M., & Saldaña, J. (2014). *Qualitative data analysis: A methods sourcebook*. Thousand Oaks, CA: Sage.

Nicholson, N., & Björnberg, Å. (2006). Critical leader relationships in family firms. In K. Smyrnios, P. Poutziouris, & S. Klein (Eds.), *Handbook of research on family business* (pp. 106–124). Cheltenham: Edward Elgar.

Patton, M. Q. (2002). *Qualitative evaluation and research methods* (3rd ed.). Thousand Oaks, CA: Sage.
Payne, G., & Williams, M. (2005). Generalization in qualitative research. *Sociology, 39*(2), 295–314.
Pearce, C. L., & Sims, H. P., Jr. (2002). Vertical versus shared leadership as predictors of the effectiveness of change management teams: An examination of aversive, directive, transactional, transformational, and empowering leader behaviors. *Group Dynamics: Theory, Research, and Practice, 6*(2), 172–197.
Perry, M. L., Pearce, C. L., & Sims, H. P., Jr. (1999). Empowered selling teams: How shared leadership can contribute to selling team outcomes. *Journal of Personal Selling & Sales Management, 19*(3), 35–51.
Rau, S. B. (2014). The resource-based view of family firms. In P. Sharma, M. Nordqvist, & L. Melin (Eds.), *The Sage handbook of family business*. Thousand Oaks, CA: Sage.
Salvato, C., & Corbetta, G. (2013). Transitional leadership of advisors as a facilitator of successors' leadership construction. *Family Business Review, 26*(3), 235–255.
Sharma, P. (2004). An overview of the field of family business studies: Current status and directions for the future. *Family Business Review, 17*(1), 1–36.
Sorenson, R. L. (2000). The contribution of leadership style and practices to family and business success. *Family Business Review, 13*(3), 183–200.
Stake, R. E. (2005). Qualitative case studies. In N. K. Denzin & Y. S. Lincoln (Eds.), *The Sage handbook of qualitative research* (3rd ed., pp. 443–466). Thousand Oaks, CA: Sage.
Steier, L. P., & Miller, D. (2010). Pre- and post-succession governance philosophies in entrepreneurial family firms. *Journal of Family Business Strategy, 1*(3), 145–154.
Strauss, A. L., & Corbin, J. M. (1990). *Basics of qualitative research* (Vol. 15). Newbury Park, CA: Sage.
Taggar, S., Hackew, R., & Saha, S. (1999). Leadership emergence in autonomous work teams: Antecedents and outcomes. *Personnel Psychology, 52*(4), 899–926.
Tagiuri, R., & Davis, J. (1996). Bivalent attributes of the family firm. *Family Business Review, 9*(2), 199–208.
Ulhoi, J. P., & Müller, S. (2014). Mapping the landscape of shared leadership: A review and synthesis. *International Journal of Leadership Studies, 8*(2), 66–87.
Upenieks, V. (2000). The relationship of nursing practice models and job satisfaction outcomes. *Journal of Nursing Administration, 30*(6), 330–335.
Varkey, P., Karlapudi, S. P., & Hensrud, D. D. (2008). The impact of a quality improvement program on employee satisfaction in an academic microsystem. *American Journal of Medical Quality, 23*(3), 215–221.
Wells, R., Ward, A. J., Feinberg, M., & Alexander, J. A. (2008). What motivates people to participate more in community-based coalitions? *American Journal of Community Psychology, 42*(1–2), 94–104.
Yin, R. K. (2018). *Case study research and applications: Design and methods* (6th ed.). Los Angeles, CA: Sage.
Yukl, G. A. (1989). Managerial leadership: A review of theory and research. *Journal of Management, 15*(2), 251–289.

Territorial Maps of Senior Entrepreneurship: A Multidimensional Analysis Based on GEM Data

José Manuel Saiz-Álvarez and Alicia Coduras-Martínez

Abstract Using APS GEM (Global Entrepreneurship Monitor) data, the authors use a multidimensional analysis based on a regression analysis of a nonlinear (cubic) polynomial equation between senior entrepreneurship and the United Nations' human development index to define territorial maps of senior entrepreneurship (SE). The objective of analyzing these maps is to know (a) which are the strongest nations of the world concerning SE, (b) if SE differs among countries, and (c) which are the main factors affecting SE. Our results suggest that SE will increase in the coming years due to the aging of the population ("Papy boom"), especially in Europe and to a lesser extent in some regions of the United States and Japan. Finally, and related to SE, four groups of countries can be formed.

Keywords Global entrepreneurship monitor · Senior entrepreneurship · Papy boom · Adult population · National experts · Entrepreneurial activity

1 Introduction

The Global Entrepreneurship Monitor (GEM) was created by the London Business School (Michael Hay, Ph.D.) and Babson College (William D. Bygrave, Ph.D.) to fill the information gap existing on entrepreneurship around the world and know the significant contribution of entrepreneurs to countries' GDP. The project was initiated in 1997, the first GEM report was launched in 1999 with ten pilot countries, and GEM was opened to the world in the year 2000 to grow up to 100 countries in 2018.

J. M. Saiz-Álvarez (✉)
EGADE Business School-Tecnologico de Monterrey, Zapopan, Jalisco, Mexico
e-mail: jmsaiz@tec.mx

A. Coduras-Martínez
Global Entrepreneurship Research Association, London Business School, London, UK

J. M. Saiz-Álvarez et al. (eds.), *Entrepreneurship and Family Business Vitality*,
Studies on Entrepreneurship, Structural Change and Industrial Dynamics,
https://doi.org/10.1007/978-3-030-15526-1_8

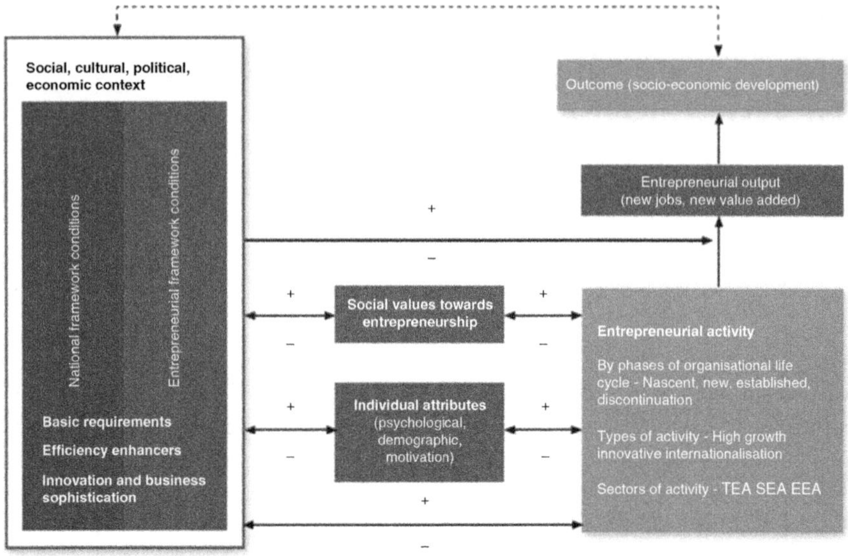

Fig. 1 The GEM theoretical framework. Source: GEM Global Report 2016

But not all nations participate every year, because each team must find the necessary resources to do the surveys.

Formed by research teams (50+ annually) representing countries, regions, and cities, the GEM is unique as it focuses mainly on individual profiles, attitudes, and aspirations designed for filling this information gap. As a result, GEM provides data on the main aspects or areas of entrepreneurship to offer global, national, and "special topic" reports describing the main features and results of the entrepreneurial sector. Also, the GEM offers harmonized academic research products to the market and distributes free data for public use subject to the GEM data release policy. All these features make GEM the most extended source of information worldwide to study senior entrepreneurship (aged 50+) in early-stage activities, that is, when starting up or consolidating a new business aged less than 42 months.

Sustained on two informational tools, constantly updated data sustains the GEM theoretical framework (Fig. 1). These tools are:

1. The Adult Population Survey (known as the APS): each participating team conducts a minimum of 2000 interviews to generate a random and representative sample of the population aged 18–64. Some countries implement the project in subnational regions and create bigger samples (e.g., Saudi Arabia around 4000 and Spain around 28,000 interviews/year). The APS collects data to calculate a wide set of indicators with the goal of describing empirically the theoretical framework devoted to social values toward entrepreneurship, individual attributes, entrepreneurial activity, and entrepreneurial output.
2. The National Expert Survey (known as the NES): each participating team interviews at least 36 experts divided into 4 groups of 9 framework conditions

(financing, government policies, government programs, entrepreneurial education and training, R&D transfer, commercial and professional infrastructure, internal market, physical infrastructure, and social and cultural norms) to generate a convenience sample to assess the general context where entrepreneurs operate. The NES provides information to calculate a wide set of indicators to estimate entrepreneurial frameworks and the average state of their main components.

We used the APS data to analyze senior entrepreneurship (SE), also known as gray entrepreneurship (Harms, Luck, Kraus, & Walsh, 2014), that mainly links to solving long-term senior unemployment. Sixteen percent of the world's population is over 55 years old (Rodríguez-Aceves, Saiz-Álvarez, & García-Caballero, 2019), and more than 1.2 billion work in economic activities based on SE. The aging process is being accelerated worldwide, as seen in Table 1.

Aware of this aging process, seniors prefer opportunity than necessity entrepreneurship and are primarily internally motivated for entrepreneurship (Perenyi, Zolin, & Maritz, 2018). However, the literature differs on the age to start SE, as seen in Table 2. As we use GEM data, we set 50 years of age for SE.

In most countries, SE is especially intense in SMMEs (small, micro, and medium enterprises) as they contribute between 50% and 60% to GDP and over 60% of employment. When these ventures replicate products or services already present in the market or innovate, they tend to find blue or purple oceans, seas, and lakes

Table 1 Population aged 60 years and over and aged 80 years or over for regions (years 2030 and 2050)

	Aged 60+				Aged 80+			
	2030		2050		2030		2050	
	Mill.	%	Mill.	%	Mill.	%	Mill.	%
Africa	105.4	7.5	220.3	10.5	9.3	4.6	22.2	5.1
Asia	844.5	60.2	1293.7	61.8	103.7	51.4	255.7	58.8
Europe	217.2	15.5	242.0	11.6	46.1	22.8	71.0	16.4
Latin American and the Caribbean	121.0	8.6	200.0	9.6	18.7	9.3	44.8	10.3
Oceania	9.6	0.7	13.2	0.6	2.0	1.0	3.6	0.8
Northern America	104.8	7.5	122.7	5.9	22.0	10.9	37.2	8.6
World	1402.5	100	2091.9	100	201.8	100	466.9	100

Source: Authors' own table adapted from United Nations (2015, p. 10)

Table 2 Age to start SE according to the literature

Age	Authors
45	Figueiredo and Paiva (2018)
50	Cerveny, Pilkova, and Rehak (2016); Maritz and Eager (2017); Tervo (2014); Van Solinge (2014); Maâlaoui, Fayolle, Castellano, Rossi, and Safraou (2012), Kenny and Rossiter (2018), and GEM
55	Rossi (2009)

Source: Authors' own table

(Saiz-Álvarez & Colvin-Díez, 2015). As a result, SE is the vehicle to improve job, revenue, innovation, and productivity by changing and adapting business models and processes.

Our research questions deal with knowing (a) which are the strongest nations of the world concerning SE, and if SE differs among countries, and (b) which are the main factors affecting SE. Finally, and mainly using 2016 APS GEM data, the objective of this chapter is to describe the keys to define, compare, and impulse SE.

To cope with this goal, first, we analyze the GEM theoretical background and information tools. Second, we study and describe the senior early-stage entrepreneurial activity (TEA) in 65 GEM countries by applying linear and nonlinear (cubic and quadratic) regression analyses.

We combine these results in a multiple linear regression with the final goal of describing senior TEA with the help of territorial maps. We finish with some practical conclusions.

2 Data and Methodology

The 2016 APS GEM data used in this chapter, the most recent database available at individual level, is formed by 194,824 cases, of which 133,942 are people from 18 to 49 years old (68.5%), 60,797 are from 50 to 99 years old (31.2%), and 535 people do not provide their age (0.3%). In Table 3 we define the age distribution for seniors. We complement the GEM data used in this chapter with information and data extracted from reputed secondary sources of information, like the Global Competitiveness Report, UN statistics, OECD data, the World Bank Reports, and others. In this chapter, we use the most recent data available for research at the global level (2016 APS GEM Database) to describe and analyze the magnitude and main features of SE.

Descriptive statistics' results show in Table 3 that, approximately, 30% of the countries have rates higher than 10%, which are more than significantly valued for the population of 50 and over who recently carried out entrepreneurial-based activities.

Regarding the distribution of the SE among 65 GEM countries (Table 4), 44.61% of countries show a TEA senior rate's value above the GEM average (6.6%), while 55.39% show rates below the GEM average. It is important to note that the position in the ranking relates neither to the country development nor to the geographical

Table 3 Age distribution for senior entrepreneurship according to GEM ($n = 60{,}797$)

	Age		Age
Mean	59.47	Standard deviation	7.71
Median	58	Range	49
Mode	50	Minimum	50
		Maximum	99

Source: Authors' own table

Table 4 Senior TEA as percentage of 50+ population according to GEM ($n = 66$)

	In %		In %
Mean	7.80	Standard deviation	5.12
Median	6.05	Range	22.50
Mode	4	Minimum	1.20
		Maximum	23.70

Source: Authors' own table

location, as there is a negative relationship between development and senior TAE, as the richest countries tend to be less prone to entrepreneurship (Table 5). Moreover, business growth increases the entry barriers to the market, except for innovators who reinvent products or services, or who create new products and services capable of competing in the consumer-oriented market.

To study the ranking shown in Table 5, we use a cubic curve adjusted to a third-degree polynomial regression, where higher GDP (in purchasing power parity, PPP) decreases senior TEA to a level where it grows again (last part of the curve) due to the surplus reinvested in R&D and innovation with the goal of boosting entrepreneurship-based activities.

3 Results

Before studying the relationship between senior TEA and GDP per capita (in terms of PPP), we firstly analyze how GDP impacts on start-ups. The results show a relatively low coefficient of determination ($R^2 = 21.22\%$) which shows a weak relationship between these two variables and an S-shaped smoothed curve (cubic curve) characteristic of a regression analysis of a third-degree polynomial equation (Fig. 2).

To analyze how social and economic variables have effects on senior TEA, instead of using GDP per capita, we choose the human development index (HDI) to study the relationship between the countries' development level and SE. The HDI is a statistic composite index of life expectancy, education, and per capita income indicators, which are used to rank countries into four tiers of human development. Results show that the cubic model, as before, generates the best fit, although the explanatory capacity of the model is moderate ($R^2 = 33.12\%$). In other words, as shown in Fig. 3, the HDI explains 33.12% of the senior TEA, having a negative sign, so high HDI reduces SE. However, 66.88% of the variability of senior TEA is not explained by the development level. Therefore, while Chile, Slovakia, Ireland, Turkey, and Israel have a high SE, it is lower than in some poorer countries, such as Burkina Faso and Cameroon.

The capacity of the HDI to explain SE is discrete because, although countries with ratios higher than 15% are developing countries located in Africa (Burkina Faso and Cameroon) and, mainly, in Latin America and the Caribbean (Belize, Peru, Colombia, Ecuador, and Chile), not all the entrepreneurial impulse of people aged over 50 appears from the lack of job opportunities. Also, population aging, the

Table 5 Rank of the 2016 senior TEA rate (GEM countries)

Country	Rank	Senior TEA (%)	World region
Burkina Faso	1	23.7	Africa
Belize	2	23.0	Latin America and the Caribbean
Peru	3	19.8	Latin America and the Caribbean
Cameroon	4	18.9	Africa
Colombia	5	18.2	Latin America and the Caribbean
Ecuador	6	18.1	Latin America and the Caribbean
Chile	7	15.0	Latin America and the Caribbean
Brazil	8	14.9	Latin America and the Caribbean
Guatemala	9	14.0	Latin America and the Caribbean
Turkey	10	12.8	Asia
Slovakia	11	11.3	Europe
Indonesia	12	11.2	Asia
Lebanon	13	11.2	Asia
Panama	14	10.6	Latin America and the Caribbean
Thailand	15	10.4	Asia
El Salvador	16	10.3	Latin America and the Caribbean
Ireland	17	10.2	Europe
Israel	18	9.5	Asia
UAE	19	9.3	Asia
South Korea	20	9.0	Asia
Australia	21	8.8	Oceania
India	22	8.8	Asia
Egypt	23	8.5	Africa
Canada	24	8.4	North America
Kazakhstan	25	8.3	Asia
Qatar	26	8.2	Asia
Argentina	27	7.7	Latin America and the Caribbean
Cyprus	28	7.2	Europe
United States	29	6.8	North America
GEM average		6.6	
Austria	30	6.2	Europe
Luxembourg	31	6.2	Europe
Puerto Rico	32	6.1	Latin America and the Caribbean
Mexico	33	6.0	Latin America and the Caribbean
Greece	34	5.9	Europe
Jordan	35	5.7	Asia
Saudi Arabia	36	5.5	Asia
Iran	37	5.3	Asia
Georgia	38	5.3	Europe
Jamaica	39	5.2	Latin America and the Caribbean
Portugal	40	5.1	Europe
Sweden	41	5.0	Europe

(continued)

Table 5 (continued)

Country	Rank	Senior TEA (%)	World region
China	42	5.0	Asia
Germany	43	4.9	Europe
Hong Kong	44	4.8	Asia
Netherlands	45	4.7	Europe
Croatia	46	4.3	Europe
Switzerland	47	4.2	Europe
United Kingdom	48	4.2	Europe
Estonia	49	4.2	Europe
Latvia	50	4.1	Europe
Uruguay	51	4.1	Latin America and the Caribbean
Italy	52	4.0	Europe
Poland	53	4.0	Europe
Morocco	54	4.0	Africa
Hungary	55	3.9	Europe
Finland	56	3.8	Europe
Taiwan	57	3.4	Asia
Spain	58	3.1	Europe
Macedonia	59	2.9	Europe
South Africa	60	2.7	Africa
Bulgaria	61	2.6	Europe
Russia	62	2.5	Europe
France	63	2.2	Europe
Slovenia	64	2.0	Europe
Malaysia	65	1.2	Asia

Source: Authors' own table

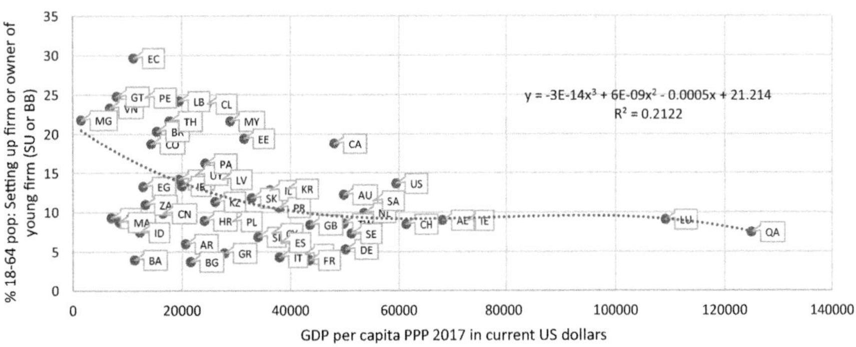

Legend: AE (UAE), AR (Argentina), AS (Austria), AU (Australia), BE (Belize), BF (Burkina Faso), BU (Bulgaria), BZ (Brazil), CA (Canada), CH (China), CL (Chile), CM (Cameroon), CO (Colombia), CR (Croatia), CY (Cyprus), DE (Germany), EC (Ecuador), EG (Egypt), ES (Spain), ET (Estonia), FI (Finland), FR (France), GE (Georgia), GR (Greece), GU (Guatemala), HK (Hong Kong), HU (Hungary), IL (Israel), IN (India), IL (Ireland), IR (Iran), IS (Indonesia), IT (Italy), JA (Jamaica), JO (Jordan), KA (Kazakhstan), KS (Saudi Arabia), LE (Lebanon), LT (Latvia), LU (Luxembourg), MC (Macedonia), ML (Malaysia), MO (Morocco), MX (Mexico), NT (Netherlands), PA (Panama), PE (Peru), PO (Poland), PR (Puerto Rico), PT (Portugal), QA (Qatar), RU (Russia), SA (El Salvador), SD (Sweden), SF (South Africa), SK (South Korea), SL (Slovakia), SV (Slovenia), SW (Switzerland), TH (Thailand), TK (Turkey), TW (Taiwan), UK (United Kingdom), UR (Uruguay), US (USA)

Fig. 2 TEA vs. GDP per capita (in terms of PPP) (In current USD for 2017)

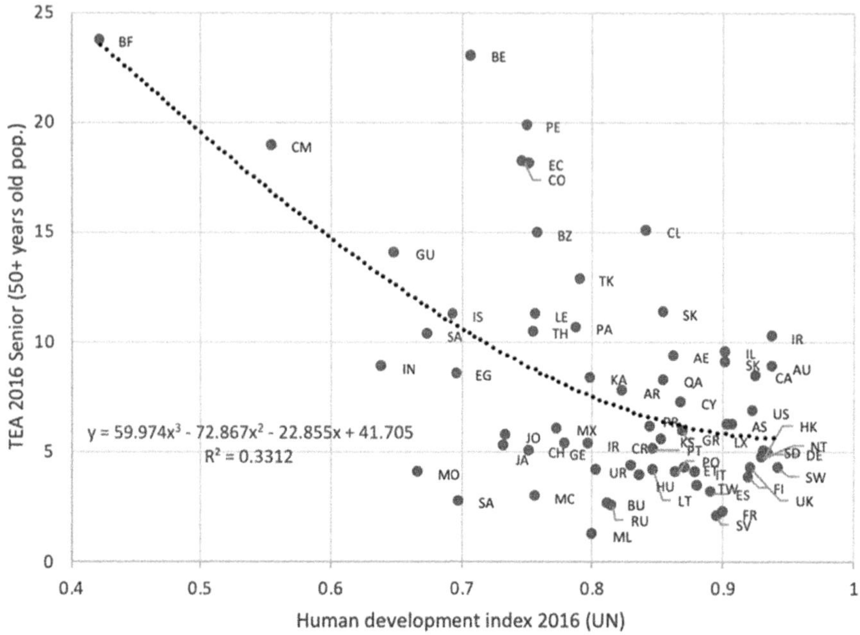

Legend: AE (UAE), AR (Argentina), AS (Austria), AU (Australia), BE (Belize), BF (Burkina Faso), BU (Bulgaria), BZ (Brazil), CA (Canada), CH (China), CL (Chile), CM (Cameroon), CO (Colombia), CR (Croatia), CY (Cyprus), DE (Germany), EC (Ecuador), EG (Egypt), ES (Spain), ET (Estonia), FI (Finland), FR (France), GE (Georgia), GR (Greece), GU (Guatemala), HK (Hong Kong), HU (Hungary), IL (Israel), IN (India), IL (Ireland), IR (Iran), IS (Indonesia), IT (Italy), JA (Jamaica), JO (Jordan), KA (Kazakhstan), KS (Saudi Arabia), LE (Lebanon), LT (Latvia), LU (Luxembourg), MC (Macedonia), ML (Malaysia), MO (Morocco), MX (Mexico), NT (Netherlands), PA (Panama), PE (Peru), PO (Poland), PR (Puerto Rico), PT (Portugal), QA (Qatar), RU (Russia), SA (El Salvador), SD (Sweden), SF (South Africa), SK (South Korea), SL (Slovakia), SV (Slovenia), SW (Switzerland), TH (Thailand), TK (Turkey), TW (Taiwan), UK (United Kingdom), UR (Uruguay), US (USA)

Dependent variable	Early Stage Senior Entrepreneurial Activity Rate	
Independent variable	Human Development Index	
Goodness of fit	$R^2 = 33.12\%$	
Adjusted model	$Y^* = 59.974x^3 - 72.867x^2 - 22.855x + 41.705$	
ANOVA test	F = 15.612	P-value = 0.000
Ho: The magnitude of senior TEA depends, to some degree, on country development		
Result: Hypothesis accepted		

Fig. 3 Nonlinear (cubic) regression analysis between senior TEA and HDI (2016 GEM data). Source: Authors' own figure and table

appearance of a strong entrepreneurial culture, the delay of the retirement age, and loss of employment for people near retirement age are factors that explain senior TEA. This behavior is observed where ratios are higher than 10%, as happens in some countries in Asia (Turkey, Indonesia, Lebanon, and Thailand) and Europe (Slovakia and Ireland), as shown in Table 5.

Despite this fact, the need for survival is the main driver for senior self-employment that is influenced by the annual rate of business abandonment, the 7-K (know-how, know-when, know-why, know-who, know-where, know-whom, and know-whose) (Saiz-Alvarez, Coduras, & Cuervo-Arango, 2017), previous training, and work experience. Drivers that are especially important as seniors have lost their jobs with an age close to retirement. When the unemployed are over 50 years of age, their chances of returning to the labor market are very low, especially in periods of economic crisis and nations with high unemployment rates.

Complementary to the analysis between HDI and senior TEA, also it is interesting to study the relationship between the discontinuation of business and senior TEA. At this respect, we also apply a regression analysis to analyze the early-stage SE activity rate, as the dependent variable, and the percentage of the 18–64 population that discontinued a business the last 12 months, as the independent variable. Results show that there is a linear regression adjustment based on OLS (ordinary least squares) and good results obtained with an ANOVA test ($F = 63.764$) with a significant (P value $= 0.000$) and acceptable goodness of fit ($R^2 = 50.3\%$) and a positive slope ($a = 1.5373$). As a result, when the discontinuation of business increases 1%, senior TEA augments 1.5373%, on average. Moreover, and according to 2016 GEM data, business volatility increases SE, being Belize (12.7%), Cameroon (10.8%), Egypt (9.5%), Ecuador (9.2%), Colombia (7.8%), Iran (7.8%), Burkina Faso (7.7%), and Chile (7.3%) the countries with the highest dropout rates.

Using the individual perception to entrepreneurship index (IPEI) as a proxy of the cultural background or the degree of embeddedness of entrepreneurial social values (defined by the combination of entrepreneurial networks, opportunity perception to undertake, and disposal of knowledge and skills to start a business), we apply a nonlinear (cubic) regression analysis for every country of the sample to analyze the percentage of the total population in terms of IPEI (Fig. 4).

Results show that IPEI for Saudi Arabia (KS point, right hand in Fig. 5) in 2016 with a low value of 5.5% is an outlier of the regression curve (Fig. 5) because the average age of the population in Saudi Arabia has around 35 years of age. As a result, there is a nonlinear (cubic) regression adjustment and good results obtained with an ANOVA test ($F = 13.922$) with a significant (P value $= 0.000$) and acceptable goodness of fit ($R^2 = 40.64\%$), higher than with HDI.

Finally, age is a key factor to explain senior TEA. To analyze the relationship among the degree of aging of the population and senior TEA with 2016 United Nations data, we use as the dependent variable the early-stage senior entrepreneurial activity rate and the total populations' average age, as the independent variable. In this occasion, we apply a nonlinear (quadratic) regression analysis.

Results show that there is a nonlinear (quadratic) regression adjustment and good results obtained with an ANOVA test ($F = 23.188$) with a significant (P value $= 0.000$) and acceptable goodness of fit ($R^2 = 42.79\%$), higher than with HDI and IPEI. As the adjustment is negatively sloped, there is a negative relationship between the populations' average age and senior TEA (Fig. 6). Consequently, higher populations' average age reduces senior TEA.

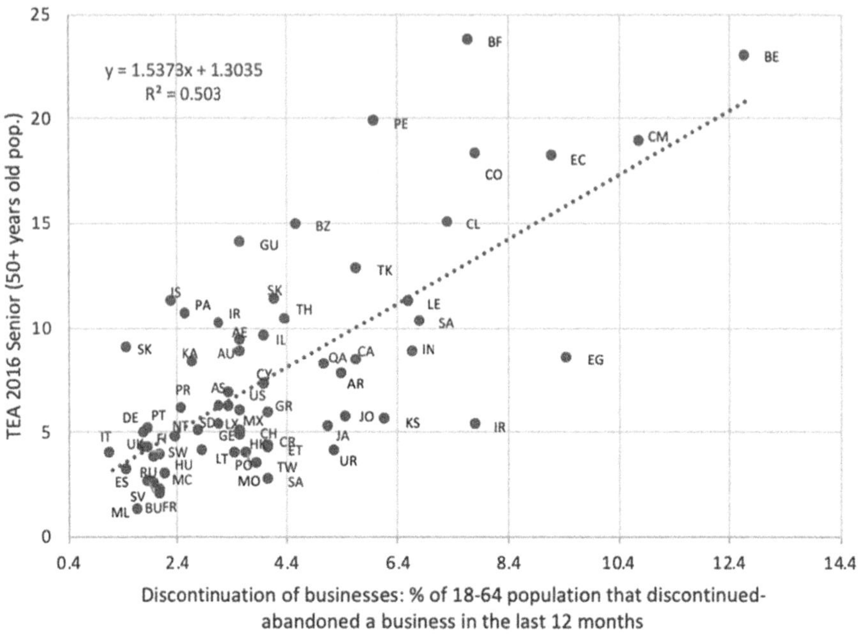

Legend: AE (UAE), AR (Argentina), AS (Austria), AU (Australia), BE (Belize), BF (Burkina Faso), BU (Bulgaria), BZ (Brazil), CA (Canada), CH (China), CL (Chile), CM (Cameroon), CO (Colombia), CR (Croatia), CY (Cyprus), DE (Germany), EC (Ecuador), EG (Egypt), ES (Spain), ET (Estonia), FI (Finland), FR (France), GE (Georgia), GR (Greece), GU (Guatemala), HK (Hong Kong), HU (Hungary), IL (Israel), IN (India), IL (Ireland), IR (Iran), IS (Indonesia), IT (Italy), JA (Jamaica), JO (Jordan), KA (Kazakhstan), KS (Saudi Arabia), LE (Lebanon), LT (Latvia), LU (Luxembourg), MC (Macedonia), ML (Malaysia), MO (Morocco), MX (Mexico), NT (Netherlands), PA (Panama), PE (Peru), PO (Poland), PR (Puerto Rico), PT (Portugal), QA (Qatar), RU (Russia), SA (El Salvador), SD (Sweden), SF (South Africa), SK (South Korea), SL (Slovakia), SV (Slovenia), SW (Switzerland), TH (Thailand), TK (Turkey), TW (Taiwan), UK (United Kingdom), UR (Uruguay), US (USA)

Dependent variable	Early stage senior entrepreneurial activity rate	
Independent variable	% of the 18-64 population that discontinued a business the last 12 months	
Goodness of fit	$R^2 = 50.3\%$	
Adjusted model	$Y^* = 1.5373x + 1.3035$	
ANOVA test	$F = 63.764$	P-value = 0.000
Ho: The magnitude of senior TEA depends, to some degree, on the annual business discontinuation rate of the country.		
Result: Hypothesis accepted		

Fig. 4 Senior TEA (50+) vs. discontinuation of businesses: linear regression (2016 GEM Data). Source: Authors' own figure and table

This variable explains the differential behavior of some European countries, such as Slovakia and Ireland, which have higher entrepreneurial activity rates (11.30% and 10.20%, respectively) and lower middle ages (38.9 and 35.9 years, respectively), compared to the rest of Europe (39 years in average), except Cyprus (35.9 years),

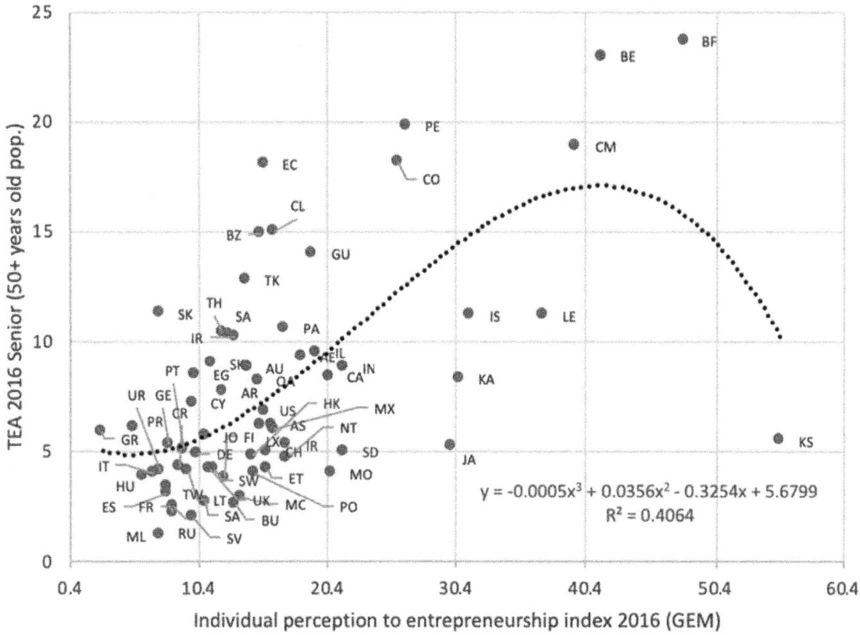

Legend: AE (UAE), AR (Argentina), AS (Austria), AU (Australia), BE (Belize), BF (Burkina Faso), BU (Bulgaria), BZ (Brazil), CA (Canada), CH (China), CL (Chile), CM (Cameroon), CO (Colombia), CR (Croatia), CY (Cyprus), DE (Germany), EC (Ecuador), EG (Egypt), ES (Spain), ET (Estonia), FI (Finland), FR (France), GE (Georgia), GR (Greece), GU (Guatemala), HK (Hong Kong), HU (Hungary), IL (Israel), IN (India), IL (Ireland), IR (Iran), IS (Indonesia), IT (Italy), JA (Jamaica), JO (Jordan), KA (Kazakhstan), KS (Saudi Arabia), LE (Lebanon), LT (Latvia), LU (Luxembourg), MC (Macedonia), ML (Malaysia), MO (Morocco), MX (Mexico), NT (Netherlands), PA (Panama), PE (Peru), PO (Poland), PR (Puerto Rico), PT (Portugal), QA (Qatar), RU (Russia), SA (El Salvador), SD (Sweden), SF (South Africa), SK (South Korea), SL (Slovakia), SV (Slovenia), SW (Switzerland), TH (Thailand), TK (Turkey), TW (Taiwan), UK (United Kingdom), UR (Uruguay), US (USA)

Dependent variable	Early stage senior entrepreneurial activity rate	
Independent variable	Individual perception to entrepreneurship index	
Goodness of fit	$R^2 = 40.64\%$	
Adjusted model	$Y^* = -0.0005x^3 + 0.0356x^2 - 0.3254x + 5.6799$	
ANOVA test	F = 13.922	P-value = 0.000
Ho: The magnitude of senior TEA depends to some degree of the individual perception to entrepreneurship index		
Result: Hypothesis accepted		

Fig. 5 Senior TEA (50+) vs. IPEI: nonlinear (cubic) regression (2016 GEM Data). Source: Authors' own figure and table

Georgia (38.1 years), Macedonia (37.8 years), and Russia (38.5 years). Excluding Cyprus, these nations were capitalists after the collapse of the Soviet Union on December 8, 1991, which can have implications on the vision of entrepreneurship exerted by the elderly living in these countries.

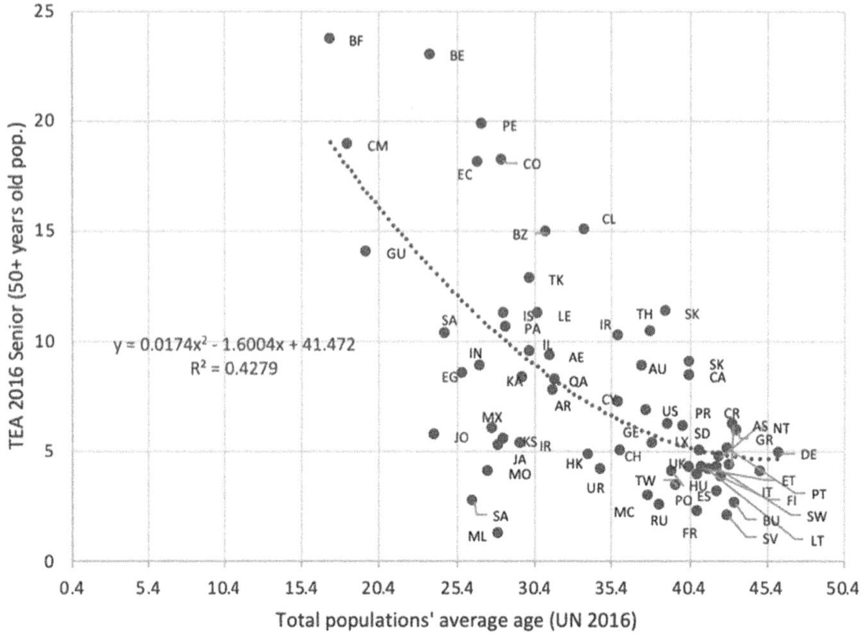

Legend: AE (UAE), AR (Argentina), AS (Austria), AU (Australia), BE (Belize), BF (Burkina Faso), BU (Bulgaria), BZ (Brazil), CA (Canada), CH (China), CL (Chile), CM (Cameroon), CO (Colombia), CR (Croatia), CY (Cyprus), DE (Germany), EC (Ecuador), EG (Egypt), ES (Spain), ET (Estonia), FI (Finland), FR (France), GE (Georgia), GR (Greece), GU (Guatemala), HK (Hong Kong), HU (Hungary), IL (Israel), IN (India), IL (Ireland), IR (Iran), IS (Indonesia), IT (Italy), JA (Jamaica), JO (Jordan), KA (Kazakhstan), KS (Saudi Arabia), LE (Lebanon), LT (Latvia), LU (Luxembourg), MC (Macedonia), ML (Malaysia), MO (Morocco), MX (Mexico), NT (Netherlands), PA (Panama), PE (Peru), PO (Poland), PR (Puerto Rico), PT (Portugal), QA (Qatar), RU (Russia), SA (El Salvador), SD (Sweden), SF (South Africa), SK (South Korea), SL (Slovakia), SV (Slovenia), SW (Switzerland), TH (Thailand), TK (Turkey), TW (Taiwan), UK (United Kingdom), UR (Uruguay), US (USA)

Dependent variable	Early stage senior entrepreneurial activity rate	
Independent variable	Total populations' average age	
Goodness of fit	$R^2 = 42.79\%$	
Adjusted model	$Y^* = 0.0174x^2 - 1.6004x + 41.472$	
ANOVA test	F = 23.188	P-value = 0.000
Ho: The magnitude of senior TEA depends, to some degree, on the individual perception to the entrepreneurship index		
Result: Hypothesis accepted		

Fig. 6 Senior TEA (50+) vs. total populations' average age: nonlinear (quadratic) regression (2016 UN Data). Source: Authors' own figure and table

In short, four factors explain SE in the 65 GEM countries for 2016: the business discontinuation annual rate, total populations' average age, IPEI, and HDI. As can be seen in Table 6, the annual rate of business abandonment is the variable with the greatest explanatory capacity of senior TEA ($R^2 = 50.30\%$), followed by the average

Table 6 Sign and variability of the senior TEA

Factor	Type of model	Sign	R^2 (%)
Business discontinuation annual rate	Linear	Positive	50.30
Total populations' average age	Quadratic	Negative	42.79
IPEI	Cubic	Positive	40.64
HDI	Cubic	Negative	33.12

Source: Authors' own table

Table 7 Results of a multiple linear regression model estimation for senior TEA

Dependent variable	Early-stage senior entrepreneurial activity rate			
Independent variables	Business discontinuation annual rate			
	Total populations' average age			
	Individual perception to entrepreneurship index			
	Human development index			
Method	Stepwise multiple linear regression			
Variables in	*B* coefficients	Beta coefficients	*t*	*P* value
Constant	0.392		0.410	0.683
Business discontinuation annual rate	1.225	0.565	5.625	0.000*
Individual perception to e-ship index	0.135	0.268	2.670	0.010*
Goodness of fit: adjusted R^2	54.0%	ANOVA test: F	38.546	0.000*
Variables out	B coefficients	Tolerance	*t*	*P* value
Total populations' average age	−0.192	0.471	−1.575	0.120
HDI	−0.152	0.633	−1.440	0.155

*$p < 0.05$
Source: Authors' own table

age of the population ($R^2 = 42.79\%$), IPEI ($R^2 = 40.64\%$), and HDI ($R^2 = 33.12\%$). When the rate of abandonment and the entrepreneurial spirit of a society grows, so makes the senior TEA. But, when the population age and the level of development increase, the senior TEA tends to decrease.

Using these four factors as independent variables to explain the early-stage senior entrepreneurial activity rate as a dependent variable, we estimate a multiple linear regression model which results are shown in Table 7.

Multiple regression results indicate that the constant is not significant (*P* value = 0.683) and the annual business discontinuation rate is the most significant variable (*P* value = 0.000) and weights the most to explain senior TEA. Also, the IPEI is significant but has less weight to explain the dependent variable. Both variables show positive regression coefficients. In average, when the business discontinuation rate increases by 1%, senior TEA grows 1.225%, and, when the rate of the population with a high perception of entrepreneurial values increases 1%, senior TEA augments, in average, 0.135%. Results suggest that market competitiveness and nonprofitable or noncompetitive business failure increase SE, being satisfactory the explanatory capacity of this model, as the goodness of fit, measured by the adjusted R^2, is 46%.

Table 8 Results of the principal component analysis and the 2016 senior TEA

Original variables	Extraction commonalities	Component 1 Rotated score correlation	Component 2 Rotated score correlation
Business discontinuation annual rate	0.683	−0.626	0.540
Total populations' average age	0.880	0.850	−0.397
IPEI	0.941	−0.257	0.935
HDI	0.885	0.921	−0.191
Variance captured by Component 1	50.715%		
Variance captured by Component 2	34.011%		
Total variance captured by Components 1 and 2	84.726%		

Source: Authors' own table

To visualize the magnitude and variability of the factors affecting senior SE, we apply a principal component analysis to take advantage of the multicollinearity existing between them (which has been detected and eliminated in the multiple linear regression analysis). As a result, we will take advantage of all the information contained in the four variables to prepare the positioning maps of the GEM countries in relation to SE. As seen in Table 8, and related to senior TEA, these four factors are being divided into two groups, one with a negative sign (average age of the populations and HDI) and another with a positive sign (annual rate of business abandonment and IPEI), and we have extracted two main components for collecting the information from both groups. The percentage of the original variance accumulated by both main components is very acceptable (84.726%) in linking the level of country development and entrepreneurship.

Results in Table 8 show that the first principal component (formed by HDI and the populations' average age) captures the biggest part of the variance (50.715%), while the second component (composed by the business discontinuation annual rate and IPEI) captures less variance (34.011%). This fact means that the first variables, at least for the year 2016, weight more than the second variables to explain the senior TEA variability. Also, the IPEI (0.935) is much more representative than the discontinuation rate (0.540), as it shows a much higher correlation with the second principal component. Thus, the territorial maps, showed in Figs. 7 and 8, must be read under this new and interesting light, where the role of the level of development and the entrepreneurial background of the nations appear as evident.

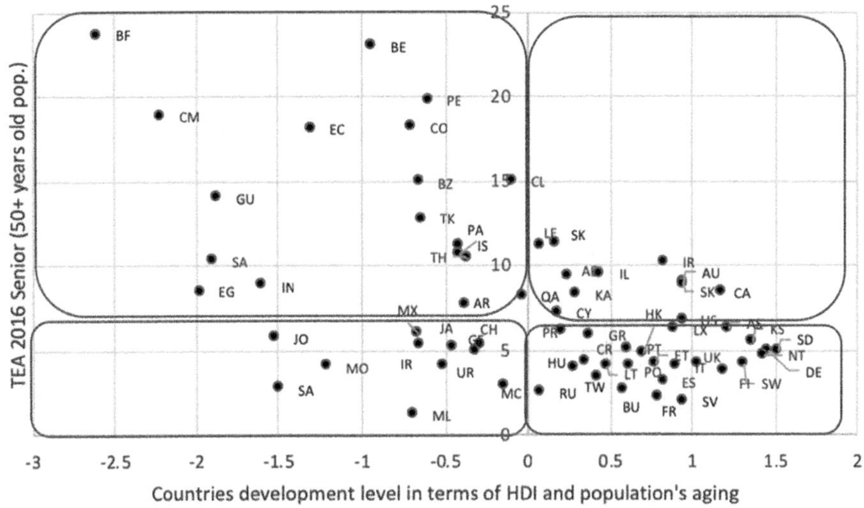

Legend: AE (UAE), AR (Argentina), AS (Austria), AU (Australia), BE (Belize), BF (Burkina Faso), BU (Bulgaria), BZ (Brazil), CA (Canada), CH (China), CL (Chile), CM (Cameroon), CO (Colombia), CR (Croatia), CY (Cyprus), DE (Germany), EC (Ecuador), EG (Egypt), ES (Spain), ET (Estonia), FI (Finland), FR (France), GE (Georgia), GR (Greece), GU (Guatemala), HK (Hong Kong), HU (Hungary), IL (Israel), IN (India), IL (Ireland), IR (Iran), IS (Indonesia), IT (Italy), JA (Jamaica), JO (Jordan), KA (Kazakhstan), KS (Saudi Arabia), LE (Lebanon), LT (Latvia), LU (Luxembourg), MC (Macedonia), ML (Malaysia), MO (Morocco), MX (Mexico), NT (Netherlands), PA (Panama), PE (Peru), PO (Poland), PR (Puerto Rico), PT (Portugal), QA (Qatar), RU (Russia), SA (El Salvador), SD (Sweden), SF (South Africa), SK (South Korea), SL (Slovakia), SV (Slovenia), SW (Switzerland), TH (Thailand), TK (Turkey), TW (Taiwan), UK (United Kingdom), UR (Uruguay), US (USA)

Fig. 7 Countries' positioning of the 2016 senior TEA concerning their development level and population aging. Source: Authors' own figure

4 Conclusions

While the HDI better explains SE in the developing countries, the business dropout rate explains better what happens in countries affected by economic crises, and the IPEI helps to explain both the SE in developing countries, mainly guided by necessity entrepreneurship, and in nations (e.g., Ireland, Israel, and the United States) endowed with a high level of entrepreneurial culture, regardless of their high level of economic development.

It is expected that SE will increase in the coming years due to the aging of the population ("Papy boom") (Maâlaoui et al., 2012), which mainly affects Europe, and to a lesser extent, affects some regions of the United States and Japan. Medical advances, better diet, and higher levels of life reached by the adult population worldwide, among other factors, lead to a nearly doubled number of estimated senior citizens aged 60+ (1402.5 in 2030 and 2091.9 in 2050) and more than doubled for aged 80+ (201.8 in 2030 and 466.9 in 2050), as seen in Table 1.

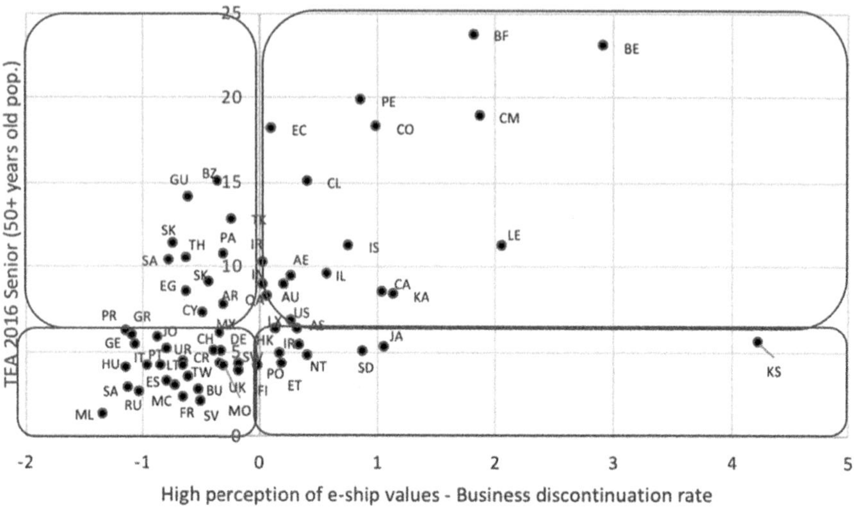

Legend: AE (UAE), AR (Argentina), AS (Austria), AU (Australia), BE (Belize), BF (Burkina Faso), BU (Bulgaria), BZ (Brazil), CA (Canada), CH (China), CL (Chile), CM (Cameroon), CO (Colombia), CR (Croatia), CY (Cyprus), DE (Germany), EC (Ecuador), EG (Egypt), ES (Spain), ET (Estonia), FI (Finland), FR (France), GE (Georgia), GR (Greece), GU (Guatemala), HK (Hong Kong), HU (Hungary), IL (Israel), IN (India), IL (Ireland), IR (Iran), IS (Indonesia), IT (Italy), JA (Jamaica), JO (Jordan), KA (Kazakhstan), KS (Saudi Arabia), LE (Lebanon), LT (Latvia), LU (Luxembourg), MC (Macedonia), ML (Malaysia), MO (Morocco), MX (Mexico), NT (Netherlands), PA (Panama), PE (Peru), PO (Poland), PR (Puerto Rico), PT (Portugal), QA (Qatar), RU (Russia), SA (El Salvador), SD (Sweden), SF (South Africa), SK (South Korea), SL (Slovakia), SV (Slovenia), SW (Switzerland), TH (Thailand), TK (Turkey), TW (Taiwan), UK (United Kingdom), UR (Uruguay), US (USA)

Fig. 8 Countries' positioning of the 2016 senior TEA concerning the population's high level of perception of entrepreneurship values and business discontinuation rate. Source: Authors' own figure

With respect to the relationship between aging and senior TEA, GEM countries can be classified into four groups: (1) low population aging and low senior TEA (Jamaica, Jordan, Morocco, Mexico, etc.); (2) high population aging and low senior TEA (France, Germany, Spain, Sweden, the United Kingdom, etc.); (3) low population aging and high senior TEA (Belize, Burkina Faso, Cameroon, Chile, Ecuador, Peru, etc.); and (4) high population aging and high senior TEA (Australia, Cyprus, Ireland, Latvia, Qatar, Slovakia, the UAE, the United States, etc.).

Regarding the relationship between entrepreneurial values, business closure, and senior TEA, GEM countries can be divided into four groups: (1) nations with a high perception of entrepreneurial values, low senior TEA, and low business closure (China, Germany, Hungary, Malaysia, Slovenia, Spain, Uruguay, etc.); (2) nations with a high perception of entrepreneurial values, high senior TEA, and low business closure (Brazil, Egypt, Guatemala, Panama, Thailand, etc.); (3) nations with a high perception of entrepreneurial values, low senior TEA, and high business closure (Finland, Ireland, Jamaica, Saudi Arabia, Sweden, The Netherlands, etc.); and (4) nations with a high perception of entrepreneurial values, high senior TEA, and high business closure (Belize, Burkina Faso, Cameroon, Chile, Colombia, Ecuador, Peru, the United Arab Emirates, the United States, etc.).

Finally, GEM countries do not show a unique combination of factors to determine senior TEA's variability, so a profound analysis on other specific features of each society should be planned to design effective policies to foster SE. In some countries, the working experience of retired entrepreneurs is combined with young initiatives. As a result, some retired entrepreneurs work for some hours with young entrepreneurs helping them to deal with the initial steps and stages of their entrepreneurial activities, a formula that works quite well to benefit start-ups without the stress of assuming risks and low-paid hard work.

Acknowledgments We thank EGADE Business School and the National Council on Science and Technology (CONACYT) (Mexico) for their financial support.

References

Cerveny, J., Pilkova, A., & Rehak, J. (2016). Senior entrepreneurship in European context: Key determinants of entrepreneurial activity. *Ekonomicky Casopis/Journal of Economics, 64*(2), 99–117.

Figueiredo, E., & Paiva, T. (2018). Senior entrepreneurship and qualified senior unemployment: The case of the Northern Portuguese region. *Journal of Small Business and Enterprise Development*. https://doi.org/10.1108/JSBED-01-2018-0006

Harms, R., Luck, F., Kraus, S., & Walsh, S. (2014). On the motivational drivers of gray entrepreneurship: An exploratory study. *Technological Forecasting and Social Change, 89*, 358–365.

Kenny, B., & Rossiter, I. (2018). Transitioning from unemployment to self-employment for over 50s. *International Journal of Entrepreneurial Behaviour and Research, 24*(1), 234–255.

Maâlaoui, A., Fayolle, A., Castellano, S., Rossi, M., & Safraou, I. (2012). L'entrepreneurial des seniors. *Revue Française de Gestion, 38*(227), 69–80.

Maritz, A., & Eager, B. (2017). Senior entrepreneurship themes: An Australian perspective. *International Journal of Organizational Innovation, 9*(4), 206–221.

Perenyi, A., Zolin, R., & Maritz, A. (2018). The perceptions of Australian senior entrepreneurs on the drivers of their entrepreneurial activity. *International Journal of Entrepreneurial Behavior and Research, 24*(1), 81–103.

Rodríguez-Aceves, L., Saiz-Álvarez, J.M., & García-Caballero, L. (2019). Emprendimiento femenino senior: una valoración para México. In Felix, C.M., & Vázquez, J.C. (Eds.), *Leadership, entrepreneurship, and gender. Engines of transformation [from Spanish, Liderazgo, Emprendimiento y Género. Motores de transformación]* (in press).

Rossi, M. (2009). Motivation and entrepreneurial intentions among potential seniors' entrepreneurs (55+) in Switzerland. *International Journal of Knowledge, Culture, and Change Management, 9*(8), 181–185.

Saiz-Álvarez, J. M., Coduras, A., & Cuervo-Arango, C. (2017). Has the first global financial crisis changed the entrepreneurial values in a digitalized marketing-based society? The case of GEM Latin American countries. *Revista EAN*, (82), 37–59.

Saiz-Álvarez, J. M., & Colvin-Díez, J. (2015). Purple oceans and the mergers and acquisitions virtuous circle. New concepts for the theory of mergers and acquisitions. In A. Tavidze (Ed.), *Progress in economic research* (Vol. 32, pp. 139–154). New York: Nova Science.

Tervo, H. (2014). Starting a new business later in life. *Journal of Small Business and Entrepreneurship, 27*(2), 171–190.

United Nations, Department of Economic and Social Affairs, Population Division. (2015). *World Population Ageing 2015* (ST/ESA/SER.A/390).

Van Solinge, H. (2014). Who opts for self-employment after retirement? A longitudinal study in the Netherlands. *European Journal of Ageing, 11*(3), 261–272.

Relationship Conflicts in Family Firms: An Empirical Analysis

Ismael Barros-Contreras, Juan Hernangómez-Barahona, and Natalia Martín-Cruz

Abstract Relationship conflicts between family members can have disastrous consequences on the performance of the family firm (FF) and even endanger its continuity. This study examines the relationship between family influence, relationship conflicts, and the organizational effectiveness of FF. Using a sample of 102 Spanish FFs, the authors analyzed the data using a partial least squares structural equation model. The results show that the involvement of family members in the ownership and on the boards of governance and management enhance the incorporation of the family values and culture into the firm and thus reduce relationship conflicts. More importantly, we find a negative relation between relationship conflicts and the effectiveness of FF.

Keywords Relationship conflict · Family firm · Involvement and essence approaches · Familiness · Organizational effectiveness

1 Introduction

Family firms (FFs) play a significant role in the global economy (Anderson & Reeb, 2003); therefore, understanding the factors that influence their objectives, strategic behaviors, and performance is a matter of importance (Chrisman, Chua, & Sharma, 2005). Prior literature on FF has focused primarily on the differences between family and nonfamily firms (NFFs) (Chrisman et al., 2005). Previous studies show that family involvement in the firm provides advantages compared with NFF, including a

I. Barros-Contreras (✉)
Universidad Austral de Chile, Puerto Montt, Chile
e-mail: ismaelbarros@uach.cl

J. Hernangómez-Barahona · N. Martín-Cruz
University of Valladolid, Valladolid, Spain
e-mail: jhernan@eco.uva.es; ambiela@eco.uva.es

J. M. Saiz-Álvarez et al. (eds.), *Entrepreneurship and Family Business Vitality*, Studies on Entrepreneurship, Structural Change and Industrial Dynamics, https://doi.org/10.1007/978-3-030-15526-1_9

longer horizon (Miller & Le Breton-Miller, 2006), better relationships with suppliers and customers based on trust (Carney, 2005) and loyalty (Tagiuri & Davis, 1996), development of social capital among workers (Pearson, Carr, & Shaw, 2008), better performance (Anderson & Reeb, 2003), and the creation of unique resources and capabilities that result from the interactions of family members both within the family and in the business (Habbershon & Williams, 1999).

In addition to the numerous advantages, the relationships and emotions shared by family members both in the family and in the firm can produce adverse effects (Pieper, Astrachan, & Manners, 2013). Affective family bonds are one of the main characteristics of this type of organization (Sorenson, 1999), and relationship conflicts between family members (Tagiuri & Davis, 1996) can provoke disastrous results for the firm and the family (Levinson, 1971). The dominant presence of the family and the combination of family and corporate roles create fertile grounds for conflict (Harvey & Evans, 1994).

Relationship conflicts can occur if the family and firm's governance systems operate according to different principals (Pieper et al., 2013) or by a different set of communication rules that make the interaction between the family and the firm difficult (Davis, 1983). When these two systems, family and firm, contradict one another, conflict is likely to occur in both systems (Eddleston & Kellermanns, 2007). Disharmony between family members (Kellermanns & Eddleston, 2004) can limit innovation and entrepreneurship behavior, because personal conflict significantly affects the processes of communication and decision-making (Filbeck & Smith, 1997).

Conflict is also frequent in FF as a result of changes and disagreements in family relationships, such as sibling rivalry, marital problems, and divorce, or children's desire for independence from their parents (Eddleston & Kellermanns, 2007). Nepotism and altruistic behavior are also sources of conflict (Schulze, Lubatkin, & Dino, 2003). The addition of successive generations of family members can also magnify some conflicts (Gersick, Davis, McCollom, & Lansberg, 1997), which can compromise the continuity of the family firm, especially when succession processes are affected (De Massis, Chua, & Chrisman, 2008).

The prior literature shows that a reduction of conflict can, under certain circumstances, improve performance in the FF (Kellermanns & Eddleston, 2007). Conversely, relationship conflicts cause satisfaction and performance to deteriorate because negative emotions such as discontent, frustration, and irritation affect organizational behavior (Jehn, 1997). Previous research focuses on identifying the causes (Davis & Harveston, 1999, 2001; Eddleston & Kellermanns, 2007; Eddleston, Otondo, & Kellermanns, 2008; Ensley, Pearson, & Sardeshmukh, 2007) and effects (Kellermanns & Eddleston, 2004, 2007) of conflict and conflict management in FF (Sorenson, 1999). Prior empirical studies primarily use conflict analysis at the cognitive level (task and process) but neglect the examination of relationship conflicts in family firms. Thus, research that examines relationship conflicts in FF is limited, and empirical studies that consider the interaction of FF systems and the cause and consequences are scarce (Eddleston & Morgan, 2014); for exceptions, see Nosé, Korunka, Frank, and Danes (2015), Eddleston et al. (2008),

Eddleston and Kellermanns (2007), Kellermanns and Eddleston (2007), and Ensley et al. (2007).

This research fills this gap in the literature by using the involvement and essence approaches (Chrisman et al., 2005) to provide empirical evidence that broadens the understanding of the effects of family influence on relationship conflicts and the organizational effectiveness of FF. The study provides an in-depth analysis of the variables that enhance or limit the development of relationship conflicts and their impact on the achievement of organizational effectiveness.

We developed a research model that investigates how family involvement and essence, relationship conflicts, and organizational effectiveness are related. We used the Spanish context to evaluate the research hypotheses. The data was obtained using a survey questionnaire of unlisted FF because research on small- and medium-sized family businesses is still limited and relationship effects are likely higher in smaller firms (Sharma & Carney, 2012). Furthermore, as recommended by the recent research of family business literature, we evaluated the data with a partial least squares (PLS) structural equation model.

This study provides several contributions to the literature. First, this research contributes to the field of FF by expanding the understanding of how family involvement and essence are related to relationship conflicts (Eddleston & Morgan, 2014) as antecedents of the behavior and performance of the FF (Astrachan, 2010). Second, we add to the extensive empirical evidence on the impact of emotions, particularly regarding the causes and consequences of relationship conflicts in family firms (Morgan & Gómez-Mejía, 2014). We also contribute to the discussion on the relationship between family involvement and essence, conflict in relationships, and organizational effectiveness. Finally, this study provides evidence about the behavior of unlisted family businesses (Sharma & Carney, 2012).

The remainder of this chapter is organized as follows. Section 2 provides a literature review and development of the hypotheses. Section 3 describes the data, variables, and empirical model. Section 4 discusses the results. Finally, Sect. 5 presents the conclusions, implications, and ideas for future research.

2 Literature Review

2.1 Conflict in Organizations

The study of organizational level conflict has received significant attention in the literature (e.g., Amason & Schweiger, 1994; Bantel & Jackson, 1989; Guetzkow & Gyr, 1954; Hackman, 1987; Jehn, 1994, 1995; Jehn & Bendersky, 2003; Jehn & Mannix, 2001; March & Simon, 1958; Pinkley, 1990; Pondy, 1967; Priem & Price, 1991; Van de Vliert & De Dreu, 1994; Wall & Nolan, 1986). Conflict is inevitable in groups and organizations due to the complexity and interdependence of organizational life (Jehn, 1995). Jehn and Bendersky (2003) defined conflict as the perceived incompatibility or differing views among stakeholders. Initially, the literature emphasized the negative relation between conflict, performance, and job satisfaction (March & Simon, 1958; Pondy, 1967). However, subsequent studies have examined the benefits of organizational conflict and methods to stimulate productive conflict (Amason & Schweiger, 1994; Jehn, 1994, 1995; Van de Vliert & De Dreu, 1994). For example, Jehn (1995) found that conflicts or functional tasks are beneficial, especially as they add to the creativity of the members of the task involved; these conflicts can contribute to the cognitive diversity of the team, which is associated with innovation and skills needed to solve complex and unusual problems (Bantel & Jackson, 1989).

Prior literature identifies different types of conflict that affect performance differently (Jehn & Bendersky, 2003). Guetzkow and Gyr (1954) distinguished the tasks based on conflict generated from the interpersonal relationships of group conflict. Likewise, Priem and Price (1991), Pinkley (1990), and Wall and Nolan (1986) characterized conflict arising from disagreements unrelated to tasks such as cognitive conflict and socioemotional conflict. Jehn (1997) identified three types of conflict: tasks, processes, and relationships. The first, also called cognitive conflict, involves disagreement among group members about the tasks performed. This type of conflict is based on the conflict of ideas within a group and disagreement about the content of the task, including differences in points of view, ideas, and opinions (Jehn & Bendersky, 2003). The conflict of the processes relates to the means or strategy to perform a specific task, not the task itself (Jehn, 1997). Finally, conflict in personal relationships occurs when incompatibilities exist between members of a group (e.g., personal differences of opinion and preferences regarding issues not related to tasks) (Jehn & Bendersky, 2003). In particular, research on organizational conflict shows that, although conflict in the workplace can be beneficial to performance (Amason & Schweiger, 1994; Jehn, 1995; Jehn & Mannix, 2001), conflict in relationships based on personal confrontations and interpersonal antagonism is detrimental to team performance (Jehn, 1995). Relationship conflicts cause negative emotional behaviors in the members of an organization such as irritation, suspicion, and resentment (Jehn, 1997), resulting in poor personal relationships that damage team synergy (Hackman, 1987) and harm the moral performance of the group (Jehn, 1997).

The distinction between types of conflicts and their impact on performance is particularly relevant in the context of the FF, where the strong bonds of and the close interaction between family members within the company generate an environment that fosters conflict (Harvey & Evans, 1994). Relationship conflicts can be particularly harmful in these organizations, because they can weaken the quality of the family members' interactions both in the family and in the firm, thereby affecting firm performance (Eddleston et al., 2008; Eddleston & Kellermanns, 2007). Therefore, how the family's influence affect the development of conflict in relationships and thus the performance and effectiveness of the FFs is a relevant matter.

2.2 How Family Affects Behavior in the Family Firms

As previously noted, in recent decades, research has employed the involvement and essence approaches to work out how the family influences strategic behavior and performance of family firms (Astrachan, 2010; Chrisman et al., 2005). The structural components of the involvement approach (Chua, Chrisman, & Sharma, 1999) include the family's direct involvement in ownership, management, and generational transfer. This approach assumes that family involvement is sufficient for a firm to be considered a FF. Application of this approach, which has been primarily used to differentiate between family and NFF (Miller, Le Breton-Miller, Lester, & Cannella, 2007), provides contradictory results (Rutherford, Kuratko, & Holt, 2008).

Firms with a high degree of family involvement are likely to have members that closely identify with the firm (Donnelley, 1964). Family firms with consistency between family values and the degree of family involvement in the ownership and management of the firm can create governance structures that facilitate organizational goals that create sustainability and high performance (Sharma & Nordqvist, 2007). However, according to the agency theory, altruism and managerial entrenchment, combined with intentions to maintain family control, can influence the behavior of FF, leading to a decline in existing capacity, a delay in the development of new skills, and dysfunctional relationships (Gómez-Mejía, Núñez-Nickel, & Gutiérrez, 2001).

The essence approach (Chua et al., 1999) considers the need to incorporate features that convey intangible values, family culture, and the desire to keep the firm in family control over multiple generations (Chrisman et al., 2005). This approach assumes that family involvement is necessary but not sufficient to define a firm as a FF; that is, such participation must also be manifested in the behavior and commitment to the company as a hallmark of a FF (Chua et al., 1999). Thus, the two approaches complement one another to capture the diversity of FFs (Chrisman, Chua, Pearson, & Barnett, 2012).

Increased ownership and family involvement create greater psychological ties to the firm, increasing both commitment and intention of transgenerational family control (Zellweger & Astrachan, 2008). Hence, when family involvement in ownership and the boards of governance and management increases, the desire to maintain control increases family members' affective commitment to the firm. Intergenerational involvement is the most viable and sustainable control mechanism that also increases commitment (Chrisman et al., 2012). The involvement of several generations in decision-making can increase power due to group cohesion (Ensley & Pearson, 2005). However, family members of different generations often hold different views, and these differences can lead to conflict (Gersick et al., 1997).

2.3 Conflict in Family Firms

Family and business systems are interdependent in FFs, and this interaction creates an environment that favors the existence of conflicts (Kellermanns & Eddleston, 2004). The family's social system creates strong emotional ties (Davis, 1983), and these affective relationships play out both in the family and the firm (Daily & Dollinger, 1992). The close interactions between family and firm become increasingly complex with each generation as the dispersion of ownership and the personal dynamics among family members change (Sharma, Chrisman, & Chua, 1997).

Despite the importance of conflict in the FF, empirical research thus far is limited (Benavides-Velasco, Quintana-García, & Guzmán-Parra, 2013). Prior empirical studies can be grouped into three streams of research.

First, some previous research examines the factors that lead to conflict within family and NFFs. Prior studies find that numerous factors affect conflicts in FFs, including number of family/generations involved in the firm's ownership and management (Davis & Harveston, 1999, 2001; Wakefield & Sebora, 2004), family dynamics (Davis & Harveston, 1999), altruism (Eddleston & Kellermanns, 2007), family social interactions (Davis & Harveston, 1999, 2001; Wakefield & Sebora, 2004), gender (Danes, Leichtentritt, Metz, & Huddleston-Casas, 2000; Thurairajah, 2013), and family welfare (Danes, Zuiker, Kean, & Arbuthnot, 1999).

Second, prior research on conflict in FFs investigates the effects of the conflict. For example, Kellermanns and Eddleston (2007) and Eddleston and Kellermanns (2007) studied the effect of cognitive and process conflicts and relationship conflicts, respectively, on firm performance. Ensley et al. (2007) examined the relationship between payment dispersions to members of the senior management team, emotional conflicts, and firm performance. Kwan, Lau, and Au (2012) investigated whether the type of firm (family vs. nonfamily) moderates the relation between family conflicts within the firm and job satisfaction. Karofsky et al. (2001) studied frustration at work as a predictor of anxiety, and Smyrnios et al. (2003) examined the causes of job stress-related anxiety of American and Australian owners of FFs; Danes et al. (2000) looked at how business tensions negatively affect family members' quality of life, and Nosé et al. (2015) evaluated how the family atmosphere counteracts the adverse effects of relationship conflicts. Memili, Chang, Kellermanns, and Welsh (2015) studied reciprocal altruism in the context of conflict between family members.

Finally, the third stream of research focuses on conflict resolution. This line of study argues that conflict is inevitable in FFs. Consequently, the conflict must be managed effectively. For example, Sorenson (1999) examined the effect of conflict management strategies and their impact on the family and the firm. Pinkley (1990) categorized prior studies according to the types of conflicts, identifying them as either task (cognitive) and relationship conflicts. In line with Pinkley's results, Table 1 shows that most investigations study cognitive, or task-related, conflicts, whereas few analyze the effects of relationship conflict in family firms.

Hence, in FFs, the dominant role of the family in establishing norms and the lack of formalized systems and structures promotes an environment in which conflicts,

Table 1 Study streams and types of conflict in the family firm

	Research trends	
	Tasks	Relations
Factors that lead to family and nonfamily conflicts	Danes et al. (1999), Davis and Harveston (2001), Wakefield and Sebora (2004), Eddleston et al. (2008), Thurairajah (2013)	Eddleston and Kellermanns (2007), Eddleston et al. (2008)
Effects of conflict	Karofsky et al. (2001), Eddleston and Kellermanns (2007), Ensley et al. (2007), Kwan et al. (2012), Memili et al. (2015)	Eddleston and Kellermanns (2007), Ensley et al. (2007), Nosé et al. (2015)
Conflict resolution	Sorenson (1999)	

Source: Authors' own table

particularly relationship conflicts, can occur (Kellermanns & Eddleston, 2004). Relationships that tend to be a significant source of conflict in FFs include marital disagreements, sibling rivalry, the desire of children to separate from their parents, the dispersion of ownership among family members (Schulze et al., 2003), the misalignment of the interests between the family and the firm, conflicts of law, and conflict in succession (Danes et al., 1999).

2.4 *Family Influence and Relationship Conflicts*

As previously stated, empirical evidence shows that family influence (involvement and essence) affects the behavior (Chua et al., 1999) and strategic fit of FFs (Lindow, Stubner, & Wulf, 2010). Hall, Melin, and Nordqvist (2006) found that the interaction between family members plays an essential role in defining the strategy, implementation, and achievement of organizational objectives. They also emphasized the negative side of family influence, including relationship conflicts, which can negatively affect the behavior of the business and jeopardize its continuity.

The literature distinguishes two significant dimensions that characterize family firms and have a different effect on conflict: generational involvement and concentration of control (Kellermanns & Eddleston, 2004). Because family involvement is a precondition to family essence, when family involvement in ownership and governance and management boards increases, the family's capacity to retain control and transfer transgenerational control also increases (Chrisman et al., 2012). The concentration of control, defined as the level of power held by the members of a FF (Gersick et al., 1997), influences the occurrence of relationship conflicts. A high degree of concentration of control indicates that the firm is under the control of a single owner, and low levels of concentration of control indicate that several individuals (dispersal of ownership) are involved in the decision-making process. Because power differences can create stress and disruption in an organization (Cliff, 1987), increases in ownership and high levels of concentration of control can create more conflicts in relationships in FFs (Kellermanns & Eddleston, 2004). Prior studies showed that these control differences could lead to the use of threats and punishment by the controlling family member (De Dreu & Van Kleef, 2004), frustration, and adverse effects (Eisenhardt & Bourgeois, 1988).

However, the family is also a social system that cares for its members. Members develop emotional ties and a sense of loyalty and responsibility (Kepner, 1991), but the level of cohesion and strength of the links between family members differ (Lansberg & Astrachan, 1994). Depending on the degree of cohesion, a firm may foster a more individual or a more familiar environment (Lansberg & Astrachan, 1994). Increased involvement allows for a higher transmission of family values to the business, which has a positive impact on the culture of FFs. Family involvement and essence promote cohesion that creates a more collective orientation so that interactions among family members are characterized by reciprocal altruism, which links the welfare of each family member with other members (Schulze, Lubatkin, Ling, & Dino, 2002). Because reciprocity discourages favoritism and provides family members with incentives to exercise self-control (Schulze et al., 2002), it mitigates self-interest and limits the potential for relationship conflicts (Kellermanns & Eddleston, 2004). When family members engage in positive relationships, they are more productive, manage information better, make better decisions (Kellermanns & Eddleston, 2004), and are more likely to promote the long-term vision and preservation of the family's socioemotional wealth (Gómez-Mejía, Haynes, Núñez-Nickel, Jacobson, & Moyano-Fuentes, 2007). Given this discussion, we pose the following hypothesis:

Hypothesis 1 Essence has a mediating effect on the relationship between ownership and relationship conflicts in family firms.

According to Gersick et al. (1997), the complexity of FFs increases with the development of the family, business, and ownership subsystems. For example, the ownership structure of FFs commonly changes from the initial stage of a sole owner to a consortium of siblings and cousins. The evolution of the family system through marriage, parenthood, sibling relationships, political relationships, communication patterns, and family roles and development of the firm through new businesses, expansion, and maturity involves new family members with different motivations, values, skills, interests, priorities, and levels of closeness in the workplace. The addition of these new members can increase the possibility of disagreements in the decision-making, goals, and other critical aspects of the firm.

The dynamics of the family and firm subsystems in FFs often lead to greater participation and a more significant number of current generations because members want to control in decision-making (Kellermanns & Eddleston, 2004). Increased involvement makes the process of decision-making more complex. Although transgenerational participation in decision-making can improve control and increase the family commitment to the firm (Chrisman et al., 2012), family members of different generations often have varying views, and these differences can lead to conflict (Gersick et al., 1997).

Prior research shows that the addition of family members to ownership and management is related to the development of relationship conflicts in family firms. For example, Davis and Harveston (1999) found that the likelihood of conflict in family firms increases when new generations enter the firm. Eddleston et al. (2008) found a negative relation between participative decision-making and relationship conflicts in FFs. Similarly, Kellermanns and Eddleston (2007) showed that the dispersion of ownership across generations moderates the relation between conflict and performance. Therefore, we formulate the following hypothesis:

Hypothesis 2 The entry of new generations to the ownership and management of the firm moderates the relation between essence and relationship conflicts in family firms.

2.5 *Organizational Effectiveness*

Organizational effectiveness denotes the efficiency of an organization in achieving its objectives (Daft, 2006). It is the result of the excellent decision-making that allows a firm to capture a greater market share, improve results, and grow and innovate faster than competitors (Zheng, Yang, & McLean, 2010). Because organizational culture is based on the assumptions and values shared by the organization's members (Schein, 1985), its standards can be a source of sustainable competitive advantage (Barney, 1991) and an essential factor for organizational effectiveness (Denison, 1990). Consequently, FFs' unique characteristics of resources and capabilities (e.g., commitment, shared values, culture, trust, reputation) can explain their long-term success (Habbershon & Williams, 1999).

However, these same idiosyncratic features can also have negative implications. For example, nepotism and altruistic behavior can be sources of conflict (Schulze et al., 2003) that mainly affect the emotional relationships between family members. The cross contacts between the family and the firm make FFs especially vulnerable to the negative consequences of relationship conflicts (Kellermanns & Eddleston, 2004). These conflicts, which are often unavoidable in family firms, directly affect the firm's organizational effectiveness.

Dysfunctional relationships caused by conflicts negatively affect organizational effectiveness and performance (Eddleston & Kellermanns, 2007). Because relationship conflicts interfere with work efforts by negatively affecting group cohesion (Jehn, 1997), they constitute a barrier to productivity. Interpersonal family conflicts increase adverse reactions and cause complacency among family members (Chirico & Salvato, 2008). They limit communication and prevent change, which thus allows the dysfunctional relationships to continue (Eddleston & Kellermanns, 2007). An organizational environment develops including animosity, stress, anxiety, hostile behavior, and the perception of other family members as antagonistic (Simons & Peterson, 2000). These negative consequences are amplified by family members' positions in ownership and management, which give them access to important information and power in decision-making (Sorenson, 1999), and thus the ability to affect the effectiveness and continuity of the family firm seriously. Therefore, we propose the following hypothesis:

Hypothesis 3 A negative relation exists between relationship conflicts and organizational effectiveness in family firms.

3 Empirical Research

3.1 Data Collection and Sample

The database is taken from the *Actualidad Económica* magazine's ranking of the 5000 largest firms in Spain, based on sales volume. The Spanish environment is selected because of its relative importance: 2.9 million FFs produce more than 70% of the GDP and create 13.9 million jobs (Casado & Rodríguez, 2009). The sample is composed of medium and large non-listed FFs. The literature on this segment of firms is scarce; over 80% of the previous studies focus on listed FFs (Sharma & Carney, 2012). Two restrictions are established to determine the firms that are included in the investigation. First, listed family firms are omitted because their ownership, structure, and management have a defined organization that separates the family from the firm and thus limits the opportunity for relational bonds to impact the firm. Also, listed FFs do not generally maintain the familiarity that characterizes the organization in their early history due to the dilution of ownership caused by segmentation (Basco & Pérez Rodríguez, 2009).

Second, because Spain lacks official statistics on FFs and no common definition of FFs exists in the literature (Cruz & Nordqvist, 2012), this study imposes particular parameters to identify FFs (Astrachan, Klein, & Smyrnios, 2002; Chua et al., 1999). Following prior literature that defines FFs to include a family commitment to the firm (Basco & Pérez Rodríguez, 2011; Chua et al., 1999; Claver, Rienda, & Quer, 2009), we develop an operational definition. Individually, firms must meet two characteristics to be defined as FF: first, family members must be committed in the ownership of the firm and the boards of governance and management; and, second, the family must have intentions of transgenerational control. These elements are recognized ex post in agreement with the collection of the study's data (Claver et al., 2009). The final sample included 1656 firms.

Because the information required for the model is not available in the database, a questionnaire was prepared and conducted to obtain the necessary data. The questionnaire was created according to prior literature related to the research variables and validated according to the usual methods. A total of 135 surveys were received, representing a response rate of 8.15%, which is similar to other studies of family firms (Lindow et al., 2010; Zellweger, Kellermanns, Chrisman, & Chua, 2012). Of the 125 valid questionnaires received, 23 were omitted because they were identified as nonfamily (17) or listed family (6) firms, resulting in 102 usable questionnaires. Of these questionnaires, 100% belong to non-listed FFs according to the first sample restriction, and 99% meet the FF definition, by the second sample restriction. Specifically, 95% of the sample firms have family members present at management meetings, 98% have a presence on the board of directors, and 93% expect the future CEO of the firm to be a family member.

To check the bias of no answer, the sample is divided into three groups, and the first group that answered the survey is compared with the last group that answered the survey. The underlying assumption is that the group that answered last is similar to those who did not answer. The analysis of variance does not show significant statistical differences between the first and last groups (99% confidence level). Hence, the absence of the no answer bias is confirmed.

Another possible limitation is the main informant, whose subjective evaluation biases the common method (Doty & Glick, 1998). Harman's individual factor test was applied, and the results showed that no factor registers a significant portion of the variance; therefore, the variance of the common method was not a problem. Also, to avoid the reduction of the validity of the construct due to the main informant, we followed Podsakoff, MacKenzie, Lee, and Podsakoff (2003) suggestion to keep the questions as simple as possible and separate the dependent from the independent variables. The results show that the sample possesses quality.

3.2 *Variables and Measures*

3.2.1 Familiness

As previously stated, we followed prior studies to define the concept of FFs (Basco & Pérez Rodríguez, 2011; Chua et al., 1999; Claver et al., 2009) based on two characteristics: (1) involvement of family members in ownership and governance and management and boards and (2) the intention of transgenerational family control. After applying the operational definition to identify FFs, we used the Family Influence on Power, Experience, and Culture scale (Astrachan et al., 2002; Holt, Rutherford, & Kuratko, 2010; Klein, Astrachan, & Smyrnios, 2005; Rutherford et al., 2008), a widely used tool in research, to measure the involvement and essence of the family in the firm, that is, their familiness.

Family Involvement

We applied variables that are most commonly used in the literature on family involvement (Astrachan et al., 2002; Chrisman et al., 2012; Chua et al., 1999; Klein et al., 2005). Family involvement is measured by power and family experience. Power considers direct and indirect control through the ownership of the business (business shares held by the family) and through the management or control of the firm through the management or participation of family members on the boards of governance and management (Klein et al., 2005). That is, family influence is manifested directly through the involvement of family members in the ownership, administration, and management of the firm (Astrachan et al., 2002) and indirectly through other companies or the appointment of family or nonfamily members to the governance and management boards (Klein et al., 2005). Power is measured using two items of the sub-power scale of the F-PEC, based on survey responses: (1) the percentage of family members involved directly or indirectly on the management board and (2) the percentage of family members who are directly or indirectly involved in the direction of the board.

The more experience family members have over generations in the ownership, management, and direction of the firm, the more opportunities they have to create important family memories (Klein et al., 2005). Thus, family influence on a business through experience is related to leadership succession, the number of active generations, and the number of family members who contribute to the firm. Prior literature shows that each generation adds significant and valuable business experience to the family and the firm (Astrachan et al., 2002). Experience is measured by asking each respondent how many generations are present in the ownership, management, and direction of the firm (Holt et al., 2010; Rutherford et al., 2008). Following Astrachan et al. (2002), Klein et al. (2005), Rutherford et al. (2008), and Holt et al. (2010), we weighted the experience subscale so that most experience transfers from the first to the second generation and so on. Experiences were measured using three items of the subscale of F-PEC experience, based on survey responses: (1) the number of family generations involved in the ownership of the company, (2) the number of family generations involved in the board of directors, and (3) the number of generations involved in the management board.

Family Essence

Essence is reflected in the extent to which the family's objectives and values align or overlap with those of the firm (Astrachan et al., 2002; Holt et al., 2010; Klein et al., 2005). Thus, family influence, from the essence, affects the extent to which the firm shares the family's objectives and values.

To measure family essence, we used a version of the culture subscale of the F-PEC. The representative elements of the culture subscale of the F-PEC are whether family members (1) feel loyal to the family business; (2) agree with the objectives of the family firm, plans, and policies; (3) care about the fate of the business; and (4) are willing to make great efforts to help the business succeed (Chrisman et al., 2012; Holt et al., 2010). We measured the four items using a Likert scale from 1 (strongly/always disagree) to 5 (strongly/always agree).

3.2.2 Relationship Conflicts

Relationship conflicts were measured using an adaptation of the scale proposed by Jehn (1995) and identified family members who (1) have personal problems, (2) have apparent personality conflicts, (3) have strained relations, (4) are often at odds with the views of the CEO, (5) have frequent conflicts on the various proposals put forward in the business, (6) have conflicts with family members over business decisions, and (7) have differences of opinion about the business. We measured the four items using a Likert scale from 1 (strongly/always disagree) to 5 (strongly/always agree).

3.2.3 Organizational Effectiveness

This variable was constructed following the micro-fundamentals proposed by Teece (2007). The items identified organizational effectiveness through ongoing development activities and organizational processes of (1) internal research and development activities; (2) activities to identify changing needs of customers; (3) processes to take advantage of technological developments; (4) adaptation processes of the business model; (5) asset management processes; (6) job rotation activities, regular meetings at different levels, newsletters/blogs, and configuration of multifunctional devices; and (7) processes that adapt resources to seize new opportunities. Prior literature recognizes these routines as evidence of organizational effectiveness (Gold, Malhotra, & Segars, 2001; Zheng et al., 2010). We measured the four items using a Likert scale from 1 (strongly/always disagree) to 5 (strongly/always agree).

3.2.4 Control Variables

We included three control variables that are commonly used in prior literature on the behavior of FFs: age, size, and industrial sector (Chrisman, Chua, & Litz, 2004). The age of business was measured according to the years of operation. The family may have a greater attachment to the business over time (Zellweger & Astrachan, 2008), which can strengthen family members' commitment and limit the likelihood of relationship conflicts. The size was evaluated according to the number of employees. The increased presence of family members in the business can increase the potential for conflicts in relationships (Chirico & Salvato, 2008). Finally, research indicates that family businesses compete better in some industries than in others (Pollak, 1985), which can affect their behavior and predisposition to relationship conflicts. The industry was measured by classifying the companies according to the SIC code. The categories were agriculture, construction, manufacturing, transportation, trade, services, and others.

The primary industries were manufacturing (43%) and services (29%). Concerning age, 28.4% of the companies in the sample were less than 25 years old, and 55.9% are between 26 and 75 years old. Concerning size, 34.3% of companies had between 51 and 250 employees, and 51.9% had more than 250 employees.

4 Results

We used a PLS structural equation model (SEM) to validate our research model (Ringle, Wende, & Will, 2005). The PLS-SEM is increasingly used in the areas of research in management, strategy, marketing (Sattler, Völckner, Riediger, & Ringle, 2010), and research on FFs (Chua et al., 1999; Vallejo, 2009). PLS-SEM can analyze structural models with multi-item constructs and direct and indirect relations (Vallejo, 2009). Finally, this model is most appropriate during the early stages of theory development and thus supports confirmatory and exploratory research (Fornell & Bookstein, 1982) and complex investigations in which theoretical knowledge is limited (Wold, 1982) as in our research. We used the software 2.0 SmartPLS M3 (Ringle et al., 2005).

We ran multiple and straightforward regressions to complete the PLS estimation. To run PLS regressions, the sample must meet the requirements of the most complex multiple regression (Barclay, Higgins, & Thompson, 1995). We determined the sample size by multiplying by ten the more significant result obtained from the following options: (1) the number of indicators of the most complex formative construct and (2) the most significant number of structural routes directed to any of the constructs of the model (Chin, 1998). Because our model contained only structural reflective constructs and two routes to any construct, the minimum size required for the sample is 20. Therefore, our sample of 102 observations is adequate.

4.1 Measurement Model

Before estimating the structural model, we performed a confirmatory factor analysis to verify the measurement model. This analysis supports our measurement model by clearly identifying factors representing the F-PEC scale, namely, relationship conflicts and organizational effectiveness.

The research model shows only measures associated with the reflective constructs. The PLS estimation determines the reflective indicators by the construct and covary at this level (Hulland, 1999). Table 2 summarizes the parameters obtained in the analysis of the measurement model.

We evaluated the measurement model by looking at the reliability, internal consistency, and convergent and discriminant validity of each item (Roldán & Leal, 2003). The internal reliability of each item is determined by the loadings and is expressed as the percentage of the variance related item construct. For good reliability of the item, all loads must be greater than 0.7 (Carmines & Zeller, 1979).

Table 2 Latent variable, item measurement, composed reliability, average variance extracted (AVE), and Cronbach's α

Construct indicator	Factor loading/ weight path	*t*-stat	Composed reliability	AVE	Cronbach's α
Power			0.923	0.857	0.841
Pow_1	0.891	5.509			
Pow_2	0.960	8.209			
Experience			0.971	0.918	0.956
Exp_1	0.946	8.250			
Exp_2	0.968	8.971			
Exp_3	0.961	8.817			
Essence			0.845	0.578	0.761
Ess_1	0.772	7.651			
Ess_2	0.759	7.234			
Ess_3	0.668	4.018			
Ess_4	0.833	10.860			
Relationship conflicts			0.914	0.606	0.894
Relcon_1	0.870	20.526			
Relcon_2	0.845	21.052			
Relcon_3	0.812	12.656			
Relcon_4	0.679	7.128			
Relcon_5	0.737	9.279			
Relcon_6	0.776	13.347			
Relcon_7	0.711	7.622			
Organizational effectiveness			0.899	0.567	0.884
Orgeff_1	0.610	3.423			
Orgeff_2	0.879	5.044			
Orgeff_3	0.809	5.102			
Orgeff_4	0.789	4.975			
Orgeff_5	0.541	3.149			
Orgeff_6	0.662	3.992			
Orgeff_7	0.905	5.012			
Control variables					
Firm_age	0.130	1.146			
Firm_size	0.238	2.661			
Firm_ind	0.170	1.816			

Source: Authors' own table
Note: See this table for the definition of variables

All loads of items exceed the limit of 0.7 except one of the essence constructs and three items of organizational effectiveness construct, whose loads are close to 0.6, which is considered acceptable when the scales are in the early stages of development (Chin, 1998).

We evaluated the internal consistency of the constructs by examining the Cronbach's alpha and composite reliability. Indicators exceed 0.8 and 0.7 for the composite and Cronbach alpha reliability, respectively, suggesting that both measures are acceptable (Nunnally, 1978). The convergent construct validity is expressed in the degree that all items of a construct are measured on the same basis and are evaluated by examining the average variance extracted (AVE). In our analysis, the AVE indicator exceeds the 0.5 recommended by Fornell and Larcker (1981). We assessed the discriminant validity by examining the extent to which the square root of AVE is higher than the inter-construct correlations. All indicators have good measurement properties.

Finally, regarding the control variables used, the size of the firm measured by the number of employees was significant with a coefficient of 0.238 ($p = 2.661$), suggesting that the growth of the firm affects conflicts in relationships in family firms. For example, a larger size may lead to an increase in interactions between family members and increase the likelihood of relationship conflicts (Eddleston & Kellermanns, 2007), thus impacting organizational effectiveness.

4.2 Structural Model

Figure 1 shows the sample variance explained (R^2) in the dependent path constructs and the β coefficients for the model. Following Chin (1998), we used a bootstrapping (1000 samples) method to generate standard errors and t statistics.

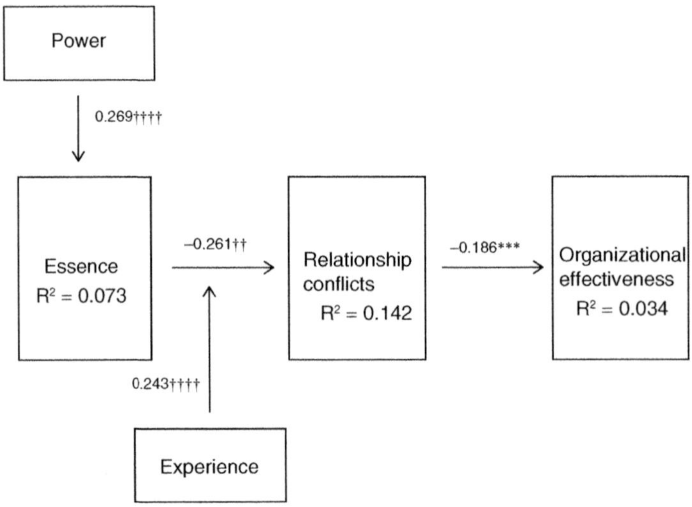

Fig. 1 Empirical model on the relationship conflicts in the family firms. Note: ***$p < 0.01$ (t-statistic one tailed). ††††$p < 0.01$; ††$p < 0.05$ (t-statistic two tailed). Source: Authors' own figure

Table 3 Power mediator effect → essence → relationship conflicts

Structural route	Model 1	Model 2	Model 3	Model 4
Power → relationship conflicts	−0.161			0.051
	(2.622***)			(0.706)
Power → essence		0.285		0.267
		(3.196***)		(2.568**)
Essence → relationship conflicts			−0.353	−0.324
			(4.922***)	(3.560***)

Source: Authors' own table
Note: ***$p < 0.01$; **$p < 0.02$ (t-statistic two tailed)

The R^2 for the endogenous variables, essence, relationship conflicts, and organizational effectiveness, were 0.073, 0.142, and 0.034, respectively.

Regarding hypothesis H1, the structural path power → essence → relationship conflicts has a significantly negative coefficient −0.261 ($t = 2.111$). However, to verify the mediating effect of the essence in the relationship between power and relationship conflicts, we performed further analysis, as suggested by Baron and Kenny (1986). Table 3 provides the results.

Table 3 provides several findings regarding the power component. Model 1 establishes a negative relationship between power (the independent variable) and relationship conflicts (the dependent variable) with a coefficient of −0.161 ($t = 2.622$). Model 2 directly relates essence to power (the variable mediator) with a coefficient of 0.285 ($p = 3.196$). Model 3 indicates a negative relation between essence and relationship conflicts with a coefficient of −0.353 ($t = 4.922$). Finally, Model 4 shows a simultaneous relation between power, essence, and relationship conflicts. The relation between power and relationship conflicts dramatically reduces its significance when essence is incorporated as the mediating variable, with a coefficient of 0.051 ($t = 0.706$); the other structural routes retain their significance. Therefore, essence full mediates the relation between power and relationship conflicts. These findings support hypothesis H1.

Regarding hypothesis H2, we performed a moderation analysis by incorporating the interactive effects analysis of the research model. Following the product term approach (Henseler & Fassott, 2010) and based on the principal component model, we analyze the moderating effect of the experience on the relation between essence and relationship conflicts. Structural path essence * experience (E * ES) conflict in relationships is positive and significant with a coefficient of 0.243 ($t = 2.763$). Furthermore, the R^2 of relationship conflicts increased from 0.085 to 0.142 when the interactive effect (the experience-moderating variable) is introduced. Therefore, the experience component positively moderates the relation between essence and relationship conflicts. That is, the addition of new family generations to the business negatively affects the relationship between essence and relationship conflicts. These results support hypothesis H2.

Regarding hypothesis H3, the results provided evidence of a negative and significant relation between relationship conflicts and organizational effectiveness, with a coefficient of −0.186 ($t = 3.088$). Therefore, our findings support the hypothesis H3.

5 Discussion and Conclusions

This research provides empirical evidence that broadens the understanding of the effects of family influence on relationship conflicts within and thus the effectiveness of FFs. Specifically, by applying the involvement and essence approaches, we first examined how essence mediates the relation between the involvement of family members in the ownership and the boards of directors and management and relationship conflicts. In line with Kellermanns and Eddleston (2004) and Chrisman et al. (2012), the results indicate that family involvement has a direct impact on the transmission of family goals and values to the business, making relationship conflicts less likely within FFs. In line with Ensley and Pearson (2005) and Eddleston et al. (2008), our results confirm the negative relation between family influence and relationship conflicts. The close and long-term ties between family members allow them to develop effective communication patterns, which promotes participative decision-making (Eddleston et al., 2008) and productive discussions (Ensley & Pearson, 2005), and reduce relationship conflicts. These results support hypothesis H1 that essence has a mediating effect on the relationship between ownership and relationship conflicts in FFs.

Second, in line with Kellermanns and Eddleston (2007), our results show that incorporating successive family generations positively moderates the adoption of family objectives and values in the firm by increasing family members' commitment (Chrisman et al., 2012), the proximity and affective ties among family members, and the power of the group (Ensley & Pearson, 2005). This finding supports the hypothesis H2 that the entry of new generations to the ownership and management of the firm moderates the relation between essence and relationship conflicts in family firms.

Finally, our results provide empirical evidence for hypothesis H3 that a negative relationship exists between relationship conflicts and organizational effectiveness in family firms. These results are in line with Eddleston and Kellermanns (2007) and Nosé et al. (2015) who found that relationship conflicts cause devastating effects on organizational effectiveness and performance because they cause negative feelings that inhibit communication and prevent families from benefiting from the closeness of family relationships. Our results are also in line with Gold et al. (2001) and Zheng et al. (2010) who reported that effectiveness contributes to organizational performance. Our analyses indicate a positive and significant relationship between organizational effectiveness and performance in FFs, with a coefficient of 0.301 ($t = 3.773$). These findings are relevant because the behavior of the family firms is enhanced by the proximity, communication, and commitment of family members to the business, which may explain their results.

Given the limited prior research on relationship conflicts in FFs (Benavides-Velasco et al., 2013), this study provides contributions to advance research in this field. First, it provides quantitative evidence of the relation between family influence, relationship conflicts, and the effectiveness of family firms (Eddleston & Morgan, 2014). Thus, following Astrachan (2010), this study increases our understanding of how involvement and essence of family businesses affect strategic behavior and performance. Second, in line with Morgan and Gómez-Mejía (2014), we extend the study of the impact of emotions in the context of relationship conflicts in family firms. Third, this study contributes to the literature on organizational effectiveness of family firms, adding evidence to the discussion about family involvement and essence as a source of capability across generations in family firms. Finally, this research extends the study of non-listed family firms, a little-discussed topic in this field (Sharma & Carney, 2012). These contributions, taken together, add to the theory of the family firms and improve our understanding of the behavior, performance, and heterogeneity of family firms.

Our results also have implications for managers of FFs, who can benefit from knowing the causes and consequences of relationship conflicts in FFs. Managers should understand that FFs are fertile ground for conflict, especially for relationship conflicts among family members, and discern the harmful consequences of such conflicts. Managers should strive to obtain the benefits of the closeness and bonding of family members by fostering an environment conducive to collaboration, sharing, and communication among members of FFs. Managers must also understand how idiosyncratic resources of FFs transfer to the business to provide the necessary incentives for this process occur. A climate of trust and emotional commitment facilitates the interaction of the members of the firm and the family, reducing as much as possible inevitable relationship conflicts, especially between family members. Also, managers have the task of developing close relations across different generations in the context of the business to that multiple generations can endorse the vision and organizational values, thus ensuring the continuity of the firm.

This research has some limitations. First, this study is cross-sectional, which is particularly problematic when measuring phenomena in time. Second, using surveys to collect data is also somewhat problematic. However, the characteristics of the study variables and the unavailability of appropriate databases make the application of this type of instrument necessary. Third, another methodological limitation is the subjective evaluation of a key informant. However, we followed the literature to correct the bias, which should eliminate the problem. Finally, the use of the PLS methodology establishes predictability, not causality, between the independent and dependent variables because it is a flexible model. Nevertheless, due to the early stage of development of the theory and the model's complexity, this methodology is adequate to evaluate our study.

This research encourages the development of new studies to obtain further evidence on the causes and consequences of relationship conflicts in family firms. The study of this phenomenon is highly important as it extends our understanding of family firm across generations and thus helps to ensure their longevity and survival.

References

Amason, A. C., & Schweiger, D. M. (1994). Resolving the paradox of conflict, strategic decision making, and organizational performance. *International Journal of Conflict Management, 5*(3), 239–253.

Anderson, R. C., & Reeb, D. M. (2003). Founding-family ownership and firm performance: Evidence from the S&P 500. *The Journal of Finance, 58*(3), 1301–1327.

Astrachan, J. H. (2010). Strategy in family business: Toward a multidimensional research agenda. *Journal of Family Business Strategy, 1*(1), 6–14.

Astrachan, J. H., Klein, S. B., & Smyrnios, K. X. (2002). The F-PEC scale of family influence: A proposal for solving the family business definition problem. *Family Business Review, 15*(1), 45–58.

Bantel, K. A., & Jackson, S. E. (1989). Top management and innovations in banking: Does the composition of the top team make a difference? *Strategic Management Journal, 10*(S1), 107–124.

Barclay, D., Higgins, C., & Thompson, R. (1995). The partial least squares (PLS) approach to causal modeling: Personal computer adoption and use as an illustration. *Technology Studies, 2* (2), 285–309.

Barney, J. B. (1991). Firm resources and sustained competitive advantage. *Journal of Management, 17*(1), 99–120.

Baron, R. M., & Kenny, D. A. (1986). The moderator-mediator variable distinction in social psychological research: Conceptual, strategic, and statistical considerations. *Journal of Personality and Social Psychology, 51*(6), 1173–1182.

Basco, R., & Pérez Rodríguez, M. J. (2009). Studying the family enterprise holistically evidence for integrated family and business systems. *Family Business Review, 22*(1), 82–95.

Basco, R., & Pérez Rodríguez, M. J. (2011). Ideal types of family business management: Horizontal fit between family and business decisions and the relationship with family business performance. *Journal of Family Business Strategy, 2*(3), 151–165.

Benavides-Velasco, C. A., Quintana-García, C., & Guzmán-Parra, V. F. (2013). Trends in family business research. *Small Business Economics, 40*(1), 41–57.

Carmines, E. G., & Zeller, R. A. (1979). *Reliability and validity assessment* (Vol. 17). Thousand Oaks, CA: Sage.

Carney, M. (2005). Corporate governance and competitive advantage in family-controlled firms. *Entrepreneurship: Theory and Practice, 29*(3), 249–265.

Casado, F., & Rodríguez, M. Á. (2009). *La RSE en la gran empresa familiar española*. Madrid.

Chin, W. W. (1998). The partial least squares approach for structural equation modeling. In G. A. Marcoulides (Ed.), *Modern methods for business research* (pp. 295–336). Mahwah, NJ: Lawrence Erlbaum Associates.

Chirico, F., & Salvato, C. (2008). Knowledge integration and dynamic organizational adaptation in family firms. *Family Business Review, 21*(2), 169–181.

Chrisman, J. J., Chua, J. H., & Litz, R. A. (2004). Comparing the agency costs of family and non-family firms: Conceptual issues and exploratory evidence. *Entrepreneurship: Theory and Practice, 28*(4), 335–354.

Chrisman, J. J., Chua, J. H., Pearson, A. W., & Barnett, T. (2012). Family involvement, family influence, and family-centered non-economic goals in small firms. *Entrepreneurship: Theory and Practice, 36*(2), 267–293.

Chrisman, J. J., Chua, J. H., & Sharma, P. (2005). Trends and directions in the development of a strategic management theory of the family firm. *Entrepreneurship: Theory and Practice, 29*(5), 555–576.

Chua, J. H., Chrisman, J. J., & Sharma, P. (1999). Defining the family business by behavior. *Entrepreneurship: Theory and Practice, 23*(4), 19–39.

Claver, E., Rienda, L., & Quer, D. (2009). Family firms' international commitment. *Family Business Review, 22*(2), 125–135.

Cliff, G. (1987). Managing organizational conflict. *Management Review, 70*(5), 51–53.
Cruz, C., & Nordqvist, M. (2012). Entrepreneurial orientation in family firms: A generational perspective. *Small Business Economics, 38*(1), 33–49.
Daft, R. (2006). Organization theory and design (9th ed.). Mason, OH: Thomson Higher Education.
Daily, C. M., & Dollinger, M. J. (1992). An empirical examination of ownership structure in family and professionally managed firms. *Family Business Review, 5*(2), 117–136.
Danes, S. M., Leichtentritt, R., Metz, M., & Huddleston-Casas, C. (2000). Effects of conflict styles and conflict severity on quality of life of men and women in family businesses. *Journal of Family and Economic Issues, 21*(3), 259–286.
Danes, S. M., Zuiker, V., Kean, R., & Arbuthnot, J. (1999). Predictors of family business tensions and goal achievement. *Family Business Review, 12*(3), 241–252.
Davis, P. S. (1983). Realizing the potential of the family business. *Organizational Dynamics, 12*(1), 47–56.
Davis, P. S., & Harveston, P. D. (1999). In the founder's shadow: Conflict in the family firm. *Family Business Review, 12*(4), 311–323.
Davis, P. S., & Harveston, P. D. (2001). The phenomenon of substantive conflict in the family firm: A cross-generational study. *Journal of Small Business Management, 39*(1), 14–30.
De Dreu, C. K., & Van Kleef, G. A. (2004). The influence of power on the information search, impression formation, and demands in negotiation. *Journal of Experimental Social Psychology, 40*(3), 303–319.
De Massis, A., Chua, J. H., & Chrisman, J. J. (2008). Factors preventing intra-family succession. *Family Business Review, 21*(2), 183–199.
Denison, D. R. (1990). *Corporate culture and organizational effectiveness*. New York: Wiley.
Donnelley, R. G. (1964). The family business. *Harvard Business Review, 42*(4), 93–105.
Doty, D. H., & Glick, W. H. (1998). Common methods bias: Does common methods variance really bias results? *Organizational Research Methods, 1*(4), 374–406.
Eddleston, K. A., & Kellermanns, F. W. (2007). Destructive and productive family relationships: A stewardship theory perspective. *Journal of Business Venturing, 22*(4), 545–565.
Eddleston, K. A., & Morgan, R. M. (2014). Trust, commitment and relationships in family business: Challenging conventional wisdom. *Journal of Family Business Strategy, 5*(3), 213–216.
Eddleston, K. A., Otondo, R. F., & Kellermanns, F. W. (2008). Conflict, participative decision-making, and generational ownership dispersion: A multilevel analysis. *Journal of Small Business Management, 46*(3), 456–484.
Eisenhardt, K. M., & Bourgeois, L. J. (1988). Politics of strategic decision making in high-velocity environments: Toward a midrange theory. *Academy of Management Journal, 31*(4), 737–770.
Ensley, M. D., & Pearson, A. W. (2005). An exploratory comparison of the behavioral dynamics of top management teams in family and nonfamily new ventures: Cohesion, conflict, potency, and consensus. *Entrepreneurship: Theory and Practice, 29*(3), 267–284.
Ensley, M. D., Pearson, A. W., & Sardeshmukh, S. R. (2007). The negative consequences of pay dispersion in family and non-family top management teams: An exploratory analysis of new venture, high-growth firms. *Journal of Business Research, 60*(10), 1039–1047.
Filbeck, G., & Smith, L. L. (1997). Team building and conflict management: Strategies for family businesses. *Family Business Review, 10*(4), 339–352.
Fornell, C., & Bookstein, F. L. (1982). Two structural equation models: LISREL and PLS applied to consumer exit-voice theory. *Journal of Marketing Research, 19*(4), 440–452.
Fornell, C., & Larcker, D. F. (1981). Evaluating structural equation models with unobservable variables and measurement error. *Journal of Marketing Research, 18*(1), 39–50.
Gersick, K. E., Davis, J. A., McCollom, M., & Lansberg, I. (1997). *Generation to generation life cycles of the family business*. Boston, MA: Harvard Business School Press.
Gold, A. H., Malhotra, A., & Segars, A. H. (2001). Knowledge management: An organizational capabilities perspective. *Journal of Management Information Systems, 18*(1), 185–214.
Gómez-Mejía, L. R., Haynes, K. T., Núñez-Nickel, M., Jacobson, K. J. L., & Moyano-Fuentes, J. (2007). Socioemotional wealth and business risks in family-controlled firms: Evidence from Spanish olive oil mills. *Administrative Science Quarterly, 52*(1), 106–137.

Gómez-Mejía, L., Núñez-Nickel, M., & Gutiérrez, M. I. (2001). The role of family ties in agency contracts. *Academy of Management Journal, 44*(1), 81–95.

Guetzkow, H., & Gyr, J. (1954). An analysis of conflict in decision-making groups. *Human Relations, 7*(3), 367–381.

Habbershon, T. G., & Williams, M. L. (1999). A resource-based framework for assessing the strategic advantages of family firms. *Family Business Review, 12*(1), 1–25.

Hackman, J. R. (1987). *The design of work teams*. Englewood Cliffs, NJ: Prentice Hall.

Hall, A., Melin, L., & Nordqvist, M. (2006). Understanding strategizing in the family business context. In P. Poutziouris, K. X. Smyrnios, & S. B. Klein (Eds.), *Handbook of research on family business* (pp. 253–268). Cheltenham: Edward Elgar.

Harvey, M., & Evans, R. E. (1994). Family business and multiple levels of conflict. *Family Business Review, 7*(4), 331–348.

Henseler, J., & Fassott, G. (2010). Testing moderating effects in PLS path models: An illustration of available procedures. In W. W. Chin, V. E. Vinzi, J. Henseler, & H. Wang (Eds.), *Handbook of partial least squares: Concepts, methods, and applications in marketing and related fields* (pp. 713–735). Berlin: Springer.

Holt, D. T., Rutherford, M. W., & Kuratko, D. F. (2010). Advancing the field of family business research: Further testing the measurement properties of the F-PEC. *Family Business Review, 23* (1), 76–88.

Hulland, J. (1999). Use of partial least squares (PLS) in strategic management research: A review of four recent studies. *Strategic Management Journal, 20*(2), 195–204.

Jehn, K. A. (1994). Enhancing effectiveness: An investigation of advantages and disadvantages of value-based intragroup conflict. *International Journal of Conflict Management, 5*(3), 223–238.

Jehn, K. A. (1995). A multimethod examination of the benefits and detriments of intragroup conflict. *Administrative Science Quarterly, 40*(2), 256–282.

Jehn, K. A. (1997). A qualitative analysis of conflict types and dimensions in organizational groups. *Administrative Science Quarterly, 42*(3), 530–557.

Jehn, K. A., & Bendersky, C. (2003). Intragroup conflict in organizations: A contingency perspective on the conflict-outcome relationship. *Research in Organizational Behavior, 25*(1), 187–242.

Jehn, K. A., & Mannix, E. A. (2001). The dynamic nature of conflict: A longitudinal study of intragroup conflict and group performance. *Academy of Management Journal, 44*(2), 238–251.

Karofsky, P., Millen, R., Yilmaz, M. R., Smyrnios, K. X., Tanewski, G. A., & Romano, C. A. (2001). Work-family conflict and emotional well-being in American family businesses. *Family Business Review, 14*(4), 313–324.

Kellermanns, F. W., & Eddleston, K. A. (2004). Feuding families: When conflict does a family firm good. *Entrepreneurship: Theory and Practice, 28*(3), 209–228.

Kellermanns, F. W., & Eddleston, K. A. (2007). A family perspective on when conflict benefits family firm performance. *Journal of Business Research, 60*(10), 1048–1057.

Kepner, E. (1991). The family and the firm: A coevolutionary perspective. *Family Business Review, 4*(4), 445–461.

Klein, S. B., Astrachan, J. H., & Smyrnios, K. X. (2005). The F-PEC scale of family influence: Construction, validation, and further implication for theory. *Entrepreneurship Theory and Practice, 29*(3), 321–339.

Kwan, H. K., Lau, V. P., & Au, K. (2012). Effects of family-to-work conflict on business owners: The role of family business. *Family Business Review, 25*(2), 178–190.

Lansberg, I., & Astrachan, J. H. (1994). Influence of family relationships on succession planning and training: The importance of mediating factors. *Family Business Review, 7*(1), 39–59.

Levinson, H. (1971). Conflicts that plague family businesses. *Harvard Business Review, 49*(2), 90–98.

Lindow, C. M., Stubner, S., & Wulf, T. (2010). Strategic fit within family firms: The role of family influence and the effect on performance. *Journal of Family Business Strategy, 1*(3), 167–178.

March, J. G., & Simon, H. A. (1958). *Organizations*. New York: Wiley.

Memili, E., Chang, E. P. C., Kellermanns, F. W., & Welsh, D. H. B. (2015). Role conflicts of family members in family firms. *European Journal of Work and Organizational Psychology, 24*(1), 143–151.

Miller, D., & Le Breton-Miller, I. (2006). Family governance and firm performance: Agency, stewardship, and capabilities. *Family Business Review, 19*(1), 73–87.

Miller, D., Le Breton-Miller, I., Lester, R. H., & Cannella, A. A., Jr. (2007). Are family firms really superior performers? *Journal of Corporate Finance, 13*(5), 829–858.

Morgan, T. J., & Gómez-Mejía, L. R. (2014). Hooked on a feeling: The affective component of socioemotional wealth in family firms. *Journal of Family Business Strategy, 5*(3), 280–288.

Nosé, L., Korunka, C., Frank, H., & Danes, S. M. (2015). Decreasing the effects of relationship conflict on family businesses: The moderating role of family climate. *Journal of Family Issues, 38*(1), 25–51.

Nunnally, J. C. (1978). *Psychometric theory* (2nd ed.). New York: McGraw-Hill.

Pearson, A. W., Carr, J. C., & Shaw, J. C. (2008). Toward a theory of familiness: A social capital perspective. *Entrepreneurship: Theory and Practice, 32*(6), 949–969.

Pieper, T. M., Astrachan, J. H., & Manners, G. E. (2013). Conflict in family business: Common metaphors and suggestions for intervention. *Family Relations, 62*(3), 490–500.

Pinkley, R. L. (1990). Dimensions of conflict frame: Disputant interpretations of conflict. *Journal of Applied Psychology, 75*(2), 117–126.

Podsakoff, P. M., MacKenzie, S. B., Lee, J.-Y., & Podsakoff, N. P. (2003). Common method biases in behavioral research: A critical review of the literature and recommended remedies. *Journal of Applied Psychology, 88*(5), 879–903.

Pollak, R. A. (1985). A transaction cost approach to families and households. *Journal of Economic Literature, 23*(2), 581–608.

Pondy, L. R. (1967). Organizational conflict: Concepts and models. *Administrative Science Quarterly, 12*(2), 296–320.

Priem, R. L., & Price, K. H. (1991). Process and outcome expectations for the dialectical inquiry, devil's advocacy, and consensus techniques of strategic decision making. *Group & Organization Management, 16*(2), 206–225.

Ringle, C. M., Wende, S., & Will, S. (2005). *SmartPLS 2.0 (M3)*. Hamburg: University of Hamburg.

Roldán, J. L., & Leal, A. (2003). A validation test of an adaptation of the DeLone and McLean's model in the Spanish EIS field. In J. J. Cano (Ed.), *Critical reflections on information systems. A systemic approach* (pp. 66–84). Hershey, PA: IGI Global.

Rutherford, M. W., Kuratko, D. F., & Holt, D. T. (2008). Examining the link between 'familiness' and performance: Can the F-PEC untangle the family business theory jungle? *Entrepreneurship Theory and Practice, 32*(6), 1089–1109.

Sattler, H., Völckner, F., Riediger, C., & Ringle, C. M. (2010). The impact of brand extension success drivers on brand extension price premiums. *International Journal of Research in Marketing, 27*(4), 319–328.

Schein, E. H. (1985). *Organizational culture and leadership: A dynamic view*. San Francisco, CA: Jossey-Bass.

Schulze, W. S., Lubatkin, M. H., & Dino, R. N. (2003). Exploring the agency consequences of ownership dispersion among the directors of private family firms. *Academy of Management Journal, 46*(2), 179–194.

Schulze, W., Lubatkin, M., Ling, Y., & Dino, R. (2002). *For love and money: Altruism and agency in private and family owned and managed firms* (Working Paper).

Sharma, P., & Carney, M. (2012). Value creation and performance in private family firms: Measurement and methodological issues. *Family Business Review, 25*(3), 233–242.

Sharma, P., Chrisman, J. J., & Chua, J. H. (1997). Strategic management of the family business: Past research and future challenges. *Family Business Review, 10*(1), 1–35.

Sharma, P., & Nordqvist, M. (2007). A typology for capturing the heterogeneity of family firms. *Academy of Management Proceedings, 2007*(1), 1–6.

Simons, T. L., & Peterson, R. S. (2000). Task conflict and relationship conflict in top management teams: The pivotal role of intragroup trust. *Journal of Applied Psychology, 85*(1), 102–111.

Smyrnios, K. X., Romano, C. A., Tanewski, G. A., Karofsky, P. I., Millen, R., & Yilmaz, M. R. (2003). Work-family conflict: A study of American and Australian family businesses. *Family Business Review, 16*(1), 35–51.

Sorenson, R. L. (1999). Conflict management strategies used by successful family businesses. *Family Business Review, 12*(4), 325–339.

Tagiuri, R., & Davis, J. (1996). Bivalent attributes of the family firm. *Family Business Review, 9*(2), 199–208.

Teece, D. J. (2007). Explicating dynamic capabilities: The nature and microfoundations of (sustainable) enterprise performance. *Strategic Management Journal, 28*(13), 1319–1350.

Thurairajah, K. (2013). Work-family conflict and its impact on career and relation to gender. *European Journal of Business and Management, 5*(30), 1–12.

Vallejo, M. C. (2009). Analytical model of leadership in family firms under transformational theoretical approach. *Family Business Review, 22*(2), 136–150.

Van de Vliert, E., & De Dreu, C. K. W. (1994). Optimizing performance by conflict stimulation. *International Journal of Conflict Management, 5*(3), 211–222.

Wakefield, M. W., & Sebora, T. C. (2004). An examination of antecedents of conflict over money, management, vision, and control in family businesses. *Journal of Business and Entrepreneurship, 16*(2), 91–114.

Wall, V. D., & Nolan, L. L. (1986). Perceptions of inequity, satisfaction, and conflict in task-oriented groups. *Human Relations, 39*(11), 1033–1051.

Wold, H. (1982). Systems under indirect observation using PLS. In C. Fornell (Ed.), *A second generation of multivariate analysis* (Method) (Vol. I, pp. 325–347). New York: Praeger.

Zellweger, T. M., & Astrachan, J. H. (2008). On the emotional value of owning a firm. *Family Business Review, 21*(4), 347–363.

Zellweger, T. M., Kellermanns, F. W., Chrisman, J. J., & Chua, J. H. (2012). Family control and family firm valuation by family CEOs: The importance of intentions for transgenerational control. *Organization Science, 23*(3), 851–868.

Zheng, W., Yang, B., & McLean, G. N. (2010). Linking organizational culture, structure, strategy, and organizational effectiveness: Mediating role of knowledge management. *Journal of Business Research, 63*(7), 763–771.

Part III
Family Firms: Innovation

Commitment to Learning, Knowledge, and Strategic Renewal: Do Family Firms Manage Them Differently?

Marta Pérez-Pérez and Remedios Hernández-Linares

Abstract Nowadays, knowledge is considered a critical resource through which organizations can develop sustainable competitive advantages and obtain superior results by allowing to transform themselves and to adapt to their environment. Hence, this research has a double purpose: first, to explore how commitment to learning determines the development of knowledge management practices (mainly, generation, flow, and storage) and how such practices impact small-sized and midsized firms' strategic renewal and, second, to explore if previous relationships are different for family and nonfamily firms. To test our model, we conducted an empirical study based on a sample of 238 Spanish small- and medium-sized enterprises. Structural equation modeling in the form of partial least squares was used to test the measurement model and hypotheses. In order to assess the moderating effects of organizational context (differences among family and nonfamily firms), we adopted a multi-group approach using two subsamples. Results show that commitment to learning and knowledge management practices are the main undercurrent of strategic renewal. Furthermore, family and nonfamily firms are less heterogeneous than we expected at first sight.

Keywords Knowledge management · Family firms · Organizational learning · SMEs · Partial least squares

M. Pérez-Pérez (✉)
University of Cantabria, Santander, Spain
e-mail: perezpm@unican.es

R. Hernández-Linares
University of Extremadura, Mérida, Spain
e-mail: remedioshl@unex.es

J. M. Saiz-Álvarez et al. (eds.), *Entrepreneurship and Family Business Vitality*,
Studies on Entrepreneurship, Structural Change and Industrial Dynamics,
https://doi.org/10.1007/978-3-030-15526-1_10

1 Introduction

The advent of the "new knowledge economy" has led to an increased emphasis on knowledge as the main strategic resource of companies (Biscotti, D'Amico, & Monge, 2018; Carayannis, Samara, & Bakouros, 2015) allowing organizations to obtain superior results (Oliva, 2014) and develop sustainable competitive advantages (Davenport & Prusak, 1998; Grant, 1996; Mustafa, Lundmark, & Ramos, 2016). Thus, businesses are paying more and more attention to knowledge management (KM) (Calvo-Mora, Navarro-García, Rey-Moreno, & Perianez-Cristobal, 2016; Hussinki, Kianto, Vanhala, & Ritala, 2017), defined as "the organized process of creating, capturing, storing, disseminating, and using knowledge within and between organization" (Jayasingam, Ansari, Ramayah, & Jantan, 2013, p. 256). Extant literature argues that KM constitutes the primary origin of corporate entrepreneurship (Martín-Rojas, García-Morales, & Bolívar-Ramos, 2013; Sakhdari, 2016), understood as the incremental process through which organizations adapt to the environment and explore opportunities to invoke changes, conceive new strategies, remake themselves, and undertake transformational activities for redefining their industries (Albert, Kreutzer, & Lechner, 2015; Floyd & Lane, 2000; Huff, Huff, & Thomas, 1992; Zahra, 2015). Among the different variables that have been proposed to explain failure or success in adapting to changing environments, strategic renewal, a dynamic management process, is attracting increasing attention by research (Pratap & Saha, 2018; Schmitt, Raisch, & Volberda, 2018) due to its potential for shedding light on the corporate entrepreneurship phenomenon (Albert et al., 2015).

Organizational learning and KM practices might be the main undercurrent of strategic renewal (Crossan & Berdrow, 2003; Simsek & Heavey, 2011). However, research testing these relationships is still limited (Lloria & Peris-Ortiz, 2014; Riviere, Suder, & Bass, 2018; Sciascia, Alberti, & Salvato, 2009) and is mostly focused on the relationship between a specific KM practice and corporate entrepreneurship (e.g., Bojica, Arroyo, & Fuentes, 2012; Bojica & Fuentes-Fuentes, 2012). However, neither all types of KM practices have been simultaneously explored nor all of them seem to have the same potential to boost corporate entrepreneurship (Shane & Venkataraman, 2000; Sullivan & Marvel, 2011). Moreover, KM processes are conditioned by the characteristics of the organization and its members (Argote, McEvily, & Reagans, 2003; Bojica, Fuentes-Fuentes, & Fernández, 2017). In this regard, family firms share specific characteristics, such as the close relationships among their members, which facilitate knowledge sharing (Zahra, Neubaum, & Larrañeta, 2007) and may have a considerable influence on their entrepreneurial activities (Naldi, Nordqvist, Sjöberg, & Wiklund, 2007) because both the family firm's knowledge and how it is used can significantly promote entrepreneurship (Zahra, 2012).

To contribute to address these research gaps, this study aims to analyze how commitment to learning, known as an organization's cultural value that reflects the degree to which such organization is likely to promote a learning culture (Sackmann,

1991; Sinkula, Baker, & Noordewier, 1997), determines the KM practices and how such practices impact strategic renewal. More specifically, this study considers that commitment to learning is related to the intensity of the learning in an organization, while its effective transformation into corporate entrepreneurship needs to be adequately managed through the KM practices. We also explore if such relationships are different for family firms and nonfamily firms with the aim to capture a possible different effect arising from the organizational context. To reach our research purposes, we conducted an empirical study based on a sample of 238 Spanish small- and medium-sized enterprises (SMEs henceforth). We focus on SMEs by three main reasons. First, because of their significant share in the business landscape (Ayyagari, Beck, & Demirguc-Kunt, 2007; Stoian & Gilman, 2017). Second, because research on KM in the SMEs' context is still fragmented and quite limited as was revealed by Durst and Edvardsson (2012) in their literature review and has been emphasized by more recent studies (e.g., Villar, Alegre, & Pla-Barber, 2014). Finally, because SMEs face unique challenges because they have fewer options regarding resources, capabilities, and market power (Brettel & Rottenberger, 2013; Drnevich & Kriauciunas, 2011; Jones & Macpherson, 2006; Sawers, Pretorius, & Oerlemans, 2008). Hence, they are more vulnerable to environmental changes (Wade & Hulland, 2004), making strategic renewal especially important for them.

Our work makes at least three contributions to the literature. We first add to the limited research on KM practices in the SMEs' context (e.g., Durst & Edvardsson, 2012) by empirically exploring the complex relationship between commitment to learning and different KM practices, mainly, KM generation, KM flow, and KM storage practices. In particular, our work shows that commitment to learning has more influence on KM storage practices than on the rest of KM practices analyzed. Similarly, our work adds to the scant research exploring how KM practices contribute to SMEs' strategic renewal (e.g., Jones & Macpherson, 2006). Finally, and although a couple of articles have explored the overall learning orientation and its relationship with other strategic orientations (e.g., Hernández-Linares, Kellermanns, & López-Fernández, 2018a), our work is pioneering in researching the individual influence of one of the learning orientation's dimensions, i.e., commitment to learning, on KM practices in the family business setting by emphasizing the relevance of such commitment. This also represents a theoretical contribution to the KM perspective due to the unique nature of family firms and, hence, enhances our understanding of the direct and conditional effects of this view across different settings. Consequently, our study also has a practical implication for family firms, which should have an awareness of the importance of knowledge and organizational learning to preserve it as an organization's advantage.

This chapter is divided into five sections. This introduction is followed by the "Theoretical background, research model, and hypotheses" section, where we review the key literature about the topic of this study and we justify the research hypotheses. In the third section, we discuss the methodology used in the empirical study. The fourth section presents the results of the empirical analysis. The chapter closes with a discussion and conclusions section, where findings are discussed and, compared with previous studies, research limitations are mentioned and new avenues for future research are suggested.

2 Theoretical Background, Research Model, and Hypotheses

Most organizations need to transform themselves at one time or another to adapt to the environment they operate. For this reason, in strategic management research, there is a long history of researching variables that help explain organizational failure and success in adapting to changing environments (Ginsberg & Venkatraman, 1992). Strategic renewal constitutes a promising attempt to shed light on this phenomenon (Albert et al., 2015) because it is considered a dynamic management process of modifying or replacing an organization's current business model to address emerging environmental opportunities and risks for long-term survival and prosperity (Lester & Parnell, 2002; Schmitt et al., 2018). Consequently, strategic renewal has drawn sustained interest from strategy scholars during the last years (Al Humaidan & Sabatier, 2017; Pratap & Saha, 2018; Schmitt et al., 2018), especially in key research domains such as competitive strategy (Agarwal & Helfat, 2009; Capron & Mitchell, 2009), corporate entrepreneurship (Kuratko & Audretsch, 2009, 2013; Verbeke, Chrisman, & Yuan, 2007; Zahra, 1996), and strategy process (Volberda, Baden-Fuller, & Van Den Bosch, 2001).

The widespread attention paid to strategic renewal seems to indicate that it constitutes an emergent, vibrant, and flourishing research area (Klammer, Gueldenberg, Kraus, & O'Dwyer, 2017; Schmitt et al., 2018). However, we are only beginning to understand how firms can undertake such strategic renewal (Capron & Mitchell, 2009). Thus, to improve our knowledge about how firms face the important challenge of exploring new ways while simultaneously exploiting what they have already learned (Crossan & Berdrow, 2003), more research is required (Glaser, Fourné, & Elfring, 2015; Riviere et al., 2018). To narrow this research gap and convinced that organizations adapt only as fast as they learn (Mavondo, Chimhanzi, & Stewart, 2005) and that knowledge is a core competency (Liu, Chan, Zhao, & Liu, 2018), we propose the research model depicted in Fig. 1. Hypotheses included in Fig. 1 are discussed with detail below.

2.1 *Commitment to Learning and Knowledge Management Practices*

Commitment to learning constitutes an organization's cultural value that reflects the degree to which such organization is likely to promote a learning culture (Sackmann, 1991; Sinkula et al., 1997). Thus, if an organization considers learning as a crucial

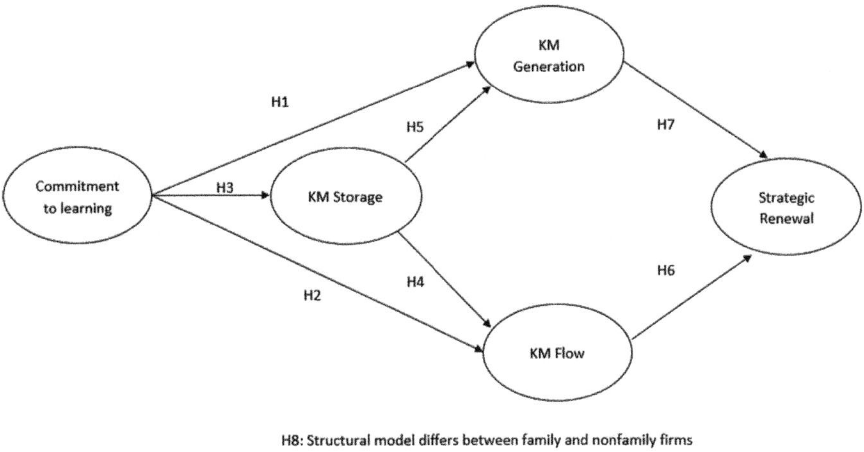

Fig. 1 Model proposal. Source: Authors' own figure

investment for survival, the more likely it is that learning occurs, whereas if an organization places little value on learning and does not encourage the development of knowledge, employees will not be motivated to pursue learning activities (Calantone, Cavusgil, & Zhao, 2002; Sinkula et al., 1997). Therefore, we consider that commitment to learning will promote the different KM practices. However, in our view, the influence of commitment to learning on KM practices may be different for different practices. To address this possibility, and in line with Yang, Nomoto, and Kurokawa's (2013), we analyze three types of KM practices: generation, flow, and storage practices. KM generation practices refer to developing new knowledge content or replacing existing content in the organization's explicit or tacit knowledge pool (Alavi & Leidner, 2001). KM flow practices refer to the integration of knowledge from different sources to develop organizational capability through mechanisms based on routines, norms, or decision-making in specific situations, as well as the application of existing knowledge to organizational activities and problem-solving (Grant, 1996; Zack, McKeen, & Singh, 2009). KM flow practices also include those activities that permit organization's members to share, disseminate, and replicate information, spreading this information to locations that need and can put to good effect the organization's existing knowledge. Finally, KM storage practices are those practices that include the organization, structuring, and retrieval of organizational knowledge and allow the firm to maintain an organizational memory (Donate & Sánchez de Pablo, 2015).

"In general, organizational learning inevitably includes the discovery and correction of errors" (Klammer et al., 2017, p. 743). Therefore, business organizations that are committed to learning tend to recognize the need to understand both the cause and effect of their actions. This, in turn, is a necessary condition for businesses are able to regularly detect and correct errors in their theories in use (Brachos, Kostopoulos, Soderquist, & Prastacos, 2007; Crossan, Lane, & White, 1999), which is in line with Hanvanich, Sivakumar, and Hult (2006), who argue that commitment to learning promotes new knowledge generation in all levels of the organization. Moreover, some studies relate executive commitment to learning to the success of knowledge codification (LeBrasseur, Whissell, & Ojham 2002; Swift & Hwang, 2008). If we understand the executive commitment to learning as an expression of the organization's commitment to learning, and considering that knowledge codification facilitates both the exchange and storage of knowledge, it seems reasonable to think that commitment to learning boosts the knowledge management flow and storage practices. Therefore, we formally state the following hypotheses:

Hypothesis 1 *Commitment to learning is positively associated to knowledge management generation of the firm.*

Hypothesis 2 *Commitment to learning is positively associated to knowledge management flow of the firm.*

Hypothesis 3 *Commitment to learning is positively associated to knowledge management storage of the firm.*

2.2 Relationship Between KM Storage and KM Flow/Generation

In SMEs, knowledge is often retained at the individual level, mostly in a small number of managers (Wong & Aspinwall, 2005). Knowledge storage practices allow the firm to remember what the company already knows (Donate & Sánchez de Pablo, 2015) because such practices are about filing, structuring, or gathering data, information, and organizational knowledge, which may reside in different forms such as written documentation, electronic databases, codified human knowledge stored in expert systems, or tacit knowledge acquired by individuals and networks of individuals, among others (Alavi & Tiwana, 2003; Donate & Sánchez de Pablo, 2015; Zack, 1999). Empirical evidence reveals that repositories of codified knowledge permit the company to transfer, use, and integrate knowledge modules (Purvis, Sambamurthy, & Zmud, 2001). Similarly, the development of an adequate mapping of knowledge in storage devices has been reported to be useful for knowledge sharing and transfer (Lai, Wang, & Chou, 2009). All previous arguments lead us to think that the existence of KM storage practices promote both KM flow practices and KM generation practices. Therefore, we formally propose the following two research hypotheses:

Hypothesis 4 *Knowledge management storage is positively associated to knowledge management flow.*

Hypothesis 5 *Knowledge management storage is positively associated to knowledge management generation.*

2.3 Relationship Between KM Flow/Generation and Strategic Renewal

In organizations, there are three patterns of knowledge flow: collecting new knowledge, which intensifies its vertical flow; codifying knowledge requiring both horizontal and vertical flows; and combining new and old knowledge (Sher & Lee, 2004). To properly manage these flows, it is essential to develop KM flow practices, which include systems or initiatives to codify tacit into explicit knowledge. Although the shorter lines of interaction within the smaller firms make the dissemination of tacit knowledge easier than it is in larger firms (Koskinen & Vanharanta, 2002), we think that such KM flow practices positively impact on the business' strategic renewal.

Moreover, resource-based view (Barney, 1991) and knowledge-based view (Leonard-Barton, 1992) propose that knowledge is the primary strategic resource of any organization. Thus, when it is appropriately managed, it allows the organization to create value for its exploitation and production (DeCarolis & Deeds, 1999; Zack et al., 2009). In our view, this proper management begins with the KM generation practices, which include cross-functional teamwork, employees' participation, as well as reward and recognition, and promotes the employees' participation in problem-solving (Aldakhil, 2016); in this case, the adaptation to the environment is the problem to resolve. Thus, we formally hypothesize:

Hypothesis 6 *Knowledge management flow is positively associated to strategic renewal.*

Hypothesis 7 *Knowledge management generation is positively associated to strategic renewal.*

2.4 Knowledge Management in FF and NFF

The ongoing evolutionary nature of strategic renewal implies that system-inherent characteristics influence whether firms engage in strategic renewal (Albert et al., 2015). In this sense, literature reports that trusted work settings facilitate knowledge sharing and transfer, as well as the knowledge creation (Chen, Elnaghi, & Hatzakis, 2011), and that strong relationships promote the codification of knowledge in a common language (Bojica et al., 2017). Similarly, the existence of strong ties constitutes a significant complement to the transfer of codified knowledge (Bojica et al., 2017), because in the case of strong relationship, the transmitter of knowledge seems to be more attentive and willing to try to ensure that the receiver of knowledge understands and can use the knowledge acquired (Hansen, 1999; Levin & Cross, 2004).

Family firms constitute a peculiar organizational context where the identity overlap between the family and the firm tends to affect the KM process (Biscotti et al., 2018), thus suggesting the relevance to explore this unique context (Andersen, 2015; Fang, Kotlar, Memili, Chrisman, & De Massis, 2018; Gupta & Bhattacharya, 2016). Specifically, the differences between family and nonfamily firm are justified by at least one if not both of the following reasons. First, family firms are characterized by an "ability-willingness paradox" (Casprini, De Massis, Di Minin, Frattini, & Piccaluga, 2017; De Massis, Di Minin, & Frattini, 2015) being usually characterized by adopting an internal oriented approach, investing less in R&D, and being more reluctant to acquire new technology (Kotlar, De Massis, Frattini, Bianchi, & Fang, 2013). Whereby, family firms are traditionally expected to have less capacity to collect and store knowledge (Aldrich & Herker, 1977; Andersen, 2015; DiPasquale & McInerney, 2010). Second, family firms are considered as an organizational context often characterized by idiosyncratic strategic behaviors (Biscotti et al., 2018; Hernández-Linares & López-Fernández, 2018; Miller & Le Breton-Miller, 2014), mostly driven by its long-term orientation (Fang et al., 2018; Higginson, 2010) and the strong ties among their members. Also, the cohesiveness and emotional attachment among family members may contribute to their capacity to transfer knowledge-based resources (Chirico & Salvato, 2016). That is, family firms are motivated to place a higher priority on enhancing the communication, sharing, and integration of knowledge, leading to greater value creation (Chirico & Salvato, 2008, 2016), and to preserve and extend organization's competitive advantage (Bjuggren & Sund, 2001; Cabrera-Suárez, De Saá-Pérez, & García-Almeida, 2001; Jaskiewicz, Uhlenbruck, Balkin, & Reay, 2013; Kellermanns & Eddleston, 2004). As a result, it could be expected that family firms develop a further enhancement of commitment to learning which the primary goal is to promote the implementation of KM generation, KM storage, and KM flow practices to enhance strategic renewal than nonfamily firms. Hence, we hypothesize:

Hypothesis 8 *Structural relationships between commitment to learning, knowledge management practices, and strategic renewal differ for family and nonfamily firms.*

3 Methodology

3.1 Population and Sample Selection

We studied SMEs from Spain compiled from the SABI database (Iberian Balance Sheets Analysis System—*Sistema de Análisis de Balances Ibéricos*), which provides detailed data of the financial statements filed in commercial registries and has been used by previous studies (e.g., Bojica et al., 2017; Cruz, Gómez-Mejía, & Becerra, 2010; Hernández-Linares et al., 2018a; Hernández-Linares, Kellermanns, & López-Fernández, 2018b). We operationalize private SMEs as non-listed businesses with 10–249 employees (Hernández-Linares et al., 2018a, 2018b). In order to obtain a representative sample of the population, and in line with previous studies (Sánchez-

Famoso, Maseda, & Iturralde, 2014), we eliminated companies affected by particular situations, such as sind-up, liquidation, insolvency, or zero activity.

Given the nature of this research and the consequent lack of secondary information, data used in this paper, which are part of a more extensive study, were collected using a survey instrument, consistent with previous studies (Bojica et al., 2017; Carrasco-Hernández & Jiménez-Jiménez, 2016; Hernandez-Perlines, 2018). Before launching the survey, five pretesting with executives of companies, not included in the final sample, and academics took place to validate the questionnaire. Such pretests guaranteed that the questions raised were perceived and result from simple drafting of the respondent, being able to respond naturally and spontaneously. Then, during the month of December of 2017, questionnaires were applied by telephone to CEOs, since they are the executives with the highest information access (Hernández-Perlines, 2016) from a wide range of departments and are considered a reliable source in upper-echelon research (Eddleston, Kellermanns, Floyd, Crittenden, & Crittenden, 2013; Sharma, Chrisman, & Chua, 2003). Finally, 238 questionnaires were fully completed. Non-response bias is tested by analyzing differences between respondents and non-respondents for a given set of variables.

3.2 *Measures*

Among the different measures appeared in the literature for assessing KM practices, this study uses the Donate and Sánchez de Pablo's (2015) scale, which measures five types of KM practices identified by Donate and Sánchez de Pablo (2015). However, these five types were grouped in three constructs following Yang et al.'s (2013) arguments: KM generation practices (acquisition and creation practices), KM flow practices (application and transfer practices), and KM storage practices. All of them were measured using a Likert-type scale with a five-point response ranging from 1 = "totally disagree" to 5 = "totally agree."

Commitment to learning and strategic renewal were measured following Sinkula et al. (1997) and Burgers and Covin (2016), respectively. We identified family firms through a subjective criterion: we asked the SMEs' CEOs whether or not they perceived their firm as a family business (Cooper, Upton, & Seaman, 2005), which allowed us to capture the essence of being a family firm (Chua, Chrisman, & Sharma, 1999). According to the CEOs' self-perception, 181 firms were classified as family firms, the remaining being classified as nonfamily firms.

3.3 *Data Analysis*

This study employs variance-based structural equation modeling (partial least squares—PLS) to test the proposed research model (Fig. 1). Two main reasons justify this decision. First, the study is exploratory, so PLS is considered the most appropriate tool (Hair, Sarstedt, Hopkins, & Kuppelwieser, 2014; Hemmert, Kim, Kim, & Cho, 2016). Second, this study tests a research model with a complex structure which makes PLS appropriate (Calvo-Mora, Ruiz-Moreno, Picón-Berjoyo, & Cauzo-Bottala, 2014; Chowdhury & Quaddus, 2017; Henseler, Ringle, & Sinkovics, 2009).

Specifically, Smart PLS software, version 3, was used to develop a multi-group analysis that considers family firm as a moderator variable (dummy variable). Notably, the multi-group analysis divides the whole sample into two subsamples: family firms (181 firms) and nonfamily firms (58 firms). Considering Cohen's power tables (1988) both samples meet the minimum sample size criteria to obtain a power of 0.80 ($\alpha = 0.05$).

4 Empirical Analysis

This section presents the results of the PLS-SEM analysis. The procedure to test the model depicted in Fig. 1 includes two steps: first, a measurement model assessment for guarantying scale validity and reliability, and second, a structural model analysis.

4.1 Measurement Model Assessment

The first stage of the measurement model assessment consists of observing the indicators' loading values in the models of both subsamples: the model for family firms and the model for nonfamily firms. Table 1 shows the parameters.

It was found that the loading factors of all items exceeded 0.6 (Hair, Anderson, Tatham, & Black, 1999), and the composite reliability measures for the scales surpassed the recommended minimum 0.7 threshold (Carmines & Zeller, 1979). By its part, average variance extracted (AVE) rates also exceeded from the recommended minimum 0.5 (Fornell & Larcker, 1981). These values support the convergent validity of the composite scales of both models.

Also, Table 2 shows the results of the heterotrait-monotrait ratio (HTMT), which is used to assess discriminant validity. Results were well below the 0.90 thresholds (Hair et al., 2014; Henseler, Ringle, & Sarstedt, 2015), thus confirming discriminant validity.

As a result, Tables 1 and 2 support the reliability and validity of the measurement model, both for the model that represents the whole sample of companies and for the family and nonfamily firm's subsamples.

Table 1 Composites and measures

		FF			NFF		
	Items	Outer loadings	Composite reliability	AVE	Outer loadings	Composite reliability	AVE
CL	CL1	0.841	0.911	0.673	0.850	0.911	0.674
	CL2	0.869			0.898		
	CL3	0.865			0.910		
	CL4	0.873			0.855		
	CL5	0.833			0.830		
KMF	KMF1	0.930	0.927	0.863	0.943	0.932	0.872
	KMF2	0.928			0.921		
KMG	KMG1	0.877	0.824	0.701	0.857	0.786	0.650
	KMG2	0.873			0.850		
KMS	KMS1	0.806	0.854	0.539	0.695	0.836	0.507
	KMS2	0.795			0.733		
	KMS3	0.760			0.779		
	KMS4	0.756			0.670		
	KMS5	0.726			0.708		
SR	SR1	0.903	0.902	0.697	0.892	0.916	0.732
	SR2	0.877			0.857		
	SR3	0.873			0.850		
	SR4	0.869			0.898		

Source: Authors' own table

AVE average variance extracted, *CL* commitment to learning, *FF* family firms, *KMF* knowledge management flow, *KMG* knowledge management generation, *KMS* knowledge management storage, *NFF* nonfamily firms, *SR* strategic renewal

4.2 *Structural Model Analysis*

After measurement model assessment, the structural model analysis confirms that commitment to learning has a positive and significant effect on KM practices and that KM practices have a positive and significant effect on strategic renewal, thus supporting H1–H7 (see Table 3). F^2 column shows the size of these effects ($F^2 > 0.02$ weak effect, $F^2 > 0.15$ moderated effect and $F^2 > 0.35$ strong effect).

With regard to goodness-of-fit of the model, Henseler et al. (2014), taking as reference the goodness-of-fit criteria proposed in SEM based on covariances, developed and empirically validated an overall measure of goodness-of-fit applicable in PLS, called standardized root mean square residual (SRMR). This measure represents the Euclidean distance between the empirical correlation matrix and the model-implied correlation matrix (Hu & Bentler, 1999). In our study, the value of the SRMR indicator is 0.07 ($R^2 = 0.357$) below the 0.08 recommending threshold (Henseler et al., 2014), which confirms that the goodness-of-fit of the model is satisfactory.

Table 2 Heterotrait-monotrait ratio (HTMT)

	Group					FF					NFF				
	CL	KMF	KMG	KMS	SR	CL	KMF	KMG	KMS	SR	CL	KMF	KMG	KMS	SR
CL															
KMF	0.599					0.597					0.603				
KMG	0.541	0.730				0.613	0.748				0.298	0.685			
KMS	0.565	0.763	0.708			0.516	0.793	0.709			0.712	0.669	0.702		
SR	0.492	0.647	0.585	0.604		0.534	0.718	0.602	0.633		0.374	0.453	0.535	0.518	

Source: Authors' own table

CL commitment to learning, *FF* family firms, *KMF* knowledge management flow, *KMG* knowledge management generation, *KMS* knowledge management storage, *NFF* nonfamily firms, *SR* strategic renewal

Table 3 Results of the structural model

	B	*p*-values	F^2
Commitment to learning → KM flow	0.287	0.000	0.116
Commitment to learning → KM generation	0.201	0.002	0.043
Commitment to learning → KM storage	0.476	0.000	0.293
KM flow → Strategic renewal	0.354	0.000	0.109
KM generation → Strategic renewal	0.124	0.030	0.017
KM storage → KM flow	0.487	0.000	0.336
KM storage → KM generation	0.390	0.000	0.161

Source: Authors' own table
CL commitment to learning, *FF* family firms, *KMF* knowledge management flow, *KMG* knowledge management generation, *KMS* knowledge management storage, *NFF* nonfamily firms, *SR* strategic renewal

4.3 Multi-group Analysis

The multi-group analysis follows the testing of the structural model. However, the previous guarantee of metric invariance across groups is necessary. To this end, the MICOM (measurement invariance of composite models) procedure is recommended (Henseler et al., 2015).

The MICOM procedure can be undertaken in three steps: (1) configural invariance, (2) compositional invariance, and (3) the equality of composite mean values and variances. If configural and compositional invariances are established, partial measurement invariance is confirmed, which allows one to compare path coefficient estimates across the groups. Besides, if partial measurement invariance holds and the composite's mean values and variances are equal across the groups, full measurement invariance is confirmed, which supports the pooled data analysis (Schlägel & Sarstedt, 2016).

Table 4 summarizes the results of the first step in the MICOM procedure, which involves examining configural invariance (Henseler, Ringle, & Sarstedt, 2016). The assessment of configural invariance consists of an evaluation of the measurement models for all groups to determine if the same basic factor structure exists in all the groups (same number of constructs as well as items for those constructs). In this regard, the results of Table 4 confirm that configural invariance is established—items were designed as equivalent across groups (Henseler et al., 2016).

The second step of the MICOM procedure examines, through the use of non-parametric permutation tests (Henseler et al., 2016), compositional invariance, which occurs when composite scores are created equally across groups (Dijkstra & Henseler, 2011). To this end, permutation test compares the composite scores of the first and second groups to determine if the original correlation is equal to or or greater than the 5.00% quantile correlations (shown in the 5% column). Results, summarized in Table 5, confirm compositional invariance—the original correlations being equal to or higher than the 5.00% quantile correlations (shown in the 5% column).

Table 4 MICOM Step 1 procedure configural invariance

	Items	Outer loadings-diff (|FF − NFF|)	*p*-value (FF vs. NFF)
CL	CL1	0.020	0.426
	CL2	0.048	0.901
	CL3	0.021	0.647
	CL4	0.025	0.620
	CL5	0.073	0.294
KMF	KMF1	0.012	0.765
	KMF2	0.011	0.512
KMG	KMG1	0.011	0.512
	KMG2	0.046	0.402
KMS	KMS1	0.101	0.151
	KMS2	0.017	0.453
	KMS3	0.083	0.281
	KMS4	0.119	0.910
	KMS5	0.035	0.405
SR	SR1	0.012	0.377
	SR2	0.034	0.821
	SR3	0.006	0.583
	SR4	0.059	0.774

Source: Authors' own table

CL commitment to learning, *FF* family firms, *KMF* knowledge management flow, *KMG* knowledge management generation, *KMS* knowledge management storage, *NFF* nonfamily firms, *SR* strategic renewal

Table 5 MICOM Step 2 results report

	Original correlation	Correlation permutation mean	5.0%	Permutation *p*-values	Compositional invariance?
CL	1.000	0.997	0.993	0.921	Yes
KMF	1.000	1.000	0.999	0.303	Yes
KMG	0.997	0.993	0.972	0.492	Yes
KMS	0.998	0.994	0.983	0.769	Yes
SR	1.000	0.998	0.995	0.943	Yes

Source: Authors' own table

CL commitment to learning, *KMF* knowledge management flow, *KMG* knowledge management generation, *KMS* knowledge management storage, *SR* strategic renewal

The third step of the MICOM procedure consists of assessing the constructs' equality of mean values and variances across the groups (see Table 6). For invariance to be established, the first column (mean original difference or variance original difference) must be a number that falls within the 95% confidence interval. This is assessed by comparing the mean original difference or variance original difference to the lower (2.5%) and upper (97.5%) boundaries shown in columns three and four. If mean and variance values are within the range of the lower and upper boundaries, then the equality of composite mean values and variances are assessed.

Table 6 MICOM Step 3 results report

	Mean – original difference (FF – NFF)	Mean – permutation mean difference (FF – NFF)	2.5%	97.5%	Permutation *p*-values	Equal mean values?
CL	0.058	0.003	−0.284	0.303	0.711	Yes
KMF	0.035	0.002	−0.295	0.302	0.817	Yes
KMG	0.209	0.003	−0.283	0.313	0.168	Yes
KMS	0.071	0.006	−0.285	0.297	0.639	Yes
SR	0.056	0.000	−0.288	0.302	0.696	Yes
	Variance – original difference (FF – NFF)	Variance – permutation mean difference (FF – NFF)	2.5%	97.5%	Permutation *p*-values	Equal variances?
CL	−0.018	0.029	−0.591	0.651	0.955	Yes
KMF	−0.189	0.022	−0.365	0.432	0.353	Yes
KMG	−0.049	0.018	−0.307	0.392	0.776	Yes
KMS	0.075	0.017	−0.332	0.388	0.685	Yes
SR	−0.122	0.018	−0.329	0.406	0.501	Yes

Source: Authors' own table

CL commitment to learning, *FF* family firm, *KMF* knowledge management flow, *KMG* knowledge management generation, *KMS* knowledge management storage, *NFF* nonfamily firms, *SR* strategic renewal

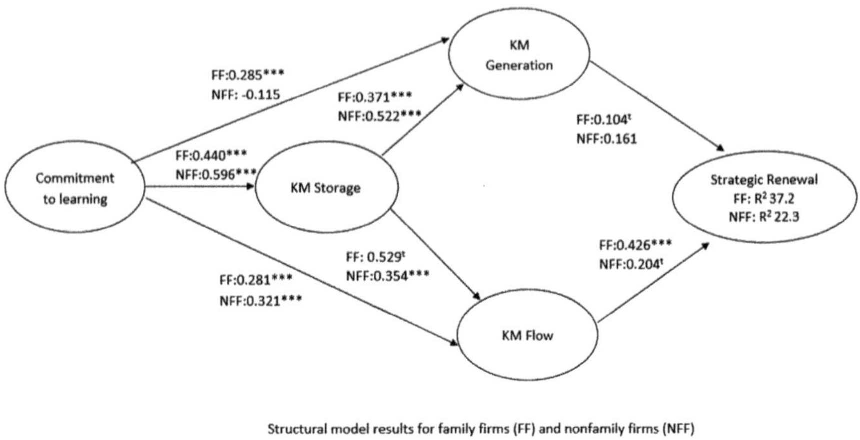

Fig. 2 A structural model for FF and NFF. Source: Authors' own figure

Table 7 Bootstrapping FF versus NFF path values

	Path coefficients (FF)	Path coefficients (NFF)	*p*-values (FF)	*p*-values (NFF)
CL → KMF	0.281	0.321	0.000	0.002
CL → KMG	0.285	−0.115	0.000	0.246
CL → KMS	0.440	0.596	0.000	0.000
KMF → SR	0.426	0.204	0.000	0.091
KMG → SR	0.104	0.161	0.097	0.116
KMS → KMF	0.529	0.354	0.000	0.003
KMS → KMG	0.371	0.522	0.000	0.000

Source: Authors' own table
CL commitment to learning, *FF* family firm, *KMF* knowledge management flow, *KMG* knowledge management generation, *KMS* knowledge management storage, *NFF* nonfamily firms, *SR* strategic renewal

Overall, results of Tables 4, 5, and 6 confirm the three types of invariance. Thus, full measurement invariance is confirmed. Once invariance is established, the multi-group analysis is therefore possible. Subsequently, PLS estimates paths' coefficients for family firms and nonfamily firms' subsamples (see Fig. 2) for determining if the path coefficients of the theoretical model are significantly different among these two groups (Table 7).

As noted in Table 7, two relationships of the proposed model indicate differences across groups. First, the relationship between commitment to learning and KM generation is significant for family firms (p-value = 0.000) and is not for nonfamily firms (p-value = 0.246). Second, the relationship between KM generation and strategic renewal is significant for family firms (p-value = 0.097) and not for nonfamily firms (p-value = 0.116). The other relationships do not indicate a major difference between family and nonfamily firms.

The last necessary step for confirming that the dummy variable has a moderating effect is to test if the differences identified in Table 7 are significant. Thus, permutation tests and PLS-MGA were employed. Results of both tests are summarized in Table 8. A permutation *p*-value of less than or equal to 0.10 designates a significant difference between the two groups of interest (Matthews, 2017). A PLS-MGA test *p*-value of less than or equal to 0.05 or greater than 0.95 designates significant difference.

As Table 8 shows, it could be confirmed that the relationship between commitment to learning and KM generation practices relationship is positively moderated by being a family firm, even though the intensity of the moderating effect is weak ($F^2 = 0.08$). This result partially supports H8, suggesting that organizational context moderates only one of the relationships proposed in the structural model. In this regard, difference between family firms and nonfamily firms is lesser than this study initially expected.

5 Discussion and Conclusions

This study had a double purpose. First, it tries to analyze how commitment to learning determines the KM practices and how such practices impact strategic renewal (H1–H7). Second, this study explores if previous relationships are different for family and nonfamily firms with the aim to capture differences arising from particular organizational contexts (H8).

Regarding the first purpose, and accordant to our initial expectation, the empirical results confirm direct effects represented by the hypotheses H1–H7. In this regard, results of this study support that the promotion of commitment to learning may create a set of opportunities and advantages that can stimulate learning attitude and affect the enhancement of KM practices, thus having a positive and significant effect on their development (supporting H1, H2, and H3). The advantages mentioned above may take the form of activities of knowledge generation, knowledge flow, or knowledge storage, which can also be decisive for creating an internal organizational climate that supports strategic renewal process (H6 and H7). More specifically, commitment to learning has a stronger effect on the development of KM storage and KM flow practices and a lesser effect on KM generation practices (see Table 3). By its part, among the different KM practices that have been proposed to explain failure or success in adapting to changing environments, strategic renewal, KM flow appears as the main pivotal KM practice (see Table 3).

Overall, these findings suggest that both commitments to learning and KM practices implementation are the main undercurrent of the strategic renewal process. Thus, organizations should realize the relevance of promoting both of them to achieve growth and development through the potential of strategic renewal (Crossan & Berdrow, 2003; Jain & Moreno, 2015). This result is particularly relevant for SMEs, where in many cases there is no formal knowledge management strategy (Durst & Edvardsson, 2012). In this regard, strategic renewal is strongly shaped by

Table 8 Permutation and PLS-MGA test report results

	Permutation test							PLS-MGA test	
	Path coefficients' original (FF)	Path coefficients' original (NFF)	Path coefficients' original difference (FF – NFF)	Path coefficients' permutation mean difference (FF – NFF)	2.5%	97.5%	Permutation *p*-values	Path coefficients – diff (|FF – NFF|)	*p*-value (EF vs. NFF)
CL → KMF	0.281	0.322	−0.040	0.003	−0.243	0.262	0.762	0.040	0.638
CL → KMG	0.284	−0.128	0.412	0.001	−0.320	0.332	0.014	0.412	0.014
CL → KMS	0.440	0.596	−0.156	−0.012	−0.263	0.257	0.260	0.156	0.919
KMF → SR	0.428	0.208	0.220	0.003	−0.357	0.383	0.244	0.220	0.117
KMG → SR	0.104	0.159	−0.055	−0.002	−0.319	0.315	0.734	0.055	0.650
KMS → KMF	0.529	0.353	0.176	−0.005	−0.242	0.237	0.150	0.176	0.109
KMS → KMG	0.371	0.536	−0.165	−0.010	−0.321	0.325	0.317	0.165	0.859

Source: Authors' own table

CL commitment to learning, *FF* family firm, *KMF* knowledge management flow, *KMG* knowledge management generation, *KMS* knowledge management storage, *NFF* nonfamily firms, *SR* strategic renewal proactive knowledge strategies that promote knowledge activities that permit organization's members to share, disseminate, and replicate information, spreading this information to locations that need and can put to good effect the organization's existing knowledge. Also, and in line with previous studies (Donate & Sánchez de Pablo, 2015; Lai et al., 2009; Purvis et al., 2001), the analysis also confirmed the relevance of KM storage to promote both KM flow and KM generation practices (supporting H4 and H5). Thus, suggesting managers should also promote KM storage activities—such as written documentation, information stored in electronic databases, codified human knowledge stored in expert systems, or documented organizational procedures—to maintain an organizational memory, which encompasses knowledge that resides in various forms.

Regarding the second purpose, the results show that although family firms have been characterized by either an "ability-willingness paradox" (Casprini et al., 2017; De Massis et al., 2015) that reduce their capacity to acquire knowledge or an idiosyncratic strategic behavior (Biscotti et al., 2018; Miller & Le Breton-Miller, 2014), mostly driven by its long-term orientation and the strong ties among their members that promotes knowledge sharing (Cunningham, Seaman, & McGuire, 2017; Fang et al., 2018; Higginson, 2010), the results ultimately fail to offer evidence in support of this hypothesis. Results show that the differences between family and nonfamily firms are less pronounced than we expected at first sight (H8 was partially supported). The only significant difference identified by this study is noted in the relationship between commitment to learning and KM generation (Table 8). In other words, within the family firms' group, the promotion of a commitment to learning culture is a better effective way of obtaining strategic renewal via the exploitation of KM generation. This result suggests a valuable managerial implication for family firm owners and managers by suggesting that family firms can overcome critical barriers that traditionally surround its KM generation (Duran, Kammerlander, Van Essen, & Zellweger, 2016; Fosfuri & Tribó, 2008) by promoting a commitment to learning the culture. This is an interesting result that deserves much more investigation in the future, thus opening the door to new research. For example, our study reports that being a family firm impacts on the relationships between commitment to learning, KM practices, and strategic renewal. In this regard, it would be interesting that future studies explore if these previous relationships vary across different types of family firms, in order to which taxonomies or archetypes appeared in literature could be a starting point [for a full review of taxonomies appeared in literature, see Hernández-Linares, Sarkar, and López-Fernández (2017)].

Similarly, we call for researching the influence of family governance on learning mechanisms and relationships researched in this work. More specifically, it would be interesting to explore if the succession process of family firms affects the enhancement of a learning culture that promotes KM practices, thus comparing family firms in the first generation with family firms in second or later generations. Recent theoretical contributions (Cabrera-Suárez, García-Almeida, & De Saá-Pérez, 2018; Scuotto, Giudice, Holden, & Mattiacci, 2017) support this proposal by suggesting that predecessors consider the transfer of knowledge as a critical resource for keeping the competitive advantage of the family firm by enhancing the successor's development.

Despite the contributions of this study to the family business, knowledge management, and strategic renewal literature, it is also important to acknowledge its limitations. First, this study is cross-sectional and uses subjective measures. Although cross-sectional designs are standard in strategic literature (e.g., Bojica et al., 2017; Klammer et al., 2017), employing a cross-sectional design constrains the strength of the causal inferences that can be made. Hence, a longitudinal design might help to elucidate the findings further; for example, whether the effect of commitment to learning on different KM practices changes over time as the economic situation of Spain evolves. To overcome the single informant bias, the study follows the recommendations in Dal Zotto and Van Kranenburg (2008). Second, this research is limited to one country under investigation (Spain), and although globalization seems to lead to similarities in business conduct across countries (e.g., Carr, 2005), we recognize that organizations may be affected by national cultures (Hofstede, 2001) and can offer different answers to the same problem depending on the cultural factors that surround them. Hence, to extend our research to other countries and cultural contexts would enrich our results. In particular, and in line with recent studies (Hernández-Linares & López-Fernández, 2018; López-Fernández, Serrano-Bedia, & Pérez-Pérez, 2016), we call to replicate our research in countries with a different conception of the family, this being the case of many African countries, where kinship is understood to go beyond the nuclear family and include a more extensive network of relatives (Khayesi, George, & Antonakis, 2014). Third, the generalizability of our findings is also limited by the nature of the sample used in this study, and it remains for future studies to determine whether these results will hold for larger or listed companies.

References

Agarwal, R., & Helfat, C. E. (2009). Strategic renewal of organizations. *Organization Science, 20* (2), 281–293.

Al Humaidan, S., & Sabatier, V. (2017). Strategic renewal in times of environmental scarcity: The mediating role of technology in business model evolution. *Journal of Organizational Change Management, 30*(1), 106–120.

Alavi, M., & Leidner, D. E. (2001). Knowledge management and knowledge management systems: Conceptual foundations and research issues. *MIS Quarterly, 25*(1), 107–136.

Alavi, M., & Tiwana, A. (2003). Knowledge management: The information technology dimension. In M. Easterby-Smith & M. A. Lyles (Eds.), *Organizational learning and knowledge management* (pp. 104–121). London: Blackwell.

Albert, D., Kreutzer, M., & Lechner, C. (2015). Resolving the paradox of interdependency and strategic renewal in activity systems. *Academy of Management Review, 40*(2), 210–234.

Aldakhil, A. M. (2016). Linking quality management practices and effective knowledge integration to new product development (NPD): An empirical study of Saudi-firms. *International Journal of Financial Research, 7*(2), 1–10.

Aldrich, H., & Herker, D. (1977). Boundary spanning roles and organization structure. *Academy of Management Review, 2*(2), 217–230.

Andersen, J. (2015). The absorptive capacity of family firms: How familiness affects potential and realized absorptive capacity. *Journal of Family Business Management, 5*(1), 73–89.

Argote, L., McEvily, B., & Reagans, R. (2003). Managing knowledge in organizations: An integrative framework and review of emerging themes. *Management Science, 49*(4), 571–582.

Ayyagari, M., Beck, T., & Demirguc-Kunt, A. (2007). Small and medium enterprises across the globe. *Small Business Economics, 29*(4), 415–434.

Barney, J. (1991). Firm resources and sustained competitive advantage. *Journal of Management, 17* (1), 99–120.

Biscotti, A. M., D'Amico, E., & Monge, F. (2018). Do environmental management systems affect the knowledge management process? The impact on the learning evolution and the relevance of organisational context. *Journal of Knowledge Management, 22*(3), 603–620.

Bjuggren, P. O., & Sund, L. G. (2001). Strategic decision making in intergenerational successions of small-and medium-size family-owned businesses. *Family Business Review, 14*(1), 11–23.

Bojica, A. M., & Fuentes-Fuentes, M. M. (2012). Knowledge acquisition and corporate entrepreneurship: Insights from Spanish SMEs in the ICT sector. *Journal of World Business, 47*(3), 397–408.

Bojica, A. M., Arroyo, M. R., & Fuentes, M. D. M. F. (2012). La adquisición de conocimiento a través de relaciones interorganizativas y la orientación emprendedora: el papel mediador del capital social de segundo orden. *Cuadernos de Economía y Dirección de la Empresa, 15*(3), 141–153.

Bojica, A. M., Fuentes-Fuentes, M. M., & Fernández, V. (2017). Corporate entrepreneurship and codification of the knowledge acquired from strategic partners in SMEs. *Journal of Small Business Management, 55*(S1), 205–230.

Brachos, D., Kostopoulos, K., Soderquist, E. K., & Prastacos, G. (2007). Knowledge effectiveness, social context and innovation. *Journal of Knowledge Management, 11*(5), 31–44.

Brettel, M., & Rottenberger, J. D. (2013). Examining the link between entrepreneurial orientation and learning processes in small and medium-sized enterprises. *Journal of Small Business Management, 51*(4), 471–490.

Burgers, J. H., & Covin, J. G. (2016). The contingent effects of differentiation and integration on corporate entrepreneurship. *Strategic Management Journal, 37*(3), 521–540.

Cabrera-Suárez, M. K., De Saá-Pérez, P., & García-Almeida, D. J. (2001). The succession process from a resource-and knowledge-based view of the family firm. *Family Business Review, 14*(1), 37–48.

Cabrera-Suárez, M. K., García-Almeida, D. J., & De Saá-Pérez, P. (2018). A dynamic network model of the successor's knowledge construction from the resource-and knowledge-based view of the family firm. *Family Business Review, 31*(2), 178–197.

Calantone, R. J., Cavusgil, S. T., & Zhao, Y. (2002). Learning orientation, firm innovation capability, and firm performance. *Industrial Marketing Management, 31*(6), 515–524.

Calvo-Mora, A., Navarro-García, A., Rey-Moreno, M., & Perianez-Cristobal, R. (2016). Excellence management practices, knowledge management and key business results in large organisations and SMEs: A multi-group analysis. *European Management Journal, 34*(6), 661–673.

Calvo-Mora, A., Ruiz-Moreno, C., Picón-Berjoyo, A., & Cauzo-Bottala, L. (2014). Mediation effect of TQM technical factors in excellence management systems. *Journal of Business Research, 67*(5), 769–774.

Capron, L., & Mitchell, W. (2009). Selection capability: How capability gaps and internal social frictions affect internal and external strategic renewal. *Organization Science, 20*(2), 294–312.

Carayannis, E. G., Samara, E. T., & Bakouros, Y. L. (2015). Innovation and competitiveness: Case study. In E. G. Carayannis (Ed.), *Innovation and entrepreneurship. Innovation, technology, and knowledge management* (pp. 47–72). Heidelberg: Cham.

Carmines, E. G., & Zeller, R. A. (1979). *Reliability and validity assessment* (Vol. 17). Thousand Oaks, CA: Sage.

Carr, C. (2005). Are German, Japanese and Anglo-Saxon strategic decision styles still divergent in the context of globalization? *Journal of Management Studies, 42*(6), 1155–1188.

Carrasco-Hernández, A. J., & Jiménez-Jiménez, D. (2016). Knowledge management, flexibility and firm performance: The effects of family involvement. *European Journal of Family Business, 6* (2), 108–117.

Casprini, E., De Massis, A., Di Minin, A., Frattini, F., & Piccaluga, A. (2017). How family firms execute open innovation strategies: The Loccioni case. *Journal of Knowledge Management, 21* (6), 1459–1485.

Chen, W., Elnaghi, M., & Hatzakis, T. (2011). Investigating knowledge management factors affecting Chinese ICT firms' performance: An integrated KM framework. *Information Systems Management, 28*(1), 19–29.

Chirico, F., & Salvato, C. (2008). Knowledge integration and dynamic organizational adaptation in family firms. *Family Business Review, 21*(2), 169–181.

Chirico, F., & Salvato, C. (2016). Knowledge internalization and product development in family firms: When relational and affective factors matter. *Entrepreneurship: Theory and Practice, 40* (1), 201–229.

Chowdhury, M., & Quaddus, M. (2017). Supply chain resilience: Conceptualization and scale development using dynamic capability theory. *International Journal of Production Economics, 188*, 185–204.

Chua, J. H., Chrisman, J. J., & Sharma, P. (1999). Defining the family business by behavior. *Entrepreneurship: Theory and Practice, 23*(4), 19–39.

Cohen, J. (1988). *Statistical power analysis for the behavioural sciences*. Abingdon: Taylor & Francis.

Cooper, M. J., Upton, N., & Seaman, S. (2005). Customer relationship management: A comparative analysis of family and nonfamily business practices. *Journal of Small Business Management, 43* (3), 242–256.

Crossan, M. M., & Berdrow, I. (2003). Organizational learning and strategic renewal. *Strategic Management Journal, 24*(11), 1087–1105.

Crossan, M. M., Lane, H. W., & White, R. E. (1999). An organizational learning framework: From intuition to institution. *Academy of Management Review, 24*(3), 522–537.

Cruz, C. C., Gómez-Mejía, L. R., & Becerra, M. (2010). Perceptions of benevolence and the design of agency contracts: CEO-TMT relationships in family firms. *Academy of Management Journal, 53*(1), 69–89.

Cunningham, J., Seaman, C., & McGuire, D. (2017). Perceptions of knowledge sharing among small family firm leaders: A structural equation model. *Family Business Review, 30*(2), 160–181.

Dal Zotto, C., & Van Kranenburg, H. (2008). *Management and innovation in the media industry*. Cheltenham: Edward Elgar.

Davenport, T. H., & Prusak, L. (1998). *Working knowledge: How organizations manage what they know*. Boston, MA: Harvard Business Press.

De Massis, A., Di Minin, A., & Frattini, F. (2015). Family-driven innovation: Resolving the paradox in family firms. *California Management Review, 58*(1), 5–19.

DeCarolis, D. M., & Deeds, D. L. (1999). The impact of stocks and flows of organizational knowledge on firm performance: An empirical investigation of the biotechnology industry. *Strategic Management Journal, 20*(10), 953–968.

Dijkstra, T. K., & Henseler, J. (2011). Linear indices in nonlinear structural equation models: Best fitting proper indices and other composites. *Quality & Quantity, 45*(6), 1505–1518.

DiPasquale, J., & McInerney, C. R. (2010). Knowledge management in small-and medium-sized enterprises. *Journal of Information & Knowledge Management, 9*(04), 341–353.

Donate, M. J., & Sánchez de Pablo, J. D. (2015). The role of knowledge-oriented leadership in knowledge management practices and innovation. *Journal of Business Research, 68*(2), 360–370.

Drnevich, P. L., & Kriauciunas, A. P. (2011). Clarifying the conditions and limits of the contributions of ordinary and dynamic capabilities to relative firm performance. *Strategic Management Journal, 32*(3), 254–279.

Duran, P., Kammerlander, N., Van Essen, M., & Zellweger, T. (2016). Doing more with less: Innovation input and output in family firms. *Academy of Management Journal, 59*(4), 1224–1264.

Durst, S., & Edvardsson, I. R. (2012). Knowledge management in SMEs: A literature review. *Journal of Knowledge Management, 16*(6), 879–903.

Eddleston, K. A., Kellermanns, F. W., Floyd, S. W., Crittenden, V. L., & Crittenden, W. F. (2013). Planning for growth: Life stage differences in family firms. *Entrepreneurship: Theory and Practice, 37*(5), 1177–1202.

Fang, H., Kotlar, J., Memili, E., Chrisman, J. J., & De Massis, A. (2018). The pursuit of international opportunities in family firms: Generational differences and the role of knowledge-based resources. *Global Strategy Journal, 8*(1), 136–157.

Floyd, S. W., & Lane, P. J. (2000). Strategizing throughout the organization: Managing role conflict in strategic renewal. *Academy of Management Review, 25*(1), 154–177.

Fornell, C., & Larcker, D. F. (1981). Evaluating structural equation models with unobservable variables and measurement error. *Journal of Marketing Research, 18*(1), 39–50.

Fosfuri, A., & Tribó, J. A. (2008). Exploring the antecedents of potential absorptive capacity and its impact on innovation performance. *Omega, 36*(2), 173–187.

Ginsberg, A., & Venkatraman, N. (1992). Investing in new information technology: The role of competitive posture and issue diagnosis. *Strategic Management Journal, 13*(S1), 37–53.

Glaser, L., Fourné, S. P., & Elfring, T. (2015). Achieving strategic renewal: The multi-level influences of top and middle managers' boundary-spanning. *Small Business Economics, 45* (2), 305–327.

Grant, R. M. (1996). Toward a knowledge-based theory of the firm. *Strategic Management Journal, 17*(S2), 109–122.

Gupta, P. D., & Bhattacharya, S. (2016). Impact of knowledge management processes for sustainability of small family businesses: Evidences from the Brassware Sector of Moradabad (India). *Journal of Information & Knowledge Management, 15*(04), 1650040.

Hair, J. F., Anderson, R. E., Tatham, R. L., & Black, W. C. (1999). *Análisis multivariante*. Madrid: Prentice Hall.

Hair, F. J., Jr., Sarstedt, M., Hopkins, L., & Kuppelwieser, V. G. (2014). Partial least squares structural equation modeling (PLS-SEM): An emerging tool in business research. *European Business Review, 26*(2), 106–121.

Hansen, M. T. (1999). The search-transfer problem: The role of weak ties in sharing knowledge across organization subunits. *Administrative Science Quarterly, 44*(1), 82–111.

Hanvanich, S., Sivakumar, K., & Hult, G. T. M. (2006). The relationship of learning and memory with organizational performance: The moderating role of turbulence. *Journal of the Academy of Marketing Science, 34*(4), 600–612.

Hemmert, M., Kim, D., Kim, J., & Cho, B. (2016). Building the supplier's trust: Role of institutional forces and buyer firm practices. *International Journal of Production Economics, 180*, 25–37.

Henseler, J., Dijkstra, T. K., Sarstedt, M., Ringle, C. M., Diamantopoulos, A., Straub, D. W., & Calantone, R. J. (2014). Common beliefs and reality about PLS: Comments on Rönkkö and Evermann (2013). *Organizational Research Methods, 17*(2), 182–209.

Henseler, J., Ringle, C. M., & Sarstedt, M. (2015). A new criterion for assessing discriminant validity in variance-based structural equation modeling. *Journal of the Academy of Marketing Science, 43*(1), 115–135.

Henseler, J., Ringle, C. M., & Sarstedt, M. (2016). Testing measurement invariance of composites using partial least squares. *International Marketing Review, 33*(3), 405–431.

Henseler, J., Ringle, C. M., & Sinkovics, R. R. (2009). The use of partial least squares path modeling in international marketing. In R. R. Sinkovics & P. N. Ghauri (Eds.), *New challenges to international marketing* (pp. 277–319). Bingley: Emerald.

Hernández-Linares, R., Kellermanns, F. W., & López-Fernández, M. C. (2018a). A note on the relationships between learning, market, and entrepreneurial orientations in family and nonfamily firms. *Journal of Family Business Strategy, 9*(3), 192–204.

Hernández-Linares, R., Kellermanns, F. W., & López-Fernández, M. C. (2018b). Dynamic capabilities and SME performance: The moderating effect of market orientation. *Journal of Small Business Management.* https://doi.org/10.1111/jsbm.12474

Hernández-Linares, R., & López-Fernández, M. C. (2018). Entrepreneurial orientation and the family firm: Mapping the field and tracing a path for future research. *Family Business Review, 31*(3), 318–351.

Hernández-Linares, R., Sarkar, S., & López-Fernández, M. C. (2017). How has the family firm literature addressed its heterogeneity through classification systems? An integrated analysis. *European Journal of Family Business, 7*(1–2), 1–13.

Hernández-Perlines, F. (2016). Entrepreneurial orientation in hotel industry: Multi-group analysis of quality certification. *Journal of Business Research, 69*(10), 4714–4724.

Hernandez-Perlines, F. (2018). Moderating effect of absorptive capacity on the entrepreneurial orientation of international performance of family businesses. *Journal of Family Business Management, 8*(1), 58–74.

Higginson, N. (2010). Preparing the next generation for the family business: Relational factors and knowledge transfer in mother-to-daughter succession. *Journal of Management and Marketing Research, 4*, 1–18.

Hofstede, G. (2001). *Culture's consequences: Comparing values, behaviors, institutions and organizations across nations*. Thousand Oaks, CA: Sage.

Hu, L. T., & Bentler, P. M. (1999). Cutoff criteria for fit indexes in covariance structure analysis: Conventional criteria versus new alternatives. *Structural Equation Modeling: A Multidisciplinary Journal, 6*(1), 1–55.

Huff, J. O., Huff, A. S., & Thomas, H. (1992). Strategic renewal and the interaction of cumulative stress and inertia. *Strategic Management Journal, 13*(S1), 55–75.

Hussinki, H., Kianto, A., Vanhala, M., & Ritala, P. (2017). Assessing the universality of knowledge management practices. *Journal of Knowledge Management, 21*(6), 1596–1621.

Jain, A. K., & Moreno, A. (2015). Organizational learning, knowledge management practices and firm's performance: An empirical study of a heavy engineering firm in India. *The Learning Organization, 22*(1), 14–39.

Jaskiewicz, P., Uhlenbruck, K., Balkin, D. B., & Reay, T. (2013). Is nepotism good or bad? Types of nepotism and implications for knowledge management. *Family Business Review, 26*(2), 121–139.

Jayasingam, S., Ansari, M. A., Ramayah, T., & Jantan, M. (2013). Knowledge management practices and performance: Are they truly linked? *Knowledge Management Research & Practice, 11*(3), 255–264.

Jones, O., & Macpherson, A. (2006). Inter-organizational learning and strategic renewal in SMEs: Extending the 4I framework. *Long Range Planning, 39*(2), 155–175.

Kellermanns, F. W., & Eddleston, K. A. (2004). Feuding families: When conflict does a family firm good. *Entrepreneurship: Theory and Practice, 28*(3), 209–228.

Khayesi, J. N., George, G., & Antonakis, J. (2014). Kinship in entrepreneur networks: Performance effects of resource assembly in Africa. *Entrepreneurship: Theory and Practice, 38*(6), 1323–1342.

Klammer, A., Gueldenberg, S., Kraus, S., & O'Dwyer, M. (2017). To change or not to change-antecedents and outcomes of strategic renewal in SMEs. *International Entrepreneurship and Management Journal, 13*(3), 739–756.

Koskinen, K. U., & Vanharanta, H. (2002). The role of tacit knowledge in innovation processes of small technology companies. *International Journal of Production Economics, 80*(1), 57–64.

Kotlar, J., De Massis, A., Frattini, F., Bianchi, M., & Fang, H. (2013). Technology acquisition in family and nonfamily firms: A longitudinal analysis of Spanish manufacturing firms. *Journal of Product Innovation Management, 30*(6), 1073–1088.

Kuratko, D. F., & Audretsch, D. B. (2009). Strategic entrepreneurship: Exploring different perspectives of an emerging concept. *Entrepreneurship: Theory and Practice, 33*(1), 1–17.

Kuratko, D. F., & Audretsch, D. B. (2013). Clarifying the domains of corporate entrepreneurship. *International Entrepreneurship and Management Journal, 9*(3), 323–335.

Lai, J. Y., Wang, C. T., & Chou, C. Y. (2009). How knowledge map fit and personalization affect success of KMS in high-tech firms. *Technovation, 29*(4), 313–324.

LeBrasseur, R., Whissell, R., & Ojha, A. (2002). Organisational learning, transformational leadership and implementation of continuous quality improvement in Canadian hospitals. *Australian Journal of Management, 27*(2), 141–162.

Leonard-Barton, D. (1992). Core capabilities and core rigidities: A paradox in managing new product development. *Strategic Management Journal, 13*(S1), 111–125.

Lester, D. L., & Parnell, J. A. (2002). Aligning factors for successful organizational renewal. *Leadership & Organization Development Journal, 23*(2), 60–67.

Levin, D. Z., & Cross, R. (2004). The strength of weak ties you can trust: The mediating role of trust in effective knowledge transfer. *Management Science, 50*(11), 1477–1490.

Liu, Y., Chan, C., Zhao, C., & Liu, C. (2018). Unpacking knowledge management practices in China: Do institution, national and organizational culture matter? *Journal of Knowledge Management*. https://doi.org/10.1108/JKM-07-2017-0260

Lloria, M., & Peris-Ortiz, M. (2014). Knowledge creation. The ongoing search for strategic renewal. *Industrial Management & Data Systems, 114*(7), 1022–1035.

López-Fernández, M. C., Serrano-Bedia, A. M., & Pérez-Pérez, M. (2016). Entrepreneurship and family firm research: A bibliometric analysis of an emerging field. *Journal of Small Business Management, 54*(2), 622–639.

Martín-Rojas, R., García-Morales, V. J., & Bolívar-Ramos, M. T. (2013). Influence of technological support, skills and competencies, and learning on corporate entrepreneurship in European technology firms. *Technovation, 33*(12), 417–430.

Matthews, L. (2017). Applying multigroup analysis in PLS-SEM: A step-by-step process. In H. Latan & R. Noonan (Eds.), *Partial least squares path modeling* (pp. 219–243). Cham: Springer.

Mavondo, F. T., Chimhanzi, J., & Stewart, J. (2005). Learning orientation and market orientation: Relationship with innovation, human resource practices and performance. *European Journal of Marketing, 39*(11/12), 1235–1263.

Miller, D., & Le Breton-Miller, I. (2014). Deconstructing socioemotional wealth. *Entrepreneurship: Theory and Practice, 38*(4), 713–720.

Mustafa, M., Lundmark, E., & Ramos, H. M. (2016). Untangling the relationship between human resource management and corporate entrepreneurship: The mediating effect of middle managers' knowledge sharing. *Entrepreneurship Research Journal, 6*(3), 273–295.

Naldi, L., Nordqvist, M., Sjöberg, K., & Wiklund, J. (2007). Entrepreneurial orientation, risk taking, and performance in family firms. *Family Business Review, 20*(1), 33–47.

Oliva, F. (2014). Knowledge management barriers, practices and maturity model. *Journal of Knowledge Management, 18*(6), 1053–1074.

Pratap, S., & Saha, B. (2018). Evolving efficacy of managerial capital, contesting managerial practices, and the process of strategic renewal. *Strategic Management Journal, 39*(3), 759–793.

Purvis, R. L., Sambamurthy, V., & Zmud, R. W. (2001). The assimilation of knowledge platforms in organizations: An empirical investigation. *Organization Science, 12*(2), 117–135.

Riviere, M., Suder, G., & Bass, A. E. (2018). Exploring the role of internationalization knowledge in fostering strategic renewal: A dynamic capabilities perspective. *International Business Review, 27*(1), 66–77.

Sackmann, S. A. (1991). *Cultural knowledge in organizations: Exploring the collective mind.* Newbury Park, CA: Sage.

Sakhdari, K. (2016). Corporate entrepreneurship: A review and future research agenda. *Technology Innovation Management Review, 6*(8), 5–18.

Sánchez-Famoso, V., Maseda, A., & Iturralde, T. (2014). The role of internal social capital in organisational innovation. An empirical study of family firms. *European Management Journal, 32*(6), 950–962.

Sawers, J. L., Pretorius, M. W., & Oerlemans, L. A. (2008). Safeguarding SMEs dynamic capabilities in technology innovative SME-large company partnerships in South Africa. *Technovation, 28*(4), 171–182.

Schlägel, C., & Sarstedt, M. (2016). Assessing the measurement invariance of the four-dimensional cultural intelligence scale across countries: A composite model approach. *European Management Journal, 34*(6), 633–649.

Schmitt, A., Raisch, S., & Volberda, H. W. (2018). Strategic renewal: Past research, theoretical tensions and future challenges. *International Journal of Management Reviews, 20*(1), 81–98.

Sciascia, S., Alberti, F. G., & Salvato, C. (2009). Firm-level entrepreneurial contents for strategic renewal: A knowledge-based perspective. In G. T. Lumpkin & J. A. Katz (Eds.), *Entrepreneurial strategic content* (pp. 41–75). Bingley: Emerald.

Scuotto, V., Giudice, M. D., Holden, N., & Mattiacci, A. (2017). Entrepreneurial settings within global family firms: Research perspectives from cross-cultural knowledge management studies. *European Journal of International Management, 11*(4), 469–489.

Shane, S., & Venkataraman, S. (2000). The promise of entrepreneurship as a field of research. *Academy of Management Review, 25*(1), 217–226.

Sharma, P., Chrisman, J. J., & Chua, J. H. (2003). Succession planning as planned behavior: Some empirical results. *Family Business Review, 16*(1), 1–15.

Sher, P. J., & Lee, V. C. (2004). Information technology as a facilitator for enhancing dynamic capabilities through knowledge management. *Information & Management, 41*(8), 933–945.

Simsek, Z., & Heavey, C. (2011). The mediating role of knowledge-based capital for corporate entrepreneurship effects on performance: A study of small-to medium-sized firms. *Strategic Entrepreneurship Journal, 5*(1), 81–100.

Sinkula, J. M., Baker, W. E., & Noordewier, T. (1997). A framework for market-based organizational learning: Linking values, knowledge, and behavior. *Journal of the Academy of Marketing Science, 25*(4), 305–318.

Stoian, C., & Gilman, M. (2017). Corporate social responsibility that "pays": A strategic approach to CSR for SMEs. *Journal of Small Business Management, 55*(1), 5–31.

Sullivan, D. M., & Marvel, M. R. (2011). Knowledge acquisition, network reliance, and early-stage technology venture outcomes. *Journal of Management Studies, 48*(6), 1169–1193.

Swift, P. E., & Hwang, A. (2008). Learning, dynamic capabilities and operating routines: A consumer package goods company. *The Learning Organization, 15*(1), 75–95.

Verbeke, A., Chrisman, J. J., & Yuan, W. (2007). A note on strategic renewal and corporate venturing in the subsidiaries of multinational enterprises. *Entrepreneurship: Theory and Practice, 31*(4), 585–600.

Villar, C., Alegre, J., & Pla-Barber, J. (2014). Exploring the role of knowledge management practices on exports: A dynamic capabilities view. *International Business Review, 23*(1), 38–44.

Volberda, H. W., Baden-Fuller, C., & Van Den Bosch, F. A. (2001). Mastering strategic renewal: Mobilising renewal journeys in multi-unit firms. *Long Range Planning, 34*(2), 159–178.

Wade, M., & Hulland, J. (2004). The resource-based view and information systems research: Review, extension, and suggestions for future research. *MIS Quarterly, 28*(1), 107–142.

Wong, K. Y., & Aspinwall, E. (2005). An empirical study of the important factors for knowledge-management adoption in the SME sector. *Journal of Knowledge Management, 9*(3), 64–82.

Yang, Y., Nomoto, S., & Kurokawa, S. (2013). Knowledge transfer in corporate venturing activity and impact of control mechanisms. *International Entrepreneurship and Management Journal, 9* (1), 21–43.

Zack, M. H. (1999). Managing codified knowledge. *Sloan Management Review, 40*(4), 45–58.

Zack, M., McKeen, J., & Singh, S. (2009). Knowledge management and organizational performance: An exploratory analysis. *Journal of Knowledge Management, 13*(6), 392–409.

Zahra, S. A. (1996). Governance, ownership, and corporate entrepreneurship: The moderating impact of industry technological opportunities. *Academy of Management Journal, 39*(6), 1713–1735.

Zahra, S. A. (2012). Organizational learning and entrepreneurship in family firms: Exploring the moderating effect of ownership and cohesion. *Small Business Economics, 38*(1), 51–65.

Zahra, S. A. (2015). Corporate entrepreneurship as knowledge creation and conversion: The role of entrepreneurial hubs. *Small Business Economics, 44*(4), 727–735.

Zahra, S. A., Neubaum, D. O., & Larrañeta, B. (2007). Knowledge sharing and technological capabilities: The moderating role of family involvement. *Journal of Business Research, 60*(10), 1070–1079.

The Moderating Effects of Family Farms Between Innovation, Information Systems, and Training-Learning Over Performance

Alfonso A. Rojo-Ramírez, Alicia Ramírez-Orellana, John Eddson Burgos-Burgos, and Daniel Ruiz-Palomo

Abstract This work addresses how information systems and training-learning affect the innovation of productive processes and in turn how they influence the performance of the agricultural banana companies (AC). Particularly, it analyzes the moderation effect that being a family farm exerts on these relationships. To do that we apply partial least square technique to 416 AC in the province of El Oro—Republic of Ecuador. Data were obtained by an in hand self-administered questionnaire addressed in 2017 to the owners and managers of these businesses. The results show that (1) information systems contribute significantly to the innovation of productive processes of AC. It also contributes directly and significantly to the performance of the AC as well as through the innovation of productive processes mediation; (2) training directly and significantly influences the innovation of productive processes, but not on performance, which it influences only through the mediation effect of the innovation of productive processes; (3) innovation of productive processes significantly affects the performance of the AC Further, we demonstrate the moderating effect that the family farms have on the information systems—the innovation of productive processes—performance relationship.

Keywords Family farms · Innovation · Production · Performance · Ecuador · Banana · Food · Agriculture

---

A. A. Rojo-Ramírez (✉) · A. Ramírez-Orellana
University of Almería, Almería, Spain
e-mail: arojo@ual.es; aramirez@ual.es

J. E. Burgos-Burgos
Technical University of Machala, Machala, Ecuador
e-mail: jburgos@utmachala.edu.ec

D. Ruiz-Palomo
University of Malaga, Málaga, Spain
e-mail: drp@uma.es

J. M. Saiz-Álvarez et al. (eds.), *Entrepreneurship and Family Business Vitality*,
Studies on Entrepreneurship, Structural Change and Industrial Dynamics,
https://doi.org/10.1007/978-3-030-15526-1_11

1 Introduction

According to the Food and Agriculture Organization of the United Nations (FAO, 2015), family farms are essential to ensure long-term global food security, but they are small- and medium-sized, so they have limited access to resources and low levels of productivity. FAO believes that farmers need an environment conducive to innovation, especially the support of public institutions that promote agricultural production activities, universities, and other research centers.

In the case of Latin American family businesses, Fernández Pérez, Lluch, and Barbero (2015) reveal that 85% of private companies are family-owned businesses of small size founded in the last two decades (with an average between 11 and 50 employees and with annual sales of less than 3 million dollars).

Our chapter is centered in the agricultural banana companies (AC) from the province of El Oro (Republic of Ecuador) and, in particular, the family banana companies of this region. The production of bananas (*Musa paradisiaca*) in Ecuador has allowed the country to be in the number one ranking of countries exporting this fruit in the world. This fruit occupies the fourth place of exportable fruits in the world since it is considered a staple food that contributes to food security and, in the developing countries, gives sustainability to rural populations since its production is perennial (Castro, Calvas, & Knoke, 2015).

The study of family businesses has acquired great importance (Sharma, Chrisman, & Gersick, 2012) due, on the one hand, to the relevance of these businesses in all countries and their important contribution to their economies and, on the other, to the important development of the investigation of this type of business (Padilla-Meléndez, Diéguez-Soto, & Garrido-Moreno, 2015).

In the agricultural field, the performance of companies is measured through an improvement in technical efficiency to achieve better levels of productivity (Selamat & Nasir, 2013) revealing that the innovation processes have a crucial role in performance development (Sumberg, 2005). Innovation in agriculture is usually justified by the need to satisfy a greater demand for food, since innovative activity enables the application of new technologies, the use of new crop varieties, fertilizers and chemical pesticides, and new irrigation and mechanization systems, as well as the use of skilled labor (Castro et al., 2015).

Indeed, innovation is a key factor for company competitiveness and performance. Nevertheless, the family farm innovation process is still poorly understood (López Fernández, Serrano Bedia, & Gómez López, 2016), and the current state of the literature contributes little to improving our understanding of the phenomenon (Becheikh, Landry, & Amara, 2006).

The objective of this research is to analyze how information systems and training-learning contribute to improving the performance of AC through the innovation in production processes and how to be recognized as a family farm (FF) influences these effects, at the level of market-oriented AC (Le Gal, Dugué, Faure, & Novak, 2011) in the province of El Oro, Ecuador.

Empirical work is carried out based on a survey to go through among AC in the province of El Oro, Ecuador. Four constructs are designed: information systems (IS), training-learning (TL), innovation in production processes (IPP), and performance (P), which allow us to study the proposed objective by using a partial least squares structural equation modeling (PLS-SEM). Based on the survey, the AC were classified into family farms and nonfamily farms to analyze the moderating effect that FF exerts.

Our results suggest that the innovation in production processes is considerably influenced by the information systems and training-learning finding that the involvement of the family in the AC influences these relationships. Also, information systems and training-learning do not influence performance directly, but they do indirectly through innovation in production processes that act as a full mediator variable. As predicted by the theory and previous studies, innovation in production processes exerts a positive and significant influence on the performance of the AC, which is reinforcing in the case of FF.

This study contributes, on the one hand, to broadening our theoretical knowledge of agricultural micro, small, and medium enterprises (MSMEs) and particularly the FF in developing countries, as well as to improve our understanding of how these companies manage and organize their attitude toward innovation and the improvement of their performance. Likewise, the proposed model can serve as a guide for researchers, professionals, and AC when applying in sectors of similar characteristics and can help guide public policies for the promotion of innovative agricultural development in developing countries. Besides, this study reveals the moderating effect of the family involvement on performance, as shown by previous studies, where significant differences between family and nonfamily businesses were found. This research is based on the resource-based view (RBV) framework following the most usual pattern in the researches related to the study of the companies' performance (e.g., Nieves, 2014; Ravichandran & Lertwongsatien, 2005; Terziovski, 2008) in the family firm (Habbershon & Williams, 1999).

The rest of the paper is organized as follows: The next section provides the theoretical framework for our model and hypotheses development. The third section is devoted to the empirical study, including the explanation of variables and the analysis of the data. The fourth section introduces the results. The investigation concludes with the discussion of the results and conclusions.

2 Theoretical Approach and Hypothesis

2.1 *Information Systems, Performance, and Innovation in Production Processes*

The knowledge society increasingly demands the use of new technologies, especially regarding information systems that facilitate increasing the organizational knowledge (Carneiro, 2000).

The previous literature indicates that information systems allow companies to achieve better performance, for example, by improving their productivity and efficiency (Abrego-Almazán, Sánchez-Tovar, & Medina-Quintero, 2017) through their basic competences (Bacha, 2012). However, existing empirical research (e.g., Bento, Bento, & Ferreira Wite, 2014) does not provide conclusive results (Tarafdar & Gordon, 2007).

Thus, Gorla, Somers, and Wong (2010) use the statistical technique of partial least squares (PLS-SEM) and follow the model of Mahmood and Soon (1991) to analyze the combined impact of the quality of the information systems, the quality of information, and the quality of service in the organizational performance, which they consider as a perceptive construct instead of an objective measure (e.g., financial) based on Ravichandran and Rai (2000). Their results show the three analyzed aspects of the information impact, both directly and indirectly, on the organizational performance.

Bento et al. (2014), in the context of strategic performance measurement systems and based on the study of performance measurement practices conducted by the American Institute of Certified Public Accountants (AICPA), show empirically how information systems (e.g., the use of the internet or technological tools for information) have a positive impact on the performance of the companies.

Abrego-Almazán et al. (2017) apply the statistical technique of partial least squares and the model of De Lone and McLean (1992) to apply to a convenience sample of 133 companies from the state of Tamaulipas (Mexico) to show that the quality of the information systems is the key to increasing user satisfaction and, consequently, the performance, measured by an increase in sales, market share, productivity, and process improvement, either in their capacity of operations management or in the reduction of operating and personnel costs. Consequently, according to the previous literature, we hypothesize that:

Hypothesis 1 *Information systems of AC positively influence their performance.*

For its part, innovation in production processes and methods is highly influenced by information systems and technologies (Bassellier & Benbasat, 2004), so it is necessary to understand the relationship between information systems and innovation in production processes (Tarafdar & Gordon, 2007).

Luengo and Obeso (2013) show that there is an interrelation between the information received from the industry, the government, and the university (what

Leydesdorff & Etzkowitz, 1998 call the triple helix) and the level of innovation of the company.

Previous literature suggests that it is necessary to train and learn the use of specific technologies and promote the use of information technologies to facilitate technology adoption processes (Jiménez-Zarco, González-González, Martínez-Ruíz, & Izquierdo-Yusta, 2015). Therefore, based on these contributions and the previous arguments, we hypothesize that:

Hypothesis 2 *Information systems of AC contribute positively to innovation in production processes of these companies.*

2.2 Training-Learning, Performance, and Innovation in Production Processes

Training-learning allows a company to be more productive by facilitating innovation in the workplace (Guisado González, Vila Alonso, & Guisado Tato, 2016). Usually, training in AC is based on the accumulated experience that generates a specific and informal organizational culture often recognized in what has been called socio-emotional values (Dressler & Tauer, 2015).

The challenge for these companies is how to dynamize and improve training to make them more innovative, thus improving their performance. The development of a culture of organizational learning contributes significantly to the improvement of the performance of the company thanks to the dynamism that it encourages (Hung, Yang, Lien, McLean, & Kuo, 2010).

The relationship between training and performance has been studied extensively, particularly analyzing the effect of training on productivity, showing a positive relationship between both (Reimers & Klasen, 2013; Xayavong, Kingwell, & Islam, 2016). Thus, Reimers and Klasen (2013) show through the use of different control variables, databases, and econometric methods that education has a highly significant and positive effect on agricultural productivity.

Xayavong et al. (2016) use structural equation modeling for the analysis of the relationship between farmers' training and performance in Australia, measured as a construct consisting of two economic variables: the rate of growth of property and the total productivity. Their results show that training has a positive and significant influence on human resources, which, in turn, impact the skills of managers, thus increasing their performance.

Undoubtedly, tacit or explicit knowledge is the most necessary intangible asset within organizations, since by sharing knowledge, there is an influence on the speed and quality of innovations and these have a positive relationship with the company's performance (Wang & Wang, 2012). Consequently, in this work, it is hypothesized that:

Hypothesis 3 *Training-learning of the workers in AC has a positive effect on the performance of the companies.*

The increasing complexity of AC requires the skill, knowledge, and capability of the managers and their families (Xayavong et al., 2016). The Oslo Manual (OECD, 2005) recognizes the role of human capital in innovation both at a business and aggregate level, as well as the relationship between the quality of the education system and the needs of innovative companies (González, Miles-Touya, & Pazó, 2016).

Several studies have examined the links between training, education, and the adoption of innovations that improve farmers' productivity. Lam (2005) highlights the critical role that organizations play in innovation and technological change. This author shows that different structural forms influence learning and knowledge creation, giving rise to different types of innovative capabilities.

Kraus, Pohjola, and Koponen (2012) point out that the organizational culture strongly influences the willingness to innovate since specific practices such as education and training enable the retention of employees. In the particular case of AC, previous studies such as that of Kabunga, Dubois, and Qaim (2014) have shown that the cultural tissue of an area and, in particular, technical training and institutional support are relevant for the adoption of new forms of action and end up increasing the income of the AC.

Therefore, it seems that the implementation of technological innovation depends mostly on organizational learning capabilities (Mat & Razak, 2013), that is, the capacity of the members of an organization to learn and train. In line with this, our hypothesis is as follows:

Hypothesis 4 *Training-learning of the workers of AC positively influences the innovation in production processes of the companies.*

2.3 Innovation in Production Processes and Performance of the AC

The existing literature (Clark & Guy, 1998; Price, Stoica, & Boncella, 2013; Rosenbusch, Brinckmann, & Bausch, 2011; Spielman & Birner, 2008) reveals that the performance of the companies is associated with the level of innovation, although, they do not seem conclusive. However, in general, a positive relationship is admitted between the two innovation and performance in the case of SMEs (Rosenbusch et al., 2011). This relationship is conditioned by the context, particularly the culture of the countries, as the study of Efrat (2014) reveals for 33 OECD countries, Singapore and Hong Kong as well as for the living conditions of the areas in which it is applied (Cannarella & Piccioni, 2011). However, limited literature exists about the relationship between the innovation in production processes in the family firms and the performance.

Rosenbusch et al. (2011) in the context of SMEs point out that smaller and less resourced companies benefit from innovation and find that the innovation-performance relationship depends on contextual factors such as the age of the firm, the type of innovation, and the cultural context.

Dostie and Jayaraman (2013) use a sample of Canadian companies to demonstrate that innovation in processes results in the reduction of production costs without changes in the incentives of managers. In the field of innovation in processes in developing countries, Goel and Nelson (2018) find that countries with lower economic prosperity are more prone to introduce process innovations.

Guisado González et al. (2016) find evidence that the influence of training on companies' productivity is positive and wholly significant in the Spanish manufacturing sector. They also show that radical innovation positively and significantly influences the labor productivity of companies, while incremental innovation is not statistically significant, although the sign of its influence is positive. In general, their findings follow the experience curve that considers that an increase in the utilization of productive capacity has a positive influence on the productivity of companies.

In the field of AC, Martinez Caro, Briones Peñalver, and De Nieves Nieto (2011) carried out a regression study with 118 companies and proved that, despite the importance of innovation as a sustainable competitive advantage, innovative actions developed by AC are not being reflected in their strategic results and have a low weight in economic results. In this paper, we hypothesize that:

Hypothesis 5 *Innovation in the production processes of AC has a positive influence on their performance.*

2.4 The Mediation Role of Innovation in Production Processes

As information systems influence the innovation in production processes and the last one influences performance, we argue that innovation in production processes acts as a mediation mechanism between information systems and performance. According to Hayes (2009), mediation is a way to establish the extent to which some putative causal variable, X, influences some outcome, Y, through one or more mediator variables. In this sense, we suggest the mediating effect of innovation in production processes in the process by which information systems affect performance considering that information systems in the AC have evolved from only keeping records to more complex systems supporting production management such as an enterprise resource planning (ERP).

Haberli, Oliveira, and Yanaze (2017) under the technology organization environment and diffusion of innovation theory framework propose an information systems model encouraging innovation systems based on the ERP of the Brazilian AC, which impacts the performance of the farms. Accordingly, it is hypothesized that:

Hypothesis 6a *Innovation in production processes of AC mediates the relationship between information system and performance.*

Training-learning appears to have a significant impact on agricultural productivity (Reimers & Klasen, 2013) which is more significant as more developed technological systems exist in countries. It looks that training-learning can facilitate innovation activities, which leads to improved performance.

Some authors (e.g., Xayavong et al., 2016) have discussed the mediating role of innovation as part of the process of improvement between training and performance suggesting that training-learning can facilitate innovation activities, which leads to the improvement of performance. These arguments allow to adopt the following hypothesis:

Hypothesis 6b *Innovation in production processes of AC mediates the relationship between training-learning and performance.*

2.5 The Moderation Effect of the Banana Family Farm

According to Baron and Kenny (1986), a moderating factor is a qualitative or quantitative variable that affects the direction and strength of the relationship between the independent and the dependent variables. The connection can be stronger or weaker or become negative or positive while it was positive without the intervention of the moderating variable. Moderators are generally introduced in previous studies when the relations are inconsistent. Regarding previous researches, the relation between family business and performance appears elusive (Miller, Le Breton-Miller, Lester, & Cannella, 2007; Westhead & Cowling, 1997).

Chrisman, Chua, and Kellermanns (2009) find that family influence has both a positive and a negative moderating effect on the relationships between different categories of resource stocks and performance. Specifically, family firms benefit more from resource stocks based on external relationships, while nonfamily firms benefit more from resource stocks based on functional skills.

For example, in relation with the top management team (TMT), De Massis, Kotlar, Campopiano, and Cassia (2013) show how the involvement of family members in TMT moderates the relationship between the degree of family ownership dispersion and firm performance in the case of SMEs in Italy; Kraiczy, Hack, and Kellermanns (2014) studying the relationship between TMT innovation orientation and new product portfolio performance in small- and medium-sized family firms also show a moderating effect when multiple generations are involved in the TMT.

Taking into account previous researches and considering the evidence presented in Wilkening (1954) suggesting that family relationships has little direct influence upon the acceptance of innovations or improvements in farming as well as the opinion of Rosenbusch et al. (2011) indicating that empirical research on the innovation–performance relationship in SMEs shows controversial results, it looks of interest to analyze how influence family involvement on different relationship presented previously. We hence establish the following hypothesis:

Hypothesis 7a *Banana family farm moderates the relationship between innovation in production processes and performance.*

If the family farm moderates the relationship between innovation and performance, it is also plausible that the family's characteristics might conditionally affect the strength of the indirect relationship between innovation and performance. In other words, the effect of information systems and training-learning gained from true innovations on performance (mediation effect) may be moderated by the fact of being a family farm, thereby demonstrating a moderated mediation effect. As we assume a strong association between innovation in production processes and performance when family involvement exists, we expect that being a family farm will positively moderate the mediation effects. That is, the mediation effects will be stronger when the farm is familiar, as claimed in the following hypotheses:

Hypothesis 7b *Banana family farm moderates the indirect effect of an information system on performance via innovation in production processes.*

Hypothesis 7c *Banana family farm moderates the indirect effect of training-learning on performance via innovation in production processes.*

2.6 Proposed Model

The proposed model is depicted in Fig. 1, which shows the existence of four constructs: two exogenous constructs, the information system and training-learning, and two endogenous constructs, the innovation in production processes and performance of the AC.

3 Empirical Study

3.1 Data Collection and Representativeness

A survey to 600 managers and owners of AC was carried out in the province of El Oro (Ecuador) between July and December of 2017. We rely on the agricultural centers, collection centers, and associations of banana producers from the towns of Machala, El Guabo, and Pasaje, which are the counties with the highest banana production. We visit each AC by contacting the manager and owners whom the objective of the investigation was explained. A total of 416 responses were valid. To define the convenience sample (Price et al., 2013; Smith, 2008), we started with the register available from the Tax Administration of Ecuador (Internal Revenue Service) that collects information about the taxpayers of the country and that in the

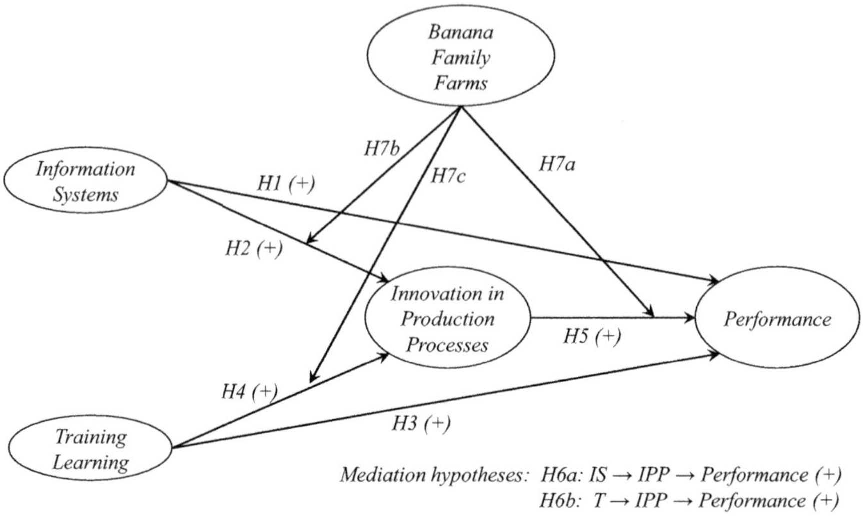

Fig. 1 Model used. Source: Authors' own figure

province of El Oro includes 1125 taxpayers who are engaged in the cultivation of the banana with more than 5 ha of farm and who are obliged to keep accounts.

Information collection follows the steps of the Delphi method recommended by Campos Climent, Melián Navarro, and Sanchis Palacio (2014). The validity and relevance of the questionnaire were assessed by experts (Reguant-Álvarez & Torrado-Fonseca, 2016). The questionnaire consisted of 45 items, of which 10 were for descriptive data identifying the characteristics of the participants and 35 for the knowledge of the aspects studied, based on a 7-point Likert scale (1: Totally disagree to 7: Totally agree).

Table 1 shows the most relevant distribution statistics of the sample. Concerning the size of the AC, 11% are considered large; 32% are medium; and 57% are small businesses. Of these, 31% are nonfamily businesses and 69% are. Also, 41% of AC managers do not belong to the family, while 59% do belong to the family. Most of the managers are above 40 years (80%). The AC surveyed can be classified as young, 45% are less than ten years old, and another 40% are between 10 and 30 years old. Likewise, most of the producers have farm size with less than 10 Has (44%) although 23% exceed more than 30 Has. Regarding the sale system, it is carried out equally between associations of producers (42%), who have contracts with exporters, and directly with exporting companies (42%), which are responsible for marketing the product.

Salazar Veloz and Del Cioppo Morstadt (2016) show that productivity (production per hectare/year) in Ecuador is rather low, (on average about 1500 boxes/ha) when compared with the international average that it is 2339 boxes/ha. The analyzed AC only 35% produce more than 2000 boxes/ha.

Table 1 Distribution of the sample

Size[a]		Family involvement	
Small: 5–20 Has	57%	Family-owned farms	69%
Medium: 20–30 Has	32%	Nonfamily-owned farms	31%
Big: >30 Has	11%	Family-managed farms	59%
Sales destination		Nonfamily-managed farm	41%
Association of producers	42%	Production/Ha/year	
Export companies	42%	Less than 1000 boxes	6%
Direct export	11%	1000–1200 boxes	16%
Manager age		1200–2000 boxes	43%
Less than 40 years	20%	More than 2000 boxes	35%
40–50 years	30%	Years of exploitation	
More than 50 years	50%	Less than 5 years	19%
Cost of production/sales		5–10 years	25%
About 70%	62%	10–30 years	40%
About 80%	28%	More than 30 years	16%
About 90%	8%		

Source: Authors' own table
[a]All agricultural firms employed up to ten workers per year

Margins (cost of production/sales) are quite large according to respondents. They indicate that it is equal to or greater than 30% (62%), while 28% report that it is between 21% and 10%. Only 8% tells us that it is less than 1%.

The final sample included two research groups: 245 family companies and 171 nonfamily companies. The percentage of family and nonfamily firms of the sample was very similar to the proportion found by other academic works for this population (Price et al., 2013). Family firms appear relatively smaller than nonfamily firms. Thus, around 66% of family firms are small businesses, while only 36% of nonfamily counterparts are small-sized firms. In contrast, 11% of nonfamily firms are large ones, while only 9% of family firms can be considered large ones. As far as business maturity is concerned, around 20% of family-managed firms are 25 years old or less in comparison to 14% of nonfamily-managed family firms, so no significant differences were found.

3.2 Measurement Variables

The selected variables are based on the conducted survey, which in turn is based on previous studies on indicators associated with innovation and performance (Daane, Francis, Oliveros, & Bolo, 2008). All the variables associated with each construct are shown in Table 2. In particular, the following constructs are part of the model:

Performance (PE) is a balanced measure that given the characteristics of small businesses (Garengo, Biazzo, & Bititci, 2005) and, in particular in the case of AC

Table 2 Questionnaire measures

Please evaluate from 1 (absolutely disagree) to 7 (absolutely agree) the following questions	
Information systems (Pérez-Méndez & Machado-Cabezas, 2015; Rao et al., 2015)	
IS1[a]	Is the use of the internet a good source to obtain information in order to innovate in the company?
IS2	Do the advances of science presented at fairs and other events favor innovation in the company?
IS3	Do the results of research carried out in universities favor innovation in the company?
IS4	Do the different levels of governments with their skills and information collaborate with companies in the sector?
IS5[a]	Do you think it is necessary to develop a web page for the company to inform customers and suppliers?
IS6	Does the information generated in technological R&D centers contribute to the innovative production processes of the firm?
IS7[a]	Is the information about the ecological situation, forests, soil resources, and available water grounded to manage the company?
Training-Learning (Wang & Wang, 2012)	
TL1	Is training a key to the development of the company?
TL2	Is learning a key to improve production processes in the company?
TL3[a]	Is knowledge management a key in the company?
TL4[a]	Is attending events/fairs a key to get more knowledge for the staff that works in the company?
TL5	Is the professionalization of workers and managers a key in the activities carried out by the company?
TL6	Is self-training a key to the personal and professional development of workers and managers in the company?
TL7[a]	Is the level of education a key to the relationship between workers and employers in the company?
Innovation in production processes (Bessant & Tidd, 2011; Freeman & Soete, 1997)	
IP1	Is it common for the company to reorganize the production process?
IP2[a]	Is the modernization of the infrastructure for production considered in the company?
IP3	In the company, is it preferred to use new inputs and materials for the production process?
IP4	Does the company consider to differentiate its product from other producers?
IP5[a]	Does the company take advantage of the experience of the workers in the production processes?
IP6	Is it common to find new market gaps in the company?
IP7	Are strategies to commercialize the product permanently applied in the company?
Performance (Gorla et al., 2010; Ravichandran & Rai, 2000)	
PE1[a]	In this period, did the percentage of total sales in the company improve?
PE2	Did the company's profitability increase?
PE3	Did you notice changes in the levels of productivity of the company?
PE4	Did the average salary level in the company evolve?
PE5	Is the company recognized in the local and national market?
PE6	Is the company recognized in the international market?
PE7[a]	Did the amount of rejection (waste) in the company's production decrease?

Source: Authors' own table

[a]These indicators were not included in latent variables due to convergent and discriminant criteria of consistent PLS path modeling. All the measures were Likert-type scales

with low formalization of their management, is defined as a construct consisting of seven variables (listed from PE1 to PE7) that collect operational and market measures (Ravichandran & Rai, 2000), so it becomes a subjective, organizational average (Gorla et al., 2010) of both financial and nonfinancial performance.

Innovation in Production Processes (IPP) is one of the most important multidimensional constructs with effect on the company's performance (Crossan & Apaydin, 2010) which in our case consists of seven indicators (listed from IP1 to IP7). Innovation in rural AC of developing countries has been extensively studied in development programs (e.g., Heanue & Macken Walsh, 2010) with a focus on structural changes. In this paper innovative changes are considered in a broad sense (Bessant & Tidd, 2011; Freeman & Soete, 1997), that is, innovations or improvements to increase the production and commercialization of these companies, what is typical in studies of developing countries (Gras, 2009).

Information Systems (IS) are latent variables oriented to know how AC use the information to improve the innovation in production processes and performance. The seven indicators on the questionnaire (identified from IS1 to IS7) are based on descriptive information provided by previous studies (Pérez-Méndez & Machado-Cabezas, 2015; Rao, Ken, & Chen, 2015).

Training-Learning (TL) is a latent variable constructed by seven indicators (TL1 to TL7) that try to collect different aspects of training and learning. Its inclusion is essential to measure the company capacity for innovation that contributes to an improvement in productivity (Guisado González et al., 2016), although the point of view that is taken is training-learning versus training-performance (Wang & Wang, 2012).

Family Farm (FF) The involvement of the family in business and ownership defines a firm as a family firm (Chua, Chrisman, & Sharma, 1999). The former demand is a basic requirement but an insufficient condition. The involvement of the family is a preliminary condition for a long-term shared conception of the business, which is transferred from one generation to another (Chrisman, Chua, & Sharma, 2005). Nevertheless, shared vision and goals are especially associated with the level of family involvement (Chrisman, Chua, Pearson, & Barnett, 2012). The interviewee was asked if the AC can be considered a family farm and then if the CEO is a family member in order to capture the family involvement since we do not have a direct estimation of family vision and goals (Diéguez-Soto, López-Delgado, & Rojo-Ramírez, 2015). Then, we use a dummy variable that takes value one whether the interviewee recognized the AC ownership is familiar and the CEO is a family member, zero otherwise. This variable has also been measured and used in previous studies to consider the influence of the family in the company through management positions (among others, Schmid, Achleitner, Ampenberger, & Kaserer, 2014).

3.3 Statistical Remedies for Bias

To test for the validity of the survey, we analyzed two types of bias: non-response and common method bias. Firstly, to test for non-response bias, we used late respondents as surrogates for nonrespondents (Nwachukwu, Vitell, Gilbert, & Barnes, 1997). We contrasted responses from firms answering the first round of interviews (81% of the sample) with those responding to the follow-up (19% of the sample) interviews. Results show no significant differences between the two groups using t and χ^2 tests. Considering these outcomes, we did not find non-response bias. Secondly, we evaluated common method bias using several statistical remedies (Mackenzie, Podsakoff, & Podsakoff, 2011; Podsakoff, MacKenzie, & Podsakoff, 2012, 2016) and partial correlation procedure (Lindell & Whitney, 2001). Results suggest that the bias of the common method variance is not relevant in our study.

3.4 Statistical Procedure

We tested our model using partial least squares (PLS), a variance-based structural equation modeling (SEM) (Reinartz, Haenlein, & Henseler, 2009). PLS-SEM is a particularly suitable technique to use in a theory development situation such as in this study (Chin, 2010). All our variables are reflective, so we applied consistent PLS (Dijkstra & Henseler, 2015a, 2015b) by using SmartPLS 3.2.7 software (Ringle, Wende, & Becker, 2017).

4 Results

4.1 Model Validation

Each latent variable in the model was measured by multiple indicators and evaluated regarding reliability, validity, and composition weights (Henseler, 2017). All the reliability and discriminant validity criteria, such as Cronbach's alpha, average variance extracted, Dijkstra-Henseler's rho (ρ_A) (Dijkstra & Henseler, 2015a, 2015b), and Jöreskog's composite reliability (ρ_C) (Ketchen, 2013), exceed their shortcuts values (Hair, Hult, Ringle, & Sarstedt, 2016; Henseler, Ringle, & Sarstedt, 2016), as shown in Table 3. Besides, we estate the relevance of measures by considering the value of outer loadings and their bootstrap significance by using a 10,000 sample bias-corrected procedure (Ketchen, 2013). Furthermore, we performed a confirmatory composite analysis test (Cepeda Carrión, Henseler, Ringle, & Roldán, 2016) following a blindfolding procedure (omission distance of 9) in order to determine the overall predictive relevance of the model as a first step in

Table 3 Reliability and convergent validity

		Load*	t			Load*	t	Q^2
Information systems (IS)				Innovation in production processes (IPP)				
	IS2	0.79	21.73		IP1	0.80	21.13	0.34
	IS3	0.71	17.91		IP3	0.77	20.3	0.34
	IS4	0.69	17.13		IP4	0.83	28.12	0.37
	IS6	0.95	36.21		IP6	0.73	19.46	0.30
					IP7	0.77	20.52	0.32
AVE: 0.62	α: 0.87	ρ_A: 0.88	ρ_C: 0.87	AVE: 0.61	α: 0.89	ρ_A: 0.89	ρ_C: 0.89	
Training/learning (TL)				Performance (PE)				
	TL1	0.84	16.03		PE2	0.47	6.13	0.06
	TL2	0.85	23.34		PE3	0.89	16.67	0.18
	TL5	0.80	19.11		PE4	0.50	6.32	0.06
	TL6	0.80	16.67		PE5	0.89	18.43	0.19
					PE6	0.73	11.87	0.13
AVE: 0.62	α: 0.87	ρ_A: 0.88	ρ_C: 0.87	AVE: 0.52	α: 0.84	ρ_A: 0.88	ρ_C: 0.84	

Source: Authors' own table
*All the loadings are significant at a $p < 0.001$ level
Significance and t statistic performed by 10,000 rep. Bootstrapping procedure. Cross-validated redundancies Stone-Geisser Q^2 performed by a 9 Distance-Blindfolding procedure
α Cronbach's alpha, ρ_A Dijkstra-Henseler's rho, ρ_C Jöreskog's composite reliability, *AVE* average variance extracted

the quality assessment, since the Q^2 values are above 0 (Chin, 2010; Sleuwaegen, 1992).

In a second stage, we assess the discriminant validity as shown in Table 4 according to Fornell and Larcker (1981) and Heterotrait-monotrait (HTMT) criteria (Henseler, Ringle, & Sarstedt, 2014) as well as cross-loadings criterion (not reported). In the third stage, path coefficients and their 10,000 resampling bootstrap significance levels are reported in Table 5 and Fig. 2. Also, Table 5 shows that constructs VIF ranged 1.04–2.88, suggesting that collinearity is not a problem. Moreover, this study assesses quality by checking that the standardized root mean square residual (SRMR) does not exceed a value of 0.08 (Hu & Bentler, 1998), while R^2 exceeds 0.1 for all the endogenous latent variables. It suggests a good fit in model specifications.

4.2 Whole Sample Results

Our results suggest that neither the use of information systems or training-learning capabilities had a significant impact on performance, so H1 and H3 are rejected. However, the use of information system and training-learning capabilities had a positive and significant impact on the innovation in production processes (β = 0.62*** and 0.25***, respectively); hence, H2 and H4 are supported.

Table 4 Discriminant validity

	IS	TL	IPP	PE
Information systems (IS)	**0.79**	0.5	0.8	0.5
Training-learning (TL)	0.55	**0.82**	0.6	0.3
Innovation in production processes (IPP)	0.76	0.59	**0.78**	0.5
Performance (PE)	0.46	0.34	0.51	**0.72**

Source: Authors' own table
HTMT ratio over the diagonal (*cursive*). Fornell-Larcker criterion: squared-root of AVE in diagonal (bold) and construct correlations below diagonal

Table 5 Whole sample results

	Path		t	Lo95	Hi95	f^2	VIF
Direct effects							
IS → IPP	0.62	***	11.29	[0.51;	0.73]	0.72	1.44
TL → IPP	0.25	***	4.19	[0.13;	0.37]	0.11	1.44
R^2: 0.62; [Adjusted R^2: 0.62]; Q^2: 0.33							
IS → PE	0.15		1.68	[−0.02;	0.34]	0.01	2.46
TL → PE	0.02		0.42	[−0.09;	0.14]	0.00	1.60
IPP → PE	0.38	***	4.16	[0.19;	0.55]	0.08	2.64
R^2: 0.28; [Adjusted R^2: 0.27]; Q^2: 0.12							
SRMR: 0.06; Chi-squared: 981.6							
Indirect effects						VAF	
IS → IPP → PE	0.24	***	3.93	[0.12;	0.36]	60.9	
TL → IPP → PE	0.10	**	2.85	[0.04;	0.17]	79.8	

Source: Authors' own table
$*p < 0.05$; $**p < 0.01$; $***p < 0.001$
Significance, t statistic and 95% bias-corrected confidence interval performed by 10,000 rep. Bootstrapping procedure. VIF: Inner model Variance Inflation Factors. VAF: proportion mediated. Constructs cross-validated redundancies Stone-Geisser Q^2 performed by a 9 Distance-Blindfolding procedure

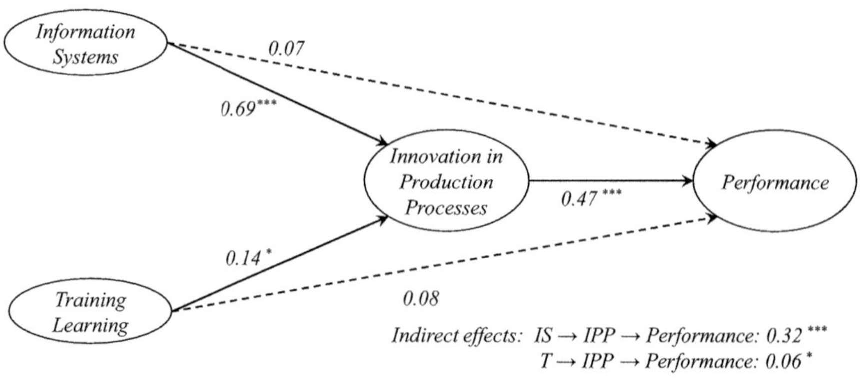

Fig. 2 Model's results. Source: Authors' own figure

Furthermore, the path coefficient from the importance of innovation through performance was positive and significant (path = 0.38***), supporting H5.

These results are in concordance of mediation hypotheses, as the total effect of information systems and learning capabilities in firm performance can be addressed by the sum of the direct and indirect effects (Alwin & Hauser, 1975), assessing mediation hypotheses (H6a and H6b) when the indirect effects are significant (Hayes, 2009). A traditional way of testing mediation hypotheses has been the Sobel test (Sobel, 1982). It is commonly indicated for a formal test of mediation in multiple linear regressions. However, such a test cannot be applied with consistent PLS because path coefficients are not independent when computed using PLS, and PLS does not provide raw unstandardized path coefficients (Sosik, Kahai, & Piovoso, 2009). Besides, Hayes (2009) indicates that the Sobel test requires the assumption that the sampling distribution of the indirect effect is normal. As an alternative, we have applied the analytical approach (Preacher & Hayes, 2008; Taylor, MacKinnon, & Tein, 2008) to test our mediation hypotheses, through a bootstrapping procedure that does not impose the assumption of normality on the sampling distribution (Chin, 2010; Preacher & Hayes, 2008), and the performance of bootstrapping is higher than the Sobel test (Mackinnon, Cumbers, & Chapman, 2002; Mackinnon, Lockwood, & Williams, 2004).

Indirect effects of information systems and training-learning on performance through the innovation are both positive and significant (product of paths = 0.24*** and 0.10**, respectively), supporting H6a and H6b. In this sense, the indirect effect of training on performance is about 79.8% of the total effect, while the indirect effect of the use of information systems on performance is a 60.9% of the total effect, suggesting both full mediations since direct effects are not significant (Baron & Kenny, 1986).

4.3 Moderation

Finally, Hypotheses H7 (H7a, H7b, and H7c) establish moderator effects of the family-managed firm on the relationships between innovation in production processes to performance and its mediation effects. We test them by implementing a multigroup analysis (MGA) and a permutation test to check any significant difference in predictor's betas between groups (Eberl, 2010; Fassott, Henseler, & Coelho, 2016; Ketchen, 2013; Wong, 2016). However, before performing MGA, measurement invariance must be assessed via measurement invariance of composites (MICOM) approach (Henseler et al., 2016), a three-step procedure which is the more suitable approach for PLS-SEM as a composite-based analysis technique (Rasoolimanesh, Roldán, Jaafar, & Ramayah, 2017). If compositional measurement invariance cannot be assessed, the MGA analysis is not meaningful (Henseler et al., 2016).

Table 6 reports the MICOM analysis results. They suggest that every construct support the full measurement invariance hypotheses. Therefore, moderation analysis

Table 6 MICOM analysis

	Step 1	Step 2		Step 3a	Step 3b	Conclusion
	Configurational	Compositional		Equal means	Equal variances	Measurement
Construct	Invariance	Invariance	*p*-value	*p*-value	*p*-value	Invariance
IS	Yes	Yes	0.104	0.584	0.342	Full
TL	Yes	Yes	0.106	0.054	0.533	Full
IPP	Yes	Yes	0.185	0.979	0.689	Full
PE	Yes	Yes	0.482	0.072	0.699	Full

Source: Authors' own table

can be done by comparing groups in our sample. As a result, we tested moderation hypotheses applying a set of procedures: MGA-PLS path difference analysis, parametric and Welch-Satterthwaite *t*-tests, and permutation-based approach.

Table 7 shows moderation analysis results via MGA-PLS and permutation tests. These results suggest that the innovation effect on performance is significantly different in family-managed firms that in nonfamily-managed business. This finding provides evidence supporting the postulate of a significant interaction between innovation in production processes and family firm. This positive and significant coefficient indicates that the slope of the line representing the link between innovation and performance is steeper when the firm is family managed, supporting H7a. Moreover, the indirect effect of an information system on performance is significantly higher in family-managed firms, supporting H7b. However, we did not find significant differences in indirect effects of training-learning on performance, so H7c is rejected.

5 Discussion and Conclusions

This research analyzes the influence of information systems and training-learning on innovation in production processes and performance, the mediating role of innovation on the relationship between information systems and training-learning on performance, as well as the moderating role of the family involvement on AC in the county of El Oro in the Republic of Ecuador. It tries to add knowledge for managers and government on how innovations affect the production processes of AC for the improvement of their performance and the role that family enterprises play.

In this region, most AC are MSMEs, and knowing the innovative processes and the performance of these AC is of interest for their effect on the economy of developing countries and for their influence on other areas of the same type in the adjoining regions or facing similar challenges since the AC are interdependent mainly due to linkage between families (Wu & Zhang, 2013).

Table 7 Moderation analyses

Panel A	Family farm			Versus	No-family farm			
	Path		t		Path		t	
Direct effects								
IS → IPP	0.69	***	12.21		0.37	***	5.61	
TL → IPP	0.14	*	2.35		0.40	***	5.77	
R^2 [Adjusted R^2]	0.73		[0.72]		0.52		[0.51]	
IS → PE	0.07		0.84		0.18		1.62	
TL → PE	0.08		1.33		0.07		0.59	
IPP → PE	0.47	***	6.15		0.18		1.89	
R^2 [Adjusted R^2]	0.39		[0.38]		0.16		[0.14]	
SRMR	0.06				0.08			
Chi-squared	862.0				628.4			
Indirect effects								
IS → IPP → PE	0.32	***	5.38		0.07		1.72	
TL → IPP → PE	0.06	*	2.22		0.07		1.76	
Panel B	MGA-PLS (Path diff)		Parametric (t)		W-S (t)		Permutation (p-value)	Moderated
Direct effects								
IS → IPP	0.32	***	3.65	***	3.66	***	0.001	Yes
TL → IPP	0.26	**	2.86	**	2.87	**	0.004	Yes
IS → PE	0.11		0.77		0.76		0.409	No
TL → PE	0.01		0.11		0.10		0.898	No
IPP → PE	0.28	**	2.35	*	2.33	*	0.026	Yes
Indirect effects								
IS → IPP → PE	0.25	***	3.24	***	3.56	***	0.001	Yes
TL → IPP → PE	0.01		0.16		0.16		0.869	No

Source: Authors' own table

*$p < 0.05$; **$p < 0.01$; ***$p < 0.001$

Panel A: PLS path model results for groups, family farms versus nonfamily farms. Significance, t statistic and 95% bias-corrected confidence interval performed by 10,000 rep. Bootstrapping procedure. Panel B: Moderation tests: (1) Path differences between groups in MGA-PLS approach; (2) Parametric test t statistic; (3) Welch-Satterthwaite test t statistic; (4) Permutation-based p-values

Our results show that both information systems (H1) and training-learning (H3) have a direct and nonsignificant influence on the performance of the AC, so our first and third hypotheses are not accepted. Indeed, these two variables affect indirectly on the performance through innovation in production processes. That is, innovation in production processes acts as a mediator between them. Thus, the results confirm the hypotheses H6a (0.24) and H6b (0.10). Furthermore, it is also demonstrating the positive, direct, and significant effect of information systems and training-learning on innovation in production processes, thus confirming the hypotheses H2 (0.62) and H4 (0.25).

These are quite exciting results. They reveal that investment processes in information systems and training-learning increase performance due to the impact they have on innovation but not by themselves. In another way round, according to previous researchers (e.g., Kraus et al., 2012; Schumpeter, 1947), the innovation of banana agricultural MSMEs positively, directly, and significantly influences performance, supporting H5 (0.38). Therefore, the use of information systems and training-learning is an instrument to innovation.

In this vein, information systems and training-learning have to be seen as associated with the daily problems and challenges that guarantee survival in SMEs (Faherty & Stephens, 2016) to develop new changes and innovate. Besides, for banana agricultural MSMEs, training-learning is carried out through the transmission of transgenerational knowledge, empowering the subjects participating in them which facilitate the innovation process and them impacting on performance.

The fact of being a banana agricultural family MSMEs has a positive and significant effect in performance which confirms H7a as previous research suggests it (e.g., Kowalewski, Talavera, & Stetsyuk, 2009; Maury, 2006). When distinguishing between family and nonfamily banana agricultural MSMEs, it is observed the positive and significant moderation that family has on the relationship between innovation in production processes and performance that support H7a as well as the relationship between information systems and innovation in production processes and between training-learning and innovation in production processes.

Moreover, the indirect effect of information systems on performance is moderated by banana agricultural family MSMEs, confirming H7b; however, the indirect effect of training on performance is not significantly different in the family or nonfamily AC, rejecting H7c. This different behavior and the counterintuitive result can be explained by considering that the family owner-managers of the AC appreciate that they incur in "costs" when carrying out training activities that reduce the benefit and the performance affecting their future which they are a commitment to preserving their heritage. Considering the knowledge in an individualized rather than collaborative way (Bhatt, 2002) by the family AC does not allow them to appreciate the relevance of the training-learning which is carried out by transgenerational knowledge.

It is of interest to highlight the relevance of the innovation that is a key factor for performance, which implies the importance to be attended by the AC, particularly considered the low level of available resources of this organization that is influenced mainly by contextual factors (Rosenbusch et al., 2011).

Summarizing, this research demonstrates that innovation in AC in the province of El Oro in the Republic of Ecuador not only has a direct impact on performance, it also acts as a driver leading investment in information systems to performance. Even more, this capacity to influence performance is reinforced in the case of banana family enterprises.

5.1 *Contributions*

This paper contributes to the literature on the measurement of innovation and performance applied to AC in the context of a developing country such as Ecuador. It also analyzes the influence of the family implication on the innovation and performance.

Academics, practitioners, and AC can benefit from this research by recognizing that innovation in production processes is a driver that is influenced by information systems (62%, 69% for family AC), which contribute to the performance of the AC. It follows that the banana companies of the province of El Oro that adapt their information systems and opt for the training-learning of their workers will contribute to transforming their production processes (production and marketing processes), improving them, and thus achieving better performance. In this process banana agricultural family MSME can take advantage.

It also reveals the role of training-learning in the AC and the deceptive role of the possible costs incurred. Undoubtedly, more research is required in this regard, but our data suggest that training-learning must be seen in the long-term (investment), playing a crucial role in innovation, particularly in the AC whose knowledge is transgenerational (e.g., family farm).

The proposed model can be used as a beneficial tool by the AC (family or nonfamily) for the evaluation of the innovative processes and their effects on performance. Manager-owners of AC who know the effects of information systems and training-learning on innovation in production processes will be able to sue the regional governments and central government support policies aimed at improving these systems.

These results can also be useful in the case of the province of El Oro of the Republic of Ecuador, where there are agricultural colleges and university centers (e.g., the Technical University of Machala) for which these results can serve as a basis for design and update training programs and for the promotion of new studies (e.g., family farm) that help to boost research on innovation in the ACs.

5.2 Limitations and Further Research

Innovation in production processes and performance are endogenous variables that are influenced not only by information systems and training-learning. In this sense, a limitation of this work is not considering an integrated conceptual model for innovation that includes both internal and external factors, including aspects such as culture (e.g., the existence of cultural differences between provinces, regions, states, and countries). Our study is carried out in the geographic context of the province of El Oro of the Republic of Ecuador, so its results are specifically contextualized, and its extrapolation must be done with caution.

Additionally, the work carried out here is cross-sectionally referred exclusively to the year 2017, the year in which the survey was carried out, which may limit its results (Xayavong et al., 2016). Consider, for example, the influence on the respondents of the prices of the banana or the expectations in the regulation of political effects.

For the family farm, it has been considered that all of them behave similarly. Nevertheless, prior research (Diéguez-Soto, 2013; Diéguez-Soto et al., 2015) stated that different types of family firms exist according to the influence that family exerts in the enterprise as well as the level of governance. These issues constitute possible limitations.

In future research, aspects such as the existence of different types of AC with different risk assessments and with different sizes and management systems that can vary widely point to the need to investigate all these aspects, both in isolation and as a whole. It is recommended in future investigations to consider the previous determinants and the fact that most of these economic units are familiar, which opens an impressive line of work of particular interest for the authors.

References

Abrego-Almazán, D., Sánchez-Tovar, Y., & Medina-Quintero, J. M. (2017). Influencia de los sistemas de información en los resultados organizacionales. *Contaduría y Administración, 62*(2), 303–320.

Alwin, D. F., & Hauser, R. M. (1975). The decomposition of effects in path analysis. *American Sociological Review, 40*(1), 37.

Bacha, E. (2012). The impact of information systems on the performance of the core competence and supporting activities of a firm. *Journal of Management Development, 31*, 752–763.

Baron, R., & Kenny, D. (1986). The moderator-mediator variable distinction in social psychological research: Conceptual, strategic, and statistical considerations. *Journal of Personality and Social Psychology, 51*(6), 1173–1182.

Bassellier, G., & Benbasat, I. (2004). Business competence of information technology professionals: Conceptual development and influence on IT-business partnerships. *MIS Quarterly, 28*(4), 673–694.

Becheikh, N., Landry, R., & Amara, N. (2006). Lessons from innovation empirical studies in the manufacturing sector: A systematic review of the literature from 1993–2003. *Technovation, 26*, 644–664.

Bento, A., Bento, R., & Ferreira Wite, L. (2014). Strategic performance management systems: Impact on business results. *Journal of Computer Information Systems, 54*(3), 25–33.
Bessant, J., & Tidd, J. (2011). *Innovation and entrepreneurship* (Vol. 31). Brighton: Wiley.
Bhatt, G. D. (2002). Management strategies for individual knowledge and organizational knowledge. *Journal of Knowledge Management, 6*(1), 31–39.
Campos Climent, V., Melián Navarro, A., & Sanchis Palacio, J. R. (2014). El método Delphi como técnica de diagnóstico estratégico. Estudio empírico aplicado a las empresas de inserción en España. *Revista Europea de Direccion y Economia de la Empresa, 23*, 72–81.
Cannarella, C., & Piccioni, V. (2011). Traditiovations: Creating innovation from the past and antique techniques for rural areas. *Technovation, 31*(12), 689–699.
Carneiro, A. (2000). How do knowledge management influence innovation and competitiveness? *Journal of Knowledge Management, 4*, 87–98.
Carrión, G. C., Henseler, J., Ringle, C. M., & Roldán, J. L. (2016). Prediction-oriented modeling in business research by means of PLS path modeling: Introduction to a JBR special section. *Journal of Business Research, 69*(10), 4545–4551.
Castro, L. M., Calvas, B., & Knoke, T. (2015). Ecuadorian banana farms should consider organic banana with low price risks in their land-use portfolios. *PLoS One, 10*(3), 1–23.
Chin, W. W. (2010). How to write up and report PLS analyses. In V. Esposito Vinzi, W. W. Chin, J. Henseler, & H. Wang (Eds.), *Handbook of partial least squares* (pp. 655–690). Heidelberg: Springer.
Chrisman, J. J., Chua, J. H., & Kellermanns, F. (2009). Priorities, resource stocks, and performance in family and nonfamily firms. *Entrepreneurship: Theory and Practice, 33*(3), 739–760.
Chrisman, J. J., Chua, J. H., Pearson, A. W., & Barnett, T. (2012). Family involvement, family influence, and family-centered non-economic goals in small firms. *Entrepreneurship: Theory and practice, 36*(2), 267–293.
Chrisman, J. J., Chua, J. H., & Sharma, P. (2005). Trends and directions in the development of a strategic management theory of the family firm. *Entrepreneurship: Theory and Practice, 29*(5), 555–575.
Chua, J. H., Chrisman, J. J., & Sharma, P. (1999). Defining the family business by behavior. *Entrepreneurship: Theory and Practice, 23*(4), 19.
Clark, J., & Guy, K. (1998). Innovation and competitiveness: A review. *Technology Analysis & Strategic Management, 10*(3), 363–395.
Crossan, M. M., & Apaydin, M. (2010). A multi-dimensional framework of organizational innovation: A systematic review of the literature. *Journal of Management Studies, 47*(6), 1154–1191.
Daane, J., Francis, J. A., Oliveros, O., & Bolo, M. (2008). Performance indicators for agricultural innovation systems in the ACP region. *Synthesis report from the international expert consultation workshop*. Technical Centre for Agricultural and Rural Cooperation (CTA), Wageningen.
De Lone, W. H., & McLean, E. R. (1992). Information systems success: The quest for the dependent variable. *Information Systems Research, 3*(1), 60–95.
De Massis, A., Kotlar, J., Campopiano, G., & Cassia, L. (2013). Dispersion of family ownership and the performance of small-to-medium size private family firms. *Journal of Family Business Strategy, 4*(3), 166–175.
Diéguez-Soto, J. (2013). Types of private family firms and firm performance: Special reference to lone founder. In *International Family Enterprise Research Academy*. St. Gallen: IFERA.
Diéguez-Soto, J., López-Delgado, P., & Rojo-Ramírez, A. (2015). Identifying and classifying family businesses. *Review of Managerial Science, 9*(3), 603–634.
Dijkstra, T. K., & Henseler, J. (2015a). Consistent and asymptotically normal PLS estimators for linear structural equations. *Computational Statistics and Data Analysis, 81*, 10–23.
Dijkstra, T. K., & Henseler, J. (2015b). Consistent partial least squares path modeling. *MIS Quarterly, 39*(2), 297–316.

Dostie, B., & Jayaraman, R. (2013). Do higher costs spur process innovations and managerial incentives? Evidence from a natural experiment. *Journal of Economics and Management Strategy, 22*(3), 529–550.
Dressler, J. B., & Tauer, L. (2015). Socioemotional wealth in the family farm. *Agricultural Finance Review, 75*(3), 403–415.
Eberl, M. (2010). An application of PLS in multi-group analysis: The need for differentiated corporate-level marketing in the mobile communications industry. In V. E. Vinzi, W. W. Chin, J. Henseler, & H. Wang (Eds.), *Handbook of partial least squares* (pp. 487–514). Heidelberg: Springer.
Efrat, K. (2014). The direct and indirect impact of culture on innovation. *Technovation, 34*, 12–20.
Faherty, U., & Stephens, S. (2016). Innovation in micro enterprises: Reality or fiction? *Journal of Small Business and Enterprise Development, 23*(2), 349–362.
FAO. (2015). *El estado mundial de la agricultura y la alimentación, 2014. La innovación en la agricultura familiar*. Roma: OECD.
Fassott, G., Henseler, J., & Coelho, P. S. (2016). Testing moderating effects in PLS path models with composite variables. *Industrial Management & Data Systems, 116*(9), 1887–1900.
Fernández Pérez, P., Lluch, A., & Barbero, M. I. (2015). *Familias empresarias y grandes empresas familiares en América Latina y España: una visión de largo plazo*. Bilbao: Fundacion BBVA.
Fornell, C., & Larcker, D. F. (1981). Evaluating structural equation models with unobservable variables and measurement error. *Journal of Marketing Research, 18*, 39–50.
Freeman, C., & Soete, L. (1997). *The economics of industrial innovation*. London: Routledge.
Garengo, P., Biazzo, S., & Bititci, U. S. (2005). Performance measurement systems in SMEs: A review for a research agenda. *International Journal of Management Reviews, 7*, 25–47.
Goel, R. K., & Nelson, M. A. (2018). Determinants of process innovation introductions: Evidence from 115 developing countries. *Managerial and Decision Economics, 2*, 1–11.
González, X., Miles-Touya, D., & Pazó, C. (2016). R&D, worker training and innovation: Firm-level evidence. *Industry and Innovation, 23*(8), 694–712.
Gorla, N., Somers, T. M., & Wong, B. (2010). Organizational impact of system quality, information quality, and service quality. *Journal of Strategic Information Systems, 19*, 207–228.
Gras, C. (2009). Changing patterns in family farming: The case of the Pampa Region, Argentina. *Journal of Agrarian Change, 9*(3), 345–364.
Guisado González, M., Vila Alonso, M., & Guisado Tato, M. (2016). Innovation, productive capacity, training and productivity. *Cuadernos de Gestion, 16*, 77–92.
Habbershon, T. G., & Williams, M. (1999). A resource-based framework for assessing the strategic advantages of family firms. *Family Business Review, 12*, 1–15.
Haberli, C., Oliveira, T., & Yanaze, M. (2017). Understanding the determinants of adoption of enterprise resource planning (ERP) technology within the agrifood context: The case of the Midwest of Brazil. *International Food and Agribusiness Management Review, 20*(5), 729–746.
Hair, J. F., Jr., Hult, G. T. M., Ringle, C., & Sarstedt, M. (2016). *A primer on partial least squares structural equation modeling (PLS-SEM)*. Thousand Oaks, CA: Sage.
Hayes, A. F. (2009). Beyond Baron and Kenny: Statistical mediation analysis in the new millennium. *Communication Monographs, 76*(4), 408–420.
Heanue, K., & Macken Walsh, Á. (2010). *The rural development programme (2007–2013) and farmer innovation: A review to date and look to the future* (No. 1007). Rural Economy and Development Programme, Teagasc.
Henseler, J. (2017). Bridging design and behavioral research with variance-based structural equation modeling. *Journal of Advertising, 46*(1), 178–192.
Henseler, J., Ringle, C. M., & Sarstedt, M. (2014). A new criterion for assessing discriminant validity in variance-based structural equation modeling. *Journal of the Academy of Marketing Science, 43*, 115–135.
Henseler, J., Ringle, C. M., & Sarstedt, M. (2016). Testing measurement invariance of composites using partial least squares. *International Marketing Review, 33*(3), 405–431.

Hu, L., & Bentler, P. (1998). Fit indices in covariance structure modeling: Sensitivity to underparameterized model misspecification. *Psychol Methods, 3*(4), 424–453.

Hung, R. Y. Y., Yang, B., Lien, B. Y. H., McLean, G. N., & Kuo, Y. M. (2010). Dynamic capability: Impact of process alignment and organizational learning culture on performance. *Journal of World Business, 45*(3), 285–294.

Jiménez-Zarco, A. I., González-González, I., Martínez-Ruíz, M. P., & Izquierdo-Yusta, A. (2015). New service innovation success: Analyzing the influence of performance indicator nature. *Computers in Human Behavior, 51*, 1024–1031.

Kabunga, N. S., Dubois, T., & Qaim, M. (2014). Impact of tissue culture banana technology on farm household income and food security in Kenya. *Food Policy, 45*, 25–34.

Ketchen, D. J. (2013). A primer on partial least squares structural equation modeling. *Long Range Planning, 46*(1–2), 184–185.

Kowalewski, O., Talavera, O., & Stetsyuk, I. (2009). Influence of family involvement in management and ownership on firm performance: Evidence From Poland. *Family Business Review, 23*, 45–59.

Kraiczy, N. D., Hack, A., & Kellermanns, F. W. (2014). New product portfolio performance in family firms. *Journal of Business Research, 67*(6), 1065–1073.

Kraus, S., Pohjola, M., & Koponen, A. (2012). Innovation in family firms: An empirical analysis linking organizational and managerial innovation to corporate success. *Review of Managerial Science, 6*, 265–286.

Lam, A. (2005). Organizational innovation. In J. Fagerberg, D. Mowery, & R. Nelson (Eds.), *The Oxford handbook of innovation*. Oxford: Oxford University Press.

Le Gal, P. Y., Dugué, P., Faure, G., & Novak, S. (2011). How does research address the design of innovative agricultural production systems at the farm level? A review. *Agricultural Systems, 104*(9), 714–728.

Leydesdorff, L., & Etzkowitz, H. (1998). The triple helix as a model for innovation studies. *Science and public policy, 25*(3), 195–203.

Lindell, M. K., & Whitney, D. J. (2001). Accounting for common method variance in cross-sectional research designs. *Journal of Applied Psychology, 86*(1), 114–121.

López Fernández, M. C., Serrano Bedia, A. M., & Gómez López, R. (2016). Determinants of innovation decision in small and medium-sized family enterprises. *Journal of Small Business and Enterprise Development, 23*(2), 408–427.

Luengo, M. J., & Obeso, M. (2013). El efecto de la triple hélice en los resultados de innovación. *Revista de Administração de Empresas, 53*, 388–399.

Mackenzie, S. B., Podsakoff, P. M., & Podsakoff, N. P. (2011). Construct measurement and validation procedures in MIS and behavioral research: Integrating new and existing techniques. *MIS Quarterly, 35*(2), 293–334.

Mackinnon, D., Cumbers, A., & Chapman, K. (2002). Learning, innovation, and regional development: A critical appraisal of recent debates. *Progress in Human Geography, 26*(3), 293–312.

Mackinnon, D. P., Lockwood, C. M., & Williams, J. (2004). Confidence limits for the indirect effect: Distribution of the product and resampling methods. *Multivariate Behavioral Research, 39*(1), 99–128.

Mahmood, M. A., & Soon, S. K. (1991). A comprehensive model for measuring the potential impact of information technology on organizational strategic variables. *Decision Sciences, 22*(4), 869–897.

Martinez Caro, E., Briones Peñalver, A. J., & De Nieves Nieto, C. (2011). Responsabilidad social, cooperación empresarial e innovación en agronegocios. *Revista Europea de Dirección y Economía de la Empresa, 20*, 63–76.

Mat, A., & Razak, R. C. (2013). Technological innovation implementation: A proposed model on organizational learning capability with moderating effect of knowledge complexity. *African Journal of Business Management, 7*(12), 926–935.

Maury, B. (2006). Family ownership and firm performance: Empirical evidence from Western European corporations. *Journal of Corporate Finance, 12*(2), 321–341.

Miller, D., Le Breton-Miller, I., Lester, R. H., & Cannella, A. A., Jr. (2007). Are family firms really superior performers? *Journal of corporate finance, 13*(5), 829–858.

Nieves, J. (2014). Relaciones sociales, capacidades dinámicas e innovación: un análisis empírico en la industria hotelera. *Revista Europea de Dirección y Economía de la Empresa, 23*, 166–174.

Nwachukwu, S. L., Vitell, S. J., Jr., Gilbert, F. W., & Barnes, J. H. (1997). Ethics and social responsibility in marketing: An examination of the ethical evaluation of advertising strategies. *Journal of Business Research, 39*(2), 107–118.

OECD. (2005). *Oslo manual: Guidelines for collecting and interpreting innovation data* (3th ed.). Madrid: Tragsa.

Padilla-Meléndez, A., Diéguez-Soto, J., & Garrido-Moreno, A. (2015). Empirical research on innovation in family business: Literature review and proposal of an integrative framework. *Review of Business Management, 17*(56), 1064–1089.

Pérez-Méndez, J. A., & Machado-Cabezas, Á. (2015). Relationship between management information systems and corporate performance. *Revista de Contabilidad, 18*, 32–43.

Podsakoff, P. M., MacKenzie, S. B., & Podsakoff, N. P. (2012). Sources of method bias in social science research and recommendations on how to control it. *Annual Review of Psychology, 63*, 539–569.

Podsakoff, P. M., MacKenzie, S. B., & Podsakoff, N. P. (2016). Recommendations for creating better concept definitions in the organizational, behavioral, and social sciences. *Organizational Research Methods, 19*(2), 159–203.

Preacher, K. J., & Hayes, A. F. (2008). Asymptotic and resampling strategies for assessing and comparing indirect effects in multiple mediator models. *Behavior Research Methods, 40*(3), 879–891.

Price, D. P., Stoica, M., & Boncella, R. J. (2013). The relationship between innovation, knowledge, and performance in family and non-family firms: An analysis of SMEs. *Journal of Innovation and Entrepreneurship, 2*, 2–20.

Rao, Y., Ken, H. G., & Chen, Y. (2015). Information systems maturity, knowledge sharing, and firm performance. *International Journal of Accounting & Information Management, 23*, 106–127.

Rasoolimanesh, S. M., Roldán, J. L., Jaafar, M., & Ramayah, T. (2017). Factors influencing residents' perceptions toward tourism development: Differences across rural and urban world heritage sites. *Journal of Travel Research, 56*(6), 760–775.

Ravichandran, T., & Lertwongsatien, C. (2005). Effect of information systems resources and capabilities on firm performance: A resource-based perspective. *Journal of Management Information Systems, 21*(4), 237–276.

Ravichandran, T., & Rai, A. (2000). Total quality management in information systems development: Key constructs and relationships. *Journal of Management Information Systems, 16*(3), 119–155.

Reguant-Álvarez, M., & Torrado-Fonseca, M. (2016). El método Delphi. *Revista d' Innovació i Recerca em Educació, 9*, 87–102.

Reimers, M., & Klasen, S. (2013). Revisiting the role of education for agricultural productivity. *American Journal of Agricultural Economics, 95*(1), 131–152.

Reinartz, W., Haenlein, M., & Henseler, J. (2009). An empirical comparison of the efficacy of covariance-based and variance-based SEM. *International Journal of Research in Marketing, 26*(4), 332–344.

Ringle, C., Wende, S., & Becker, J. (2017). *SmartPLS 3*. Boenningstedt: SmartPLS GmbH.

Rosenbusch, N., Brinckmann, J., & Bausch, A. (2011). Is innovation always beneficial? A meta-analysis of the relationship between innovation and performance in SMEs. *Journal of Business Venturing, 26*, 441–457.

Salazar Veloz, R., & Del Cioppo Morstadt, J. (2016). *Ecuador: Exportación de banano (Musa sp.) Estudio sectorial del banano ecuatoriano de exportación*. Milagro (Ecuador): The Agrarian University of Ecuador.

Schmid, T., Achleitner, A. K., Ampenberger, M., & Kaserer, C. (2014). Family firms and R&D behavior-New evidence from a large-scale survey. *Research Policy, 43*(1), 233–244.
Schumpeter, J. A. (1947). Theoretical problems of economic growth. *The Journal of Economic History, 7*, 1–9.
Selamat, Z., & Nasir, A. M. (2013). Efficiency measurement of malaysian agriculture firms. *International Journal of Trade, Economics, and Finance, 4*(2), 79–85.
Sharma, P., Chrisman, J. J., & Gersick, K. E. (2012). 25 Years of family business review: Reflections on the past and perspectives for the future. *Family Business Review, 25*(1), 5–15.
Sleuwaegen, L. (1992). Advances in international marketing. *International Journal of Research in Marketing, 9*(4), 319–323.
Smith, M. (2008). Differences between family and non-family SMEs: A comparative study of Australia and Belgium. *Journal of Management and Organization, 14*, 40–58.
Sobel, M. E. (1982). Asymptotic confidence intervals for indirect effects in structural equation models. *Sociological Methodology, 13*, 290–312.
Sosik, J. J., Kahai, S. S., & Piovoso, M. J. (2009). Silver bullet or voodoo statistics?: A primer for using the partial least squares data analytic technique in group and organization research. *Group and Organization Management, 34*(1), 5–36.
Spielman, D. J., & Birner, R. (2008). *How innovative is your agriculture? Using innovation indicators and benchmarks to strengthen national agricultural innovation systems*. Washington, DC: The World Bank.
Sumberg, J. (2005). Systems of innovation theory and the changing architecture of agricultural research in Africa. *Food Policy, 30*, 21–41.
Tarafdar, M., & Gordon, S. R. (2007). Understanding the influence of information systems competencies on process innovation: A resource-based view. *The Journal of Strategic Information Systems, 16*(4), 353–392.
Taylor, A. B., MacKinnon, D. P., & Tein, J. Y. (2008). Tests of the three-path mediated effect. *Organizational Research Methods, 11*(2), 241–269.
Terziovski, M. (2008). Innovation practice and its performance implications in small and medium enterprises (SMEs) in the manufacturing sector: A resource-based view. *Strategic Management Journal, 31*(8), 892–902.
Wang, Z., & Wang, N. (2012). Knowledge sharing, innovation, and firm performance. *Expert Systems with Applications, 39*, 8899–8908.
Westhead, P., & Cowling, M. (1997). Performance contrasts between family and non-family unquoted companies in the UK. *International Journal of Entrepreneurial Behavior & Research, 3*(1), 30–52.
Wilkening, E. A. (1954). Change in farm technology as related to familism, family decision making, and family integration. *American Sociological Review, 19*(1), 29–37.
Wong, K. K. (2016). Mediation analysis, categorical moderation analysis, and higher-order constructs modeling in partial least squares structural equation modeling (PLS-SEM): A B2B example using SmartPLS. *The Marketing Bulletin, 26*, 1–22.
Wu, B., & Zhang, L. (2013). Farmer innovation diffusion via network building: A case of winter greenhouse diffusion in China. *Agriculture and Human Values, 30*(4), 641–651.
Xayavong, V., Kingwell, R., & Islam, N. (2016). How training and innovation link to farm performance: A structural equation analysis. *The Australian Journal of Agricultural and Resource Economics, 60*(2), 227–242.

The Effect of CEO Attributes on the Internationalization-Performance Relationship in Private Family Firms

Jonathan Bauweraerts

Abstract This chapter explores the influence of CEO attributes on the internationalization-performance relationships of private family firms. Drawing on the upper echelon theory and the socioemotional wealth perspective, this research posits that CEOs play a crucial role in the internationalization of private family firms and that some of their attributes have moderating effects on the internationalization-performance relationship. Using cross-sectional data of 319 private family firms that expanded abroad, we find that both the family and the generational status of the CEO moderate the relationship between internationalization and firm performance.

Keywords Family firms · Internationalization · Performance · CEO · Socioemotional wealth

1 Introduction

The relationship between internationalization and performance has attracted considerable attention in the literature (Marano, Arregle, Hitt, Spadafora, & van Essen, 2016). While some scholars argue that operating across borders allows the firm to acquire new capabilities and benefit from economies of scale and a better access to new resources and capital (Bartlett & Ghoshal, 1989; Dunning, 1988), others claim that operating internationally is very challenging since the firm must face and learn about new customers and regulatory environments while supporting additional investments (Johanson & Vahlne, 1977; Zaheer, 1995). As a result, a large amount of studies has tried to determine the shape and the sign of the internationalization-performance relationship (e.g., Contractor, 2012; Cuervo-Cazurra, Ciravegna,

J. Bauweraerts (✉)
Control, Accounting, Risk Management, and Entrepreneurship Department, University of Mons, Mons, Belgium
e-mail: jonathan.bauweraerts@umons.ac.be

J. M. Saiz-Álvarez et al. (eds.), *Entrepreneurship and Family Business Vitality*, Studies on Entrepreneurship, Structural Change and Industrial Dynamics, https://doi.org/10.1007/978-3-030-15526-1_12

Melgarejo, & Lopez, 2018; Marano et al., 2016). Despite the abundance of analyses, little is known about the drivers of this relationship in the family business context (Arregle, Duran, Hitt, & Van Essen, 2017), which is quite surprising considering their specificities and their predominant role in the worldwide economy (De Massis, Frattini, Majocchi, & Piscitello, 2018). More specifically, few works have investigated how top executives affect the operation of family firms' internationalization and subsequent performance.

This chapter tries to address the research gap by analyzing the influence of the attributes of chief executive officers (CEOs) on the internationalization-performance relationship in private family firms. When private family firms move into new international markets, the CEO plays a crucial role in shaping the internationalization strategy because of his/her central position in the decision-making team (Miller & Dröge, 1986). Prior research reveals that the attributes of CEO impact the firm's ability to manage to internationalization process (Cuervo-Cazurra et al., 2018). Indeed, upper echelon theorists suggest that executives should possess characteristics that enable them to manage international complexity and ambiguity (Nielsen & Nielsen, 2011). According to that perspective, CEO attributes, such as age (Herrmann & Datta, 2005), educational level (Tihanyi, Ellstrand, Daily, & Dalton, 2000), tenure (Herrmann & Datta, 2005), and international experience (Kirca, Hult, Deligonul, Perryy, & Cavusgil, 2012), represent proxies for their cognitive orientation and knowledge base (Hambrick & Mason, 1984) and should therefore have an impact on the firm's internationalization performance. This study focuses on the family and generational status of the CEO as potential moderators of the internationalization-performance relationship in family firms.

Considering that family CEOs differ from nonfamily CEOs because of the greater emphasis they place on nonfinancial goals, this chapter draws on the socioemotional wealth (SEW) model (Gómez-Mejía, Haynes, Núñez-Nickel, Jacobson, & Moyano-Fuentes, 2007) to develop a consistent theoretical frame. According to that perspective, family firms are loss averse with respect to SEW, that is, the nonfinancial utility the family derives from its participation in the business, including family control and influence, emotional attachment and identification with the firm, binding social ties, the perpetuation of the family legacy, and the firm's long-term success (Berrone, Cruz, & Gómez-Mejia, 2012). Several scholars claim that SEW encompasses a bright side and a dark side (Kellermanns, Eddleston, & Zellweger, 2012). Indeed, recent works highlight that SEW preservation can lead to favorable outcomes (e.g., employee commitment, emotional attachment, long-term investments) but also outcomes (e.g., altruism, incompetent family managers, inefficient use of firm resources) (see Kalm & Gómez-Mejia, 2016 for a review).

This study argues that the dark side of SEW will predominate when a family CEO leads the firm, thereby altering the internationalization-performance relationship. The underlying assumption is that, although family CEOs' desire to preserve SEW by passing a healthy business onto subsequent generations may encourage them to develop a long-term orientation that enhances internationalization (Liang, Wang, & Cui, 2014), their propensity to preserve SEW may deprive the organization of essential resources and capabilities (Naldi, Cennamo, Corbetta, & Gómez-Mejia,

2013) to capture the financial benefits of internationalization. In other words, family CEOs' long-term orientation derived from SEW is not a sufficient condition to realize the value-creating potential of internationalization, the lack of resources, and capabilities outweighing its advantage. Considering that the salience of SEW tends to diminish when leadership positions are held by later generations of the family (Cruz & Nordqvist, 2012), this research also proposes to distinguish between family-founder and later generation family CEOs to determine how generational differences in CEO position drive the internationalization-performance relationship among family-led firms.

This chapter contributes to the literature in several ways. First, while prior works stress the importance of CEO attributes in the internationalization-performance relationship (e.g., Cuervo-Cazurra et al., 2018; Kirca et al., 2012), this issue has been largely overlooked in the family business context. This study offers fresh insights into this problematic by analyzing how specific family attributes of the CEO affect the internationalization-performance link. Second, this study combines the upper echelon theory and the socioemotional wealth perspective to explore how CEO attributes affect the ability of the firm to convert international initiatives into performance gains, whereas most studies referred to these theoretical approaches to study the antecedents of international behaviors (Banalieva & Eddleston, 2011; Scholes, Mustafa, & Chen, 2016). By so doing, we extend the relevance of both theoretical lenses to the understanding of the internationalization-performance relationship in family firms.

2 Theoretical Background and Hypotheses Development

2.1 The Internationalization-Performance Relationship in Family Firms

Internationalization is an essential pathway for firm growth and long-term value creation (Sapienza, Autio, George, & Zahra, 2006). Operating in foreign countries enables the firm to increase its market power (Kogut, 1985), realize economies of scale and scope (Dunning, 1988), and reduce input costs (Dunning, 1988). Internationalizing is also a strategic move that allows the firm to exploit its intangible assets in international markets. For instance, setting up subsidiaries in multiple countries increases the firm's knowledge base, capabilities, and competitiveness through experiential learning in the host countries (Barkema & Vermeulen, 1998), enabling the firm to create a competitive advantage compared to companies that restrict their activities to their domestic market. Expanding into new geographic markets enhances the firm's ability to reconfigure and adjust its resources for other markets, making it more likely to develop dynamic capabilities that facilitate the implementation of internationalization strategies (Sapienza et al., 2006). However, entering new geographic markets is not free of costs and challenges. Indeed, internationalizing firms typically face specific costs associated with the liabilities of foreignness (Zaheer, 1995) and newness (Stinchcombe, 1965). While the liability of foreignness refers to the difficulties encountered by new entrants such as unfamiliarity with local culture, lack of local information, and discriminatory treatment by host governments, customers, and suppliers (Zaheer, 1995), the liability of newness is related to the new rules and business methods internationalization imposes (Stinchcombe, 1965). As a result, operating internationally fosters organizational and environmental complexity, which implies higher governance and coordination needs and hence higher transaction costs (Reid, 1983).

Considering the advantages and the drawbacks of internationalization, the study of the internationalization-performance relationship has become a central reflection point in the international business literature (Powell, 2014). Despite the large number of studies in the field (see Marano et al., 2016 for a meta-analysis), there is still no consensus on the sign or the shape of the internationalization-performance link. While some scholars find a positive relationship (e.g., Chen & Tan, 2012; Elango & Sethi, 2007), others show a negative (e.g., Wan & Hoskisson, 2003), U-shaped (e.g., Lu & Beamish, 2001), inverted U-shaped (e.g., Brida, Driha, Ramón-Rodriguez, & Such-Devesa, 2016; Gomes & Ramaswamy, 1999), S-shaped (e.g., Ruigrok, Amann, & Wagner, 2007), or W-shaped link (Fernández-Olmos, Gargallo-Castel, & Giner-Bagües, 2016). Marano et al. (2016) argue that these inconsistencies result from the omitted impact of theory-driven moderators or the methodological approaches such as differences in the time frames examined, endogeneity controls, and operationalizations of the main variables of interest.

Despite this growing attention for the internationalization-performance relationship, few studies address this problem in the family business context (Fernández-Olmos et al., 2016). Most works try to explain how the distinctive nature of family firms drives differences in internationalization strategies between family and nonfamily firms (see Arregle et al., 2017 for a meta-analysis) but neglect to analyze how family-specific factors enhance or constrain the pecuniary realization of internationalization. However, exploring this issue is crucial since family firms present unique characteristics that could affect the internationalization-performance relationship in different ways (Arregle, Naldi, Nordqvist, & Hitt, 2012). Not exhaustively, family member's emotional attachment to the business enhances commitment, trusted relationship, and a long-term orientation that fosters organizational learning and the construction of dynamic capabilities (Zahra, Hayton, Neubaum, Dibrell, & Craig, 2008), two factors that facilitate the conversion of international initiatives into profits (Fernández-Olmos et al., 2016). In contrast, family firms' inclination toward the protection of family control deprives the organization of the managerial and financial resources required to cope with the demands of internationalization strategies (Arregle et al., 2012). Indeed, family firms are often reluctant to hire competent nonfamily collaborators or to raise external funds because family members perceive these decisions as potential threats to family control (Gómez-Mejía et al., 2007).

Considering that family firms present different characteristics depending on the degree and the type of family influence in the business (Nordqvist, Sharma, &

Chirico, 2014), we can expect that the internationalization performance is contingent on family-related sources of heterogeneity. Therefore, we ascribe to the contingency view of the internationalization-performance relationship and propose to explore the moderating effects of specific family attributes of the CEO on this relationship.

2.2 *The Effect of Family CEO*

Most studies focusing on the CEO and his/her impact on strategy and performance rely on the upper echelon theory which suggests that the idiosyncrasies, characteristics, and behaviors of executives determine strategic choices and reflect firm performance since they are the most powerful actors in the organization (Hambrick & Mason, 1984). According to that perspective, performance and strategic differences arise from CEO attributes that reflect CEOs' cognition and values (Musteen, Barker, & Baeten, 2006). Previous works confirm this assumption by showing that a large variety of CEO attributes affects the firm's strategic choices and performance (e.g., Cuervo-Cazurra et al., 2018; Herrmann & Datta, 2005; Kirca et al., 2012).

In the context of family firms, various studies explore how CEO attributes affect performance and strategies (e.g., Boling, Pieper, & Covin, 2016; Miller, Le Breton-Miller, Minichilli, Corbetta, & Pittino, 2014), including internationalization (Scholes et al., 2016). However, little is known about the effect of the CEO on the internationalization-performance relationship despite his/her crucial role in the implementation of the firm's international strategy. Indeed, CEOs are responsible for the strategic management of the firm (Carpenter, Geletkanycz, & Sanders, 2004) and must, therefore, ensure that internationalization decisions are oriented toward the survival of the firm (Nielsen & Nielsen, 2011). This task is particularly complex in private family firms where the CEO is often a family member that also considers the family's socioemotional wealth (SEW), that is, the nonfinancial endowment of the firm meeting the family's affective needs, such as emotional attachment, reputation, ability to exercise control influence, and perpetuation of the family dynasty, when making decisions (Gómez-Mejía et al., 2007). According to the SEW perspective, family decision-makers are risk-averse concerning SEW and hence take decisions that mitigate SEW losses (Gómez-Mejía et al., 2007). Prior works advocate that the salience of SEW in decision-making depends on the nature and the extent of family involvement in the firm (Berrone et al., 2012). In private family firms, where family involvement in ownership is usually high, the appointment of a family CEO reinforces the ability of the family to protect the family's SEW (Naldi et al., 2013). As a result, SEW preservation is more likely to play a crucial role in the decision-making process of family-led firms.

Since SEW preservation represents the pivotal reference frame in family-led firms, its impact on the internationalization-performance relationship cannot be underestimated. Following recent advancements suggesting that SEW encompasses a bright side and a dark side (Kellermanns et al., 2012), we now illustrate how both aspects of SEW affect the conversion of international strategies into profits in family-led firms. On the bright side, family CEOs' desire to preserve SEW by passing the business onto the subsequent generations may encourage them to develop a long-term orientation that drives international behaviors and growth (Liang et al., 2014). Accordingly, they can rely on the family support to sustain international initiatives that contribute to the safeguard of the future family SEW (Alessandri, Cerrato, & Eddleston, 2018). However, this greater inclination toward internationalization may not be enough to realize the economic potential of international strategies that also require specific capabilities and resources.

Beyond long-term aspirations, protecting SEW implies that family CEOs place high importance on preserving family control and exercising family influence, which makes family CEOs less inclined to professionalize the organization by hiring outside managers and delegating authority (Gómez-Mejía et al., 2007). Limiting managerial positions to family members can be problematic since it increases the likelihood of appointing incompetent executives, whereas internationalizing firms require superior managerial expertise and coordination capabilities to face the increased complexity of international activities (Arregle et al., 2012). Additionally, the willingness of family CEOs to maintain family control makes them particularly reluctant to external funding (Lardon, Deloof, & Jorissen, 2017), depriving the organization of essential financial resources to realize the economic potential of international activities (Alessandri et al., 2018). Altruistic behaviors represent another SEW aspect that can provoke detrimental effects when family power is exacerbated (Schulze, Lubatkin, & Dino, 2003), which is typically the case in private family-led firms where the dominant family coalition has no opposition (Lubatkin, Schulze, Ling, & Dino, 2005). In that context, family altruism allows the family to free ride by exploiting the firm's resources for personal benefits and privileges to family members (Schulze et al., 2003), reducing the bunch of resources available for the implementation of international initiatives.

Preserving SEW also implies binding social ties (Berrone et al., 2012). As such family CEOs engage in enduring relationships with external stakeholders that allow the family to build a good image over time. Most family CEOs develop connections with other business leaders that are geographically close, making them benefit from local network ties (Banalieva & Eddleston, 2011). Since international success requires the establishment of relevant and strong networks outside the country of origin (Zhang, Ma, Wang, Li, & Huo, 2016), family CEOs may lack the personal connections required for effectively entering new international markets. Due to their emotional attachment to the organization, family CEOs are also more likely to emphasize the historical foundations of the firm, which can hamper the pecuniary realization of international moves that require the adaptation of the traditional methods of operation to the reality of the new international markets (Alessandri et al., 2018).

Taken together, the abovementioned arguments seem to indicate that the dark side of SEW is more likely to outweigh the bright side in family-led firms. While the bright side motivates to internationalize, the dark side reduces the capabilities and resources available to operate internationally, which would hamper the internationalization-performance relationship in family-led firms. Therefore, the following hypothesis is posed:

Hypothesis 1 *The presence of a family CEO negatively moderates the internationalization-performance relationship.*

2.3 The Effect of Family-Founder CEOs

Beyond the distinction between family and nonfamily CEOs, the family business literature stresses the importance to account for generational differences in CEO position by distinguishing between family firms run by the founding generation and family firms led by later generations (Cruz & Nordqvist, 2012; Fang et al., 2018; Miller, Le Breton-Miller, & Lester, 2011). Prior research suggests that the family's emotional attachment to the firm is highest when the family founder leads the firm, whereas it tends to decline when leadership positions are passed onto subsequent generations (Cruz & Nordqvist, 2012). As a result, the salience of SEW is more likely to vary depending on the generation leading the business (Berrone et al., 2012). In what follows, we try to understand how generational differences in CEO position affect the salience of SEW prerogatives to explain variation in the internationalization-performance relationship.

Family-founder CEOs have often invested considerable amounts of time, energy, and money in the business since its setting up and are hence characterized by a strong personal attachment, commitment, and identification with the firm (Miller et al., 2011). As a result, they are more likely to engage in long-term growth initiatives, including internationalization, with the aim of preserving SEW through the development of a healthy company for the next generations (Liang et al., 2014). Despite this willingness to internationalize, the dark side of SEW can alter the financial consequences of internationalization when the family founder runs the firm. Indeed, family-founder CEOs tend to place a greater emphasis on the historical foundations of the firm and are thus particularly reluctant to change the traditional methods of operation of the business (Cruz & Nordqvist, 2012). The consequence is that the firm can encounter some difficulties in managing internationalization since it requires the adaptation of the structures and management policies to the reality of the new international markets (Sapienza et al., 2006). Additionally, the strong emotional ties of family-founder CEOs to the business model they have created may make them reluctant to build international connections and networks that could induce significant changes to it, depriving the organization of critical business relationships to convert international initiatives into profits (Johanson & Vahlne, 1977). Furthermore, the stronger concern of family founders for maintaining family control and influence can considerably reduce the financial and human resources available to ensure the financial success of international initiatives (Fang et al., 2018).

In contrast, later generation family CEOs tend to deemphasize SEW preservation when making decisions. The emergence of family branches when leadership passes out of the hands of the founding generation weakens family ties and identification with the firm, making later generation family CEOs more concerned with the economic well-being of their own family (Miller et al., 2011). As a result, they show lower levels of attachment and commitment to the organization, reducing the aversion to the loss of family control associated with external funding and human capital as well as the loss of traditionality associated with the historical foundations of the business. Therefore, the dark side of SEW could diminish when the firm is led by later generation family CEOs that are more likely to dispose of the required resources to adapt the organization to the specific needs of internationalization.

In sum, the dark side of SEW seems to be more prominent in family firms led by a family founder, as compared to later generation run family firms, which is likely to alter the internationalization-performance relationship. Accordingly, the following hypothesis is proposed:

Hypothesis 2 *Among family-led firms, the presence of family-founder CEO negatively moderates the internationalization-performance relationship.*

3 Method

3.1 Sample Description

This study uses empirical data from a survey in 2015 to investigate internationalization and governance issues within private family firms in Belgium. Studying the performance implications of family firm internationalization is particularly relevant in this country. Indeed, Belgium is a small open economy with a natural propensity to operate internationalization: more than one-third of private firms in Belgium records exports, which is well above the average of the European Union (Onkelinx, Manolova, & Edelman, 2016). Furthermore, more than 50% of private firms are family-owned in this national setting (Crutzen & Pirnay, 2014).

To build our sample, we obtained information about a population of 3136 exporting private firms from the Walloon Agency for exportation. We sent mail questionnaires to the CEO of these companies to gather information on the firm's internationalization strategy as well as the ownership, managerial, and governance structures. After two rounds, we collected 372 responses and removed 26 incomplete surveys, resulting in a sample of 346 potential private family firms. Twenty-seven questionnaires were excluded from the analysis because these firms did not meet the family business definition used in this study, that is, the firm is owned by multiple family members of the same family (i.e., the majority of equity is owned by the family).

To reduce common method bias, we used both the primary data from the survey and secondary data for financial and accounting variables extracted from the Belfirst database (Podsakoff, MacKenzie, & Podsakoff, 2012). We also tested for potential nonresponse bias using several procedures that did not show any significant differences between responding and nonresponding firms as well as between earliest and latest respondents.

3.2 *Variable Description*

Dependent Variables Consistent with prior works on internationalization and firm performance, an accounting-based measure of firm performance (ROA) is used as the dependent variable. ROA is calculated as net income divided by total assets. This measure presents several advantages. First, it improves comparison with previous studies that used the same dependent variable (i.e., Banalieva & Eddleston, 2011; Cuervo-Cazurra et al., 2018). Second, ROA is a good indicator of how well economies of scale that is often associated with internationalization are achieved (Dunning, 1988). Third, given our focus on the moderating effect of CEO attributes, ROA represents an appropriate measure of performance since it is often used to assess executives' effectiveness and efficiency (Robins & Wiersema, 1995).

Independent Variables Considering the large variety of indicators measuring the degree of internationalization of a firm, this study uses two measures. First, to capture the scale of internationalization that assesses the firm's dependence on foreign markets and resources, two common variables of foreign sales to total sales (FSTS) and foreign assets to total assets (FATA) are integrated into a composite measure of internationalization because of their strong correlation ($r = 0.91$, $p < 0.01$) (Sanders & Carpenter, 1998) and, second, to assess the scope of internationalization that captures cultural and institutional variety, the number of foreign countries in which SMEs received sales during 3 years (Dai, Maksimov, Gilbert, & Fernhaber, 2014).

Moderators Family CEO is a dummy variable equaling 1 if a family member holds CEO position, 0 otherwise (Banalieva & Eddleston, 2011). Family-founder CEO is a dummy variable coded 1 if the family founder is the CEO, 0 otherwise (Miller et al., 2011).

Control Variables In line with prior works (Cuervo-Cazurra et al., 2018), additional CEO attributes are included in the model, that is, CEO tenure, age, education, international experience, and CEO duality. CEO tenure corresponds to the number of years for which the firm's CEO has been in that position. CEO age is computed as the age of the CEO. CEO education is measured on a six-point scale, reflecting the highest level of education attained by the CEO (1 = elementary school, 2 = junior high school, 3 = high school, 4 = 3-year college, 5 = master's degree, 7 = Ph.D. degree). Three sources of international exposure measure CEO international experience. The CEO was asked whether (1) he/she has expatriated experience or has worked outside Belgium in some professional capacity, (2) he/she has been responsible for a firm's international market, and (3) he/she was educated outside Belgium. These three proxies were measured as dummy variables and were highly correlated

($r = 0.88$, $p < 0.01$). Following Reuber and Fischer (1997), we incorporated them into a single measure of CEO international experience. CEO duality is computed as a dummy variable equaling 1 if the CEO of the firm is the chairman of the board, 0 otherwise. This study also controls for firm size (total employees transformed by the natural logarithm), leverage (total debts divided by total assets), and industry affiliation by integrating five industry dummies for manufacturing, service, retail, high-technology, and wholesale. Following prior works in the internationalization literature (George, Wiklund, & Zahra, 2005), we used a 3-year lag between the dependent variable and the independent variables to mitigate reverse causality concerns and allow time for the internationalization efforts of family firms to materialize.

4 Results

4.1 Descriptive Statistics

Descriptive statistics and correlations are presented in Tables 1 and 2. Table 1 reports the descriptive statistics and correlations for the entire sample of family firms, and Table 2 presents the same figures for the subsample of family-led firms. Both internationalization scale ($p < 0.001$) and scope ($p < 0.001$) are positively and significantly correlated to performance in the entire sample of family firms and the subsample of family-led firms. Interestingly enough, Tables 1 and 2 show positive and significant correlations between CEO education and performance ($p < 0.001$), internationalization scale ($p < 0.05$), and scope ($p < 0.05$), while CEO international experience is positively and significantly correlated to performance ($p < 0.001$), internationalization scale ($p < 0.01$), and scope ($p < 0.01$). To test further for the effects of multicollinearity, we computed the variance inflation factors (VIF). The highest VIF is 2.7, which is well below the threshold of 10, suggesting that multicollinearity is not a problem.

4.2 Regression Analysis

The multiple OLS regression analyses are presented in Tables 3 and 4. We tested our hypotheses using two sets of six regressions. Table 3 reports the results of internationalization scale, and Table 4 illustrates the results of internationalization scope. Models 4–6 of Table 3 and Models 10–12 of Table 4 present the results of our subsample of family-led firms. All models in both Tables 3 and 4 are significant, and each has a reasonable explanatory power. Furthermore, the results of the Breusch-Pagan/Cook-Weisberg and White tests to check for heteroscedasticity are $\chi^2(1) = 2.89$; $p\ (\chi^2) = 0.1417$ and $\chi^2 = 88.97$; $p = 0.2452$, respectively, indicating that heteroscedasticity is not a concern. While the former determines whether the

Table 1 Descriptive statistics and correlation matrix (family- and nonfamily-led firms)

Variables	Mean	S.D.	1	2	3	4	5	6	7	8	9	10	11
1. ROA	0.061	0.054	1.00										
2. International scale	0.3247	0.162	0.341***	1.00									
3. International scope	2.953	1.112	0.243***	0.264***	1.00								
4. Family CEO	0.880	0.424	−0.102	−0.094	−0.106	1.00							
5. CEO tenure	7.422	2.847	0.094	−0.123*	−0.131*	0.109	1.00						
6. CEO age	49.34	5.245	−0.086	−0.084	−0.079	0.110	0.143*	1.00					
7. CEO education	4.145	2.314	0.245***	0.134*	0.156*	−0.124*	0.084	−0.056	1.00				
8. CEO international experience	1.262	0.419	0.227***	0.184**	0.187**	−0.126*	0.097	0.094	0.136*	1.00			
9. CEO duality	0.731	0.176	−0.141*	−0.141*	−0.132*	0.177**	0.054	0.067	−0.068	0.032	1.00		
10. Firm size	4.867	1.978	0.094	0.052	0.098	0.074	−0.064	0.072	−0.086	0.044	0.034	1.00	
11. Leverage	0.426	0.184	0.189**	0.103	0.104	−0.142*	0.041	0.052	−0.049	−0.094	0.057	0.127*	1.00

Source: Author's own table

$*p < 0.05$, $**p < 0.01$, $***p < 0.001$, $N = 319$

Table 2 Descriptive statistics and correlation matrix (family-led firms)

Variables	Mean	S.D.	1	2	3	4	5	6	7	8	9	10	11
1. ROA	0.053	0.044	1.00										
2. International scale	0.294	0.147	0.308***	1.00									
3. International scope	2.147	1.041	0.232***	0.259***	1.00								
4. Family-founder CEO	0.423	0.102	−0.112	−0.102	−0.084	1.00							
5. CEO tenure	7.317	2.847	0.096	−0.127*	−0.141*	0.172**	1.00						
6. CEO age	48.41	4.847	−0.074	−0.079	−0.085	0.104	0.138*	1.00					
7. CEO education	3.941	1.984	0.232***	0.129*	0.148*	−0.125*	0.074	−0.063	1.00				
8. CEO international experience	1.106	0.402	0.214***	0.177**	0.194**	−0.131*	0.088	0.074	0.132*	1.00			
9. CEO duality	0.823	0.189	−0.142*	−0.139*	−0.137*	0.184**	0.061	0.084	−0.094	0.047	1.00		
10. Firm size	4.841	1.942	0.084	0.067	0.089	0.066	−0.042	0.068	−0.042	0.037	0.038	1.00	
11. Leverage	0.386	0.141	0.175**	0.094	0.085	−0.151*	0.052	0.046	−0.037	−0.088	0.049	0.141*	1.00

Source: Author's own table

$*p < 0.05$, $**p < 0.01$, $***p < 0.001$, $N = 281$

Table 3 Regression analyses (internationalization scale, ROA, and CEO attributes)

Variables	Model 1	Model 2	Model 3	Model 4	Model 5	Model 6
Intercept	0.064** (0.011)	0.062** (0.010)	0.072** (0.012)	0.077** (0.011)	0.080** (0.014)	0.081** (0.016)
CEO tenure	0.004 (0.001)	0.006 (0.002)	0.007 (0.002)	0.010 (0.009)	0.011 (0.009)	0.013 (0.010)
CEO age	−0.024 (0.018)	−0.031 (0.028)	−0.033 (0.029)	−0.061 (0.055)	−0.074 (0.063)	−0.068 (0.054)
CEO education	0.019** (0.005)	0.021** (0.006)	0.017** (0.004)	0.031** (0.009)	0.038** (0.010)	0.041** (0.012)
CEO international experience	0.021** (0.005)	0.023** (0.004)	0.026** (0.003)	0.047** (0.005)	0.054** (0.007)	0.061** (0.008)
CEO duality	−0.054 (0.048)	−0.066 (0.052)	−0.057 (0.049)	−0.047 (0.036)	0.041 (0.033)	−0.074 (0.065)
Firm size	0.066 (0.059)	0.068 (0.060)	0.071 (0.064)	0.104 (0.099)	0.110 (0.108)	0.106 (0.097)
Leverage	0.044** (0.010)	0.048** (0.012)	0.051** (0.014)	0.084** (0.014)	0.091** (0.015)	0.093** (0.016)
Internationalization scale		0.023*** (0.004)	0.018*** (0.003)		0.031*** (0.004)	0.034*** (0.004)
Family CEO		−0.014 (0.010)	−0.023 (0.018)			
Family-founder CEO					−0.026 (0.018)	−0.018 (0.011)
Internationalization scale*family CEO			−0.010*** (0.001)			
Internationalization scale*family-founder CEO						−0.014*** (0.002)
Industry dummies	Yes	Yes	Yes	Yes	Yes	Yes
R^2	0.084	0.110	0.143	0.079	0.104	0.138
Adjusted R^2	0.067	0.084	0.102	0.059	0.082	0.010
F-stat	2.472**	2.849**	3.046***	2.252**	2.741**	2.947***
N	319	319	319	281	281	281

Source: Author's own table
$*p < 0.05$, $**p < 0.01$, $***p < 0.001$

estimated variance of the residuals from a regression depends on the values of the independent variables, the latter tests whether the residual variance of a variable in a regression model is constant.

The results show similar effects of both internationalization scale and scope on performance. Models 2 ($\beta = 0.023$, $p < 0.001$) and 5 ($\beta = 0.031$, $p < 0.001$) of Table 3 reveal that internationalization scale is positively and significantly related to performance. These findings suggest that expanding foreign markets and accessing foreign resources enhance the realization of economies of scale for family firms. Models 8 ($\beta = 0.042$, $p < 0.001$) and 11 ($\beta = 0.036$, $p < 0.001$) of Table 4 show a

Table 4 Regression analyses (internationalization scope, ROA, and CEO attributes)

Variables	Model 7	Model 8	Model 9	Model 10	Model 11	Model 12
Intercept	0.023*** (0.004)	0.034*** (0.006)	0.042*** (0.005)	0.071*** (0.005)	0.088*** (0.008)	0.091*** (0.009)
CEO tenure	0.006 (0.005)	0.007 (0.006)	0.012 (0.009)	0.018 (0.012)	0.019 (0.013)	0.023 (0.018)
CEO age	−0.018 (0.012)	−0.026 (0.023)	−0.019 (0.013)	−0.034 (0.025)	−0.041 (0.036)	−0.038 (0.031)
CEO education	0.064** (0.007)	0.076** (0.010)	0.084** (0.021)	0.095** (0.018)	0.088** (0.015)	0.076** (0.012)
CEO international experience	0.096** (0.012)	0.092** (0.010)	0.082** (0.009)	0.097** (0.013)	0.083** (0.010)	0.099** (0.014)
CEO duality	−0.014 (0.012)	−0.023 (0.019)	−0.029 (0.023)	−0.036 (0.032)	−0.041 (0.038)	−0.045 (0.041)
Firm size	0.136 (0.126)	0.152 (0.144)	0.123 (0.111)	0.081 (0.079)	0.088 (0.081)	0.091 (0.084)
Leverage	0.047** (0.005)	0.051** (0.004)	0.038** (0.003)	0.076** (0.009)	0.072** (0.008)	0.061** (0.004)
Internationalization scope		0.042*** (0.002)	0.046*** (0.002)		0.036*** (0.003)	0.038*** (0.003)
Family CEO		−0.017 (0.015)	−0.021 (0.019)			
Family-founder CEO					0.018 (0.014)	0.022 (0.019)
Internationalization scope*family CEO			−0.012*** (0.002)			
Internationalization scope*family-founder CEO						−0.014*** (0.002)
Industry dummies	Yes	Yes	Yes	Yes	Yes	Yes
R^2	0.086	0.112	0.132	0.079	0.102	0.124

Adjusted R^2	0.066	0.098	0.113	0.062	0.084	0.103
F-stat	2.142**	2.517**	2.947***	2.041**	2.418**	2.847***
N	319	319	319	281	281	281

Source: Author's own table

$^*p < 0.05$, $^{**}p < 0.01$, $^{***}p < 0.001$

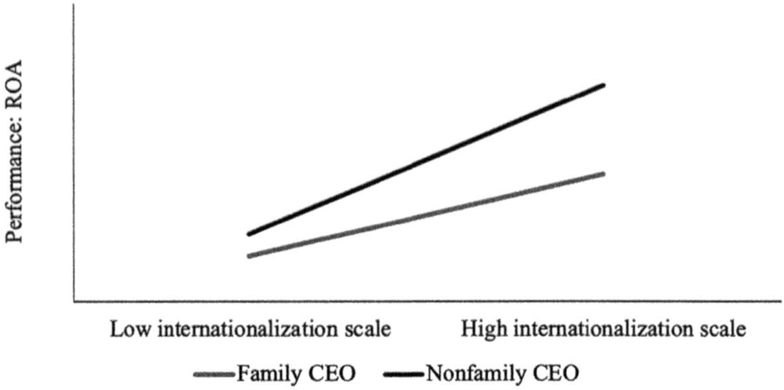

Fig. 1 The internationalization-performance relationship in family and nonfamily-led firms. Source: Author's own figure

positive and significant influence of internationalization scope on performance, implying that exporting to an increasing number of countries is beneficial for family firms' performance.

Consistent with hypothesis 1, the presence of a family CEO negatively moderates the internationalization-performance relationship. In Models 3 and 9, the interaction terms *Internationalization scale*Family CEO* ($\beta = 0.010$, $p < 0.001$) and *Internationalization scope*Family CEO* ($\beta = 0.012$, $p < 0.001$) are negatively and significantly related to performance. Our results also provide strong support for hypothesis 2 and the negative moderating effect of family-founder CEOs on the internationalization-performance relationship in family-led firms. Models 6 and 12 show negative and significant relationships between both interaction terms *Internationalization scale*Family-founder CEO* ($\beta = 0.010$, $p < 0.001$) and *Internationalization scope*Family-founder CEO* ($\beta = 0.012$, $p < 0.001$) and performance in family-led firms. Taken together, these findings suggest that family involvement in CEO positions attenuates the positive relationship between internationalization and performance and that this negative effect is even more prominent in the presence of family-founder CEO when the firm is family-led.

To better illustrate our findings, we plotted the moderating effects in Figs. 1 and 2. Figure 1 confirms that family CEOs hamper the internationalization-performance relationship, the slope of the internationalization scale-performance line being less positive when the firm is family-led. We found similar patterns for family-founder CEOs. Figure 2 reveals that the positive impact of internationalization scale on performance is attenuated in the presence of a family-founder CEO in family-led firms. Similar graphs were obtained for the internationalization scope-performance relationship.

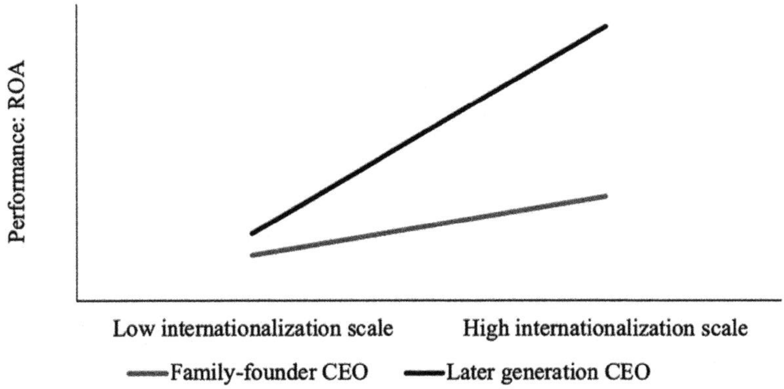

Fig. 2 The internationalization-performance relationship in family firms with a family-founder CEO and a later generation CEO. Source: Author's own figure

5 Discussion and Conclusion

The main purpose of this chapter was to investigate how the internationalization-performance relationship varies among family firms depending on CEO attributes. Based on a sample of 319 Belgian private family firms, this study combines insights from the upper echelon theory and the SEW perspective to explore the impact of specific family attributes of the CEO on this relationship. The results confirm our predictions: both family CEOs and family-founder CEOs negatively moderate the internationalization-performance link. An explanation for the detrimental effect of family CEOs lies in the fact that, although the long-term orientation derived from family CEOs' desire to perpetuate the family legacy may stimulate international initiatives, this motivation is not enough to ensure the conversion of internationalization into profits because the dark side of SEW deprives the organization of essential resources and capabilities to operate internationally. This detrimental effect is amplified in the presence of a family-founder CEO because of his/her stronger emotional attachment to the firm, as compared to later generation family CEOs, thereby explaining the negative moderating effect of family-founder CEOs on the internationalization-performance link among family-led firms.

This chapter contributes to the literature in two ways. First, prior research finds that CEO attributes play a crucial role in the internationalization-performance relationship (e.g., Cuervo-Cazurra et al., 2018; Kirca et al., 2012); however, this issue is not well-documented in the family business literature. With the aim of addressing this gap, this study integrates family-related CEO characteristics into the internationalization-performance relationship, which offers a clearer picture of how this relationship is enhanced or constrained by CEO attributes in the family business context. Second, this research relies on the upper echelon theory and the SEW perspective to study the internationalization-performance relationship in family firms. While prior works used these theoretical approaches to investigate family firms' internationalization behaviors (Banalieva & Eddleston, 2011; Scholes et al., 2016), few of them integrate them into the analysis of the internationalization-performance relationship. Extending the upper echelon theory and incorporating the SEW perspective, this study demonstrates that the financial benefits family firms can derive from internationalization depend on family CEOs inclination toward SEW preservation.

This chapter also has some practical implications. While our results demonstrate that internationalization is an appropriate strategic behavior to engender performance gains in family firms, family owners and advisors must be conscious that having a family member occupying CEO position could represent a sub-optimal solution to ensure an effective internationalization process and that the presence of a family-founder CEO even reinforces the constraints placed on the pecuniary realization of international initiatives. At the same time, family CEOs, especially family-founder CEOs, should be aware and understand that blindly preserving the family's SEW can be detrimental for the internationalization of the business.

This chapter suffers from several limitations that must be acknowledged to orientate future research. First, this study relied on cross-sectional data, while it might be interesting to replicate the models with longitudinal data to consider the time variability of the dependent and independent variables. Second, data are limited to the Belgian context. Therefore, future research in other countries could be useful to strengthen the external validity of these findings since institutional, legal, and cultural factors could affect the internationalization-performance link (Elango & Sethi, 2007). Third, this study used SEW as a primary theoretical lens to develop the hypotheses. However, we did not measure it directly. Accordingly, future research could try to measure the bright side and the dark side of SEW to determine how the different aspects of the family's nonfinancial endowment affect the pecuniary realization of internationalization in family firms.

References

Alessandri, T. M., Cerrato, D., & Eddleston, K. A. (2018). The mixed gamble of internationalization in family and nonfamily firms: The moderating role of organizational slack. *Global Strategy Journal, 8*(1), 46–72.

Arregle, J. L., Duran, P., Hitt, M. A., & Van Essen, M. (2017). Why is family firms' internationalization unique? A meta-analysis. *Entrepreneurship: Theory and Practice, 41*(5), 801–831.

Arregle, J. L., Naldi, L., Nordqvist, M., & Hitt, M. A. (2012). Internationalization of family-controlled firms: A study of the effects of external involvement in governance. *Entrepreneurship: Theory and Practice, 36*(6), 1115–1143.

Banalieva, E. R., & Eddleston, K. A. (2011). Home-region focus and performance of family firms: The role of family vs. non-family leaders. *Journal of International Business Studies, 42*(8), 1060–1072.

Barkema, H. G., & Vermeulen, F. (1998). International expansion through start-up or acquisition: A learning perspective. *Academy of Management Journal, 41*(1), 7–26.

Bartlett, C., & Ghoshal, S. (1989). *The transnational solution*. Boston: Harvard Business School Press.

Berrone, P., Cruz, C., & Gómez-Mejia, L. R. (2012). Socioemotional wealth in family firms: Theoretical dimensions, assessment approaches, and agenda for future research. *Family Business Review, 25*(3), 258–279.

Boling, J. R., Pieper, T. M., & Covin, J. G. (2016). CEO tenure and entrepreneurial orientation within family and nonfamily firms. *Entrepreneurship: Theory and Practice, 40*(4), 891–913.

Brida, J. G., Driha, O., Ramón-Rodriguez, A. B., & Such-Devesa, M. J. (2016). The inverted-U relationship between the degree of internationalization and the performance: The case of Spanish hotel chains. *Tourism Management Perspectives, 17*, 72–81.

Carpenter, M. A., Geletkanycz, M. A., & Sanders, W. G. (2004). Upper echelons research revisited: Antecedents, elements, and consequences of top management team composition. *Journal of Management, 30*(6), 749–778.

Chen, S., & Tan, H. (2012). Region effects in the internationalization-performance relationship in Chinese firms. *Journal of World Business, 47*(1), 73–80.

Contractor, F. J. (2012). Why do multinational firms exist? A theory note about the effect of multinational expansion on performance and recent methodological critiques. *Global Strategy Journal, 2*(4), 318–331.

Crutzen, N., & Pirnay, F. (2014). *L'impact de la crise sur la transmission dans les entreprises familiales en Belgique francophone*. Liege: HEC-University of Liege.

Cruz, C., & Nordqvist, M. (2012). Entrepreneurial orientation in family firms: A generational perspective. *Small Business Economics, 38*(1), 33–49.

Cuervo-Cazurra, A., Ciravegna, L., Melgarejo, M., & Lopez, L. (2018). Home country uncertainty and the internationalization-performance relationship: Building an uncertainty management capability. *Journal of World Business, 53*(2), 209–221.

Dai, L., Maksimov, V., Gilbert, B. A., & Fernhaber, S. A. (2014). Entrepreneurial orientation and international scope: The differential roles of innovativeness, proactiveness, and risk-taking. *Journal of Business Venturing, 29*(4), 511–524.

De Massis, A., Frattini, F., Majocchi, A., & Piscitello, L. (2018). Family firms in the global economy: Toward a deeper understanding of internationalization determinants, processes, and outcomes. *Global Strategy Journal, 8*(1), 3–21.

Dunning, J. H. (1988). The eclectic paradigm of international production: A restatement and some possible extensions. *Journal of International Business Studies, 19*(1), 1–31.

Elango, B., & Sethi, S. P. (2007). An exploration of the relationship between country of origin (COE) and the internationalization-performance paradigm. *Management International Review, 47*(3), 369–392.

Fang, H., Kotlar, J., Memili, E., Chrisman, J. J., & De Massis, A. (2018). The pursuit of international opportunities in family firms: Generational differences and the role of knowledge-based resources. *Global Strategy Journal, 8*(1), 136–157.

Fernández-Olmos, M., Gargallo-Castel, A., & Giner-Bagües, E. (2016). Internationalization and performance in Spanish family SMEs: The W-curve. *Business Research Quarterly, 19*(2), 122–136.

George, G., Wiklund, J., & Zahra, S. A. (2005). Ownership and the internationalization of small firms. *Journal of Management, 31*(2), 210–233.

Gomes, L., & Ramaswamy, K. (1999). An empirical examination of the form of the relationship between multinationality and performance. *Journal of International Business Studies, 30*(1), 173–187.

Gómez-Mejía, L. R., Haynes, K. T., Núñez-Nickel, M., Jacobson, K. J., & Moyano-Fuentes, J. (2007). Socioemotional wealth and business risks in family-controlled firms: Evidence from Spanish olive oil mills. *Administrative Science Quarterly, 52*(1), 106–137.

Hambrick, D. C., & Mason, P. A. (1984). Upper echelons: The organization as a reflection of its top managers. *Academy of Management Review, 9*(2), 193–206.

Herrmann, P., & Datta, D. K. (2005). Relationships between top management team characteristics and international diversification: An empirical investigation. *British Journal of Management, 16* (1), 69–78.

Johanson, J., & Vahlne, J. E. (1977). The internationalization process of the firm—A model of knowledge development and increasing foreign market commitments. *Journal of International Business Studies, 8*(1), 23–32.

Kalm, M., & Gómez-Mejia, L. R. (2016). Socioemotional wealth preservation in family firms. *Revista de Administração (São Paulo), 51*(4), 409–411.

Kellermanns, F. W., Eddleston, K. A., & Zellweger, T. M. (2012). Article commentary: Extending the socioemotional wealth perspective: A look at the dark side. *Entrepreneurship: Theory and Practice, 36*(6), 1175–1182.

Kirca, A. H., Hult, G. T. M., Deligonul, S., Perryy, M. Z., & Cavusgil, S. T. (2012). A multilevel examination of the drivers of firm multinationality: A meta-analysis. *Journal of Management, 38*(2), 502–530.

Kogut, B. (1985). Designing global strategies: Profiting from operational flexibility. *Sloan Management Review, 21*(1), 27–38.

Lardon, A., Deloof, M., & Jorissen, A. (2017). Outside CEOs, board control and the financing policy of small privately held family firms. *Journal of Family Business Strategy, 8*(1), 29–41.

Liang, X., Wang, L., & Cui, Z. (2014). Chinese private firms and internationalization: Effects of family involvement in management and family ownership. *Family Business Review, 27*(2), 126–141.

Lu, J. W., & Beamish, P. W. (2001). The internationalization and performance of SMEs. *Strategic Management Journal, 22*(6–7), 565–586.

Lubatkin, M. H., Schulze, W. S., Ling, Y., & Dino, R. N. (2005). The effects of parental altruism on the governance of family-managed firms. *Journal of Organizational Behavior, 26*(3), 313–330.

Marano, V., Arregle, J. L., Hitt, M. A., Spadafora, E., & van Essen, M. (2016). Home country institutions and the internationalization-performance relationship: A meta-analytic review. *Journal of Management, 42*(5), 1075–1110.

Miller, D., & Dröge, C. (1986). Psychological and traditional determinants of structure. *Administrative Science Quarterly, 31*(4), 539–560.

Miller, D., Le Breton-Miller, I., & Lester, R. H. (2011). Family and lone founder ownership and strategic behavior: Social context, identity, and institutional logics. *Journal of Management Studies, 48*(1), 1–25.

Miller, D., Le Breton-Miller, I., Minichilli, A., Corbetta, G., & Pittino, D. (2014). When do non-family CEO s outperform in family firms? Agency and behavioural agency perspectives. *Journal of Management Studies, 51*(4), 547–572.

Musteen, M., Barker, V. L., III, & Baeten, V. L. (2006). CEO attributes associated with attitude toward change: The direct and moderating effects of CEO tenure. *Journal of Business Research, 59*(5), 604–612.

Naldi, L., Cennamo, C., Corbetta, G., & Gómez-Mejia, L. R. (2013). Preserving socioemotional wealth in family firms: Asset or liability? The moderating role of business context. *Entrepreneurship: Theory and Practice, 37*(6), 1341–1360.

Nielsen, B. B., & Nielsen, S. (2011). The role of top management team international orientation in international strategic decision-making: The choice of foreign entry mode. *Journal of World Business, 46*(2), 185–193.

Nordqvist, M., Sharma, P., & Chirico, F. (2014). Family firm heterogeneity and governance: A configuration approach. *Journal of Small Business Management, 52*(2), 192–209.

Onkelinx, J., Manolova, T. S., & Edelman, L. F. (2016). The human factor: Investments in employee human capital, productivity, and SME internationalization. *Journal of International Management, 22*(4), 351–364.

Podsakoff, P. M., MacKenzie, S. B., & Podsakoff, N. P. (2012). Sources of method bias in social science research and recommendations on how to control it. *Annual Review of Psychology, 63*, 539–569.

Powell, K. S. (2014). From M-P to MA-P: Multinationality alignment and performance. *Journal of International Business Studies, 45*(2), 211–226.

Reid, S. (1983). Firm internationalization, transaction costs, and strategic choice. *International Marketing Review, 1*(2), 44–56.

Reuber, A. R., & Fischer, E. (1997). The influence of the management team's international experience on the internationalization behaviors of SMEs. *Journal of International Business Studies, 28*(4), 807–825.

Robins, J., & Wiersema, M. F. (1995). A resource-based approach to the multibusiness firm: Empirical analysis of portfolio interrelationships and corporate financial performance. *Strategic Management Journal, 16*(4), 277–299.

Ruigrok, W., Amann, W., & Wagner, H. (2007). The internationalization-performance relationship at Swiss firms: A test of the S-shape and extreme degrees of internationalization. *Management International Review, 47*(3), 349–368.

Sanders, W. G., & Carpenter, M. A. (1998). Internationalization and firm governance: The roles of CEO compensation, top team composition, and board structure. *Academy of Management Journal, 41*(2), 158–178.

Sapienza, H. J., Autio, E., George, G., & Zahra, S. A. (2006). A capabilities perspective on the effects of early internationalization on firm survival and growth. *Academy of Management Review, 31*(4), 914–933.

Scholes, L., Mustafa, M., & Chen, S. (2016). Internationalization of small family firms: The influence of family from a socioemotional wealth perspective. *Thunderbird International Business Review, 58*(2), 131–146.

Schulze, W. S., Lubatkin, M. H., & Dino, R. N. (2003). Toward a theory of agency and altruism in family firms. *Journal of Business Venturing, 18*(4), 473–490.

Stinchcombe, A. L. (1965). Social structure and organizations. In J. March (Ed.), *Handbook of organizations* (pp. 142–193). Chicago: Rand McNally.

Tihanyi, L., Ellstrand, A. E., Daily, C. M., & Dalton, D. R. (2000). Composition of the top management team and firm international diversification. *Journal of Management, 26*(6), 1157–1177.

Wan, W. P., & Hoskisson, R. E. (2003). Home country environments, corporate diversification strategies, and firm performance. *Academy of Management Journal, 46*(1), 27–45.

Zaheer, S. (1995). Overcoming the liability of foreignness. *Academy of Management Journal, 38* (2), 341–363.

Zahra, S. A., Hayton, J. C., Neubaum, D. O., Dibrell, C., & Craig, J. (2008). Culture of family commitment and strategic flexibility: The moderating effect of stewardship. *Entrepreneurship: Theory and Practice, 32*(6), 1035–1054.

Zhang, X., Ma, X., Wang, Y., Li, X., & Huo, D. (2016). What drives the internationalization of Chinese SMEs? The joint effects of international entrepreneurship characteristics, network ties, and firm ownership. *International Business Review, 25*(2), 522–534.

Part IV
Family Firms: Case Studies

Is Being Conservative at Home Whilst Taking Risks Abroad a Suitable Competitive Strategy? The Case of Spanish Family Firms Internationalizing to Mexico

Julen Castillo-Apraiz, Unai Arzubiaga, and Jesús Manuel Palma-Ruiz

Abstract Family firms' (FFs) importance for industrialized and developing countries and the growing competition has led to an increased interest in knowing how FFs develop their competitive strategies. Since FFs usually have a long-term vision when deciding how to compete, analyzing competitive strategies—usually linked with the long-term—makes even more sense. Furthermore, FFs' behavior is especially interesting when they have been internationalized. Thus, the purpose of our study is to improve the understanding of the competitive strategies of FFs' internationalizing to Mexico, namely, exploitation (at a national level) and exploration (at international level). Briefly, a firm's exploitation strategy is characterized by better-using firms' existing resources and knowledge, whereas a firm's exploration strategy involves exploring new ways of doing. Based on data collected from 81 CEOs of Spanish firms that have been internationalized to Mexico, we use partial least squares structural equation modeling (PLS-SEM) technique. We conclude that FFs' exploitation strategy (at a national level) has a positive impact on firms' exploration strategy (at international level). In other words, being more efficient and leveraging current knowledge at a national level help to pursue opportunities internationally actively.

Keywords Family firm · Competitive strategy · Exploitation · Exploration · Internationalization

---

J. Castillo-Apraiz (✉) · U. Arzubiaga
The University of the Basque Country UPV/EHU, Bilbao, Spain
e-mail: julen.castillo@ehu.eus; unai.arzubiaga@ehu.eus

J. M. Palma-Ruiz
Universidad Autónoma de Chihuahua, Chihuahua, Mexico
e-mail: jmpalma@uach.mx

J. M. Saiz-Álvarez et al. (eds.), *Entrepreneurship and Family Business Vitality*,
Studies on Entrepreneurship, Structural Change and Industrial Dynamics,
https://doi.org/10.1007/978-3-030-15526-1_13

1 Introduction

Due to increased international competitive pressures, firms need to decide the most effective strategy to allocate their resources (Battaglia, Neirotti, & Paolucci, 2018). In this sense, a central topic in corporate strategy has analyzed the appropriateness of the exploitation strategy and the exploration strategy (Arzubiaga, Maseda, & Iturralde, 2017). Since family firms' (FFs) resources are limited and there is usually—at least to some extent—a tension between exploitation and exploration, FFs need to think strategically about how resources are employed (Benner & Tushman, 2003; Calabrò et al., 2018; De Massis, Audretsch, Uhlaner, & Kammerlander, 2018), being the link between FFs and performance an interesting topic (Mazzi, 2011; Randerson, Bettinelli, Fayolle, & Anderson, 2015; Zellweger, 2007). In this context, there is a relevant line of research which tries to shed some light on the exploitation-exploration balance and the ability some firms are developing to explore and exploit *simultaneously*, i.e., ambidexterity (Zimmermann, Raisch, & Cardinal, 2018). Nevertheless, only few firms have the ability to pursue both strategies simultaneously, since both logics require different strategies and structures (He & Wong, 2004). Hence, how to manage the tension between exploitation and exploration is still a recurrent topic (Lin & Si, 2018).

On the one hand, exploitation refers to actions that entail refinement, choice, production, efficiency, selection, implementation, and execution (March, 1991). In this sense, an exploitation strategy enhances the refinement of existing knowledge and is related to convergent thinking and focus (Bierly, Damanpour, & Santoro, 2009; Smith & Tushman, 2005). Lin and Si (2018) point out that exploitation may be deemed as the development of new knowledge pertaining to existing markets, products, technology, and capabilities. On the other hand, exploration strategy is considered as a shift away from a firm's current knowledge base and skills, directed at new opportunities in (geographical) new markets (Alexiev, Jansen, Van den Bosch, & Volberda, 2010). This type of organization comprises the knowledge search for new organizational norms, routines, structures, and systems (Mom, Van Den Bosch, & Volberda, 2007).

Prior research has regarded exploitative and explorative innovations as complementary strategies (Kammerlander, Burger, Fust, & Fueglistaller, 2015). Nevertheless, there is still much room to investigate how these strategies are related among FFs, especially when they are involved in internationalization strategies. As such, this study pursues to illuminate how exploitative innovations influence exploratory innovations in FFs that are involved in an internationalization process, specifically investigating: How does the national exploitative innovation strategy impact on the international exploratory innovation strategy in internationalized FFs?

The authors believe this study brings a new perspective with important implications for future ambidexterity research in FF. Therefore, this chapter contributes in two important ways. First, it provides a review of what is known about ambidexterity in family firms. Second, it investigates the use of exploration and exploitation strategies in FF. To this end, an empirical study is conducted considering a sample of 81 Spanish FFs internationalized to Mexico as the setting for investigating the research question.

The rest of this chapter is organized as follows. After the introduction, we provide the theoretical background of both national exploitative innovation strategy and international exploratory innovation strategy in the context of FFs that have been engaged in internationalization processes. We also explain the influence of national exploitative innovation strategy on international exploratory innovation strategy by proposing a specific model and testing it. Finally, we enunciate some remarks about this work and its limitations and then propose avenues for future research.

2 Theoretical Background

Ambidexterity, defined in a broad sense as the ability to both use and refine existing knowledge (exploitation) while also creating new knowledge to overcome knowledge deficiencies or absences identified within the execution of the work (exploration) (Turner, Swart, & Maylor, 2013), has been a subject of enduring interest to management scholars (Koryak, Lockett, Hayton, Nicolaou, & Mole, 2018). Exploitation is typically considered to be concerned with refinement and incremental change, efficiency, whereas searching, experimentation, radical change, risk-taking, and discovery are exploration-oriented activities (Cheng & Van de Ven, 1996). Therefore, ambidextrous organizations are defined as those capable of both exploiting existing competencies and exploring new opportunities while managing an equilibrium between these two (Cao, Gedajlovic, & Zhang, 2009; O'Reilly & Tushman, 2008; Raisch & Birkinshaw, 2008).

By recognizing that firms should "engage in enough exploitation to ensure the organization's current viability and engage in enough exploration to ensure its future viability" (Levinthal & March, 1993, p. 105), studies analyzing ambidexterity at the organizational level have entered multiples areas of research (Simsek, 2009). They come from the organizational learning literature in which the concept began (Levinthal & March, 1993) to the strategic management (Jansen, George, Van den Bosch, & Volberda, 2008; Wassmer, Li, & Madhok, 2017), innovation and technology management (Chang & Hughes, 2012; Kortmann, 2015; Lin & McDonough, 2014), organization theory and behavior (Raisch & Birkinshaw, 2008; Uotila, 2018), or operation management (Adler et al., 2009) areas. Some scholars suggest that exploration and exploitation compete with each other for scarce resources (March, 1991). Yet, a more contemporary view has been presented in the literature suggesting both dimensions are complementary forces which tend to be mutually reinforcing when they co-occur over time (Raisch, Birkinshaw, Probst, & Tushman, 2009; Veider & Matzler, 2016) and stating that ambidexterity is a source of competitive advantage (Raisch & Birkinshaw, 2008) and a necessary prerequisite for prosperity, higher growth, and superior firm performance (Gupta, Smith, & Shalley, 2006; He & Wong, 2004; Lubatkin, Simsek, Ling, & Veiga, 2006; O'Reilly & Tushman, 2013), regardless of sector, size, or type of property. However, authors have recognized the difficulties in operationalizing ambidexterity as to the extent and magnitude to engage in exploration and exploitation strategies simultaneously, so have begun to characterize these strategies as independent (Gupta et al., 2006) or as initially conceived as two ends of a single continuum (March, 1991).

Family firms are widely recognized as essential contributors to both employment and wealth creation for economies around the world (Botero, Cruz, De Massis, & Nordqvist, 2015; IEF, 2015; Memili, Fang, Chrisman, & De Massis, 2015). Given its economic and social relevance and the role of the ambidexterity as a potential source of competitive advantages, the achievement of organizational ambidexterity is as important for the FFs as it is for non-family businesses (Veider & Matzler, 2016). However, the existing literature on ambidexterity in the context of the FF offers conflicting arguments about its achievement in this type of companies. Thus, while on the one hand some studies seem to confirm that FFs could be less willing to engage in risky endeavors (Bammens, Notelaers, & Van Gils, 2014; König, Kammerlander, & Enders, 2013), thus diminishing the achievement of organizational ambidexterity in the form of low exploration activities, other works suggest that the unique attributes of FFs also foster ambidexterity ability (Le Breton-Miller, Miller, & Lester, 2011) via traits such as long-term orientation of goals and investments (Cassia, De Massis, & Pizzurno, 2012), personalized control, low levels of formalization (Sirmon & Hitt, 2003), and alignment of interests between owners and managers (Carney, 2005).

Top management is responsible for designing and executing the company's overall strategy, thus dealing with the exploration and exploitation dilemma (Gibson & Birkinshaw, 2004). In addition, there's further evidence that links the involvement of frontline managers in initiating ambidextrous strategies (Zimmermann, Raisch, & Cardinal, 2018). However, little is known about ambidexterity strategies in family business and the involvement of family members in senior and frontline management in developing such strategies.

Internationalization processes play a crucial role in FFs because it facilitates setting in different markets and increasing sales. Accordingly, these processes allow FFs to increase their growth potential by operating on bigger markets with primary targets (Booltink & Saka-Helmhout, 2018). However, internationalization is not only beneficial in terms of direct sales but also because of the direct effect it has on innovation processes (Battaglia et al., 2018), being innovation critical for FFs (Casprini, De Massis, Di Minin, Frattini, & Piccaluga, 2017; Cassia et al., 2012; Classen, Carree, Van Gils, & Peters, 2014; De Massis, Frattini, Pizzurno, & Cassia, 2015). At this regard, Love and Roper (2015) suggest that there is a great complementarity between internationalization and innovation. More specifically, with the aim of competing in foreign markets, firms need to innovate by introducing important changes in organizational norms, routines, structures, and systems (Raisch et al., 2009). These improvements are usually based on the actions of search, variation, risk-taking, experimentation, play, flexibility, and discovery (Kortmann, Gelhard, Zimmermann, & Piller, 2014; March, 1991). In other words, exploratory innovations challenge institutionalized learning and offer major transformations of existing technologies that often render the prevailing product designs and technologies obsolete (Stadler, Rajwani, & Karaba, 2014). Based on the long-term orientation (Stubner, Blarr, Brands, & Wulf, 2012), the focus of exploratory innovations is on the ability to reorient organizational competencies toward new opportunities as a source of competitive advantage (Goel & Jones, 2016). These new opportunities, however, need to be complemented with exploitation to improve existing competencies and obtain better results (Shane & Venkataraman, 2000).

The competitive strategy based on exploitative innovations focuses on the refinement of products to address customers' needs. The primary goals of these exploitative innovations are closely related to refinement, choice, production, efficiency, selection, implementation, and execution (March, 1991; Stubner et al., 2012). In other words, exploitative innovations are about efficiency, increasing productivity, control, certainty, and variance reduction (O'Reilly & Tushman, 2008). This type of innovation improves existing competencies, technologies, paradigms, and extensions and brings efficiency when applied to organizational elements such as existing products and process capability (Ghemawat & Ricart Costa, 1993).

The competitive strategy based on exploratory innovations usually requires high availability of resources and long-term orientation (Moss, Payne, & Moore, 2014). However, as we say, FFs usually suffer from resource and financial constraints, which directly impact on their capacity to develop this competitive strategy. These difficulties are even higher when these exploratory innovation strategies are set in foreign countries or are an essential part of these organizations' internationalization processes. Thus, FFs may need an important capacity to create own resources through their incomes and revenues. These new cash flows, if sustainable, may need to emerge from the core and usual markets of businesses. As such, the returns emerged from exploitative innovations set in well-known national markets seem to play an important role when maintaining a good level of own finance. These resources may allow developing exploratory strategies in other countries. Based on the above, we posit that exploitative innovation strategies (at a national level) have positive effects on the exploratory innovation strategies (at international level).

Hypothesis 1 The exploitation strategy (at a national level) has a positive impact on the exploration strategy (at international level).

3 Methodology

3.1 Sample

Our population comprises Spanish FFs that have been internationalized to Mexico. This data was obtained from the Spanish Institute for Foreign Trade (ICEX, in Spanish) in 2018. We chose FFs because of their importance for both industrialized and developing countries regarding their contribution to the gross domestic product (Cowling, Liu, Ledger, & Zhang, 2015).

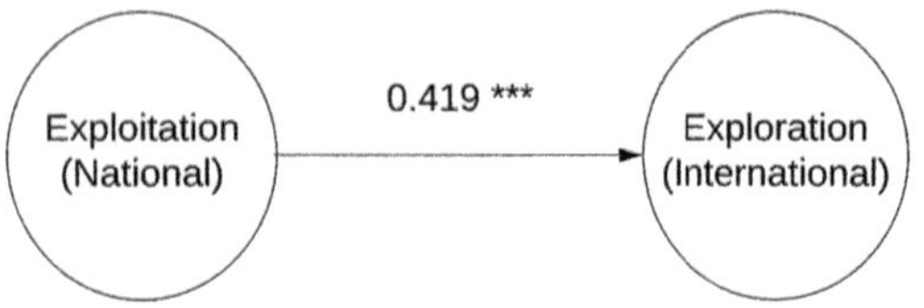

Fig. 1 Path loading and hypothesized structural model. Note: ***$p < 0.01$. Source: Authors' own figure

Specifically, we focused on Spanish FFs that have been internationalized to Mexico, since we wanted to investigate how FFs behave when there is a high level of host-home country similarity (as it is the case here) and countries are geographically far away from each other. Both Spain and Mexico have a considerable power distance (Hofstede, 1991), which is not surprising due to their shared cultural roots. Cultural similarities between Mexico and Spain are also shown in the results of the GLOBE project (House, Hanges, Javidan, Dorfman, & Gupta, 2004). We obtained 81 valid responses from Spanish family firms' CEOs who answered a short questionnaire via e-mail.

3.2 *Data Analysis*

The model presented in Fig. 1 was tested using partial least squares structural equation modeling (PLS-SEM) technique, which is a useful method in management and marketing (Hair, Hult, Ringle, & Sarstedt, 2017; Hair, Ringle, & Sarstedt, 2011; Hair, Ringle, & Sarstedt, 2012; Hair, Sarstedt, Pieper, & Ringle, 2012; Hair, Sarstedt, Ringle, & Mena, 2012). Recent studies emphasize the usefulness of this model as a research tool in the field of FFs (Binz, Patel, & Wanzenried, 2014; Sarstedt, Ringle, Smith, & Reams, 2014). PLS-SEM is especially appropriate for our study. First, this technique allows us to include latent variables with reflective indicators (Henseler, Ringle, & Sinkovics, 2009). Second, PLS-SEM can establish assumptions of normality in the data (Chin, 1998) and can be used on small samples (Kyu Kim, Yul Ryoo, & Dug Jung, 2011). Finally, it is especially appropriate due to the early phase of theorizing within the field (Richter, Cepeda, Roldán, & Ringle, 2016; Rigdon, 2016). Concretely, we used the SmartPLS 3 (Ringle, Wende, & Becker, 2014) software.

3.3 *Measurement of the Model Variables*

Since researchers agree that multiple measures offer a rich perspective, we based our research on well-known scales on measuring our constructs. Concretely, consistent with prior research, the measurement scale for exploitation (at a national level) and exploration (at international level) was based on that used by He and Wong (2004) and Cui, Walsh, and Zou (2014), respectively. Both variables are measured utilizing multiple items on 7-point Likert scales.

4 Results

4.1 Validity of the Scales

We first assessed the measurement model. Factor loadings ranged from 0.669 to 0.950. Hence, latent variables explain a substantial part of each indicator's variance (Hair et al., 2019; Henseler et al., 2009). The assessment of internal consistency showed that all the composite reliability (CR) values are well above 0.7 (Hair et al., 2019). Since all the average variance extracted (AVE) values are above 0.5, there is no evidence of a lack of convergent validity (Hair et al., 2019). We assessed the discriminant validity using the Heterotrait-monotrait (HTMT) ratio (Hair et al., 2019; Henseler, Ringle, & Sarstedt, 2015; Voorhees, Brady, Calantone, & Ramirez, 2016), which is 0.511. The HTMT value is below the threshold of 85% (Hair et al., 2019; Kline, 2011). Hence, discriminant validity has been established. Table 1 provides an overview of the results for the measurement model.

Table 2 provides an overview of the results for the inner model. Besides the path coefficients, it provides the R^2 value, the variance inflation factor (VIF), and the effect size.

Table 1 Evaluation results: measurement model

Constructs/items	Loading	Composite reliability (Cronbach's α)	AVE
Exploitation strategy (national)		0.904 (0.861)	0.702
Improve existing product quality	0.840		
Improve production flexibility	0.888		
Reduce production cost	0.832		
Improve yield or reduce material consumption	0.788		
Exploration strategy (international)		0.801 (0.574)	0.675
New approaches to developing products and processes	0.950		
Engage in developing new products	0.669		

Source: Authors' own table
AVE average variance extracted

Table 2 PLS-SEM analysis

Relationship	Path coefficient	p value	VIF	f^2	Bias-corrected 95% CI
Exploitation (national) → Exploration (international)	0.419***	0.009	1.000	0.213	[−0.424;0.552]
R^2	0.176				

Source: Authors' own table
VIF variance inflation factor, *CI* confidence interval
***$p < 0.01$

4.2 *Estimation of the Causal Model*

To test the proposed model (Fig. 1), we ran SmartPLS 3 and concluded that exploitation strategy (at a national level) has a positive impact on firms' exploration strategy (at international level), i.e., the hypothesis is supported.

5 Discussion, Conclusions, and Implications

The study aims to explain the relationship between exploitation strategy (at a national level) and exploration strategy (at international level) in FFs. Precisely, we investigate how FFs involved in international processes compete when there is a high level of host-home country similarity (as it is the case here) and countries are geographically far away from each other.

Our findings reveal that exploitation strategy (at a national level) has a positive impact on firms' exploration strategy (at international level). That is, by generating more stable performance nationally, family firms can gain returns (yet often more variable) with an international exploration strategy. Thus, generating value nationally, where the context is usually more stable and less risky, and hence pursuing opportunities internationally are appropriate competitive strategies for Spanish FF, which is the dominant business model in Europe (Björnberg, Elstrodt, & Pandit, 2015).

This study opens interesting new paths for further research. First, even when it seems accurate that thanks to the exploitation strategy (nationally) firms can gain the necessary resources to follow an exploration strategy when accomplishing internationalization processes which are usually costly (Richter, 2014; Richter et al., 2016), further research could include other countries in the analysis to analyze how the host-home country similarity affects the exploitation (national)-exploration (international) relationship. Second, new studies could include additional variables into the analysis (e.g., mediating effects such as training of personnel, see Castillo-Apraiz & Matey de Antonio, 2018). Third, further research could join the balance mentioned above and the ambidexterity lines of research.

References

Adler, P., Benner, M. J., Brunner, D. J., MacDuffie, J. P., Osono, E., Staats, B. R., & Winter, S. G. (2009). Perspectives on the productivity dilemma. *Journal of Operations Management, 27*(2), 99–113.

Alexiev, A. S., Jansen, J. J., Van den Bosch, F. A., & Volberda, H. W. (2010). Top management team advice seeking and exploratory innovation: The moderating role of TMT heterogeneity. *Journal of Management Studies, 47*(7), 1343–1364.

Arzubiaga, U., Maseda, A., & Iturralde, T. (2017). Exploratory and exploitative innovation in family businesses: The moderating role of the family firm image and family involvement in top management. *Review of Managerial Science*, 1–31.

Bammens, Y., Notelaers, G., & Van Gils, A. (2014). Implications of family business employment for employees' innovative work involvement. *Family Business Review, 28*(2), 123–144.

Battaglia, D., Neirotti, P., & Paolucci, E. (2018). The role of R&D investments and export on SMEs' growth: A domain ambidexterity perspective. *Management Decision, 56*(9), 1883–1903.

Benner, M. J., & Tushman, M. L. (2003). Exploitation, exploration, and process management: The productivity dilemma revisited. *Academy of Management Review, 28*(2), 238–256.

Bierly, P. E., III, Damanpour, F., & Santoro, M. D. (2009). The application of external knowledge: Organizational conditions for exploration and exploitation. *Journal of Management Studies, 46* (3), 481–509.

Binz, C., Patel, V. K., & Wanzenried, G. (2014). A comparative study of CB-SEM and PLS-SEM for theory development in family firm research. *Journal of Family Business Strategy, 5*(1), 116–128.

Björnberg, Å., Elstrodt, H. P., & Pandit, V. (2015). *Joining the family business: An emerging opportunity for investors* (Vol. 2, pp. 22–26). McKinsey & Company.

Booltink, L. W., & Saka-Helmhout, A. (2018). The effects of R&D intensity and internationalization on the performance of non-high-tech SMEs. *International Small Business Journal, 36*(1), 81–103.

Botero, I. C., Cruz, C., De Massis, A., & Nordqvist, M. (2015). Family business research in the European context. *European Journal of International Management, 9*(2), 139–159.

Calabrò, A., Vecchiarini, M., Gast, J., Campopiano, G., De Massis, A., & Kraus, S. (2018). Innovation in family firms: A systematic literature review and guidance for future research. *International Journal of Management Reviews, 20*(3), 1–39.

Cao, Q., Gedajlovic, E., & Zhang, H. (2009). Unpacking organizational ambidexterity: Dimensions, contingencies, and synergistic effects. *Organization Science, 20*(4), 781–796.

Carney, M. (2005). Corporate governance and competitive advantage in family-controlled firms. *Entrepreneurship: Theory and Practice, 29*(3), 249–265.

Casprini, E., De Massis, A., Di Minin, A., Frattini, F., & Piccaluga, A. (2017). How family firms execute open innovation strategies: The Loccioni case. *Journal of Knowledge Management, 21* (6), 1459–1485.

Cassia, L., De Massis, A., & Pizzurno, E. (2012). Strategic innovation and new product development in family firms: An empirically grounded theoretical framework. *International Journal of Entrepreneurial Behavior & Research, 18*(2), 198–232.

Castillo-Apraiz, J., & Matey de Antonio, J. (2018). Does quality pay in the pharmaceutical industry? The mediating role of training of personnel between quality management and performance. *Revista de Dirección y Administración de Empresas, 25*. (in press).

Chang, Y. Y., & Hughes, M. (2012). Drivers of innovation ambidexterity in small-to-medium-sized firms. *European Management Journal, 30*, 1–17.

Cheng, Y. T., & Van de Ven, A. H. (1996). Learning the innovation journey: Order out of chaos? *Organization Science, 7*(6), 593–614.

Chin, W. W. (1998). The partial least squares approach for structural equation modeling. In M. GA (Ed.), *Modern methods for business research* (pp. 295–336). Mahwah, NJ: Lawrence Erlbaun Associates.

Classen, N., Carree, M., Van Gils, A., & Peters, B. (2014). Innovation in family and non-family SMEs: An exploratory analysis. *Small Business Economics, 42*(3), 595–609.
Cowling, M., Liu, W., Ledger, A., & Zhang, N. (2015). What really happens to small and medium-sized enterprises in a global economic recession? UK evidence on sales and job dynamics. *International Small Business Journal, 33*(5), 488–513.
Cui, A. P., Walsh, M. F., & Zou, S. (2014). The importance of strategic fit between host-home country similarity and exploration-exploitation strategies on small and medium-sized enterprises' performance: A contingency perspective. *Journal of International Marketing, 22*(4), 67–85.
De Massis, A., Audretsch, D., Uhlaner, L., & Kammerlander, N. (2018). Innovation with limited resources: Management lessons from the German Mittelstand. *Journal of Product Innovation Management, 35*(1), 125–146.
De Massis, A., Frattini, F., Pizzurno, E., & Cassia, L. (2015). Product innovation in family *versus* nonfamily firms: An exploratory analysis. *Journal of Small Business Management, 53*(1), 1–36.
Ghemawat, P., & Ricart Costa, J. E. I. (1993). The organizational tension between static and dynamic efficiency. *Strategic Management Journal, 14*(S2), 59–73.
Gibson, C. B., & Birkinshaw, J. (2004). The antecedents, consequences, and mediating role of organizational ambidexterity. *Academy of Management Journal, 47*(2), 209–226.
Goel, S., & Jones, R. J., III. (2016). Entrepreneurial exploration and exploitation in the family business: A systematic review and future directions. *Family Business Review, 29*(1), 94–120.
Gupta, A. K., Smith, K. G., & Shalley, C. E. (2006). The interplay between exploration and exploitation. *Academy of Management Journal, 49*(4), 693–706.
Hair, J. F., Hult, G. T. M., Ringle, C. M., Sarstedt, M., Castillo, J., Cepeda, G., & Roldán, J. L. (2019). *Manual de Partial least squares structural equation modeling (PLS-SEM). Terrasa (Barcelona)*. España: Omnia Science.
Hair, J. F., Jr., Hult, G. T. M., Ringle, C., & Sarstedt, M. (2017). *A primer on partial least squares structural equation modeling (PLS-SEM)*. Thousand Oaks, CA: Sage.
Hair, J. F., Ringle, C. M., & Sarstedt, M. (2011). PLS-SEM: Indeed a silver bullet. *The Journal of Marketing Theory and Practice, 19*(2), 139–152.
Hair, J. F., Ringle, C. M., & Sarstedt, M. (2012). Editorial-partial least squares: The better approach to structural equation modeling? *Long Range Planning, 45*(5–6), 312–319.
Hair, J. F., Sarstedt, M., Pieper, T. M., & Ringle, C. M. (2012). The use of partial least squares structural equation modeling in strategic management research: A review of past practices and recommendations for future applications. *Long Range Planning, 45*(5–6), 320–340.
Hair, J. F., Sarstedt, M., Ringle, C. M., & Mena, J. A. (2012). An assessment of the use of partial least squares structural equation modeling in marketing research. *Journal of the Academy of Marketing Science, 40*(3), 414–433.
He, Z. L., & Wong, P. K. (2004). Exploration vs. exploitation: An empirical test of the ambidexterity hypothesis. *Organization Science, 15*(4), 481–494.
Henseler, J., Ringle, C. M., & Sarstedt, M. (2015). A new criterion for assessing discriminant validity in variance-based structural equation modeling. *Journal of the Academy of Marketing Science, 43*, 115–135.
Henseler, J., Ringle, C., & Sinkovics, R. (2009). The use of partial least squares path modeling in international marketing. *Advances in International Marketing, 20*, 277–320.
Hofstede, G. (1991). *Cultures and organizations. Intercultural cooperation and its importance for survival. The software of the mind.* London: McGraw-Hill.
House, R. J., Hanges, P. M., Javidan, M., Dorfman, P., & Gupta, V. (2004). *Culture, leadership, and organizations: The GLOBE study of 62 societies*. Thousand Oaks, CA: Sage.
IEF. (2015). *La empresa familiar en España*. Madrid: Instituto de la Empresa Familiar.
Jansen, J., George, G., Van den Bosch, F., & Volberda, H. W. (2008). Senior teams' attributes and organizational ambidexterity: The moderating role of transformational leadership. *Journal of Management Studies, 45*, 982–1007.

Kammerlander, N., Burger, D., Fust, A., & Fueglistaller, U. (2015). Exploration and exploitation in established small and medium-sized enterprises: The effect of CEOs' regulatory focus. *Journal of Business Venturing, 30*(4), 582–602.
Kline, R. B. (2011). *Principles and practice of structural equation modeling*. New York: Guilford Press.
König, A., Kammerlander, N., & Enders, A. (2013). The family innovator's dilemma: How family influence affects the adoption of discontinuous technologies by incumbent firms. *Academy of Management Review, 38*(3), 418–441.
Kortmann, S. (2015). The mediating role of strategic orientations on the relationship between ambidexterity-oriented decisions and innovative ambidexterity. *Journal of Product Innovation Management, 32*(5), 666–684.
Kortmann, S., Gelhard, C., Zimmermann, C., & Piller, F. T. (2014). Linking strategic flexibility and operational efficiency: The mediating role of ambidextrous operational capabilities. *Journal of Operations Management, 32*(7–8), 475–490.
Koryak, O., Lockett, A., Hayton, J., Nicolaou, N., & Mole, K. (2018). Disentangling the antecedents of ambidexterity: Exploration and exploitation. *Research Policy, 47*, 413–427.
Kyu Kim, K., Yul Ryoo, S., & Dug Jung, M. (2011). Inter-organizational information systems visibility in buyer-supplier relationships: The case of telecommunication equipment component manufacturing industry. *Omega, 39*(6), 667–676.
Le Breton-Miller, I., Miller, D., & Lester, R. H. (2011). Stewardship or agency? A social embeddedness reconciliation of conduct and performance in public family businesses. *Organization Science, 22*(3), 704–721.
Levinthal, D. A., & March, J. G. (1993). The myopia of learning. *Strategic Management Journal, 14*, 95–112.
Lin, H. E., & McDonough, E. F., III. (2014). Cognitive frames, learning mechanisms, and innovation ambidexterity. *Journal of Product Innovation Management, 31*, 170–188.
Lin, S., & Si, S. (2018). The influence of exploration and exploitation on born globals' speed of internationalization. *Management Decision, 57*(1), 193–210.
Love, J. H., & Roper, S. (2015). SME innovation, exporting and growth: A review of existing evidence. *International Small Business Journal, 33*(1), 28–48.
Lubatkin, M. H., Simsek, Z., Ling, Y., & Veiga, J. F. (2006). Ambidexterity and performance in small-to medium-sized firms: The pivotal role of top management team behavioral integration. *Journal of Management, 32*(5), 646–672.
March, J. G. (1991). Exploration and exploitation in organizational learning. *Organization Science, 2*(1), 71–87.
Mazzi, C. (2011). Family business and financial performance: Current state of knowledge and future research challenges. *Journal of Family Business Strategy, 2*(3), 166–181.
Memili, E., Fang, H., Chrisman, J. J., & De Massis, A. (2015). The impact of small and medium-sized family firms on economic growth. *Small Business Economics, 45*(4), 771–785.
Mom, T. J., Van Den Bosch, F. A., & Volberda, H. W. (2007). Investigating managers' exploration and exploitation activities: The influence of top-down, bottom-up, and horizontal knowledge inflows. *Journal of Management Studies, 44*(6), 910–931.
Moss, T. W., Payne, G. T., & Moore, C. B. (2014). Strategic consistency of exploration and exploitation in family businesses. *Family Business Review, 27*(1), 51–71.
O'Reilly, C. A., III, & Tushman, M. L. (2008). Ambidexterity as a dynamic capability: Resolving the innovator's dilemma. *Research in Organizational Behavior, 28*, 185–206.
O'Reilly, C. A., & Tushman, M. L. (2013). Organizational ambidexterity: Past, present, and future. *Academy of Management Perspectives, 27*(4), 324–338.
Raisch, S., & Birkinshaw, J. (2008). Organizational ambidexterity: Antecedents, outcomes, and moderators. *Journal of Management, 34*(3), 375–409.
Raisch, S., Birkinshaw, J., Probst, G., & Tushman, M. L. (2009). Organizational ambidexterity: Balancing exploitation and exploration for sustained performance. *Organization Science, 20*(4), 685–695.

Randerson, K., Bettinelli, C., Fayolle, A., & Anderson, A. (2015). Family entrepreneurship as a field of research: Exploring its contours and contents. *Journal of Family Business Strategy, 6*(3), 143–154.

Richter, N. F. (2014). Information costs in international business: Analyzing the effects of economies of scale, cultural diversity and decentralization. *Management International Review, 54*(2), 171–193.

Richter, N. F., Cepeda, G., Roldán, J. L., & Ringle, C. M. (2016). European management research using partial least squares structural equation modeling (PLS-SEM). *European Management Journal, 34*(6), 589–597.

Richter, N. F., Hauff, S., Schlaegel, C., Gudergan, S., Ringle, C. M., & Gunkel, M. (2016). Using cultural archetypes in cross-cultural management studies. *Journal of International Management, 22*(1), 63–83.

Rigdon, E. E. (2016). Choosing PLS path modeling as an analytical method in European management research: A realist perspective. *European Management Journal, 34*(6), 598–605.

Ringle, C. M., Wende, S., & Becker, J. M. (2014). *SmartPLS 3*. Hamburg: SmartPLS.

Sarstedt, M., Ringle, C. M., Smith, D., Reams, R., & Hair, J. F., Jr. (2014). Partial least squares structural equation modeling (PLS-SEM): A useful tool for family business researchers. *Journal of Family Business Strategy, 5*(1), 105–115.

Shane, S., & Venkataraman, S. (2000). The promise of entrepreneurship as a field of research. *Academy of Management Review, 25*(1), 217–226.

Simsek, Z. (2009). Organizational ambidexterity: Towards a multilevel understanding. *Journal of Management Studies, 46*, 597–624.

Sirmon, D. G., & Hitt, M. A. (2003). Managing resources: Linking unique resources, management, and wealth creation in family firms. *Entrepreneurship: Theory and Practice, 27*(4), 339–358.

Smith, W. K., & Tushman, M. L. (2005). Managing strategic contradictions: A top management model for managing innovation streams. *Organization Science, 16*(5), 522–536.

Stadler, C., Rajwani, T., & Karaba, F. (2014). Solutions to the exploration/exploitation dilemma: Networks as a new level of analysis. *International Journal of Management Reviews, 16*(2), 172–193.

Stubner, S., Blarr, W. H., Brands, C., & Wulf, T. (2012). Organizational ambidexterity and family firm performance. *Journal of Small Business & Entrepreneurship, 25*(2), 217–229.

Turner, N., Swart, J., & Maylor, H. (2013). Mechanisms for managing ambidexterity: A review and research agenda. *International Journal of Management Reviews, 15*, 317–332.

Uotila, J. (2018). Punctuated equilibrium or ambidexterity: Dynamics of incremental and radical organizational change over time. *Industrial and Corporate Change, 27*(1), 131–148.

Veider, V., & Matzler, K. (2016). The ability and willingness of family-controlled firms to arrive at organizational ambidexterity. *Journal of Family Business Strategy, 7*, 105–116.

Voorhees, C. M., Brady, M. K., Calantone, R., & Ramirez, E. (2016). Discriminant validity testing in marketing: An analysis, causes for concern, and proposed remedies. *Journal of the Academy of Marketing Science, 44*(1), 119–134.

Wassmer, U., Li, S., & Madhok, A. (2017). Resource ambidexterity through alliance portfolios and firm performance. *Strategic Management Journal, 38*(2), 384–394.

Zellweger, T. M. (2007). Time horizon, costs of equity capital, and generic investment strategies of firms. *Family Business Review, 20*(1), 1–15.

Zimmermann, A., Raisch, S., & Cardinal, L. B. (2018). Managing persistent tensions on the frontline: A configurational perspective on ambidexterity. *Journal of Management Studies, 55* (5), 739–769.

Corporate Venturing Determinants in Mexican Family Firms

Luis Arturo Torres-García, M. Concepción López-Fernández, and Ana M. Serrano-Bedia

Abstract The objective of this study is to explore whether factors related to the focus of both the ability of the CEO to interpret the environmental signals and identify business opportunities and the characteristics of the firm in terms of previous innovation experience and ability to learn from that experience can determine the decision to enter into corporate venturing (CV) in Mexican family firms. Besides, we will consider the moderating effect of family members' willingness to change on these relationships. In order to explore the proposed relationships, a theoretical framework that encompasses arguments from the resource-based view, the knowledge-based view, and the upper-echelons theory are used. To test our hypotheses, we conducted a study among CEOs in Mexican family firms of all sizes and performed a binomial logistic regression analysis based on a sample of 136 family companies across all sectors. The results obtained indicate that individual and firm variables are highly significant. All the variables except organizational learning, the effect of which is adverse, demonstrated positive effects, and this variable, also, is the only one moderated by the willingness to change.

Keywords Venturing · Family firms · Opportunity detection · Organizational learning · Innovation · Willingness to change

L. A. Torres-García
Instituto de Emprendimiento "Eugenio Garza Lagüera", Tecnologico de Monterrey, Monterrey, Mexico

M. C. López-Fernández (✉) · A. M. Serrano-Bedia
University of Cantabria, Santander, Spain
e-mail: concepcion.lopez@unican.es; serranoa@unican.es

J. M. Saiz-Álvarez et al. (eds.), *Entrepreneurship and Family Business Vitality*, Studies on Entrepreneurship, Structural Change and Industrial Dynamics,
https://doi.org/10.1007/978-3-030-15526-1_14

1 Introduction

Corporate venturing (CV) includes different activities for creating, adding to, or investing in new businesses (Kuratko & Audretsch, 2009; McGrath, Keil, & Tukiainen, 2006) in existing or new fields, markets, or industries (Narayanan, Yang, & Zahra, 2009). CV can be classified as internal (when new businesses are created and owned by the mother firm), external (when parties outside the corporation create new businesses), or cooperative (when a new business entity is created through the cooperative efforts of two or more parent firms) (Covin & Miles, 2007; Morris, Kuratko, & Covin, 2011). Given that the need of change is inherent to the current economic landscape, CV has become an essential element of corporate strategy that has a positive effect in both short-term financial and market results and long-term strategic position (Narayanan et al., 2009). However, previous research also shows that CV outcomes are context dependent, with different environments or different intra-organizational characteristics, such as those exhibited by family firms in their entrepreneurial orientation (Hernández-Linares & López-Fernández, 2018), leading to different results (Narayanan et al., 2009).

Family firms, in which a family exert their influence through their involvement in ownership, management, or governance (Hernández-Linares, Sarkar, & Cobo, 2018; Hernández-Linares, Sarkar, & López-Fernández, 2017), are companies in which CV is especially relevant (Minola, Brumana, Campopiano, Garrett, & Cassia, 2016) due to their need to guarantee the survival of the company and their capacity for wealth creation across generations. The transgenerational succession in family firms requires to adapt firms to changing competitive scenarios (Cruz & Nordqvist, 2012), and CV is an excellent instrument to offer family firms the chance to last and maintain their current and future competitive advantage while other family needs are covered such as the involvement of different generations in business (Marchisio, Mazzola, Sciascia, Miles, & Astrachan, 2010). However, previous research has also found that family firms may be change-resistant (Beckhard & Dyer, 1983; Vago, 2004; Ward, 1987) or risk-averse (Peters & Kallmuenzer, 2018; Short, Payne, Brigham, Lumpkin, & Broberg, 2009; Zellweger & Sieger, 2012).

Despite this relevance, empirical literature researching CV in family firms is very scarce and has concentrated on analyzing the influence of family variables—CEO founder duality, CEO tenure, and family involvement—on firm's predisposition to undertake CV (Greidanus & Mark, 2012; Toledano, Urbano, & Bernadich, 2010) or their moderator effect on the innovativeness–CV link (Calabrò, Minola, Campopiano, & Pukall, 2016). Another research line explores the influence of CV activities on firm performance (Marchisio et al., 2010). Consequently, prior research has not explored, so far, many relevant issues in which the family character of the firm may exert a significant influence. Firstly, several important variables, at both individual and organizational levels, have been omitted in the previous empirical studies. Secondly, the factors that could moderate the relationships between those variables that could predispose firms to undertake CV activities have been only explored in Calabrò et al. (2016). Thirdly, previous studies are mostly based on case studies from very limited geographical contexts. However, researchers need to consider the external context in which CV activities occur (Narayanan et al., 2009), because both the institutional context (Peng, 2003) and national cultures (Hofstede, 1980) influence the level of business development, strategic focus, and organizational priorities and, in turn, companies' proclivity to undertake CV.

Consequently, the objective of this study is to explore whether factors related to both the ability of the CEO to interpret the environmental signals and identify business opportunities (Shane & Venkataraman, 2000; Wiklund & Shepherd, 2003) and the characteristics of the firm in terms of previous innovation experience and ability to learn from that experience (Burgelman, 1983; Floyd & Lane, 2000; Kor & Mesko, 2013) can determine the decision to enter into CV in Mexican family firms. Besides, given that firms are forced to be open to introducing continuous changes if they wish to adapt to change and survive in the long term (Bloodgood & Morrow, 2003), we will consider the moderating effect of family members' willingness to change. To test our hypotheses, we conducted a study among top managers in Mexican family firms of all sizes and performed a binomial regression analysis based on a sample of 136 companies across all sectors.

This study makes three main contributions to research in this field. Firstly, it extends the work of Calabrò et al. (2016), which considered the influence of innovativeness, by offering insight into the influence of CEO and firm variables in the decision of conducting CV in family firms. Secondly, it extends the explorations of the influence of family firm characteristics in the decision to undertake CV by considering family members' willingness to change. Thirdly, the study addresses the decision of conducting CV in family firms in a geographical context scarcely studied, that of Mexican or Latin American companies, thus requiring further investigation (San Martin-Reyna & Duran-Encalada, 2012; San Martín-Reyna, Vázquez, & Valdés, 2012). In particular, an analysis of Mexico can be useful for the Latin American region, given their similar institutional framework characteristics as compared to the USA or European countries (Calderón-Martínez & García-Quevedo, 2013).

2 Literature Review and Hypotheses

Both theoretical and empirical literature on CV in family firms is still very scant, and most of the empirical works are of a qualitative nature. Regarding theoretical works, Hoy (2006) analyzes the effect on the CV of the existence of different life cycles that overlap in a family firm, whereas Minola et al. (2016) discuss, by drawing on family development theory, when and why family firms are motivated to engage in entrepreneurial activities. Finally, Brumana, Minola, Garrett, and Digan (2017), drawing on stewardship theory, argue that family business dynamics, and in particular the development of the ownership structure, influence how family firms pursue and make decisions related to internal corporate venturing (ICV).

Among the empirical studies, Marchisio et al.'s (2010) study analyzes through case studies how the complex social system of the family firm affects CV. Concretely, CV offers significant advantages at the individual level given that it can help increase the management abilities of those responsible for CV activities. CV also offers advantages at the family level because it gives family members the chance to exercise good judgment on the person responsible for CV without risking the original business. Possible negative aspects are also identified, both at the individual level—loss of interest in the original business—and at the family level—deterioration of relations with family members not participating in the new venture. Also by using case studies, Toledano et al. (2010) analyze the collaboration process that emerges from interactions among individuals in order to develop entrepreneurial actions within established family firms, whereas Greidanus and Mark (2012) analyze, on a qualitative study of six family businesses, the ICV goals of family firms.

The few quantitative studies identified to analyze the reason why firms that initially were very entrepreneurial became more conservative (Zahra, 2005). The reaction of stock markets to the news that listed companies are adopting CV initiatives is explored in Wong, Chang, and Chen (2010). Finally, Calabrò et al. (2016) explore whether family ownership and family influence moderate the relationship between innovativeness and national/international CV. They find that high family ownership and family influence negatively affect the positive innovativeness–national/venturing international relationships, this effect being weaker for the innovativeness–international venturing link. In all these cases, the main focus was on the influence of family-related variables on the aspects under study. By contrast, our model reflects the firm and individual attitudes and values that are expected to determine CV, as well as the moderating effect that the family members' willingness to change may exert on the firm-related variables.

Including these variables is justified because CV is a strategic decision at the highest level in the company (Narayanan et al., 2009). More specifically, we consider the influence of both the ability of the CEO to interpret the environmental signals and identify business opportunities (Shane & Venkataraman, 2000; Wiklund & Shepherd, 2003) and the characteristics of the firm in terms of previous innovation experience and ability to learn from that experience (Burgelman, 1983; Floyd & Lane, 2000; Kor & Mesko, 2013). Moreover, and considering the importance of anticipating, embracing, and inducing change to entrepreneurial thinking (Miller, 1983), we study the moderating effect of family members' willingness to change on the relationships between firm's characteristics and CV. On this basis, the following variables are included. Figure 1 provides the conceptual framework of our model. Below, we discuss the direct relationships first, and then we outline the proposed moderation effects.

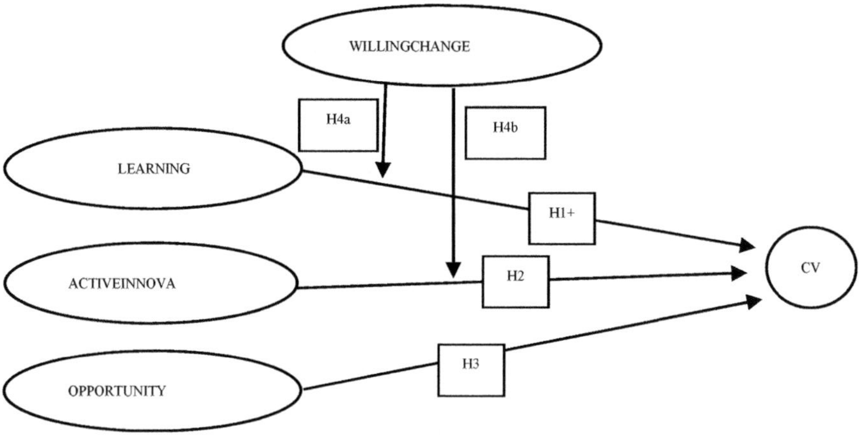

Fig. 1 Research model. Source: Authors' own figure

2.1 *Organizational Learning and CV*

Organizational learning is derived from a group of values possessed by a firm's collaborators to create, internalize, disseminate, and use knowledge (Liu, Luo, & Shi, 2002). According to the knowledge-based view of the firm, knowledge is the most important resource for organizations to develop sustainable competitive advantages (Barney, 1991; Grant, 1996; Mustafa, Lundmark, & Ramos, 2016) and obtain superior organizational performance and success (Andreeva & Kianto, 2012; Oliva, 2014; Spender, 1996). Having the ability to learn lets a company acquire and understand new ideas, and to do that it must be able to decide what information it needs to look for, classify, and place at the disposal of the organization (Hurley & Hult, 1998). Learning in a company is essential for implementing an effective development strategy and is achieved when the organization has the opportunity to learn not only from successes but also from failures (Burger-Helmchen, 2009; Carayannis & Roy, 2000; Gomezelj Omerzel & Antončič, 2008; Kautt, Walsh, & Bittner, 2007; Rerup, 2005; Rhee, Park, & Lee, 2010).

Learning new knowledge is also a crucial factor for CV development given that it fosters future entrepreneurial initiatives and also catalyzes and accelerates sustainable growth (Carayannis, Popescu, Sipp, & Stewart, 2006). In particular, Latin American corporate ventures may require that parent companies take responsibility for knowledge sharing in ventures in order to achieve growth and success (Rajagopal, 2006). Having a high level of learning is an important factor distinguishing highly entrepreneurial firms from their competitors allowing them to maintain a competitive advantage over time (Burger-Helmchen, 2009; Carayannis et al., 2006; Gomezelj Omerzel & Antončič, 2008), as they will have better tools for facing uncertainty and will more rapidly assimilate changes in the business environment (Gomezelj Omerzel & Antončič, 2008). If the organization wants to achieve successful CV, managers must be able to discover opportunities, as well as develop and execute them satisfactorily (Burger-Helmchen, 2009), none of which is possible without prior acquisition of knowledge through learning (Montes, Moreno, & Morales, 2005). Innovative firms that increase their participation in the market, as well as their technology-based knowledge (Bojica & Fuentes, 2012; Garcia-Morales, Llorens-Montes, & Verdú-Jover, 2006), can improve the results of CV activity. Other authors (Covin & Slevin, 1991) identify this process inversely, indicating that corporate entrepreneurship generates a learning orientation.

The unique configuration of resources and capabilities of family firms (Habbershon & Williams, 1999; Habbershon, Williams, & MacMillan, 2003; Sirmon & Hitt, 2003) may influence both the family firm's knowledge and how it is used to promote corporate entrepreneurship (Zahra, 2012). Thus, the limited managerial resources of family firms besides their more homogenous knowledge (Sirmon & Hitt, 2003) and their preference for cohesion may also prevent deep learning (Zahra, 2012) which may constitute a barrier to CV. However, family firms share certain characteristics, such as the close relationships among their members that facilitate knowledge sharing (Zahra, Neubaum, & Larrañeta, 2007; Zahra, Van de Velde, & Larrañeta, 2007) and exchange as well as communication (Craig, Dibrell, & Garrett, 2014; Habbershon & Williams, 1999). Moreover, their long-term orientation and their desire of passing a healthy business to the new generations foster their commitment to learning (Berrone, Cruz, & Gomez-Mejia, 2012; Zahra, 2012) which, in turn, endow family firms with a specific capability to sense opportunities and to transform them in entrepreneurial activities (Barros, Hernangómez, & Martin-Cruz, 2016; Chirico & Nordqvist, 2010). Finally, previous empirical research informs that "being a family business would strengthen the positive association between learning orientation and entrepreneurial orientation" (Hernández-Linares et al., 2018, p. 7). On this basis, the following premise is stated:

Hypothesis 1 *Organizational learning is positively related to the development of CV activities.*

2.2 Innovation Activity and CV

An important premise in our model is that behaviors more than nonbehavioral attributes are what give meaning to the entrepreneurial process or, in other words, the behavior is the central, essential element in the entrepreneurial process (Covin & Slevin, 1991). This is the reason why the model includes a firm's active involvement in innovation, which reflects an effective behavior related to one of the dimensions of corporate entrepreneurship (Kellermanns & Eddleston, 2006).

Innovation has become a permanent strategic process drawing from all firms' available resources coming from the firm itself, external acquisition, or cooperation with external agents (Faems, 2008). Although the need to innovate for all firms has never been so high (Engel, 2011) regardless of the size, sector, or ownership type, not all of them exhibit the same innovative behavior in response to their challenges and problems (Serrano-Bedia, López-Fernández, & Garcia-Piqueres, 2016). In particular, a number of literature reviews about innovation in family firms (De Massis, Frattini, & Lichtenthaler, 2013; Duran, Kammerlander, Van Essen, & Zellweger, 2016; Fuetsch & Suess-Reyes, 2017; Röd, 2016) show these firms have peculiar innovation behaviors based on their risk preferences, resource endowments, and family objectives (Classen, Carree, Van Gils, & Peters, 2014; De Massis, Frattini, Kotlar, Petruzzelli, & Wright, 2016; Kellermanns, Eddleston, Sarathy, & Murphy, 2012) which may influence not only specific dimensions of their innovation process (König, Kammerlander, & Enders, 2013; Röd, 2016) but also their innovation output and performance (Fuetsch & Suess-Reyes, 2017). More precisely, family firms tend to invest less in R&D (Duran et al., 2016) and use distinct innovation activities than nonfamily firms (Röd, 2016), more oriented to pursue exploitative innovation strategies with a focus on incremental innovations, a behavior that allows them to have a higher conversion rate from innovation input to output (Fuetsch & Suess-Reyes, 2017). These results may be highly influenced by factors such as family ownership, management, governance structures, or generational effects (Röd, 2016). Thus, several studies show the existence of a negative relationship between R&D investments and family involvement, even though a later-generation family member CEO (Duran et al., 2016) or a high diversity of members in ownership, management, and control (Fuetsch & Suess-Reyes, 2017) can support innovative behavior.

Some works point out a greater awareness among company executives (Battistini, Hacklin, & Baschera, 2013), especially those at high levels of management, of the need of having a sustained strategy for change. Along with this line, the existence of a firm's innovative behavior and good innovation performance may contribute to this end, in several ways. While some studies (Maine, 2008) analyze examples presenting the inverse relationship in which CV is a factor for exploiting radical technological innovation, factors such as the family involvement in the board may exert a negative effect on family firm's ability to turn entrepreneurial orientation into innovation (Arzubiaga, Kotlar, De Massis, Maseda, & Iturralde, 2018). Calabrò et al. (2016) also report a positive effect of family firms' innovativeness, one of the dimensions of entrepreneurial orientation, on both national and international CV, being the innovativeness–national venturing relationship negatively moderated by high family ownership and influence.

In sum, and despite the peculiar innovation behaviors of family firms influenced by aspects such as family ownership, governance structures, or generational effects, the limited empirical evidence available suggests that an active, innovative behavior of family firms may contribute to making them more inclined to become involved in CV. On this basis, the following premise is proposed:

Hypothesis 2 *The fact that a family firm is active in innovation is positively related to the development of CV activities.*

2.3 *Opportunity Detection and CV*

The entrepreneurial process involves activities and actions associated with recognizing and exploiting opportunities to create value (Bygrave & Hofer, 1992). Opportunities are frequently considered an essential trigger for generating new enterprises (Shane & Venkataraman, 2000). Busenitz et al. (2003) suggest that opportunities evolve from interactions between markets and environments involving the creation of new mean-ends relationships. Changes in the environment almost immediately create a new need in the same industry. In turn, these necessities are opportunities and the ability to recognize and take advantage of them is what generates entrepreneurship (Wiklund & Shepherd, 2003). Information asymmetry also generates opportunities in markets; eventually, these opportunities are most likely to be recognized by alert individuals and organizations with privileged access to strategic and different information (Schumpeter, 1934).

Focusing on the relationship between personality traits and opportunity discovery, Gaglio and Katz (2001) highlight that individual entrepreneurial alertness is the cognitive engine driving the opportunity recognition process. Upper-echelons theory (Hambrick, 2007; Hambrick & Mason, 1984) states that companies' strategic choices are determined and shaped by the values, experience, and personalities of the dominant players in the organization, namely by the CEO of the company. The rationale behind this premise is that the values and cognitive bases of the CEOs influence their interpretations of the situations they face, as occurs during the process of recognition of opportunities and the decision to exploit them or not.

Previous research also suggests that CEO's influence is more salient when more managerial discretion exists (Hambrick, 2007; Hambrick & Finkelstein, 1987), as is the case in non-listed family firms. CEOs in private companies can make decisions relatively free from dominant capital markets and boards of directors (Fiegener, Brown, Dreux, & Dennis Jr, 2000) and use to have fewer complex stakeholders (Jeong & Harrison, 2017; Ling, Simsek, Lubatkin, & Veiga, 2008). CEO autonomy is even more salient in family firms in which the desire to maintain the control over the company and its strategic decisions (Schulze, Lubatkin, & Dino, 2003) explains, for example, its restricted use of banks financing (Gomez-Mejia, Makri, & Kintana, 2010). Moreover, family firm ownership is highly concentrated in the hands of the dominant family, allowing them to heavily influence the firm's strategy (Zahra, 2003). Families channel their influence on the company (Audretsch, Hülsbeck, & Lehmann, 2013) through the appointment of family CEOs, who may enjoy the additional autonomy derived from being part of the controlling family (Finkelstein & Hambrick, 1990).

Finally, previous research suggested that family firms favor opportunities recognition, due to their enduring knowledge structures and their ability for knowledge combination and long-term orientation while they are expected to have a quick and flexible response in taking advantage of opportunities (Patel & Fiet, 2011). Therefore, we propose the following hypothesis:

Hypothesis 3 *The ability to detect opportunities by family firms' CEOs is positively related to the development of CV activities.*

2.4 The Moderator Effect of Family Members' Willingness to Change

The need for change is inherent in our society, given the existence of global competition, short life cycles, and constant changes in the environment. Nowadays, most firms are forced to make organizational changes and recognize and exploit opportunities, as long as they wish to survive (Bloodgood & Morrow, 2003). A family firm culture that allows facing change quickly and effectively may favor an active involvement of the firm in CV activities (Zahra, Hayton, & Salvato, 2004). Some family firms are reluctant to change (Beckhard & Dyer Jr, 1983; Ward, 2011), because they think change will be costly and cause internal conflicts, or perhaps simply due to inertia (Beckhard & Dyer Jr, 1983); they see innovation as a threat to their organizations (Miller & Friesen, 1982). This attitude may lead them to rigidity and cause difficulty in adapting (Zahra et al., 2004) when situations change, resulting in stagnation or loss of the market (Miller, Steier, & Le Breton-Miller, 2003). As a counterweight to this situation, a study reveals that, in Mexican multinational companies, the development of technological capabilities tends to facilitate lowering cognitive inertia of managers (Rajagopal, 2006). Within this context, the importance of an organizational culture promoting change to adapt rapidly and more simply to the environment stands out even more prominently (Karagozoglu & Brown, 1988; López-Fernández, Serrano-Bedia, & Gómez-López, 2011). The willingness to change (Kellermanns & Eddleston, 2006) can be an important distinguishing factor in entrepreneurial family firms. Specifically, these authors show that family firms demonstrating a greater willingness to change reach higher rates of corporate entrepreneurship (Kellermanns & Eddleston, 2006). The willingness to change can affect the degree to which organizational learning and innovation activity contribute to CV in family firms.

Congruent with the knowledge-based view of the firm, organizational learning obtained by exploring and integrating different internal and external knowledge areas makes it possible to build new skills and capabilities that could lead to family firms' competitive advantage (Chirico, 2008; Zahra et al., 2007). Learning also promotes entrepreneurial activities by enabling family firms to innovate, create new businesses, and renew their operations (Zahra, 2008). Firms that exploit their core competences by investing in building an internal stock of knowledge are better able to develop the absorptive capacity necessary for effectively combining in-house and external knowledge (Cohen & Levinthal, 1990), and these diverse knowledge bases serve firms as a foundation for entrepreneurial activities (Zahra et al., 2007). However, these processes may require a fundamental transformation of the organizational culture and systems of the firm. For this reason, the willingness to change may contribute positively to enhance the positive effect of family firms' organizational learning on CV activities.

The willingness to change appears to be directly related to "organizational learning," as this orientation to change leads firms to be interested in generating new knowledge that will trigger changes associated with improvement in products and processes and, thus, allows them to achieve sustainable growth (Luo, Olechowski, & Magee, 2014) through CV activities (Carayannis et al., 2006). Gaining new knowledge makes future CV initiatives more viable, and therefore, the desire to keep learning is an important factor in the entrepreneurial family firm culture (Carayannis et al., 2006). Therefore, we propose:

Hypothesis 4a *The relationship between organizational learning and CV is moderated by a willingness to change—precisely, the higher the willingness to change, the better the positive relationship between these two variables.*

Finally, the willingness to change may enhance the relationship between innovation and CV. The willingness to change has been directly linked to innovation (López-Fernández et al., 2011) since there cannot be innovation if there is no acceptance of change (Miller & Friesen, 1982). Performing innovation can be viewed as a way to enter new markets, hold on to market share, and adapt to industry changes, contributing to the entrepreneurial activity of the firms. However, the challenges involved in pursuing these activities conducive to CV regarding coordination, resource sharing, and corporate culture (Gibson & Birkinshaw, 2004) or entrepreneurship-led mind-set (Simpson, Siguaw, & Enz, 2006) may be demanding for firms. For these reasons, a strong predisposition to change may contribute to creating an organizational context such that the firm could be abler or motivated to address these challenges.

The willingness to change may also mitigate the resistance to the adoption of innovations that often arises in the innovating organizations (Damanpour, 1991; Hultink & Atuahene-Gima, 2000; Ram & Jung, 1991) when they focus exclusively on areas closely related to preexisting knowledge or "local search" (Teece, 2007). From this perspective, the willingness to change could be viewed as the first predictor of innovative behavior in a firm (Montalvo, 2006). Along this line, the acceptance of change encompassing the disposition to innovate has been analyzed at the individual level as one of the intangible measurements of the attitude toward innovation (*innovate human capital—IHC*) in the workplace (McGuirk, Lenihan, & Hart, 2015). Little is known about how the willingness to change impacts the tendency toward innovation (Wang & Ahmed, 2004), but based on previous arguments, the following hypothesis is formulated:

Hypothesis 4b *The relationship between active in innovation and CV is moderated by the willingness to change. Specifically, the greater the willingness to change, the higher the positive relationship between these two variables.*

3 Empirical Study

3.1 The Sample

The research was conducted from April 2013 to February 2014. Data were collected from CEOs and top managers within the targeted firms using questionnaire-based surveys, which is a common method to obtain data in studies investigating entrepreneurship and family firms (e.g., Cruz & Nordqvist, 2012; Kellermanns & Eddleston, 2006; Kellermanns, Eddleston, Barnett, & Pearson, 2008; Zahra et al., 2004). CEOs were used as key informants (Kumar, Stern, & Anderson, 1993), since they receive information from a wide range of departments and, therefore, are a very valuable source for evaluating the different variables of the organization. CEOs and top managers also play a major role in informing and molding the management process and are ultimately responsible for plotting the organization's direction and plans, as well as for guiding the actions carried out to achieve them (Westphal & Fredrickson, 2001).

No incentives were given for survey completion. We pre-tested the questionnaire with five CEOs from local firms in the cities of Queretaro and San Luis Potosí to ensure the correct wording and overall structure and understanding of the questions. Once the pre-test was completed, we used the online Qualtrics platform to administer the survey delivery and follow-up. Three different sources to gather reliable information about firms were considered. The first was an internal database of family firms provided by the *Eugenio Garza Lagüera* Entrepreneurship Institute at the Monterrey Institute of Technology in Mexico (TEC). This database contained a list of firms in Mexico, most of them with the CEOs' contact information. The second source was contact with TEC's business incubators and technological parks at four different campuses in Mexico, including Monterrey, Chihuahua, Queretaro, and San Luis Potosi. These institutions also provided us with a list of companies and their corresponding contact information. Moreover, the third source was contact with currently enrolled graduate students at the Queretaro Campus and postgraduate students at TEC's Virtual University, many of whom are CEOs or occupy top-level positions in Mexican firms.

A personalized invitation to respond to the online version of the questionnaire within the databases mentioned above was then delivered to each of the contacts. Additionally, a paper version was also offered to currently enrolled students. From the 627 invitations initially sent, we received replies from 431 firms, and after proceeding to the removal of incomplete questionnaires as well as those that were not answered by CEOs or top managers, 295 questionnaires were considered valid (response rate 47.05% including paper and online responses). TEC's special interest in developing quality research in Mexico and the close collaboration among colleagues and the researchers involved in this study were decisive in obtaining such a good response. Companies in the sample were of all sizes but only in industrial, commercial, and private service sectors. The sampling error was 5.71%.[1] In most survey research, sampling error levels typically lie between 2% and 6%, with 95% confidence limits (Patel & Read, 1996; Särndal, Swensson, & Wretman, 2003). Also, we tried to assess potential nonresponse bias by utilizing Mann–Whitney tests to determine potential differences between early and late respondents. This approach is based on the assumption that nonrespondents are more similar to late respondents than early respondents (Armstrong & Overton, 1977; Narasimhan & Das, 2001). No statistically significant differences were discovered (p-value >0.05), which mitigated the concern for potential nonresponse bias.[2]

Bearing in mind that definitions of family firms abound in the literature and definitional ambiguities persist (Voordeckers, Van Gils, & Van den Heuvel, 2007), we opted to employ a subjective criterion: self-definition. We asked the CEOs whether or not they perceived their firm as a family business (e.g., Cooper, Upton, & Seaman, 2005), which allowed us to capture the essence of the family firm (Chua, Chrisman, & Sharma, 1999). Answers were then codified using a dummy variable (0 = nonfamily firms, 1 = family firms). From the sample of 295 firms, 156 were identified as family firms from which the 136 surveys answered by CEOs were finally chosen for this study.

About the common method bias problem (Podsakoff, MacKenzie, Lee, & Podsakoff, 2003), we introduced all items pertaining to the independent, moderator, and dependent variables into a factor analysis and the factor analysis extracted six factors explaining 65.171% of the variance. The factors separated cleanly, and the first factor explained only 16.440% of the variance. We concluded that common method variance was not a major concern in the current study, particularly, since no single method factor emerged.

3.2 Measures

All constructs were measured on a five-point Likert scale anchored by "strongly disagree" to "strongly agree" and were averaged. In order to test the measurement properties of the scales used for the construction of the multi-item variables, these scales were subjected to validity and reliability by using principal component analysis and by calculating the Cronbach's alpha for each scale. The results supported the validity of these scales, as indicated by the amount of variance explained, which is very close or exceeded 0.5 (Hair, Anderson, Tatham, & Black, 1998), and the loading factors of all items within each scale which exceeded 0.5 (Hair et al., 1998). For Cronbach's alpha, typically, a threshold of 0.6–0.7 is required (Nunnally & Bernstein, 1978), but the limit in alpha depends on the number of items per construct as well as the exploratory character of the study. The Cronbach's alpha

[1]Confidence level: 95% ($z = 1.96$; $p = q = 0.5$).

[2]Results of the Mann–Whitney test: sector p-value = 0.306 and size p-value = 0.355.

measures of all the scales surpassed 0.7, which is accepted as a very good level (Nunnally & Bernstein, 1978), except in the case of the learning scale, a newly developed scale with few items. In these circumstances, levels of around 0.6 are acceptable (Cronbach, 1951; Nunnally & Bernstein, 1978).

The dependent variable CV has been measured by means of a dichotomous variable that takes the value of 1 if the firm answered affirmatively the question, "During the period of 2008–2012, have new entrepreneurial initiatives been taken in your company?," and zero when the response was negative just like has been used in other studies (Galán González, Pizarro Moreno, & Castro, 2007).

In respect to the independent variables, organizational learning (LEARNING) was measured using a four-items scale adapted from Obloj, Obloj, and Pratt (2010) in a study of transition economies. After depuration, three items were maintained (Cronbach's alpha = 0.562). To determine firms active in innovation, a dichotomous variable (ACTIVEINNOVA), which assumes a value of "1" when the respondent indicated that the family firm had performed activities conducted specifically to develop or implement any type of innovation (product innovation, process innovation, and/or management innovation) during the previous 3 years and a value of "0" otherwise (Mohnen & Röller, 2005), was constructed.

To capture the CEO's capacity of detecting new opportunities, a dichotomous variable (OPPORTUNITY) taking the value of "1" when the CEO has detected at least one opportunity a year in the period 2011–2012 and a value of "0" in the rest of the cases was constructed. The variable (Singh, Hills, Hybels, & Lumpkin, 1999) was constructed by asking, "During the period 2011–2012, how many potential opportunities did you detect?"

The moderator variable willingness to change (WILLINGCHANGE) was measured using the scale employed by Kellermanns and Eddleston (2006), which they adapted for use in family firms based on the one developed by Barrick and Mount (1991). After the depuration of the scale, three items were maintained (Cronbach's alpha = 0.810).

The study controlled for different variables that could influence the relationship between the independent variables and the CV. First, we controlled for size, as larger firms might have more slack resources to engage in corporate entrepreneurship (Kellermanns et al., 2008; Rauch, Wiklund, Lumpkin, & Frese, 2009; Zahra et al., 2004). We used a dichotomous variable for companies with less than ten employees (MICRO). Second, we controlled the company sector because different industries may differentially encourage companies' entrepreneurial and innovative behavior (Sciascia, Mazzola, & Chirico, 2013). We used a dichotomous variable that identifies companies in the industrial sector (INDUSTRY). Third, given the heterogeneity of family firms (Chrisman, Chua, Pearson, & Barnett, 2012; Nordqvist, Sharma, & Chirico, 2014), we are led to think that certain decisions, like CV, can be conditioned by the type of family firm. Then we included a dichotomous variable that identifies family firms with more than 25% of the ownership in the hands of the dominant family (OWNERSHIP+25). Fourth, we controlled by the educational level of the CEO, given that educational level is a knowledge source (Cooper, Gimeno-Gascon, & Woo, 1994) and that individuals with higher educational level report higher abilities to identify entrepreneurial opportunities (Ucbasaran, Westhead, & Wright, 2008). We included a dichotomous variable (POSTGRADUATE) that identifies CEOs with postgraduate studies.

Finally, we controlled for environmental dynamism (DYNAMISM) because firms that operate in dynamic environments need to systematically explore new entrepreneurial opportunities (Sciascia et al., 2013; Zahra & Bogner, 2000). Environmental dynamism was measured using five items employed in previous research (Casillas, Moreno, & Barbero, 2011; Lumpkin & Dess, 2001). After the depuration of the scale, four items were maintained (Cronbach's alpha = 0.761).

3.3 *Methodology*

The theoretical model proposed here is tested by the estimation of a binomial logistic regression model. The suitability of this technique derives from the nature of the dependent variable (dichotomous) and the explanatory variables (where continuous variables are combined with categorical variables). Logistic regression is a classification method, an alternative to discriminant analysis when the multivariate normal model is not justified.[3] It applies to any combination of continuous and categorical independent variables (Hair et al., 1998).

Logistic regression analysis allows us to estimate the probability of a firm deciding to carry out CV activities as a function of the company, family, and individual factors. Also included was the analysis of the effect of a moderator variable reflecting the orientation toward change in the firm regarding business variables. The regression coefficients estimate the impact of the explanatory variables on the probability of carrying out CV activities, with a positive sign for the coefficient, which means that the variable increases that probability. The aim is to establish a profile for firms engaged in CV activities.

The underlying regression has been defined as:

$$\begin{aligned}\mathrm{CV}_i = {} & \beta 1 + \beta 2\ \mathrm{LEARNING}_i + \beta 3\ \mathrm{ACTIVEINNOVA}_i + \beta 4\ \mathrm{OPPORTUNITY}_i \\ & + \beta 5\ \mathrm{WILLINGCHANGE}_i + \beta 6\ \mathrm{WILLINGCHANGE} \times \mathrm{LEARNING}_i \\ & + \beta 7\ \mathrm{WILLINGCHANGE} \times \mathrm{ACTIVEINNOVA}_i + \beta 8\ \mathrm{MICRO}_i \\ & + \beta 9\ \mathrm{INDUSTRY}_i + \beta 10\ \mathrm{OWNERSHIP} + \beta 11\ \mathrm{POSTGRADUATE}_i \\ & + \beta 12\ \mathrm{DYNAMISM}_i + \varepsilon_i\end{aligned}$$

where β are the estimated coefficients and ε_i is a normally distributed error term. The statistical software IBM SPSS v.22 was used for the analyses.

[3]The linear discriminant model is sensitive to the assumption that independent variables are normally distributed. This assumption is violated when, as in this case, several explanatory variables are qualitative.

4 Results

The means, standard deviations, and zero-order correlations are shown in Table 1. We only observed moderate levels of correlations (all smaller than 0.419) between our variables. We calculated the variance inflation factors (all smaller than 1.240), which suggested that multicollinearity was not a concern in this study (Hair et al., 1998). Besides, the variables have been Z-scored before creating the interactions also with the purpose to mitigate multicollinearity concerns (Aiken & West, 1991; Cronbach, 1987).

A description of the main characteristics of our sample is reported in Table 2.

To estimate the impact of the explanatory variables on innovation activities, logistic regression estimations have been carried out. The models included four steps to incorporate the different variables in our study (control variables in step 1, firm variables in step 2, individual variables in step 3, and the moderator effect in step 4).

The results of the logistic regression are presented in Table 3. The strength of the models is assessed through the calculation of the χ^2 and the Nagelkerke pseudo R^2. The Nagelkerke pseudo R^2 is one of the most straightforward of the various pseudo R^2 statistics proposed for assessing logistic regression models (DeMaris, 1995). The pseudo R^2 gives a rough measure of goodness of fit that can be compared across models.

In the first step, and regarding the control variables, MICRO is found to be negatively related ($\beta = -0.678$, $p = 0.002$) to the development of CV activities, which indicates that very small firms have more significant difficulties in starting CV activities. DYNAMISM was found to be positively related to CV ($\beta = 0.407$, $p = 0.077$), indicating that in dynamic environments, CV activities are more likely to be conducted. Both control variables retain their sign, although their level of significance is slightly diminished in different steps, which confirms both effects. The remaining control variables are nonsignificant. The χ^2 of the block is significant ($p = 0.002$), and the pseudo R^2 Nagelkerke value is 0.216.

In the second step, we introduce two company variables. LEARNING ($\beta = -0.269$, $p = 0.278$) is nonsignificant to CV, while ACTIVEINNOVA ($\beta = 0.508$, $p = 0.033$) is positively related to the dependent variable. The χ^2 of the block is (significant $p = 0.074$), and the pseudo R^2 Nagelkerke value is 0.269, which demonstrates a slight increase in the explanatory power of the model derived from the inclusion of the firm-associated variables. These results support hypothesis 2, while for hypothesis 1 we have not found a significant effect.

In step 3, we introduce OPPORTUNITY to test the individual effect on our model. OPPORTUNITY ($\beta = 0.937$, $p = 0.000$) is positively significant to CV, which supports hypothesis 3. The χ^2 of the block is significant ($p = 0.000$), and the pseudo R^2 Nagelkerke value is 0.410, which indicates a significant increase in the explanatory power of the model derived from the inclusion of the variable associated with the CEO's characteristics.

Table 1 Mean, standard deviation, and correlations between variables

	Mean	S.D.	1	2	3	4	5	6	7	8	9	10
Dependent variable												
1. CV	.67	.472	1									
Control variables												
2. MICRO	.23	.421	−.312**	1								
3. INDUSTRY	.34	.475	.125	−.166	1							
4. OWNERSHIP+25	.90	.295	.022	−.121	0.74	1						
5. POSTGRADUATE	.34	.475	.090	−.166	.014	.127	1					
6. DYNAMISM	3.06	.773	.200*	−.073	−.036	.014	.042	1				
Firm variables												
7. LEARNING	3.76	.604	−.019	−.073	.038	−.061	.020	.154	1			
8. ACTIVEINNOVA	.77	.421	.176*	−.254**	.160	−.101	.160	−.167	.144	1		
Individual variable												
9. OPPORTUNITY	.76	.431	.419**	−.096	−.049	−.045	.106	.167	.066	.084	1	
Moderating variable												
10. WILLINGCHANGE	3.76	.820	−.003	.045	.227*	.096	.131	.002	.313**	.140	.067	1

Source: Authors' own table

Notes: Levels of significance (two-tailed) ** 0.01; * 0.05

Table 2 Sample description ($N = 136$) (%)

Market	Local/regional = 47.1; National = 34.6; International = 18.4
Employees	<10 = 22.8; 10–50 = 34.6; 51–250 = 25.0; <250 = 17.6
Company age	5 years or less = 11.0; 6–15 years = 27.3; 16–30 years = 36.7; +30 years = 25
Sector	Agricultural = 5.9; Industrial = 27.9; Services = 66.2
CEO seniority	<10 years = 50.7; 11–25 years = 40.4; +26 years = 8.8
Family ownership	up to 25% = 9.6; 26–50% = 19.9; +50% = 70.6
Family CEO	Yes = 89; No = 11

Source: Authors' own table

In step 4, we test the moderator effect of WILLINGCHANGE on the two company variables. Of the two interaction effects, only the one affecting LEARNING is significant ($\beta = 0.784$, $p = 0.025$). The χ^2 of the block is significant ($p = 0.048$), and the global model is significant ($p = 0.000$). The pseudo R^2 Nagelkerke value is 0.463, which indicates an increase in the explanatory power of the model derived from the inclusion of moderation. To facilitate the interpretation of the moderation effects, the significant interactions are plotted in Fig. 2. Hypothesis 4a stated that WILLINGCHANGE would augment the positive relation between LEARNING and CV. Our results found that the relationship is significant and positive. However, the sign is negative, contrary to what was expected. A gradient test revealed that the negative slope between LEARNING and CV was significant for family businesses scoring low on WILLINGCHANGE ($t = -1.744$, $p = 0.0084$), whereas the positive slope for family firms with high WILLINGCHANGE was not significant ($t = -0.644$, n.s.). The interaction signifies that in our model a high WILLINGCHANGE does not significantly influence the LEARNING–CV link, whereas in companies with low WILLINGCHANGE the negative relationship between LEARNING and CV is strongest. Put in other words, the organizational learning (LEARNING) generates an aversion to CV that is more salient in companies with family members with low willingness to change.

5 Discussion and Conclusions

This chapter had the objective of exploring whether factors related to the focus of both the CEO and the company on innovation and entrepreneurship can determine the decision to enter into CV in Mexican family firms. Also, the moderator variable willingness to change was considered to identify its effect on the relationships between innovation activity/organizational learning and CV. To test our hypotheses, we conducted a study among top managers in Mexican family firms of all sizes and performed a multiple regression analysis based on a sample of 136 family CEOs from companies across all sectors. The effects considered in our hypotheses were

Table 3 Results of logistics regression for CV ($n = 113$)

Variables	Step 1			Step 2			Step 3			Step 4		
	B[a]	SE[b]	OR[c]	B[a]	SE[b]	OR[c]	B[a]	SE[b]	OR[c]	B[a]	SE[b]	OR[c]
Control variables												
1. MICRO	−.678**	.221	.508	−.602**	.229	.548	.254**	7.003	.511	−.681*	.277	.506
2. INDUSTRY	.231	.231	1.260	.187	.237	1.206	.257	1.216	1.328	.376	.280	1.457
3. OWNERSHIP+25	−.211	.259	.810	−.152	.269	.859	.263	.000	1.003	.119	.298	1.127
4. POSTGRADUATE	.251	.239	1.286	.236	.248	1.266	.277	.121	1.101	−.009	.300	.991
5. DYNAMISM	.407†	.231	1.503	.566*	.250	1.761	.260†	3.092	1.579	.461†	.275	1.586
6. LEARNING				−.269	.248	.764	−.313	.268	.731	−.601†	.345	.548
7. ACTIVEINNOVA				.508*	.239	1.662	.475†	.268	1.608	.620*	.292	1.858
Individual variable												
8. OPPORTUNITY							.937***	.257	2.552	1.111***	.295	3.037
Moderating variable												
9. WILLINGCHANGE										−.014	.266	.986
Moderating effects												
10. WILLINGCHANGE×LEARNING										.351*	2.191	
11. WILLINGCHANGE×ACTIVEINNOVA										.270	.710	.797
χ^2 Block	18.903**			5.209†			15.009***			6.084*		
χ^2 Model	18.903**			24.112**			39.121***			45.328***		
R^2 Nagelkerke	.216			.269			.410			.463		
% correct predictions	.735			.752			.770			.796		

Source: Authors' own table

Notes: Levels of significance: ***$p < 0.001$; **$p < 0.01$; *$p < 0.05$; †$p < 0.1$

[a]Estimated parameter; [b]Standard error; [c]Odds ratio

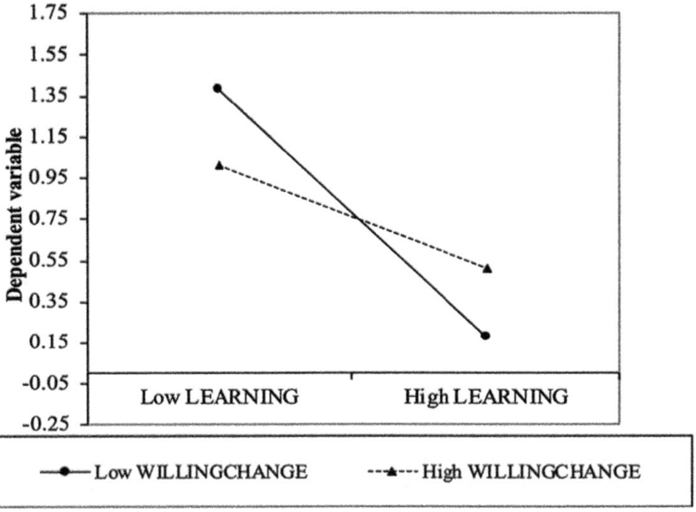

Fig. 2 Moderating effects of willingness to change on the learning–CV relationship. Source: Authors' own figure

partially supported in relation to their effect on CV. These findings are of great significance, given the lack of research on determinant factors for CV.

Through our work, we were able to sustain that the presence of innovative activity (ACTIVEINNOVA) was positively related to CV, as stated in hypothesis 2, as the actions leading to innovation are what really make a firm exercise CV activities and not merely remain at the attitudinal level (Covin & Slevin, 1991). Contrary to our expectation, organizational learning (LEARNING) turned out to be negatively related to CV activity. Although it is true that there is literature affirming that organizational learning is an important factor (Carayannis et al., 2006; Hernández-Linares et al., 2018) for CV, there are also authors who describe organizational learning as a factor that can take us in both directions (Rerup, 2005). On the one hand, previous negative experiences could boost the need to experiment with new activities that could result in CV. Nevertheless, prior activities that produced more positive results for the firm can lead it to generate organizational learning that encourages these same activities or actions in an attempt to repeat these successes, inhibiting CV in the family firm. In our study, the possibility exists that the successful firms have learned what has brought them good results and that this leads them to reject generating new initiatives, which explains why what is stated in hypothesis 1 is not fulfilled. In the recent work from Hernández-Linares et al. (2018), they found that a family business boosts the transformation of learning orientation into entrepreneurial orientation. However, they also found that this is only true for family firms that are highly learning oriented. While we do not measure the same constructs, and therefore we must be cautious with comparisons, many explanations of the differences arise. Firstly, it is possible that our sample has lower levels of organizational learning. Second, it is possible that for a company there is a difference between the orientation of doing something (namely, their entrepreneurial orientation) and the decision of compromise resources in doing so (namely launching new firms), especially when there is high risk and uncertainty regarding the results of such investments. Finally, it is also possible that in the Mexican context, the higher level of political and economic uncertainty makes family firms more cautious, preventing their involvement in new CV initiatives. Future research must explore this issue to reach a deeper understanding of CV decisions in family firms.

About the individual block variables, the CEO's capacity to detect opportunities (OPPORTUNITY) proved to be positively related to CV, just as we stated in hypothesis 3, confirming what was proposed in prior studies (Kellermanns & Eddleston, 2006), though specifically for technological opportunities. New enterprises are generated as a result of solving a problem or market need. This need or problem is also known as an opportunity. Consequently, being able to detect new opportunities is directly related to the possibility of generating CV.

Family firms are more prone to invest in CV when confronted with an environment rich in opportunities (Kellermanns & Eddleston, 2006) and that is why it is important to have the capacity to identify these opportunities and then proceed to develop the necessary competences to make use of them (Dess & Lumpkin, 2005).

Concerning the moderator variable willingness to change (WILLINGCHANGE) in relation to the firm variables block (LEARNING and ACTIVEINNOVA), we find that when WILLINGCHANGE is low, the higher the learning of the company the less likely is that CV occurs. This result is coherent with the explanation offered for the negative link between organizational learning and CV. If a company has learned something that works, and they have low willingness to change, they will be reluctant to undertake changes and launch new CV initiatives. Consequently, what is anticipated in hypothesis 4a is not fulfilled. As for hypotheses 4b, we can say that the moderating effect of willingness to change does not produce any significance between ACTIVEINNOVA and CV.

Despite the relevant results reached, this study is not without limitations, among which is the fact that data derived from a survey made at a point in time were employed, and as a result, it would be interesting to be able to incorporate longitudinal data. About future lines of research, results contrary to expectations in the matter of organizational learning suggest that in the future it will be necessary to study in greater depth these results to try to confirm them.

References

Aiken, L. S., & West, S. G. (1991). *Multiple regression: Testing an interpreting interactions.* Newbury Park, CA: Sage.

Andreeva, T., & Kianto, A. (2012). Does knowledge management really matter? Linking knowledge management practices, competitiveness and economic performance. *Journal of Knowledge Management, 16*(4), 617–636.

Armstrong, J. S., & Overton, T. S. (1977). Estimating nonresponse bias in mail surveys. *Journal of Marketing Research*, 396–402.

Arzubiaga, U., Kotlar, J., De Massis, A., Maseda, A., & Iturralde, T. (2018). Entrepreneurial orientation and innovation in family SMEs: Unveiling the (actual) impact of the board of directors. *Journal of Business Venturing, 33*(4), 455–469.

Audretsch, D. B., Hülsbeck, M., & Lehmann, E. E. (2013). Families as active monitors of firm performance. *Journal of Family Business Strategy, 4*(2), 118–130.

Barney, J. (1991). Firm resources and sustained competitive advantage. *Journal of Management, 17*(1), 99–120.

Barrick, M. R., & Mount, M. K. (1991). The big five personality dimensions and job performance: A meta-analysis. *Personnel Psychology, 44*(1), 1–26.

Barros, I., Hernangómez, J., & Martin-Cruz, N. (2016). A theoretical model of strategic management of family firms. A dynamic capabilities approach. *Journal of Family Business Strategy, 7*(3), 149–159.

Battistini, B., Hacklin, F., & Baschera, P. (2013). The state of corporate venturing: Insights from a global study. *Research-Technology Management, 56*(1), 31–39.

Beckhard, R., & Dyer, W. G., Jr. (1983). SMR forum: Managing change in the family firm–Issues and strategies. *Sloan Management Review (Pre-1986), 24*(3), 59–65.

Berrone, P., Cruz, C., & Gomez-Mejia, L. R. (2012). Socioemotional wealth in family firms: Theoretical dimensions, assessment approaches, and agenda for future research. *Family Business Review, 25*(3), 258–279.

Bloodgood, J. M., & Morrow, J. L., Jr. (2003). Strategic organizational change: Exploring the roles of environmental structure, internal conscious awareness and knowledge. *Journal of Management Studies, 40*(7), 1761–1782.

Bojica, A. M., & Fuentes, M. D. M. F. (2012). Knowledge acquisition and corporate entrepreneurship: Insights from Spanish SMEs in the ICT sector. *Journal of World Business, 47*(3), 397–408.

Brumana, M., Minola, T., Garrett, R. P., & Digan, S. P. (2017). How do family firms launch new businesses? A developmental perspective on internal corporate venturing in family business. *Journal of Small Business Management, 55*(4), 594–613.

Burgelman, R. A. (1983). A process model of internal corporate venturing in the diversified major firm. *Administrative Science Quarterly, 28*, 223–244.

Burger-Helmchen, T. (2009). Option chain and change management: A structural equation application. *European Management Journal, 27*(3), 176–186.

Busenitz, L. W., West, G. P., III, Shepherd, D., Nelson, T., Chandler, G. N., & Zacharakis, A. (2003). Entrepreneurship research in emergence: Past trends and future directions. *Journal of Management, 29*(3), 285–308.

Bygrave, W. D., & Hofer, C. W. (1992). Theorizing about entrepreneurship. *Entrepreneurship: Theory and Practice, 16*(2), 13–22.

Calabrò, A., Minola, T., Campopiano, G., & Pukall, T. (2016). Turning innovativeness into domestic and international corporate venturing: The moderating effect of high family ownership and influence. *European Journal of International Management, 10*(5), 505–533.

Calderón-Martínez, M. G., & García-Quevedo, J. (2013). Knowledge transfer and university patents in Mexico. *Academia. Revista Latinoamericana de Administración, 26*(1), 33–60.

Carayannis, E. G., Popescu, D., Sipp, C., & Stewart, M. (2006). Technological learning for entrepreneurial development (TL4ED) in the knowledge economy (KE): Case studies and lessons learned. *Technovation, 26*(4), 419–443.

Carayannis, E. G., & Roy, R. I. S. (2000). Davids vs Goliaths in the small satellite industry: The role of technological innovation dynamics in firm competitiveness. *Technovation, 20*(6), 287–297.

Casillas, J. C., Moreno, A. M., & Barbero, J. L. (2011). Entrepreneurial orientation of family firms: Family and environmental dimensions. *Journal of Family Business Strategy, 2*(2), 90–100.

Chirico, F. (2008). The creation, sharing and transfer of knowledge in family business. *Journal of Small Business & Entrepreneurship, 21*(4), 413–433.

Chirico, F., & Nordqvist, M. (2010). Dynamic capabilities and trans-generational value creation in family firms: The role of organizational culture. *International Small Business Journal, 28*(5), 487–504.

Chrisman, J. J., Chua, J. H., Pearson, A. W., & Barnett, T. (2012). Family involvement, family influence, and family-centered non-economic goals in small firms. *Entrepreneurship: Theory and Practice, 36*(2), 267–293.
Chua, J. H., Chrisman, J. J., & Sharma, P. (1999). Defining the family business by behavior. *Entrepreneurship: Theory and Practice, 23*(4), 19–39.
Classen, N., Carree, M., Van Gils, A., & Peters, B. (2014). Innovation in family and non-family SMEs: An exploratory analysis. *Small Business Economics, 42*(3), 595–609.
Cohen, W. M., & Levinthal, D. A. (1990). Absorptive capacity: A new perspective on learning and innovation. *Administrative Science Quarterly, 35*, 128–152.
Cooper, A. C., Gimeno-Gascon, F. J., & Woo, C. Y. (1994). Initial human and financial capital as predictors of new venture performance. *Journal of Business Venturing, 9*(5), 371–395.
Cooper, M. J., Upton, N., & Seaman, S. (2005). Customer relationship management: A comparative analysis of family and nonfamily business practices. *Journal of Small Business Management, 43*(3), 242–256.
Covin, J. G., & Miles, M. P. (2007). Strategic use of corporate venturing. *Entrepreneurship: Theory and Practice, 31*(2), 183–207.
Covin, J. G., & Slevin, D. P. (1991). A conceptual model of entrepreneurship as firm behavior. *Entrepreneurship: Theory and Practice, 16*(1), 7–26.
Craig, J. B., Dibrell, C., & Garrett, R. (2014). Examining relationships among family influence, family culture, flexible planning systems, innovativeness and firm performance. *Journal of Family Business Strategy, 5*(3), 229–238.
Cronbach, L. J. (1951). Coefficient alpha and the internal structure of tests. *Psychometrika, 16*(3), 297–334.
Cronbach, L. J. (1987). Statistical tests for moderator variables: Flaws in analyses recently proposed. *Psychological Bulletin, 102*(3), 414–417.
Cruz, C., & Nordqvist, M. (2012). Entrepreneurial orientation in family firms: A generational perspective. *Small Business Economics, 38*(1), 33–49.
Damanpour, F. (1991). Organizational innovation: A meta-analysis of effects of determinants and moderators. *Academy of Management Journal, 34*(3), 555–590.
De Massis, A., Frattini, F., Kotlar, J., Petruzzelli, A. M., & Wright, M. (2016). Innovation through tradition: Lessons from innovative family businesses and directions for future research. *Academy of Management Perspectives, 30*(1), 93–116.
De Massis, A., Frattini, F., & Lichtenthaler, U. (2013). Research on technological innovation in family firms: Present debates and future directions. *Family Business Review, 26*(1), 10–31.
DeMaris, A. (1995). A tutorial in logistic regression. *Journal of Marriage and Family, 57*(4), 956.
Dess, G. G., & Lumpkin, G. T. (2005). *Entrepreneurial orientation as a source of innovative strategy in innovating strategy processes* (pp. 3–9). Oxford: Blackwell.
Duran, P., Kammerlander, N., Van Essen, M., & Zellweger, T. (2016). Doing more with less: Innovation input and output in family firms. *Academy of Management Journal, 59*(4), 1224–1264.
Engel, J. S. (2011). Accelerating corporate innovation: Lessons from the venture capital model. *Research-Technology Management, 54*(3), 36–43.
Faems, D. (2008). Open innovation: Researching a new paradigm-by H. Chesbrough, W. Vanhaverbeke and J. West. *Creativity and Innovation Management, 17*(4), 334–335.
Fiegener, M. K., Brown, B. M., Dreux, D. R., & Dennis, W. J., Jr. (2000). The adoption of outside boards by small private US firms. *Entrepreneurship & Regional Development, 12*(4), 291–309.
Finkelstein, S., & Hambrick, D. C. (1990). Top-management-team tenure and organizational outcomes: The moderating role of managerial discretion. *Administrative Science Quarterly*, 484–503.
Floyd, S. W., & Lane, P. J. (2000). Strategizing throughout the organization: Managing role conflict in strategic renewal. *Academy of Management Review, 25*(1), 154–177.
Fuetsch, E., & Suess-Reyes, J. (2017). Research on innovation in family businesses: Are we building an ivory tower? *Journal of Family Business Management, 7*(1), 44–92.

Gaglio, C. M., & Katz, J. A. (2001). The psychological basis of opportunity identification: Entrepreneurial alertness. *Small Business Economics, 16*(2), 95–111.

Galán González, J. L., Pizarro Moreno, M. I., & Castro, J. O. (2007). *Corporate venturing: modo interno versus externo* (Vol. 1, p. 5). Empresa global y mercados locales: XXI AEDEM Annual Congress, King Juan Carlos University, Madrid, June 6–8.

Garcia-Morales, V. J., Llorens-Montes, F. J., & Verdú-Jover, A. J. (2006). Antecedents and consequences of organizational innovation and organizational learning in entrepreneurship. *Industrial Management & Data Systems, 106*(1), 21–42.

Gibson, C. B., & Birkinshaw, J. (2004). The antecedents, consequences, and mediating role of organizational ambidexterity. *Academy of Management Journal, 47*(2), 209–226.

Gomezelj Omerzel, D., & Antončič, B. (2008). Critical entrepreneur knowledge dimensions for the SME performance. *Industrial Management & Data Systems, 108*(9), 1182–1199.

Gomez-Mejia, L. R., Makri, M., & Kintana, M. L. (2010). Diversification decisions in family-controlled firms. *Journal of Management Studies, 47*(2), 223–252.

Grant, R. M. (1996). Toward a knowledge-based theory of the firm. *Strategic Management Journal, 17*(S2), 109–122.

Greidanus, N. S., & Märk, S. (2012). An exploration of internal corporate venturing goals in family firms. *Journal of Small Business & Entrepreneurship, 25*(2), 169–183.

Habbershon, T. G., & Williams, M. L. (1999). A resource-based framework for assessing the strategic advantages of family firms. *Family Business Review, 12*(1), 1–25.

Habbershon, T. G., Williams, M., & MacMillan, I. C. (2003). A unified systems perspective of family firm performance. *Journal of Business Venturing, 18*(4), 451–465.

Hair, J. J., Anderson, R. R., Tatham, R. R., & Black, W. (1998). *Multivariate data analysis with readings*. Upper Saddle River, NJ: Macmillan.

Hambrick, D. C. (2007). Upper Echelons theory: An update. *The Academy of Management Review*, 334–343.

Hambrick, D. C., & Finkelstein, S. (1987). Managerial discretion: A bridge between polar views of organizational outcomes. *Research in Organizational Behavior, 9*, 369–406.

Hambrick, D. C., & Mason, P. A. (1984). Upper Echelons: The organization as a reflection of its top managers. *Academy of Management Review, 9*(2), 193–206.

Hernández-Linares, R., Kellermanns, F. W., & López-Fernández, M. C. (2018). A note on the relationships between learning, market, and entrepreneurial orientations in family and nonfamily firms. *Journal of Family Business Strategy, 9*(3), 192–204.

Hernández-Linares, R., & López-Fernández, M. C. (2018). Entrepreneurial orientation and the family firm: Mapping the field and tracing a path for future research. *Family Business Review, 31*(3), 318–351.

Hernández-Linares, R., Sarkar, S., & Cobo, M. J. (2018). Inspecting the Achilles heel: A quantitative analysis of 50 years of family business definitions. *Scientometrics, 115*(2), 929–951.

Hernández-Linares, R., Sarkar, S., & López-Fernández, M. C. (2017). How has the family firm literature addressed its heterogeneity through classification systems? An integrated analysis. *European Journal of Family Business, 7*(1–2), 1–13.

Hofstede, G. (1980). Culture and organizations. *International Studies of Management & Organization, 10*(4), 15–41.

Hoy, F. (2006). The complicating factor of life cycles in corporate venturing. *Entrepreneurship Theory and Practice, 30*(6), 831–836.

Hultink, E. J., & Atuahene-Gima, K. (2000). The effect of sales force adoption on new product selling performance. *Journal of Product Innovation Management, 17*(6), 435–450.

Hurley, R. F., & Hult, G. T. M. (1998). Innovation, market orientation, and organizational learning: An integration and empirical examination. *The Journal of Marketing, 62*(3), 42–54.

Jeong, S. H., & Harrison, D. A. (2017). Glass breaking, strategy making, and value creating: Meta-analytic outcomes of women as CEOs and TMT members. *Academy of Management Journal, 60*(4), 1219–1252.

Karagozoglu, N., & Brown, W. B. (1988). Adaptive responses by conservative and entrepreneurial firms. *Journal of Product Innovation Management, 5*(4), 269–281.

Kautt, M., Walsh, S. T., & Bittner, K. (2007). Global distribution of micro-nano technology and fabrication centers: A portfolio analysis approach. *Technological Forecasting and Social Change, 74*(9), 1697–1717.

Kellermanns, F. W., & Eddleston, K. A. (2006). Corporate entrepreneurship in family firms: A family perspective. *Entrepreneurship: Theory and Practice, 30*(6), 809–830.

Kellermanns, F. W., Eddleston, K. A., Barnett, T., & Pearson, A. (2008). An exploratory study of family member characteristics and involvement: Effects on entrepreneurial behavior in the family firm. *Family Business Review, 21*(1), 1–14.

Kellermanns, F. W., Eddleston, K. A., Sarathy, R., & Murphy, F. (2012). Innovativeness in family firms: A family influence perspective. *Small Business Economics, 38*(1), 85–101.

König, A., Kammerlander, N., & Enders, A. (2013). The family innovator's dilemma: How family influence affects the adoption of discontinuous technologies by incumbent firms. *Academy of Management Review, 38*(3), 418–441.

Kor, Y. Y., & Mesko, A. (2013). Dynamic managerial capabilities: Configuration and orchestration of top executives' capabilities and the firm's dominant logic. *Strategic Management Journal, 34*(2), 233–244.

Kumar, N., Stern, L. W., & Anderson, J. C. (1993). Conducting interorganizational research using key informants. *Academy of Management Journal, 36*(6), 1633–1651.

Kuratko, D. F., & Audretsch, D. B. (2009). Strategic entrepreneurship: Exploring different perspectives of an emerging concept. *Entrepreneurship: Theory and Practice, 33*(1), 1–17.

Ling, Y., Simsek, Z., Lubatkin, M. H., & Veiga, J. F. (2008). The impact of transformational CEOs on the performance of small-to medium-sized firms: Does organizational context matter? *Journal of Applied Psychology, 93*(4), 923–934.

Liu, S. S., Luo, X., & Shi, Y. Z. (2002). Integrating customer orientation, corporate entrepreneurship, and learning orientation in organizations-in-transition: An empirical study. *International Journal of Research in Marketing, 19*(4), 367–382.

López-Fernández, M. C., Serrano-Bedia, A. M., & Gómez-López, R. (2011). Factors encouraging innovation in Spanish hospitality firms. *Cornell Hospitality Quarterly, 52*(2), 144–152.

Lumpkin, G. T., & Dess, G. G. (2001). Linking two dimensions of entrepreneurial orientation to firm performance: The moderating role of environment and industry life cycle. *Journal of Business Venturing, 16*(5), 429–451.

Luo, J., Olechowski, A. L., & Magee, C. L. (2014). Technology-based design and sustainable economic growth. *Technovation, 34*(11), 663–677.

Maine, E. (2008). Radical innovation through internal corporate venturing: Degussa's commercialization of nanomaterials. *R&D Management, 38*(4), 359–371.

Marchisio, G., Mazzola, P., Sciascia, S., Miles, M., & Astrachan, J. (2010). Corporate venturing in family business: The effects on the family and its members. *Entrepreneurship and Regional Development, 22*(3–4), 349–377.

McGrath, R. G., Keil, T., & Tukiainen, T. (2006). Extracting value from corporate venturing. *MIT Sloan Management Review, 48*(1), 50–56.

McGuirk, H., Lenihan, H., & Hart, M. (2015). Measuring the impact of innovative human capital on small firms' propensity to innovate. *Research Policy, 44*(4), 965–976.

Miller, D. (1983). The correlates of entrepreneurship in three types of firms. *Management Science, 29*(7), 770–791.

Miller, D., & Friesen, P. H. (1982). Innovation in conservative and entrepreneurial firms: Two models of strategic momentum. *Strategic Management Journal, 3*(1), 1–25.

Miller, D., Steier, L., & Le Breton-Miller, I. (2003). Lost in time: Intergenerational succession, change, and failure in family business. *Journal of Business Venturing, 18*(4), 513–531.

Minola, T., Brumana, M., Campopiano, G., Garrett, R. P., & Cassia, L. (2016). Corporate venturing in family business: A developmental approach of the enterprising family. *Strategic Entrepreneurship Journal, 10*(4), 395–412.

Mohnen, P., & Röller, L. H. (2005). Complementarities in innovation policy. *European Economic Review, 49*(6), 1431–1450.

Montalvo, C. (2006). What triggers change and innovation? *Technovation, 26*(3), 312–323.

Montes, F. J. L., Moreno, A. R., & Morales, V. G. (2005). Influence of support leadership and teamwork cohesion on organizational learning, innovation and performance: An empirical examination. *Technovation, 25*(10), 1159–1172.

Morris, M. H., Kuratko, D. F., & Covin, J. G. (2011). *Corporate entrepreneurship and innovation: Entrepreneurial development within organizations* (3rd ed.). Mason, OH: Thompson.

Mustafa, M., Lundmark, E., & Ramos, H. M. (2016). Untangling the relationship between human resource management and corporate entrepreneurship: The mediating effect of middle managers' knowledge sharing. *Entrepreneurship Research Journal, 6*(3), 273–295.

Narasimhan, R., & Das, A. (2001). The impact of purchasing integration and practices on manufacturing performance. *Journal of Operations Management, 19*(5), 593–609.

Narayanan, V. K., Yang, Y., & Zahra, S. A. (2009). Corporate venturing and value creation: A review and proposed framework. *Research Policy, 38*(1), 58–76.

Nordqvist, M., Sharma, P., & Chirico, F. (2014). Family firm heterogeneity and governance: A configuration approach. *Journal of Small Business Management, 52*(2), 192–209.

Nunnally, J. C., & Bernstein, I. (1978). *Psychometric theory* (2nd ed.). New York: McGraw-Hill.

Obloj, T., Obloj, K., & Pratt, M. G. (2010). Dominant logic and entrepreneurial firms' performance in a transition economy. *Entrepreneurship: Theory and Practice, 34*(1), 151–170.

Oliva, F. L. (2014). Knowledge management barriers, practices and maturity model. *Journal of Knowledge Management, 18*(6), 1053–1074.

Patel, P. C., & Fiet, J. O. (2011). Knowledge combination and the potential advantages of family firms in searching for opportunities. *Entrepreneurship: Theory and Practice, 35*(6), 1179–1197.

Patel, J. K., & Read, C. B. (1996). *Handbook of the normal distribution*. New York: CRC Press.

Peng, M. W. (2003). Institutional transitions and strategic choices. *Academy of Management Review, 28*(2), 275–296.

Peters, M., & Kallmuenzer, A. (2018). Entrepreneurial orientation in family firms: The case of the hospitality industry. *Current Issues in Tourism, 21*(1), 21–40.

Podsakoff, P. M., MacKenzie, S. B., Lee, J. Y., & Podsakoff, N. P. (2003). Common method biases in behavioral research: A critical review of the literature and recommended remedies. *Journal of Applied Psychology, 88*(5), 879–903.

Rajagopal. (2006). Innovation and business growth through corporate venturing in Latin America: Analysis of strategic fit. *Management Decision, 44*(5), 703–718.

Ram, S., & Jung, H. S. (1991). "Forced" adoption of innovations in organizations: Consequences and implications. *Journal of Product Innovation Management, 8*(2), 117–126.

Rauch, A., Wiklund, J., Lumpkin, G. T., & Frese, M. (2009). Entrepreneurial orientation and business performance: An assessment of past research and suggestions for the future. *Entrepreneurship: Theory and Practice, 33*(3), 761–787.

Rerup, C. (2005). Learning from past experience: Footnotes on mindfulness and habitual entrepreneurship. *Scandinavian Journal of Management, 21*(4), 451–472.

Reyna, J. M. S. M., Vázquez, R. D., & Valdés, A. L. (2012). Corporate governance, ownership structure and performance in Mexico. *International Business Research, 5*(11), 12–27.

Rhee, J., Park, T., & Lee, D. H. (2010). Drivers of innovativeness and performance for innovative SMEs in South Korea: Mediation of learning orientation. *Technovation, 30*(1), 65–75.

Röd, I. (2016). Disentangling the family firm's innovation process: A systematic review. *Journal of Family Business Strategy, 7*(3), 185–201.

San Martin-Reyna, J. M., & Duran-Encalada, J. A. (2012). Ownership structure, firm value and investment opportunities set: Evidence from Mexican firms. *Journal of Entrepreneurship, Management and Innovation, 8*(3), 35–58.

Särndal, C.E., Swensson, B., & Wretman, J. (2003). *Model assisted survey sampling.*. Springer Science & Business Media.

Schulze, W. S., Lubatkin, M. H., & Dino, R. N. (2003). Exploring the agency consequences of ownership dispersion among the directors of private family firms. *Academy of Management Journal, 46*(2), 179–194.

Schumpeter, J. A. (1934). *The theory of economic development: An inquiry into profits, capital, credit, interest, and the business cycle*. Cambridge: Harvard University Press.

Sciascia, S., Mazzola, P., & Chirico, F. (2013). Generational involvement in the top management team of family firms: Exploring nonlinear effects on entrepreneurial orientation. *Entrepreneurship: Theory and Practice, 37*(1), 69–85.

Serrano-Bedia, A. M., López-Fernández, M. C., & Garcia-Piqueres, G. (2016). Analysis of the relationship between sources of knowledge and innovation performance in family firms. *Innovation, 18*(4), 489–512.

Shane, S., & Venkataraman, S. (2000). The promise of entrepreneurship as a field of research. *Academy of Management Review, 25*(1), 217–226.

Short, J. C., Payne, G. T., Brigham, K. H., Lumpkin, G. T., & Broberg, J. C. (2009). Family firms and entrepreneurial orientation in publicly traded firms: A comparative analysis of the S&P 500. *Family Business Review, 22*(1), 9–24.

Simpson, P. M., Siguaw, J. A., & Enz, C. A. (2006). Innovation orientation outcomes: The good and the bad. *Journal of Business Research, 59*(10-11), 1133–1141.

Singh, R., Hills, G. E., Hybels, R. C., & Lumpkin, G. T. (1999). Opportunity recognition through social network characteristics of entrepreneurs. In *Frontiers of entrepreneurship research* (pp. 228–241). Wellesley, MA: Babson College.

Sirmon, D. G., & Hitt, M. A. (2003). Managing resources: Linking unique resources, management, and wealth creation in family firms. *Entrepreneurship: Theory and Practice, 27*(4), 339–358.

Spender, J. C. (1996). Making knowledge the basis of a dynamic theory of the firm. *Strategic Management Journal, 17*(S2), 45–62.

Teece, D. J. (2007). Explicating dynamic capabilities: The nature and microfoundations of (sustainable) enterprise performance. *Strategic Management Journal, 28*(13), 1319–1350.

Toledano, N., Urbano, D., & Bernadich, M. (2010). Networks and corporate entrepreneurship: A comparative case study on family business in Catalonia. *Journal of Organizational Change Management, 23*(4), 396–412.

Ucbasaran, D., Westhead, P., & Wright, M. (2008). Opportunity identification and pursuit: Does an entrepreneur's human capital matter? *Small Business Economics, 30*(2), 153–173.

Vago, M. (2004). Integrated change management: Challenges for family business clients and consultants. *Family Business Review, 17*(1), 71–80.

Voordeckers, W., Van Gils, A., & Van den Heuvel, J. (2007). Board composition in small and medium-sized family firms. *Journal of Small Business Management, 45*(1), 137–156.

Wang, C. L., & Ahmed, P. K. (2004). The development and validation of the organisational innovativeness construct using confirmatory factor analysis. *European Journal of Innovation Management, 7*(4), 303–313.

Ward, J. L. (1987). *Keeping the family business healthy: How to plan for continuing growth*. San Francisco: Jossey-Bass.

Ward, J. L. (2011). *Keeping the family business healthy: How to plan for continuing growth, profitability, and family leadership*. New York: Palgrave Macmillan.

Westphal, J. D., & Fredrickson, J. W. (2001). Who directs strategic change? Director experience, the selection of new CEOs, and change in corporate strategy. *Strategic Management Journal, 22*(12), 1113–1137.

Wiklund, J., & Shepherd, D. (2003). Aspiring for, and achieving growth: The moderating role of resources and opportunities. *Journal of Management Studies, 40*(8), 1919–1941.

Wong, Y. J., Chang, S. C., & Chen, L. Y. (2010). Does a family-controlled firm perform better in corporate venturing? *Corporate Governance: An International Review, 18*(3), 175–192.

Zahra, S. A. (2003). International expansion of US manufacturing family businesses: The effect of ownership and involvement. *Journal of Business Venturing, 18*(4), 495–512.

Zahra, S. A. (2005). Entrepreneurial risk taking in family firms. *Family Business Review, 18*(1), 23–40.

Zahra, S. A. (2008). The virtuous cycle of discovery and creation of entrepreneurial opportunities. *Strategic Entrepreneurship Journal, 2*(3), 243–257.

Zahra, S. A. (2012). Organizational learning and entrepreneurship in family firms: Exploring the moderating effect of ownership and cohesion. *Small Business Economics, 38*(1), 51–65.

Zahra, S. A., & Bogner, W. C. (2000). Technology strategy and software new ventures' performance: Exploring the moderating effect of the competitive environment. *Journal of Business Venturing, 15*(2), 135–173.

Zahra, S. A., Hayton, J. C., & Salvato, C. (2004). Entrepreneurship in family vs. non-family firms: A resource-based analysis of the effect of organizational culture. *Entrepreneurship: Theory and Practice, 28*(4), 363–381.

Zahra, S. A., Neubaum, D. O., & Larrañeta, B. (2007). Knowledge sharing and technological capabilities: The moderating role of family involvement. *Journal of Business Research, 60*(10), 1070–1079.

Zahra, S. A., Van de Velde, E., & Larrañeta, B. (2007). Knowledge conversion capability and the performance of corporate and university spin-offs. *Industrial and Corporate Change, 16*(4), 569–608.

Zellweger, T., & Sieger, P. (2012). Entrepreneurial orientation in long-lived family firms. *Small Business Economics, 38*(1), 67–84.

Determinants of the Economic Performance of Portuguese Family Firms: Is Innovation Relevant?

Aurora A. C. Teixeira and Sofia F. Correia

Abstract Family firms contribute substantially to the economy of a country. Thus, it is surprising that few studies have considered these firms as an object of analysis, especially regarding the importance of innovation to their economic performance. In an attempt to fill this gap, this paper assesses the importance of innovation and technological capabilities in the performance of family firms in Portugal. Based on a sample comprising 230 firms, 110 of which are family-owned, and on econometric estimation methods, we show that internal factors are more relevant in explaining family firms' economic performance than contextual factors. Family firms run by CEOs with a degree in engineering or with CEOs and management teams with more international experience tend, on average, to present higher levels of productivity. Additionally, the firms that are more experienced in business and more internationalized are also more productive generally. Notwithstanding family firms being less intensive in R&D than nonfamily ones, innovation is one of the most critical determinants for the performance of the former. Besides the relevance of technological- and innovation-related skills mirrored by investment in R&D, the result of innovation, reflected in the successful introduction of innovations (in marketing and combined), emerges as highly relevant statistically, playing a decisive role in the economic performance of family firms. Family firms that are located in economically less developed regions tend, on average, to present higher productivity levels. This seems to indicate that family firms may constitute a driver of regional convergence regarding dynamics and development.

Keywords Family firms · Innovation · Technological skills · Economic performance · Internationalization

A. A. C. Teixeira (✉) · S. F. Correia
University of Porto, Porto, Portugal
e-mail: ateixeira@fep.up.pt; geral@fep.up.pt

J. M. Saiz-Álvarez et al. (eds.), *Entrepreneurship and Family Business Vitality*, Studies on Entrepreneurship, Structural Change and Industrial Dynamics,
https://doi.org/10.1007/978-3-030-15526-1_15

1 Introduction

Family firms are organizations where the capital is held in part or whole by a family (Miller & Le Breton-Miller, 2006) and where the respective members are in management positions (Getz & Carlsen, 2005). These businesses play an increasingly important role in the economy of countries, generating around 70–90% of annual global GDP and creating 50–80% of jobs in most countries worldwide (Family Firm Institute, 2017).

Evidence from *European Family Businesses* reveals that family businesses are decisive in creating jobs and fostering growth in the world economy's gross domestic product, being present in all sectors of the economy and accounting for over 50% of the GDP and more than 14 million businesses providing over 60 million jobs in the private sector (EFB, 2018). In Portugal, Lourenço, Branco, and Curto (2018, p. 171) report that "family firms may account for 80–85% of the Portuguese firms, generating over 75% of new jobs and contributing with over 70% of the GDP."

The topic of family businesses has attracted extensive research, both in management and economics (Bigliardi & Galati, 2018; De Massis, Frattini, Majocchi, & Piscitello, 2018; Feranita, Kotlar, & De Massis, 2017). Several issues have been addressed within this topic, such as family succession (Le Breton-Miller, Miller, & Steier, 2004; Weng & Chi, 2019), the effect of family control on performance (Cassia, De Massis, & Kotlar, 2012a; Terlaak, Kim, & Roh, 2018), the relationship between the continuing involvement by the owner-manager in a family business over time and the continuation of the business itself (Rau, Werner, & Schell, 2018), as well as the interaction between family members and the business and its impact on the method of administration used (Kusumastuti, 2018), among others. More recently, a few studies have related the performance of such companies with internationalization (Kano & Verbeke, 2018; Kontinen & Ojala, 2010; Piva, Rossi-Lamastra, & De Massis, 2013; Swoboda & Olejnik, 2013).

Although the existing literature has focused extensively on the adaptability of such companies in changing environments and the role of new technologies (Martínez-Alonso, Martínez-Romero, & Rojo-Ramírez, 2018), innovation is still a poorly explored topic in the literature related to family businesses. In particular, little has been written and researched on how innovation can influence the performance of family businesses, not only in terms of the expenses incurred in research and development (R&D) but also the company's ability to absorb new technologies and be flexible in new environments (Alonso, O'Brien, & Kok, 2018; Siebels & Aufseß, 2012). The few studies available in the area of family firms and innovation have focused mainly on companies located in countries such as Germany, Italy, Spain, and Taiwan, analyzing the relationship between the presence of family in business and management factors that affect the success of new product development (Cassia, De Massis, & Pizzurno, 2012b; Werner, Schröder, & Chlosta, 2018), as well as the antecedents and impacts of information technology (IT) adopted by family businesses (Meroño-Cerdán, 2017; Niehm, Tyner, Shelley, & Fitzgerald, 2010).

Studies on family firms located in Portugal and the relationship between economic performance with the respective innovative dynamics are, to the best of our knowledge, nonexistent. The few studies analyzing Portuguese family firms address stock performance (Miralles-Marcelo, Miralles-Quirós, & Lisboa, 2013), internationalization paths (Jorge, Couto, Veloso, & Franco, 2017; Pacheco, 2017) and accounting reporting (Lourenço et al., 2018), control (Miralles-Marcelo, Miralles-Quirós, & Lisboa, 2014), and organizational performance (Franco & Franco, 2017), but do not tackle innovation-related issues. Carvalho and Williams (2014) analyzed the issue of innovation but related to creativity and not economic performance. The present study aims to fill in this literature gap and assess the importance of innovation and technological skills in the performance of family businesses in Portugal.

This paper is structured as follows. Section 2 presents a literature review on family firms, more specifically, the importance of innovation for the performance of these companies. Subsequently, Sect. 3 details the methodology used and describes the measures used to assess the importance of innovation in family firms in Portugal. Section 4 presents the estimation results, and the Conclusions (Sect. 5) summarize the main contributions and limitations of this study.

2 Literature Review on Economic Performance of Family Businesses and the Role of Innovation

2.1 Relevant Concepts: Family Business, Innovation, and Economic Performance

Many of the major companies we know today started as small family businesses that have grown to become the empires they represent today (Swoboda & Olejnik, 2013).

Despite the widespread use of the term family business, it is a highly arguable operational concept in theoretical terms. A consensus has yet to be reached among authors on the definition of the family business (Siebels & Aufseß, 2012). It is critical to establish the boundaries of what is understood to be a family business because, depending on the definition used, empirical results tend to diverge (Chrisman, Chua, & Sharma, 2003).

For Miller and Le Breton-Miller (2006), a family business is an organization in which the "family" is in management. Chrisman et al. (2003) state that a company is considered "family" if the family is a majority owner. Other authors consider that the family's direct involvement is necessary for day-to-day operations (Shanker & Astrachan, 1996). In the same line, there are those who argue that it is relevant if more than one family member holds a great responsibility in the company's management (Shanker & Astrachan, 1996). Somewhat distinct, Tsang (2002), in his analysis of the IDE family enterprises in China, admits that strategic decisions can be divided among family members and external members.

Table 1 Criteria to define family firm

Criteria	Indicators	Studies
Core criterion		
Ownership: Family owns the majority of the company's capital	The percentage of the company's assets is held by a given family	Litz (1995), Chua, Chrisman, and Sharma (1999), Kontinen and Ojala (2010), Swoboda and Olejnik (2013), Piva et al. (2013)
Complementary criteria		
Involvement of the family in the activities of company management	Percentage of family members who are also in management positions	Litz (1995), Chua et al. (1999), Shanker and Astrachan (1996), Miller and Le Breton-Miller (2006), Cassia et al. (2012a), Swoboda and Olejnik (2013)
	Number of active generations in company operations	Shanker and Astrachan (1996), Chrisman et al. (2003), Kontinen and Ojala (2010)
	Power over strategic decisions of the company (control votes)	Shanker and Astrachan (1996), Chrisman et al. (2003), Cassia et al. (2012a)

Source: Authors' own table

Summarizing the current contributions, we define family business as an organization owned, controlled, and managed by family members, i.e., they have power over strategic decisions and members participate in the corresponding concrete operations.

To clarify and operationalize the concept of family firms, it is critical to establish the criteria. Thus, in line with Shanker and Astrachan (1996) and Chrisman et al. (2003), the following criteria were applied (see Table 1): (1) family ownership, the company's capital is majority owned by the family of the owner (Kontinen & Ojala, 2010; Piva et al., 2013; Swoboda & Olejnik, 2013); (2) family governance, family has power over strategic firm decisions, i.e., control over votes (Cassia et al., 2012a; Chrisman et al., 2003; Shanker & Astrachan, 1996); (3) family management, family members are in management (Cassia et al., 2012a; Litz, 1995, in Labour Research, 2005; Miller & Le Breton-Miller, 2006; Shanker & Astrachan, 1996; Swoboda & Olejnik, 2013), and/or several generations of the family are actively involved in the company's daily operations (Chrisman et al., 2003; Kontinen & Ojala, 2010; Shanker & Astrachan, 1996).

With the boost of globalization, both markets and companies have become increasingly more open to outside influences, favoring the exploration of new ideas in order to ensure their survival (Giovannetti, Ricchiuti, & Velucchi, 2013).

According to Freeman (1994), innovation is responsible for 80% of productivity growth in developed countries, and this growth contributes to 80% of global GDP growth (Sternberg and Arndt, 2001). These figures clearly show the importance of innovation to improve competitiveness, growth, and consequently employment (Sternberg & Arndt, 2001).

One of the definitions given for "innovation," which dates back to Schumpeter, is a process that fosters the development of new products, processes, and business models through which companies gain competitive advantage (Cassia, De Massis, & Pizzurno, 2012b). Other related concepts have since been developed but closely related to Schumpeter's original taxonomy. For example, according to Belloc (2012), technological innovation is the development of a product or process by incorporating unique, combined, or summarized knowledge into a new object or method. It is understood here that innovation is generated by the process of collective and cumulative learning (Belloc, 2012).

The process of research and development (R&D) often plays a decisive role in innovation because it is expected to lead to the development of prototypes and the introduction of new products in the market (Kirner, Kinkel, & Jaeger, 2009). Considering the different modes of innovation processes, R&D can be assumed as a distinctive activity that can occur not only in industries or high-tech firms but also in more traditional firms, contributing to overall economic success (Kirner et al., 2009).

Firmly anchored in the relevant source for the process of innovation, Pavitt (1984) proposed a taxonomy that has been extensively used to distinguish sectors: supplier-dominated, specialized supplier, scale-intensive, and science-based. These four sectors are differentiated by technological differences and the number of technological innovations introduced. The sectors that have a higher level of innovations are considered specialized suppliers or science-based—the firms belonging to the first sector experience a constant need to improve their efficiency due to pressure from their consumers. High investments in R&D characterize those belonging to the second sector and have a strong connection to science. At a relatively smaller scale, the scale-intensive sector is distinguished from other sectors by its system of large-scale production and generates innovation through engineering departments and transmission by specialized suppliers. In the supplier-dominated sector, these introductions are in fewer in number, and most of the technological advances come from their equipment and services suppliers, among others.

Inside innovation, firms can follow different paths, develop new products, as well as create services related to these products to gain a competitive advantage because they distinguish them from competitors by offering a complete solution to the final consumer (Kirner et al., 2009).

In recent years, it has become increasingly difficult to introduce innovations in processes and products, the so-called more traditional innovations, as they require higher investment for their execution, and there is greater difficulty in removing the benefits from such investment, because of the growing shift to organizational and marketing innovations (Ortiz-Villajos, 2017; Schmidt & Rammer, 2006).

According to the 3rd edition of the *Oslo Manual* (OECD, 2005), product innovation consists in introducing new or significantly improved products or services. This includes significant changes in technical specifications, components, materials, incorporated software, user interface, or other functional characteristics. Process innovation is the implementation of new or significantly improved processes, logistics, or production of goods or services. This includes significant changes in techniques, equipment, or software. Marketing innovation is the implementation of a new marketing method involving significant changes in the design of the product or its packaging or its promotion or even in its price. Finally, organizational innovation involves the implementation of a new organizational structure, new methods to manage the company's business practices, workplace organization, or external relations (OECD, 2005).

Several studies have focused on economic performance and its determinants (Belloc, 2012; Hawawini, Subramanian, & Verdin, 2003), but only in recent years have some authors given greater importance to corporate governance in business performance, as well as their innovative capacity (Belloc, 2012; Céspedes-Lorente, Magán-Díaz, & Martínez-Ros, 2018). Many studies have focused on innovation as economic performance because the introduction of innovations can lead to better performance in the near future, but in reality, innovation is a determinant of economic performance.

From the perspective of industrial organization (Porter, 1980), factors are the main determinants of a company's industrial performance, a view based on resources, which establishes that it is the firm's internal environment that drives its competitive advantage (Nelson & Winter, 1982; Penrose, 1959).

Hawawini et al. (2003) argue that it is increasingly challenging to explain heterogeneity in intraindustrial business performance rigorously. According to Arvey and Murphy (1998), several studies have addressed the influence of ongoing changes in the structure and functions of the performance of these businesses. Firms have become less hierarchical and more decentralized, moving away from individual thinking to production methods more focused on teams (Arvey & Murphy, 1998). One of the reasons is that the traditional microeconomic theory, which relies on industrial factors, ignores that firms make appropriate choices, which are different from firm to firm within the same industry (Nelson, 1991). Thus, there are differences in corporate profits coming from different firms to create barriers to mobility and get ahead in the market. Another justification for differences in performance by firms pointed out by the resource-based theory is that the company's specific features in the accumulation and leverage of resources can be a unique and lasting source of sustainable competitive advantage (Hawawini et al., 2003). Income-generating resources explain the level of corporate profits, and for profits to be sustainable resources must be scarce, trying to replicate or replace, and difficult to trade or sell in the market (Barney, 1991). Thus, for heterodox approaches, companies are regarded as a conjunction of dynamics and specific skills that leads to differing levels of performance (Nelson, 1991).

Various dimensions and measures are used to assess a company's degree of performance, although the most common are employment growth, sales growth, and share of net assets before tax (Baum & Wally, 2003; Zahra & Bogner, 2000). Another important performance measurement used in previous studies is the return on assets (ROA) (Hawawini et al., 2003; Marco, 2012). Marco (2012) focuses on two dimensions of this indicator: growth and corporate profitability. To calculate the growth of the company, he applies indicators such as size, number of employees, and total sales value. Regarding the company's profitability, the ratios used are "return on capital used," "return on assets," and "profit per employee" based on different concepts to be able to compare performance between companies (Marco, 2012).

Cainelli, Evangelista, and Savona (2006), who studied the relationship between innovation and economic performance in services, use two main indicators: average sales growth rate and the ratio between the value of "sales" and "number of employees" as a proxy for labor productivity. According to the authors, the latter ratio would make it possible to assess the impact of the introduction of innovation processes on the economic performance of companies because they could positively influence sales value and thus the value of worker productivity. Several other authors have also considered the "number of employees" to measure the economic performance/productivity of firms (Marco, 2012).

Pantea, Munteanu, Gligor, and Sopoian (2008) consider that the indicators that determine the company's results (results of business activity) do not consider the financial structure and how this capital is acquired (cost of financing). The authors propose therefore an "economic value added" indicator which eliminates this drawback and is more comprehensive since it combines the results of the firm's operating activity with the cost of capital, profit taxation policy, and stock value enterprise, satisfying the interested parties, whether they be company shareholders, managers, creditors, or State (Pantea et al., 2008). Hamilton, Rahman, and Lee (2009) argue that the value-added economic indicator started to be used from the 1990s with the goal of improving the economic performance of companies as it provides a more accurate assessment of the residual income. This measure is based on the economic principle of residual income, meaning that companies should earn a rate of return on invested capital greater than the cost of capital (Hamilton et al., 2009).

2.2 Determinants of the Economic Performance of Firms

The available studies on the determinants of firms' economic performance propose various variables that can be aggregated into three major dimensions: (1) determinants related to these firms' management (CEO and management team, i.e., personal and professional characteristics of these individuals, such as age, training/qualifications, and experience), (2) determinants related to firm characteristics (demographic, business experience, human capital, innovative position, technological resources, ability to attract new technologies, degree of internationalization, product strategies/market culture, among others), and (3) determinants associated with context (network characteristics, sector, and region where the company operates and locates).

In the group of determinants related with the entrepreneurs/founders/managers of firms, we consider their personal and professional characteristics, such as the manager's and the management team's human capital (education and skills) and professional experience, as well as the size of the management team.

Regarding the latter aspect, it is argued that larger management teams have greater difficulty in controlling the business, as problems may arise from free-riding (Aggarwal, Evans, & Nanda, 2012). Others argue that larger management groups take longer to make decisions (Sánchez-Marín, Baixauli-Soler, & Lucas-Pérez, 2010), being less efficient and cohesive (Finkelstein & Hambrick, 1997). Boyd (1995) argues that larger groups face this difficulty because of lower flexibility associated with a lack of coordination and communication among the group. In the same line, Yermack (1996) proves that there is an inverse relationship between the size of the management team and the company's value. Based on the agency theory, some authors argue that the lower the level of supervision, the higher the compensation for top managers and, therefore, the more they will act in their interest (Sánchez-Marín et al., 2010). Hence, managers acting in their interest would also act for the good of the company. Realizing this, Jensen (1993) indicates that the firm's management should not exceed ten members.

Thus, we hypothesize that:

Hypothesis 1 *The smaller the size of the management team, the better the firms' economic performance.*

Some authors argue that a higher level of education among managers leads to better economic performance (Brown, Adams, & Amjad, 2007; Sluis, Praag, & Vijverberg, 2008). However, some argue that the economic performance of companies does not only depend on education. Ganotakis (2012), using data from 412 technology-based companies in the services and transformation sectors in the UK, studied the relationship between the human capital of their founders and their economic performance and found that technical education alone did not lead to better economic performance; instead, a combination of commercial and management experience was required. The level of education can also act as a signal of the managers' ability as well as other characteristics valued as contributing to the company's productivity, which is difficult to observe (Sluis et al., 2008). Brown et al. (2007), using data from two different but comparable construction industries from the UK and Saudi Arabia, also concluded that investment in the human capital of managers would bring benefits regarding improved economic performance. Besides its effect on productivity, education is important for signaling the value of productive capacity in markets that issue imperfect information (Riley, 2002). Marrocu and Paci (2012) consider that the existence of highly qualified individuals in a given area can be seen as a major determinant of local economic performance since other important factors such as the creation of new ideas and technology are dependent on the allocation of human capital. Typically, this feature is measured by the level of the individuals' qualifications. However, more recently, in addition to using formal education to evaluate this feature, importance has also been given to personal skills, among which the foremost are creativity, innovation, and accumulated experience (Marrocu & Paci, 2012).

Hypothesis 2a *The education level of the manager has a positive effect on the economic performance of firms.*

Hypothesis 2b *The education level of the management team has a positive effect on the economic performance of firms.*

One of the features mentioned in the literature is the variety of training areas in management (Chen, Chang, & Chang, 2012; Ganotakis, 2012). Some authors argue that the more successful management teams usually have members with a greater variety of skills (West & Noel, 2009). More specifically, Chen et al. (2012) explore the relationship between project success for research and development (R&D) and its determinants, concluding that broadening the managers' competences is positively associated with their success. One explanation for these results comes from the fact that a combination of skills enables managers to consider the problems they face daily from different perspectives because they do not specialize in just one area (Koellinger, 2008). Several studies have proved the theory that a range of skills increases the chances of a product or service being traded successfully and thus improves the economic performance of firms (Ganotakis, 2012). That said, the CEO's/management team's field of study/degree potentially exerts influence on the economic performance of firms.

Hypothesis 3a *The CEO's field of study/degree influences the economic performance of firms.*

Hypothesis 3b *The management team's field of study/degrees influences the economic performance of firms.*

Several authors have argued that the experience of CEOs is negatively associated with the firms' innovative performance and risk-taking (Stewart, Watson, Carland, & Carland, 1999; Zahra, 2005), as well as employment growth (Kellermanns, Eddleston, Barnett, & Pearson, 2008). These results can be justified by the fact that the CEOs are in power for some time and accommodate and become more resistant to change (Kellermanns et al., 2008) and to the creation of new ideas and innovative practices, ultimately "suffocating" creativity (Kellermanns et al., 2008) by questioning new ideas and practices (Zahra, Hayton, & Salvato, 2004). In contrast, other authors (e.g., Levesque & Minniti, 2006) argue that the longer a CEO is in charge, the more knowledge and experience he/she acquires, giving him/her a greater ability to take riskier entrepreneurial attitudes and therefore lead the business to act more aggressively. That is, a more experienced manager will be more skillful in making decisions, being more willing to take risks (Lin, Lin, Song, & Li, 2011). Regarding the experience of managers in family businesses, Kellermanns et al. (2008) highlight the potentially negative relationship between the CEO's business "experience" and economic performance, as the aging CEO may become more concerned with succession issues than with pursuing projects that lead to better economic performance. Despite this last note, we assume that:

Hypothesis 4a *The international experience of the manager has a positive effect on the economic performance of firms.*

Hypothesis 4b *The international experience of the management team is positively related to the economic performance of firms.*

Determinants related to the characteristics of companies include factors such as the demographics, finances, human capital, culture, innovation profile, technological resources, capacity to absorb new technologies, the degree of internationalization, and product or market strategies.

Regarding demographic factors, particularly company size, several authors are unanimous in concluding that it is positively related to internationalization and export performance (Eickelpasch & Vogel, 2011; Giovannetti et al., 2013; Majocchi, Bacchiocchi, & Mayrhofer, 2005; Piva et al., 2013), as well as employment growth (Kellermanns et al., 2008). Several authors argue that firm size has a positive impact on performance because larger companies have a greater ability to absorb the risk associated with internationalization and the exploration of new ideas, quickly overcoming the fixed costs associated with entry into new markets, and also greater ability for financing (Eickelpasch & Vogel, 2011). Larger companies have less difficulty in getting involved in R&D activities, which increases the probability of introducing innovations that boost these companies' efficiency (Barbosa & Eiriz, 2009). Some authors argue that the size of the company reflects its ability to achieve economies of scale (Barbosa & Eiriz, 2009; Kuntluru, Muppani, & Khan, 2008) and absorb market power (Kuntluru et al., 2008). Barbosa and Eiriz (2009) also argue that the learning effect (learning by doing, i.e., the ability of workers to improve their productivity due to the repetition of the same type of activity) leads to improved business efficiency. Thus:

Hypothesis 5 *Larger firms tend to have higher levels of economic performance.*

About the age of the firms, there is no consensus in the literature regarding its impact on business performance. Nevertheless, Alfred Marshall (in Kuntluru et al., 2008) suggests that older firms are more likely to stagnate and be less flexible in making quick adjustments to a contemporary setting. Zahra (2005) concludes that the age of firms is negatively and significantly associated with innovative attitudes. Authors like Majocchi et al. (2005) demonstrate that, in industrial firms, experience in the sector is an important variable and that there is a positive relationship between firm age and the corresponding export performance. These authors emphasize that the accumulation of experience in the management of international trade, the market, and the cultural conditions of foreign countries is a long and complicated process, so the company's experience in the business affects its international position.

Hypothesis 6 *The most experienced firms in the business have better economic performance.*

Spending on research and development as in the firms' technological intensity (measured, in general, by the ratio of spending on R&D in sales) is as a rule associated with the ability/competence for innovation by firms. Giovannetti et al. (2013) conclude that spending on R&D and technological intensity has a positive effect on the propensity of firms to export. Other authors (e.g., Artz, Norman, Hatfield, & Cardinal, 2010; Tsai, 2005) also reached similar conclusions, finding that companies able to support high levels of spending on R&D could benefit from increasing returns to scale to spread costs and, thus, have higher capacity to support research projects and use knowledge that could lead to an increase in product innovation. Artz et al. (2010) explore the relationship between the ability to create innovations and performance (i.e., spending on R&D) in 272 companies from 35 different industries and also found a positive relationship between firm size and sales growth, but a negative one with profitability. Thus, according to Artz et al. (2010), a higher level of innovative activity tends to result in higher sales, despite not necessarily translating into higher economic return due to possible inefficiencies typical of large enterprises.

Hypothesis 7 *The innovativeness of the firm has a positive effect on the respective economic performance.*

Regarding the output of innovation (e.g., new products, processes, access to new markets), some authors have concluded that the generation of new products is positively related to economic performance (Artz et al., 2010; Li, Su, & Liu, 2010; Roberts, 1999). Specifically, Artz et al. (2010) argue that the high profits of companies may persist if they can bring to the market many innovations over time, allowing them to enjoy a temporary monopoly while these products are new in the market. On the other hand, using a sample of 488 companies in the *Fortune Reputation Survey (FRS)*, Cho and Pucik (2005) show that the most innovative companies (index of perception of innovation taken from FRS) have higher growth rates and higher levels of economic performance (yield). Thus, the introduction of new products means that companies can overcome competition by creating barriers to entry, opening new distribution channels, and discovering new customers in order to improve their market position and underline their leadership (Roberts, 1999). Cainelli (2008) also concludes, for a set of 2821 Italian manufacturing firms, that firms with a higher propensity to innovate have better economic performance.

Hypothesis 8 *The most innovative performance (using innovations in products, processes, practices, organization, and marketing) is positively related to the economic performance of firms.*

Concerning the characteristics related to the human capital of the firms' employees, it is relatively consensual, at the macroeconomic level, that educational policies promote prosperity and boost the economic growth of nations (Ganotakis, 2012). Although at the microeconomic level the evidence is not so overwhelming, Eickelpasch and Vogel (2011), analyzing a panel of about 36,000 German service companies in the period 2003–2005, conclude that workers with higher levels of human capital are more productive, being the average productivity of the firm positively related to the intensity of the respective export. However, few studies have focused on the relationship between the stock of human capital and the economic performance of businesses and have failed to find a positive relationship between them (Collier, Green, Kim, & Peirson, 2011). Using data from 2191 British companies of both the public and private sectors, Collier et al. (2011) find a positive relationship between the level of education and the survival of the workplace, i.e., the economic performance of these companies. Herstad, Sandven, and Solberg (2013), using data on the link between workers and employers to Norwegian firms and individuals active in the country, also conclude that the growth and survival of a company are strictly related to the existence of highly qualified human resources.

Hypothesis 9 *Firms with higher average levels of human capital (skills/education and qualifications of employees) have a better economic performance.*

Recently there have been some studies relating internationalization with economic performance (Hagemejer & Kolasa, 2011; Kontinen & Ojala, 2010; Lu & Beamish, 2001; Piva et al., 2013; Swoboda & Olejnik, 2013). Hagemejer and Kolasa (2011), based on a sample of 15,000 Polish firms, find that companies entering new markets are also growing and increasing their earnings as well as bolstering the country's overall level of production. Although initially, the profitability of foreign direct investment in 164 Japanese companies had decreased, Lu and Beamish (2001) found a positive and significant relationship between this type of internationalization strategy and the economic performance of these companies. Nevertheless, Kontinen and Ojala (2010) find that family firms have a lower propensity to internationalization, and Piva et al. (2013) show that family companies in high-tech sectors are more likely to internationalize than nonfamily members of those sectors.

Hypothesis 10 *Firms exporting more have higher economic performance.*

Hausman (2005) found that partnerships with innovative companies have a positive influence on their innovative performance. In the same line, Lu and Beamish (2001) found that alliances with local partners can be a good strategy to overcome the difficulties small businesses face when they intend to expand to international markets. Small businesses are more vulnerable and deal daily with scarce resources and, thus, see these alliances as a means to overcome these difficulties, thereby benefiting from lower transaction costs, increased market power, risk diversification, and easier access to resources such as key information and capital (Lu & Beamish, 2001). Once they are placed in partnerships, small businesses have access to their partners' knowledge, thus accelerating their learning process (Lu & Beamish, 2001). Lu and Beamish (2011) pointed out that, despite the importance of partnerships in the performance of companies, membership alone does not guarantee the company's success in the internationalization process. Problems may arise such as lack of trust, conflicts of interest among the companies, problems with the division of power, as well as cultural differences (Lu & Beamish, 2001). Consequently, it is important to choose of the right partner.

Hypothesis 11 *Firms with a higher number of partnerships have a better economic performance.*

Several authors have focused on the benefits of foreign ownership in the economic performance of companies (Kimura & Kiyota, 2007; Kuntluru et al., 2008). Kuntluru et al. (2008), based on a study of 102 pharmaceutical companies in India in the period 1998–2005, concluded that foreign ownership had a positive and statistically significant impact on their financial performance. Kimura and Kiyota (2007), however, analyzed the differences between Japanese companies held by domestic and foreign capital in the 1990s and concluded that foreign-owned firms had higher growth regarding profitability and productivity. Foreign investors bring valuable firm-specific assets such as technology, management capacity, and more efficient business governance (Kimura & Kiyota, 2007; Kuntluru et al., 2008). Another advantage is access to resources from the country of origin at a lower cost as well as additional talent, resulting from their becoming part of much larger organizations with access to a more significant amount of resources (Kuntluru et al., 2008). However, the best use of these resources to achieving better economic performance depends on the proportion the subsidiary owns (Kuntluru et al., 2008).

Companies with foreign ownership have an advantage over domestic firms, contributing to improved economic performance:

Hypothesis 12 *Foreign-owned firms have better economic performance.*

There are business-related factors that influence the economic performance of companies such as network characteristics, sector, or region in which they operate. Barbosa and Eiriz (2009), analyzing the existence of productivity spillovers from FDI in the Portuguese industry, concluded that foreign companies in the same industry did not significantly affect the local companies' productivity. They found a consistent lack of horizontal spillovers between different groups of firms, with no significant differences between large and small firms, or between export-oriented firms and firms operating in the domestic market, or firms operating in R&D intensive industries, among others. Some authors suggest that the specific characteristics of each sector are crucial for productivity spillovers to occur (Barbosa & Eiriz, 2009).

Several authors have analyzed the influence of the firms' location on improved economic performance. Niehm et al. (2010) studied the antecedents and impact of the use of information technologies by small family businesses and found a positive relationship between the existence of technologies in the region and the innovation performance of firms. However, Döring and Schnellenbach (2006) stated that it is not surprising that companies try to exploit knowledge spillovers but, much as others try to appropriate knowledge, they have an incentive to protect theirs over their competitors. Hence, companies try to negotiate contracts intended to avoid this informal communication. Nevertheless, it is increasingly recognized that agglomeration is an important factor for the competitive advantage of firms (Cainelli, 2008; Döring & Schnellenbach, 2006; Vor & Groot, 2010). Several studies show that firms belonging to clusters/industrial districts have a higher propensity to innovate than other firms as well as improved performance in productivity (Cainelli, 2008; Döring & Schnellenbach, 2006). Better performance is underpinned at these hubs as they attract and retain a workforce with the skills the industry requires and thereby reduce the costs of searching for skilled labor, as well as attract suppliers and customers (Vor & Groot, 2010). Cost reductions in labor demand mean more flexibility and mobility of workers (Breschi & Lissoni, 2009). Specialization encourages the exploration of externalities of scale (Vor & Groot, 2010). Döring and Schnellenbach (2006) argued that small companies whose production function is characterized by economies of scale and that do not compete in the same market could increase their level of innovation through cooperation with other companies.

Thus, in these districts, an increase in the level of innovation led to increased profit compared to other locations lacking such market dynamics, usually characterized by informal communication (Döring & Schnellenbach, 2006).

Hypothesis 13a *Firms located in regions with greater economic development have better economic performance.*

Hypothesis 13b *Firms located in regions with greater technological capabilities have improved economic performance.*

Hypothesis 13c *The sectoral density of a region influences the economic performance of companies located therein.*

Hypothesis 13d *The degree of productive regeneration of a region (average number of births and deaths of enterprises), i.e., the region's ability to generate new business after others have ended and thus renew the entrepreneurial influence and the economic performance of companies located therein.*

3 Methodology

3.1 Target Population, Sample, and Data Collection

In Portugal, although large firms can be considered family businesses (e.g., Espírito Santo Financial Group, Sonae Group, Amorim Group, or Luís Simões and Salvador Caetano), the vast majority of family businesses in Portugal are small- and medium-sized (Jorge et al., 2017).

For convenience, because it is not possible to obtain microdata at the national level, the AICEP database was used, containing 6228 Portuguese SMEs that export or have intentions to do so soon. This group of firms was surveyed by Pedro Oliveira (Oliveira, 2011), having obtained 912 valid responses. These 912 companies were subsequently resurveyed to ascertain which ones could be classified as "family."[1] In this second round, 230 responses were obtained, of which 110 were classified as family-owned SMEs.

Data collection from the firms in the AICEP database was carried out by Pedro Oliveira as part of his dissertation at FEUP in 2012. The survey applied consisted of several parts covering relevant issues related to the characteristics of the firms' managers/founders (size of management team, managers' formal and informal qualifications, CEO's experience as well as family involvement in management positions), firms' characteristics (size, age, R&D intensity and innovation, formal

[1]We thank Pedro Oliveira for kindly providing the databases relevant to this study. His dissertation—"Segmentation of SME customers at AICEP Portugal Global: a proposal based on real data," Pedro Miguel Sousa de Oliveira, Master in Service Engineering and Management, FEUP, Faculty of Engineering, University of Porto—contains more detailed information on the characteristics of firms comprising the target population and sample (i.e., the 912 respondent companies).

and informal qualifications of employees, export profile, among others), and the region where the firm is located.

In 2013, to determine which of the 912 companies surveyed could be considered as "family" businesses, they were contacted again by email, requesting answers to four questions on the constitution of their share capital, a criterion for strict classification according to the relevant literature on family businesses: (1) percentage of share capital that was held by the majority shareholder at the time, (2) the majority shareholder of the company was also its President/CEO, (3) percentage of managers/directors who were relatives/family members of the majority partner, (4) and which majority partner's family generation (1st generation, 2nd generation, 3rd generation, or more) was managing the company.

Two criteria were selected to classify the firms as family businesses: (1) firms in which at least 50% of the share capital is held by one of the partners, and there are administrators/directors who are the principal shareholder's relatives, corresponding to whether the company's management was in a given family generation; (2) companies in which at least 50% of the share capital is held by one of the partners and managers who are administrators/directors and the family's majority shareholder.

The first criterion is more restrictive than the second because it requires information regarding which generation is running the company. Accordingly, from the 230 respondent firms in our sample, 90 are "family" businesses. The second criterion used in the estimation of the econometric models considered 110 companies "family" businesses because information obtained about the generation is not of sufficient quality.

3.2 Proxies for the Relevant Variables

Given that this study's main goal was to ascertain the extent to which the economic performance of family businesses in Portugal is determined by innovation, our dependent variable is economic performance. As a proxy for this variable, we used the gross value added per worker, commonly identified as "productivity." This indicator combines the results of the company's operating activity with the cost of capital and is thus a more robust performance indicator than sales or turnover (Hamilton et al., 2009; Pantea et al., 2008).

Based on the literature review, developed in the previous section, the proxies selected for the three main groups of determinants of economic performance of family firms in Portugal were characteristics of the management team/founder, firm characteristics, and their context.

The first group consists of the personal and professional characteristics of the firms' entrepreneurs/founders/managers and the size of their management team. The literature places particular emphasis on the level of education as a reliable indicator of an improved level of economic performance (Brown et al., 2007; Sluis et al., 2008). Thus, educational level was calculated by two proxies, a dummy variable that takes the value of 1 if the CEO has higher education or more, and 0 otherwise, and the proportion of the management team with degrees in economics and engineering.

The proxy for the CEO's area of specialization is a dummy that takes the value one if the CEO has a degree in economics and engineering (0 otherwise). For the management team, we created an "index of skill dispersion," because, according to the literature, the greater the range of skills within a company's management team, the better its performance (West & Noel, 2009). Levesque and Minniti (2006) and Li et al. (2010), among others, argued that a CEO with more time in office acquires more knowledge and becomes more experienced, increasing their ability to take riskier decisions, and have more entrepreneurial attitudes, being skillful in the company's management. Hence, two variables were used to measure the impact of experience on business performance: the CEO's and the management team's years of international experience (the average years of experience).

In the second group of determinants of performance—business characteristics—we calculated the size of firms based on the number of employees, in line with Majocchi et al. (2005) and Eickelpasch and Vogel (2011). Based on Majocchi et al. (2005), who argued that the company's experience in the sector was important for better export performance, we used the number of years the firm has been in business.

In line with Artz et al. (2010), the companies' innovation capacity is measured by R&D intensity (i.e., the ratio of spending on R&D in sales), since expenditure on R&D is considered an input to the innovation process and reflects the firm's commitment/skills in terms of innovation.

To evaluate the outcome of family businesses' innovation performance in Portugal (either *via the introduction of innovations in products, processes, organizational practices, or marketing*), we computed a dummy variable that takes the value 1 when the company has introduced (in the last 3 years) some innovation (*product, process, marketing, or organizational practices*) and 0 otherwise. Additionally, an "Innovation Index" was calculated which combines different innovations in the last 3 years by firms.

Concerning the training of employees, it was found that workers with higher levels of human capital are more productive (Eickelpasch & Vogel, 2011). In this study, the employees' level of training is measured by percentage (the total workers employed) of employees with higher education (university-level) and the weight of workers with technical courses in total workers.

In line with Eickelpasch and Vogel (2011), we used the percentage of turnover exported to assess the firm's commitment to internationalization. It is often through partnerships that companies have a better chance to grow and succeed in entering other markets. To assess whether the existence of partnerships influences the economic performance of Portuguese family businesses, the weight of exports within partnership compared to the rest was used as a proxy. To assess whether foreign capital influences the performance of family businesses, we computed a dummy variable that takes the value of 1 if the company is owned by foreign capital and 0 otherwise.

Finally, the last group of determinants covers context-related characteristics. According to Döring and Schnellenbach (2006), the knowledge that results from the clustering of companies and other organizations in a particular industry and region generates potentially dynamic externalities that enable positive returns to scale. In this study, we calculated the weight of the industry concerning total companies according to NUTIII as a proxy for the existence of sectoral spillovers.

To assess whether the level of development of the area where companies are located influences the level of productivity of firms located there, we use several indicators, namely, the synthetic index of regional development, the purchasing power per capita, and local purchasing power per capita. The weight of the region's high-tech exports was used to take account of its technological capacity, while the region's degree of regeneration at corporate level (i.e., the average number of births and deaths of enterprises in total enterprises in the region) was used to measure the region's ability to generate new businesses after others have closed and thus renew its business fabric.

4 Empirical Results

4.1 Descriptive Analysis

The group of 230 Portuguese SMEs surveyed employs 9719 workers, with an average number of approximately 42 workers per company. By the European Union's (EU) definition of SME, the sample includes 60 (26%) micro, 105 (46%) small, and 65 (28%) medium firms. With respect to the industry sector to which they belong, most of the target population fall under "manufacturing" (52%), followed by "wholesale and retail" (21%), whereas "consulting, scientific, and technical activities" has a lower weight (14%), followed by "information and communication" (4%), "agriculture, animal production, hunting, forest, and fish" (3%), "construction" (2%), and "transport and storage" (1%). Firms in the "activities of administrative and support services" (0.8%), "extractive industries" (0.4%), and "collection, treatment, and distribution water, sanitation, waste management, and pollution control" (0.4%) represent under 1% of the sample. In terms of location, and taking the NUTS III regions as a reference, accounting for a majority of the firms in our database, Greater Porto ("Grande Porto") has the highest weight (22.2%), followed by Greater Lisbon ("Grande Lisboa") (19.1%), Ave (8.7%), and Lower Vouga ("Baixo Vouga") (4.3%). Family and nonfamily firms present similar locations as we can observe in Fig. 1.

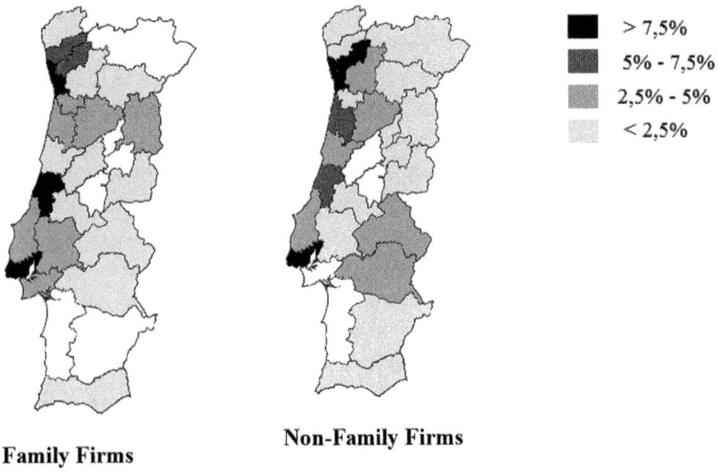

Fig. 1 Geographical distribution (% of total firms surveyed in each group) of firms. Source: Authors' own figure

4.2 *Model Estimation and Testing the Hypotheses*

Seven major groups of models were estimated (see summary in Table 2). Except for the first model (logistic regression), for each of the remaining 6 groups, 43 models were estimated in order to avoid multicollinearity caused by high correlations between some independent variables.

The first model, estimated by logistic regression, assesses the differences between family and nonfamily firms concerning the various determinants highlighted in the literature as influencing the productivity of firms, i.e., their economic performance. The remaining six models greatly facilitate assess to the determinants of economic performance of family (three models) and nonfamily (three models) businesses. In each of the three major groups of models, the difference refers to the dummy variable used to control the sector: the first group used the category of Pavitt's taxonomy, "specialized suppliers"; the second dummy variable is the industry category, "supplier-dominated"; and the third sector is controlled by the variable "manufacturing."

In comparison to nonfamily firms (NFF), the Portuguese family firms (FF) surveyed have, on average, higher levels of international experience, both the CEO and management team (see Model 0. Logistic, Table 2). Also, family firms are smaller, less intensive in R&D, but with a higher propensity to innovate regarding marketing. They have, on average, less foreign capital and tend to locate in regions (NUTS III) where the proportion of high-tech exports is lower. It is interesting to note that among the three groups of determinants of economic performance of family businesses (see Models 1–3, Table 2)—characteristics of the management team, factors relating to the company, and context factors—factors relating to companies emerge as the most important in explaining the productivity of those firms, followed by the characteristics of the respective management teams. In other words, the

Table 2 Overview of the estimates of the econometric models

	Hypothesis	Variables (proxies)	Model 0. Logistic	Model 1. Specialized suppliers sector		Model 2. Supplier-dominated sectors		Model 3. Manufacturing industry	
			FF vs. NFF	FF	NFF	FF	NFF	FF	NFF
CEO/Management team		GVA per worker (in EUR/year), in ln	−0.501						
	H1	Size of the management team (in ln)	−1.022	0.445	−0.014	0.346	−0.025	0.640	−0.080
	H2a	CEO with higher education or more (dummy variable)	1.347	1.510	−0.130	1.638*	−0.155	1.248	−0.174
	H2b	Management team—proportion (%) of graduates in engineering and economics	0.328	−2.146	0.095	−2.147	0.099	−1.865	0.231
	H3a	CEO engineer (dummy variable)	0.184	0.364*	0.903**	0.171*	0.944***	0.464*	0.948***
	H3a	CEO economics (dummy variable)	−0.110	−0.815	0.001	−0.881	0.007	−0.633	0.010
	H3b	Education backgrounds' dispersion index—management team (in ln)	0.572***	0.948	−0.505	0.783	−0.510	0.728	−0.641
	H4a	Years of international experience of the CEO (in ln)	−0.598**	0.057**	0.543***	0.122**	0.543***	0.120**	0.558***
	H4b	Average years of international experience of the management team (in ln)	−0.104	0.764***	−0.337	0.642***	−0.335	0.874***	−0.313

(continued)

Table 2 (continued)

	Hypothesis	Variables (proxies)	Model 0. Logistic	Model 1. Specialized suppliers sector		Model 2. Supplier-dominated sectors		Model 3. Manufacturing industry	
			FF vs. NFF	FF	NFF	FF	NFF	FF	NFF
Firms' characteristics	H5	Size of the firm (n° workers) (in ln)	−0.135*	0.228	0.180*	0.260	0.184*	0.305	0.245**
	H6	Firm's age (years) (in ln)	−0.280	0.531**	0.290**	0.543***	0.299**	0.595**	0.303**
	H7	R&D intensity (business volume ratio)	-7.806**	10.761*	−0.882	10.388*	−0.717	9.171*	−1.220
	H8	Introduction of new products (dummy variable)	−0.094	−0.533	−0.322	−0.601	−0.326	−0.022	−0.573
		Introduction of new processes (dummy variable)	−0.346	0.105	0.005	0.253	-0.001	0.444	−0.405
		Organizational innovation (dummy variable)	0.030	−0.087	−0.569	−0.135	−0.588	0.455	−0.798
		Marketing innovation (dummy variable)	0.657*	0.821*	−0.095	0.887*	−0.119	1.118**	−0.462
		Innovation Index (em ln)		0.327*	1.903	0.373*	1.982	2.104*	3.792
	H9	The weight of employees with bachelor's degree or more (% of total employees)	0.352	0.155	0.892	0.099	0.940	−0.243*	0.722
		The weight of employees with technical courses (% of total employees)	−1.707*	−2.434**	−1.728**	−2.410**	−1.736**	−2.057**	−1.682**

	H10	Volume business exported (proportion business volume)	−0.227	0.939**	0.616	1.154**	0.599	1.058**	0.714
	H11	Export made in partnership (total exports ratio)	0.064	−0.998	−0.570	−0.984	−0.572	−0.678	−0.582
	H12	Foreign capital (total share capital ratio)	−3.056**	0.244	−0.241	−0.151	−0.237	0.443	−0.247
Context	H13	Sector spillovers (companies of the sector/total NUTIII companies)	0.699	1.838	−1.025	0.222	−1.005	−1.654*	−2.169*
		Synthetic index regional development (100: Portugal)	1.001	−9.651**	−1.274	−9.493**	−1.256	−8.457**	−0.744
		Purchasing power per capita in NUTIII where the company is located (100: Portugal)	−0.010	1.581	1.192	1.000	1.160	1.090	1.019
		Purchasing power municipality per capita at NUTIII where the company is located (100: Portugal)		−0.766*	0.371*	−0.897*	0.389*	−0.850*	0.252
		High-tech export in the NUTIII region (in the proportion of regional total exports)	−4.344***	0.616	7.731	−0.565	7.520	3.533	9.633*
		The degree of regeneration of the NUTIII region where the company is located [(birth of companies + mortality	−5.499	15.948	−20.167	24.261	−19.795	12.564	−23.387

(continued)

Table 2 (continued)

	Hypothesis	Variables (proxies)	Model 0. Logistic	Model 1. Specialized suppliers sector		Model 2. Supplier-dominated sectors		Model 3. Manufacturing industry	
			FF vs. NFF	FF	NFF	FF	NFF	FF	NFF
		of companies)/2]/total companies in the region in%							
		Specialized supplier sector/sector dominated by suppliers/ manufacturing industry (dummy that assumes value one if the company belongs to this sector)		0.180	0.108	−0.930*	−0.035	−1.091**	−0.677*
		Hosmer and Lemeshow test (*p*-value)	10.619 (0.224)						
		% Correct [adjusted R^2]	67.8	0.173	0.122	0.203	0.121	0.200	0.147

Dependent variable Models 1–3: productivity (gross value added per worker in logarithm)
Notes: *** (**) [*] statistically significant at 1% (5%) [10%]. Source: Authors' own table

sample showed that internal factors to the firm are more relevant in explaining their economic performance than context factors, particularly those associated with the characteristics of the regions where the companies are located.

Now focusing on the assumptions made in the literature review for which the estimates reveal various levels of significance (1%, 5%, or 10%), the estimation results (see Table 2) yield the following conclusions. Family firms with a higher proportion of CEOs from engineering (H3a) and most experienced CEOs (H4a) and management teams in international terms (H4B) tend, on average, all else equal, to have higher levels of productivity. Additionally, the international experience of the management team emerges as more relevant in explaining the economic performance of family businesses than of the nonfamily ones. There is also some evidence (in Model 2) that family businesses have more skilled CEOs and, on average, a higher level of economic performance (H2a). These results are in line with the more general literature on the economic performance of firms (Brown et al., 2007; Sluis et al., 2008), which argues that education can act as a signal of the capabilities of managers as well as other characteristics highlighted as contributing to the higher productivity of firms (Sluis et al., 2008). The best allocation of human capital, both concerning education, skills, and experience, can also allow the creation of new ideas and technology (Marrocu & Paci, 2012).

Our results concerning the experience level of the CEO and management team is in line with Lin et al. (2011) and Levesque and Minniti (2006), who argue that greater experience is associated with a higher capacity for decision-making, greater willingness to take risks, and, therefore, better economic results, that is, higher levels of productivity.

Regarding the characteristics of the company, the results of the econometric estimations corroborate some of the assumptions made, particularly those relating to innovation, and are even surprising. We found that family businesses (and also nonfamily ones) with more experience in the business (on the market for more years) are on average more productive (H6), which is in line with the more general literature on the economic performance of companies (Majocchi et al., 2005).

Surprisingly, not only does investment in R&D contribute positively to the performance of family firms as compared to the results obtained for the nonfamily group, this factor is only discriminating in terms of productivity in the case of family businesses (i.e., for this sample, there is no evidence that family firms that invest more in R&D show higher economic performance than those investing less). Thus, although family firms are less intensive in R&D than nonfamily ones (cf. Model 0), R&D emerges as more relevant for the entire group of family firms than for nonfamily group, considering discrimination by best performance separately.

The positive contribution of R&D activities to economic performance is in line with the literature, including studies by Tsai (2005), Artz et al. (2010), and more recently Giovannetti et al. (2013). The latter authors concluded that spending on R&D and technological intensity had a positive effect on the propensity of firms to export (Giovannetti et al., 2013). Companies that can support high levels of spending on R&D could benefit from increasing returns to scale to distribute costs and thus bolster their capacity to support research projects and use the knowledge that could lead to higher product innovation (Artz et al., 2010; Tsai, 2005).

Besides the relevance of technological and innovative skills boosted by investment in R&D, innovation, reflected in the successful introduction of innovations, emerges as very significant statistically and has a positive effect on the economic performance of family businesses (however, there is enough evidence to say the same for the group of nonfamily businesses in our sample). Indeed, family businesses that claimed to have introduced innovations in marketing and various types of innovation together in the last 3 years are, on average, more productive (*H8*). These results generally confirm the literature which argues that innovation (e.g., new products, processes, entering new markets) is positively related to economic performance (Artz et al., 2010; Li et al., 2010; Roberts, 1999), adding evidence regarding family businesses that are often identified as moderately innovative (Block, Miller, Jaskiewicz, & Spiegel, 2013). The introduction of innovations leads firms in general and the family in particular to overcoming competition, creating barriers to entry, opening new distribution channels, enlisting new customers in order to improve their market position and economic performance (Roberts, 1999). The relevance of the firm's marketing strategy and focus on the market should also be noted since innovation performance through marketing rather than using products and processes is evident in our findings. This may be associated with the need to reposition their products/services, whether in the domestic or international market.

Contrary to the majority of existing empirical studies, we found that family businesses employing more workers with higher levels of human capital (i.e., higher levels of education and training) tend, on average, to have poorer economic performance (lower productivity per employee). Although it is difficult to explain this counterintuitive result, it is likely that this is partly because these firms' competitive strategy is related to product/service differentiation through marketing. Schmidt and Rammer (2006) showed that despite a positive relationship between the product innovation process and the educational level of workers, this result does not arise in the case of organizational and marketing innovations. Thus, indirectly, we can explain why *H9* is not corroborated in our study.

Family firms with higher export intensity are, on average, more competitive and productive than other family businesses (note that this variable is not discriminating in the case of nonfamily firms). This result is consistent with the literature analyzed in this area (e.g., Lu & Beamish, 2001; Kontinen & Ojala, 2010; Hagemejer & Kolasa, 2011; Swoboda & Olejnik, 2013; Piva et al., 2013) thus confirming *H10*. The impact of exports/international performance and innovation (capabilities and output) on economic performance is particularly evident for the family business group but is not statistically significant in the nonfamily group. We can, therefore, conclude that innovation and internationalization are important for the economic performance of most companies, but they are discriminating factors for performance only in the family business group, which makes these factors even more critical for this group. This argument is partly supported by Piva et al.'s (2013) study, which showed that family firms in high-tech sectors are more likely to internationalize than nonfamily firms in these sectors.

Regarding the context-related factors, we note that, contrary to our postulate in *H13*, family businesses that are located in economically underdeveloped regions, as reflected by regional development and local purchasing power indicators, tend, on average, to have higher levels of productivity. This result, although surprising concerning the literature, is interesting because it suggests that family businesses can be seen here as an engine of regional convergence regarding development.

Finally, a word on the matter of the sector of business activity: We found that family firms belonging to the so-called "supplier-dominated" and "manufacturing" sectors are, on average, less productive than other family businesses. Thus, it is important that these studies consider the sectoral trajectories which companies follow.

5 Conclusion

The main purpose of this study was to contribute empirically to the literature on family businesses, adding evidence for an underexplored case, Portugal, where family firms represent between 70 and 80% of the corporate network and contribute to 60% of employment and 50% of gross domestic product. We further proposed to explore the role of the capabilities and outputs of innovation in the economic performance of these firms, often identified as laggards concerning innovation dynamics (Block et al., 2013).

To prepare this study, a database consisting of nearly 6000 exporting or potentially exporting SMEs was used. Of the 230 respondent firms that constituted our sample, 110 were classified as "family businesses."

The econometric estimations made found that innovation (capacity and performance) matters significantly for the economic performance of family firms: on average, all else equal, family firms that invest more in R&D and innovate globally (i.e., introduce product, process, organizational, and marketing innovations in combination) and/or through marketing are more productive. Other results are also worth summarizing here. We found that firms with CEOs with higher qualification levels had higher levels of economic performance, particularly those whose CEOs were graduates in engineering. The international experience factor—the CEO and management team—was also proven as an important enabler of economic performance of family businesses. It was surprising to find that family firms located in less developed regions have higher levels of productivity. This result may indicate that this type of business does not depend on the region for their survival but rather can be seen as an engine of regional convergence regarding development.

For future research in this area, it would be important to understand why innovation regarding marketing is more relevant to the firms' economic performance and why their employees' human capital does not seem to contribute to productivity. Networking among enterprises in regional terms was relatively neglected in this work as a factor, and it would undoubtedly be an interesting aspect to explore in the future given the importance of social relationships and tacit knowledge in the business development of family businesses (Miller & Le Breton-Miller, 2006; Zahra, Hayton, Neubaum, Dibrell, & Craig, 2008).

References

Aggarwal, R. K., Evans, M. E., & Nanda, D. (2012). Non-profit boards: Size, performance, and managerial incentives. *Journal of Accounting and Economics, 53*, 466–487.

Alonso, A. D., O'Brien, S., & Kok, S. (2018). Innovation, dynamic capabilities, and family firms operating in an emerging economy. *Journal for International Business and Entrepreneurship Development, 11*(3), 221–242.

Artz, K. W., Norman, P. M., Hatfield, D. E., & Cardinal, L. B. (2010). A longitudinal study of the impact of R&D, patents, and product innovation on firm performance. *The Journal of Product Innovation Management, 27*, 725–740.

Arvey, R., & Murphy, K. (1998). Performance evaluation in work settings. *Annual Review of Psychology, 49*, 141–168.

Barbosa, N., & Eiriz, V. (2009). Linking corporate productivity to foreign direct investment: An empirical assessment. *International Business Review, 18*(1), 1–13.

Barney, J. (1991). Firm resources and sustained competitive advantage. *Journal of Management, 17* (1), 99–120.

Baum, J., & Wally, S. (2003). Strategic decision speed and firm performance. *Strategic Management Journal, 24*(1), 107–1129.

Belloc, F. (2012). Corporate governance and innovation: A survey. *Journal of Economic Surveys, 26*(5), 835–864.

Bigliardi, B., & Galati, F. (2018). Family firms and collaborative innovation: Present debates and future research. *European Journal of Innovation Management, 21*(2), 334–358.

Block, J., Miller, D., Jaskiewicz, P., & Spiegel, F. (2013). Economic and technological importance of innovations in large family and founder firms: An analysis of patent data. *Family Business Review, 26*(2), 180–199.

Boyd, B. (1995). CEO duality and firm performance: A contingency model. *Strategic Management Journal, 16*, 301–312.

Breschi, S., & Lissoni, F. (2009). Mobility of skilled workers and co-invention networks: An anatomy of localized knowledge flows. *Journal of Economic Geography, 9*(4), 439–468.

Brown, A. W., Adams, J. D., & Amjad, A. A. (2007). The relationship between human capital and time performance in project management: A path analysis. *International Journal of Project Management, 25*, 77–89.

Cainelli, G. (2008). Spatial agglomeration, technological innovations, and firm productivity: Evidence from Italian industrial districts. *Growth and Change, 39*(3), 414–435.

Cainelli, G., Evangelista, R., & Savona, M. (2006). Innovation and economic performance in services: A firm-level analysis. *Cambridge Journal of Economics, 30*, 435–458.

Carvalho, L., & Williams, B. (2014). Let the cork fly: Creativity and innovation in a family business. *International Journal of Entrepreneurship and Innovation, 15*(2), 127–133.

Cassia, L., de Massis, A., & Kotlar, J. (2012a). Exploring the effect of family control on the characteristics of SMEs in northern Italy. *International Journal of Engineering Business Management, 4*(16), 1–8.

Cassia, L., De Massis, A., & Pizzurno, E. (2012b). Strategic innovation and new product development in family firms: An empirically grounded theoretical framework. *International Journal of Entrepreneurial Behaviour & Research, 18*(2), 198–232.

Céspedes-Lorente, J. J., Magán-Díaz, A., & Martínez-Ros, E. (2018). Information technologies and downsizing: Examining their impact on economic performance. *Information and Management*. https://doi.org/10.1016/j.im.2018.09.012.

Chen, Y. S., Chang, K. C., & Chang, C. H. (2012). Nonlinear influence on R&D project performance. *Technological Forecasting and Social Change, 79*, 1537–1547.

Cho, H. J., & Pucik, V. (2005). Relationship between innovativeness, quality, growth, profitability, and market value. *Strategic Management Journal, 26*(6), 555–575.

Chrisman, J. J., Chua, J. H., & Sharma, P. (2003). Current trends and future directions in family business management studies: Toward a theory of the family business. *Coleman White Paper series*, unpublished.

Chua, J., Chrisman, J., & Sharma, P. (1999). Defining the family business by behavior. *Entrepreneurship: Theory and Practice, 23*(4), 19–39.

Collier, W., Green, F., Kim, Y. B., & Peirson, J. (2011). Education, training and economic performance: Evidence from establishment survival data. *Journal of Labor Research, 32*, 336–361.

De Massis, A., Frattini, F., Majocchi, A., & Piscitello, L. (2018). Family firms in the global economy: Toward a deeper understanding of internationalization determinants, processes, and outcomes. *Global Strategy Journal, 8*(1), 3–21.

Döring, T., & Schnellenbach, J. (2006). What do we know about geographical knowledge spillovers and regional growth?: A survey of the literature. *Regional Studies, 40*(3), 375–395.

EFB. (2018). *The New Europe: The family business vision*. Retrieved from http://www.europeanfamilybusinesses.eu/uploads/Modules/Mediaroom/pp%2D%2D-the-new-europe-v3.pdf

Eickelpasch, A., & Vogel, A. (2011). Determinants of the export behavior of German, business services companies. *The Service Industries Journal, 31*(3–4), 513–526.

Family Firm Institute. (2017). *Global data points*. Retrieved from http://www.ffi.org/page/globaldatapoints

Feranita, F., Kotlar, J., & De Massis, A. (2017). Collaborative innovation in family firms: Past research, current debates, and agenda for future research. *Journal of Family Business Strategy, 8*(3), 137–156.

Finkelstein, S., & Hambrick, D. (1997). Strategic leadership: Top executives and their effects on organizations. *Australian Journal of Management, 22*(2), 221–224.

Franco, M., & Franco, S. (2017). Organizational commitment in family SMEs and its influence on contextual performance. *Team Performance Management, 23*(7–8), 364–384.

Freeman, C. (1994). Technological infrastructure and international competitiveness. *Industrial and Corporate Change, 13*(3), 541–569.

Ganotakis, P. (2012). Founders' human capital and the performance of UK new technology-based firms. *Small Business Economics, 39*(2), 495–515.

Getz, D., & Carlsen, J. (2005). Family business in tourism – State of art. *Annals of Tourism Research, 32*(1), 237–258.

Giovannetti, G., Ricchiuti, G., & Velucchi, M. (2013). Location, internationalization and performance of firms in Italy: A multilevel approach. *Applied Economics, 45*, 2665–2673.

Hagemejer, J., & Kolasa, M. (2011). Internationalization and economic performance of enterprises: Evidence from polish firm-level data. *The World Economy, 34*(1), 74–100.

Hamilton, J., Rahman, S., & Lee, A. C. (2009). EVA: Does size matter? *Review of Pacific Basin Financial Markets and Policies, 12*(2), 267–287.

Hausman, A. (2005). Innovativeness among small businesses: Theory and propositions for future research. *Industrial Marketing Management, 34*, 773–782.

Hawawini, G., Subramanian, V., & Verdin, P. (2003). Is performance driven by industry or firm-specific factors? A new look at the evidence. *Strategic Management Journal, 24*, 1–16.

Herstad, S., Sandven, T., & Solberg, E. (2013). Location, education and enterprise growth. *Applied Economics Letters, 20*(10), 1019–1022.

Jensen, M. (1993). The modem industrial revolution, exit, and the failure of internal control systems. *Journal of Applied Corporate Finance, 6*, 4–23.

Jorge, M., Couto, M., Veloso, T., & Franco, M. (2017). When family businesses go international: Management sets the path. *Journal of Business Strategy, 38*(1), 31–38.

Kano, L., & Verbeke, A. (2018). Family firm internationalization: Heritage assets and the impact of bifurcation bias. *Global Strategy Journal, 8*(1), 158–183.

Kellermanns, F., Eddleston, K., Barnett, T., & Pearson, A. (2008). An exploratory study of family member characteristics and involvement: Effects on entrepreneurial behavior in the family firm. *Family Business Review, 21*(1), 1–14.

Kimura, F., & Kiyota, K. (2007). Foreign-owned versus domestically-owned firms: Economic performance in Japan. *Review of Development Economics, 11*(1), 31–48.

Kirner, E., Kinkel, S., & Jaeger, A. (2009). Innovation paths and the innovation performance of low-technology firms – An empirical analysis of German industry. *Research Policy, 38*, 447–458.

Koellinger, P. (2008). Why are some entrepreneurs more innovative than others? *Small Business Economics, 31*, 21–37.

Kontinen, T., & Ojala, A. (2010). Internationalization pathways of family SMEs: Psychic distance as a focal point. *Journal of Small Business and Enterprise Development, 17*(3), 437–454.

Kuntluru, S., Muppani, V., & Khan, M. (2008). Financial performance of foreign and domestic owned companies in India. *Journal of Asia-Pacific Business, 9*(1), 28–54.

Kusumastuti, R. (2018). Understanding social capital that leads to strategic ambidexterity practice in family firm business. *Journal of Engineering and Applied Sciences, 13*, 5317–5321.

Le Breton-Miller, I., Miller, D., & Steier, L. (2004). Toward an integrative model of effective FOB succession. *Entrepreneurship: Theory and Practice, 28*(4), 305–328.

Levesque, M., & Minniti, M. (2006). The effect of aging on entrepreneurial behavior. *Journal of Business Venturing, 21*, 177–194.

Li, Y., Su, Z., & Liu, Y. (2010). Can strategic flexibility help firms profit from product innovation? *Technovation, 30*, 300–309.

Lin, C., Lin, P., Song, F., & Li, C. (2011). Managerial incentives, CEO characteristics and corporate innovation in China's private sector. *Journal of Comparative Economics, 39*, 176–190.

Litz, R. A. (1995). The family business: Toward definitional clarity. *Family Business Review, 8*, 71–81.

Lourenço, I. C., Branco, M. C., & Curto, J. D. (2018). Timely reporting and family ownership: The Portuguese case. *Meditari Accountancy Research, 26*(1), 170–192.

Lu, J., & Beamish, P. (2001). Internationalization and performance of SMEs. *Strategic Management Journal, 22*, 565–586.

Majocchi, A., Bacchiocchi, E., & Mayrhofer, U. (2005). Firm size, business experience and export intensity in SMEs: A longitudinal approach to complex relationships. *International Business Review, 14*, 719–738.

Marco, R. (2012). Gender and economic performance: Evidence from the Spanish hotel industry. *International Journal of Hospitality Management, 31*, 981–989.

Marrocu, E., & Paci, R. (2012). Education or creativity: What matters most for economic performance? *Economic Geography, 88*(4), 369–401.

Martínez-Alonso, R., Martínez-Romero, M. J., & Rojo-Ramírez, A. A. (2018). Technological innovation and socioemotional wealth in family firm research: Literature review and proposal of a conceptual framework. *Management Research, 16*(3), 270–301.

Meroño-Cerdán, A. L. (2017). Perceived benefits of and barriers to the adoption of teleworking: Peculiarities of Spanish family firms. *Behavior and Information Technology, 36*(1), 63–74.

Miller, D., & Le Breton-Miller, I. (2006). Family governance and firm performance: Agency, stewardship, and capabilities. *Family Business Review, 19*(1), 73–87.

Miralles-Marcelo, J. L., Miralles-Quirós, M. M., & Lisboa, I. (2013). The stock performance of family firms in the Portuguese market. *Applied Financial Economics, 23*(22), 1721–1732.

Miralles-Marcelo, J. L., Miralles-Quirós, M. D. M., & Lisboa, I. (2014). The impact of family control on firm performance: Evidence from Portugal and Spain. *Journal of Family Business Strategy, 5*(2), 156–168.

Nelson, R. (1991). Why do firms differ, and how does it matter? *Strategic Management Journal, 12*, 61–74.

Nelson, R. R., & Winter, S. G. (1982). *An evolutionary theory of economic change*. Cambridge, MA: Harvard University Press.

Niehm, L. S., Tyner, K., Shelley, M. C., & Fitzgerald, M. A. (2010). Technology adoption in small family-owned businesses: Accessibility, perceived advantage, and information technology literacy. *Journal of Family and Economic Issues, 31*, 498–515.

OECD. (2005). *Oslo manual: Guidelines for collecting and interpreting innovation data*, 3rd ed. Retrieved from https://www.oecd-ilibrary.org/science-and-technology/oslo-manual_9789264013100-en

Oliveira, P. (2011). *Segmentation of SME clientes at AICEP Portugal Global: A proposal based on real data*. Dissertação de Mestrado em Engenharia de Serviços e Gestão, FEUP – Faculdade de Engenharia da Universidade do Porto (Portugal).

Ortiz-Villajos, J. M. (2017). Forms of innovation throughout time: Insights from the British business elite. *Innovation: Management, Policy, and Practice, 19*(4), 428–451.

Pacheco, L. M. (2017). Internationalization vs. family ownership and management: The case of Portuguese wine firms. *International Journal of Wine Business Research, 29*(2), 195–209.

Pantea, M. I., Munteanu, V., Gligor, D., & Sopoian, D. (2008). The managerial performances evaluation through the economic value added. *European Research Studies, 21*(4), 83–100.

Pavitt, K. (1984). Sectoral patterns of technical change: Towards a taxonomy and a theory. *Research Policy, 13*, 353–369.

Penrose, E. T. (1959). *The theory of the growth of the firm*. New York: Wiley.

Piva, E., Rossi-Lamastra, C., & De Massis, A. (2013). Family firms and internationalization: An exploratory study on high-tech entrepreneurial ventures. *Journal of International Entrepreneurship, 10*(1), 109–129.

Porter, M. E. (1980). *Competitive strategy: Techniques for analyzing industries and competitors*. New York: Free Press.

Rau, S. B., Werner, A., & Schell, S. (2018). Psychological ownership as a driving factor of innovation in older family firms. *Journal of Family Business Strategy*. https://doi.org/10.1016/j.jfbs.2018.03.001.

Riley, J. (2002). Weak and strong signals. *Scandinavian Journal of Economics, 104*(2), 213–236.

Roberts, W. (1999). Product innovation, product-market competition, and persistent profitability in the U.S. pharmaceutical industry. *Strategic Management Journal, 20*(7), 655–670.

Sánchez-Marín, G., Baixauli-Soler, J. S., & Lucas-Pérez, M. E. (2010). When much is not better? Top management compensation, board structure, and performance in Spanish firms. *The International Journal of Human Resource Management, 21*(15), 2778–2797.

Schmidt, T., & Rammer, C. (2006). *The determinants and effects of technological and non-technological innovations. Evidence from the German CIS IV*. Retrieved from http://www.oecd.org/dataoecd/10/43/37450197.pdf

Shanker, M., & Astrachan, J. (1996). Myths and realities: Family businesses' contribution to the US economy. A framework for assessing family business statistics. *Family Business Review, 9*(2), 107–123.

Siebels, J., & Aufseß, D. (2012). A review of theory in family business research: The implications for corporate governance. *International Journal of Management Reviews, 14*, 280–304.

Sluis, J., Praag, M., & Vijverberg, W. (2008). Education and entrepreneurship selection and performance: A review of the empirical literature. *Journal of Economic Surveys, 22*(5), 795–841.

Sternberg, R., & Arndt, O. (2001). The firm or the region: What determines the innovation behaviour of European firms. *Economic Geography, 77*, 364–382.

Stewart, W. H., Watson, W. E., Carland, J. A., & Carland, J. W. (1999). A proclivity for entrepreneurship: A comparison of entrepreneurs, small business owners, and corporate managers. *Journal of Business Venturing, 14*, 189–214.

Swoboda, B., & Olejnik, E. (2013). A taxonomy of small- and medium-sized international family firms. *Journal of International Entrepreneurship, 11*(2), 130–157.

Terlaak, A., Kim, S., & Roh, T. (2018). Not good, not bad: The effect of family control on environmental performance disclosure by business group firms. *Journal of Business Ethics, 153*(4), 977–996.

Tsai, H. (2005). R&D productivity and firm size: A nonlinear examination. *Technovation, 25*(7), 795–803.

Tsang, E. (2002). Learning from overseas venturing experience, the case of Chinese family businesses. *Journal of Business Venturing, 17*, 21–40.

Vor, F., & Groot, H. L. F. (2010). Agglomeration externalities and localized employment growth: The performance of industrial sites in Amsterdam. *The Annals of Regional Science, 44*, 409–431.

Weng, T. C., & Chi, H. Y. (2019). Family succession and business diversification: Evidence from China. *Pacific Basin Finance Journal, 53*, 56–81.

Werner, A., Schröder, C., & Chlosta, S. (2018). Driving factors of innovation in family and non-family SMEs. *Small Business Economics, 50*(1), 201–218.

West, G., & Noel, T. (2009). The impact of knowledge resources on new venture performance. *Journal of Small Business Management, 47*, 1–22.

Yermack, D. (1996). Higher market valuation of companies with a small board of directors. *Journal of Financial Economics, 40*(2), 185–211.

Zahra, S., & Bogner, W. (2000). Technology strategy and software new ventures' performance exploring the moderating effect of the competitive environment. *Journal of Business Venturing, 15*, 135–173.

Zahra, S., Hayton, J., & Salvato, C. (2004). Entrepreneurship in family vs. non-family firms: A resource-based analysis of the effect of organizational culture. *Entrepreneurship: Theory and Practice, 28*(4), 363–381.

Zahra, S. A. (2005). Entrepreneurial risk-taking in family firms. *Family Business Review, 18*(1), 23–40.

Zahra, S. A., Hayton, J. C., Neubaum, D. O., Dibrell, C., & Craig, J. (2008). Culture of family commitment and strategic flexibility: The moderating effect of stewardship. *Entrepreneurship: Theory and Practice, 32*(6), 1035–1054.

RISE Model: Its Application on Diving Enterprises Located in the San Andres Archipelago (Colombia)

María del Pilar Ramírez-Salazar, Rafael Ignacio Pérez-Uribe, Carlos Salcedo-Pérez, and Julieth Paola Juffington-Smith

Abstract This research aimed to identify the level of fulfillment of the four sustainability dimensions included in the RISE model, in three diving enterprises located in the Archipelago of San Andres. This model was developed at EAN University by the G3Pymes Research Group, which is rated A1 by Colciencias (Administrative Department of Science Technology and Innovation in Colombia). The model is composed of a diagnosis matrix that includes the following factors: innovation, sustainable production, leadership, strategic direction, organizational culture, collaborative processes, recognition, governance, new markets, technology, and financial indicators. Each factor is analyzed under the following four dimensions: (1) environmental, (2) economic, (3) social, and (4) managerial. The matrix measures the maturity level of each enterprise related to each dimension and factor. The results provided by the matrix, along with interviews performed in each enterprise, lead to a path for innovation and corporate sustainability. This path contains specific activities tailored to make improvements in each factor and dimension for which results were low. The expectation of performing this study is to motivate academic, industrial, and government institutions to use this model in order to boost best social, environmental, managerial, and economic practices.

Keywords Innovation · Corporate sustainability · Diagnosis matrix · Leadership · Strategic direction · Financial indicators · Collaborative processes · Organizational culture

---

M. del Pilar Ramírez-Salazar (✉) · R. I. Pérez-Uribe · C. Salcedo-Pérez · J. P. Juffington-Smith
Universidad EAN, Bogotá, Colombia
e-mail: mpramirezs@universidadean.edu.co; riperez@universidadean.edu.co; casalcedo@universidadean.edu.co; jhuffing527@universidadean.edu.co

J. M. Saiz-Álvarez et al. (eds.), *Entrepreneurship and Family Business Vitality*, Studies on Entrepreneurship, Structural Change and Industrial Dynamics, https://doi.org/10.1007/978-3-030-15526-1_16

1 Introduction

In this changing global world, enterprises compete and move toward new challenges. The business environment grows more unstable, changing, competitive, and innovative, so therefore, entrepreneurial growth and evolution become a challenge. Blázquez, Dorta, and Verona (2006) define business growth as the process of adaptation to changes posed by the environment or boosted by the entrepreneurial spirit of the manager, for which, the enterprise needs to develop or increase its production capacity by adjusting the use or acquisition of new resources.

This research focuses on the application of a model which is a path for innovation and corporate sustainability. This model is a practical tool that helps enterprises to grow. This study shows three cases of three Colombian diving enterprises. The companies belong to the tourism industry. This industry, according to the World Tourism Organization (2017),[1] is an economic activity that has been growing uninterruptedly through time. The number of tourists worldwide has gone from 25 million in 1950 to 278 million in 1980, to 674 million in 2000 to 1.235 billion in 2016. Also, the income generated by international tourism worldwide has gone up from USD2 billion in 1950 to USD104 billion, to 495 billion in 2000, to USD1.22 trillion in 2016 (World Tourism Organization, 2017).

ANATO (Colombian Association of Travel and Tourism Agencies) mentions that Colombia received around 4.4 million foreign visitors by the end of 2015, an increase of about 6% compared to 2014, growing 2% more than the world average (Diario El Heraldo, 2016). In 2016, 5,093,052 visitors arrived in Colombia; the tourism industry in Colombia grew 28.3% compared to 2016, thanks to the 6,535,182 visitors who arrived in the country (Revista Dinero, 2018).

This study focuses on the Municipality of Providencia y Santa Catalina, where tourism has shown considerable growth in the last 3 years. A total of 92,325 domestic and foreign tourists visited it in 2015, 101,589 in 2016, and 114,693 in 2017 according to data from CITUR-Centro de Información Turística (2018).

Tastes and preferences of travelers have changed. According to Trekksoft (2016), since the 1990s tourists started showing new trends when traveling; there is a new demand for postmodern tourists who look for adventures and get excited about cultural and natural activities. *Millennials*,[2] at-home vacations also called "staycations," tourism targeted to the Chinese public, gastronomic tourism, sustainable tourism, adventure travel, mobile photography, and women traveling alone, among others, are current tourism trends (Coppola, 2016). Adventure travel refers to the activity by which the user challenges his/her physical abilities in natural environments (land, water, air) (Entorno Turístico, 2018). As the UNWTO (2016)

[1]The UNWTO has a virtual library, source of information available to member states. Its website is https://www.e-unwto.org/.

[2]Mark McCrindle describes millennials as those youngsters who turned adults in the year 2000. He is an advisor, expert in millennial's behavior. He described them as completely digital, who look for new experiences and who are sensitive toward the environment and the ecology.

explains, more and more destinations try to position themselves in that segment because they recognize its environmental, cultural, and economic values.

Based on calculations from the Adventure Travel Trade Association (ATTA) (Hosteltur, 2015), adventure travel generates an estimated global income of USD263 billion. This data indicates that adventure travel is continuously growing, and it is positioning more and more especially when it comes to natural environment destinations.

Colombia has a high potential for adventure travel, with activities such as horse riding, camping, fishing, surf, paragliding, biking, trekking, rafting, zip-lining, rappel, or diving. The practice of extreme diving requires to dive in beaches, rivers, lakes, and caves, among others, having the adequate equipment and training which allows breathing and free movement underwater (El Clima, 2018; James & Márquez, 2011). Diving is considered a sport as well as a recreational activity (El Clima, 2018; James & Márquez, 2011). There are some techniques such as sports diving, night diving, deep water diving/sunk ships, cave diving, and scuba diving. It is required to have the necessary certifications according to the difficulty and depth level at which the diver will descend.[3] The following are some of the existing certifications: Certificación Open Water Dive, Advanced Open Water Diver, Rescue Diver, and Master Scuba Diver (PADI, 2018).

The publication *Cinco lugares para bucear en Colombia* (Alba Torres, 2015) mentions beautiful Colombian places where diving is worth to be practiced: Barú, Malpelo, Taganga, Isla Gorgona, and Providencia. The latter is located in the place where this research was conducted. The San Andrés, Providencia and Santa Catalina Archipelago was declared a Biosphere Reserve by the United Nations Educational, Scientific and Cultural Organization (UNESCO, 2000). This Reserve was named "Seaflower" (Sánchez-Jabba, 2012) after the ship that brought the first English settlers to such area, and with 180,000 square kilometers, it became the largest Biosphere Reserve. In 2005, the Colombian Government, recognizing its environmental importance, declared 65,000 square kilometers of the reserve as the "Seaflower Protected Sea Area," making it one of the most wanted places by tourism operators (Prato & Newball, 2015).

This research focuses on three diving enterprises operating in the Municipality of Providencia y Santa Catalina with the aim of identifying their scope in innovation and sustainability toward environmental processes and actions in an environment characterized by fragile marine ecosystems.

Inhabitants of the islands are worried continuously to preserve their environment. Sometimes, enterprises that operate there are not conscious about flora and fauna of the place, and consequently, sometimes they unconsciously damage the sea life and the environment of the island and its surroundings.

---

[3]With appropriate experience and training, recreational diving's limit is 40 m/130 ft. Beginners must stay at less than 18 m/60 ft. Even when those are the limits, some of the most popular dives are not farther than 12 m/40 ft, where water is hotter and colors are brighter (PADI, 2018).

Four objectives guided this research. First, a theoretical framework about the (1) social, (2) environmental, (3) managerial, and (4) economic dimensions contained in the intervention model used. Second, a description of the RISE model (Path for innovation and corporate sustainability) was applied in the diving enterprises chosen for the research. Third, results were analyzed, comparing maturity levels between enterprises. Finally, a Path for innovation and corporate sustainability was designed, so enterprises can improve those factors in which they performed low.

1.1 Research Problem

Enterprises must adapt themselves to changes in the environment. The National Center for Environmental Education of Spain, CENEAM, emphasizes that enterprises must render environmental, social, and economic services without harming the natural environment (Salvo & Kitsos, 2016). Operating in a world where irreversible problems that harm well-being and life conditions are growing, enterprises have taken a more relevant and conscious position toward the production of sustainable goods and services.

According to Berrone (2016), savage capitalism is not the trend anymore, and those enterprises that do not take an environmentally friendly strategy are due to fail. The previous sentence emphasizes on the importance of resource preservation; to produce irresponsibly, without caring for the environment, is not a priority, and enterprises must incorporate sustainability into their processes of strategic planning if they want to increase their success and competitiveness standards. The concept of sustainable enterprise relates to the general concept of sustainable development as the progress that satisfies present needs without compromising the capacity of future generation to fulfill their own needs (ILO, 2012). In Colombia, managers are getting more educated in topics of innovation and corporate sustainability (Epstein & Mantilla, 2009).

The Development Plan of San Andres Island (Gobernación Departamento Archipielago de San Andres, Providencia y Santa Catalina 2016) found out that there are difficulties related to:

1. Environment: mostly related to solid waste, since there is no separation in the source, there is a high amount of solid waste and an inadequate handling of their final disposal. Besides, people do not recycle, there are water and sewing problems, agricultural production is scarce, and the basket of goods and energy prices are expensive.
2. Social problems: dealing with security and prevention of environmental and health emergencies.
3. Cultural issues: there is neither an organization nor standardization to promote indigenous cultural events.

It is necessary to act to solve those problems. Such touristic place must be preserved so it can still be chosen because of its favorable conditions; therefore, it is mandatory to start with the assessment and intervention of all enterprises in the island. Diving enterprises are responsible for protecting the environment; flora and fauna must be cared for. This research starts with diving enterprises located in the San Andres Archipelago. The researchers expect to be able to apply this research to other touristic enterprises from the region in the future.

2 Theoretical Framework

The Brundtland Report (UNESCO, 2006) introduces the concept of sustainable development as "development that meets the needs of the present without compromising the ability of future generations to meet their own needs." Therefore, sustainable development offers environmental, social, and economic services to all members of a community without risking natural, built, and social environments (Eizenberg & Jabareen, 2017).

The 1992 Rio de Janeiro Earth Summit boosted sustainable development through three types of sustainability: environmental, social, and economic, recognizing not only the environmental crisis and its different issues but also that such crisis is revolving around social and economic systems. Based on the definition of sustainable development, the following characteristics are considered: to pursuit the integrity of processes, cycles, and times of nature (Shiva & Bandyopadhyay, 1989); to achieve sustainability of human, physical, environmental, and nonrenewable resources (Eizenberg & Jabareen, 2017); to protect natural resources and to sustain consumption levels (Redclift, 1987); and to sustain production levels (Naredo, 1990).

According to Naredo (1990) and Redclift (1987), a *sustainable activity* is one that uses renewable products or at least starts a project that ensures both the renewable production of a substitute good and the handling of waste without harming the environment; governance then arises, being it a dimension that plays an important role when orienting strategic planning. Aguilar (2014) describes the following: The *New Governance*, with less hierarchy, command, and control, in which ideas, actions, and resources of social and economic organizations are more influential, with more direct involvement, going further than traditional instruments of participation such as popular vote, tax contributions, and public opinion.

Sustainability was an unknown topic, and people related it only to environmental matters; it has gained importance nowadays, and it is considered valuable for human evolution. It is composed by three pillars which are economic, environmental, and social; however, for this research, a fourth pillar is taken, managerial, which plays a unique role in the strategy and operation of enterprises. Therefore, the four dimensions of sustainability of the RISE model become the main focus of this research.

Environmental Dimension[4] It is necessary to analyze how enterprises are affecting the environment (in physical, economic, and social matters) by their emissions to the atmosphere, as well as water, energy, and stable waste handling. This dimension refers to the circular economy, a system designed to be restorative and regenerator, which proposes keeping products, components, and materials at their highest use levels (Cerdá & Khalilova, 2016). There is a search for eco-innovation, the action to search for a more competitive, equal, and sustainable economy in which there is improvement in the use of resources, satisfying productive processes using fewer materials and energy; it minimizes the environmental harm due to the use of natural resources, less pollution, and because it creates new demand for goods and services, therefore generating new jobs and entrepreneurial activities (Álvarez, Fernández, & Romera, 2014).

According to ISO 14006 Standard, *eco-design* is known as the integration of environmental aspects in the design and development of products, aimed at reducing adverse impacts to the environment during their life cycles (Rieradevall, Gabarrell, & García, 2009). In the 1992 Rio de Janeiro Earth Summit, it was recognized that *sustainable consumption and production* represents an essential topic, in which environmental and development challenges are tied. During the Soria Moria Conference held in Oslo in February 1994, sustainable consumption was defined as "the use of goods and services that respond to basic needs and bring a better quality of life, while minimizing the use of natural resources, toxic materials and emissions of waste and pollutants over the life cycle, so as not to jeopardize the needs of future generations" (United Nations, 1994).

Green businesses have arisen as an economical option. A green business is an economic activity by which innovation-based goods or services are offered, generating direct environmental benefits (León, 2010). Technology is the main ally to obtain a green, ecological, environmental-friendly product. It is at this point when there is evidence of clean techs, aimed to reduce and avoid pollution by modifying the process and product (Pérez, 2006).

Social Dimension[5] Social, a word originated from the Latin word "Sociales" ("related to or that belongs to a society" or "related to or that belongs to a company or society, the partners or fellow"). Enterprises must consider the human factor; therefore, workers, shareholders, suppliers, competitors, community, workers' families, government institutions, and customers will be the first stakeholders to be benefited by the actions taken by the enterprise, both directly and indirectly. There must be a good governance code, containing clear acting norms and principles. Such governance code is usually composed by recommendations about the conduct of corporations and their members; the idea is that the market positively values its compliance, which encourages enterprises to follow such norms and principles (Ferruz, Marco, & Acero, 2010).

[4]According to Collins Dictionary, environmental "means concerned with the protection of the natural world of land, sea, air, plants, and animals."

[5]Social: it refers to the human factor and the company's stakeholders.

According to Nelson and Winter (1982), people require to have a considerable change in the way they are used to do things if they want to be innovative inside an enterprise. It is necessary to generate new capacities to think and create, which is a quantum (not incremental) leap, coming from the execution of a nondeterministic project that starts with an idea and evolves into different phases (from the generation of an idea to its commercialization), framed by a favorable organizational environment. To succeed, it is necessary to have good leadership, to be able to change paradigms, and to get people involved in collaborative work with more innovative and sustainable processes and in such way creating an optimal working environment for human development (Pérez-Uribe, 2015; Zarate, 2015).

It is necessary to create and consolidate healthy organizational cultures so that stakeholders can find a social dimension well cared for. *Organizational culture* must be guided toward specific objectives, projects, and goals planned (García Álvarez, 2006). According to Pérez-Uribe (2012), organizational culture is an attribute or internal characteristic of the organization, and it is a proper environment for human talent to develop all of its capacities to be able to align with organizational values. To have a healthy social dimension, enterprises must promote a culture in which suppliers are aligned with the enterprises' objectives; it is recommended to have clear and transparent tenders, with standardized regulations to build trust among parties (Aranda, 2016; Concha & Solikova, 2000).

Generations in the twenty-first century are different to twentieth-century generations regarding knowledge and use of technology. The arrival of millennials (who became adults in the year 2000, are around 36 years old now, and are occupying managerial positions) has brought changes in organizations. Twenty-first-century generations have a unique way to work, to act, and to live, and managers must learn to understand and work with them. Technology is part of their life; traveling, experiencing live, and communicating via social media are easy tasks for them (McCrindle & Wolfinger, 2010; Ramírez-Salazar & Pérez-Uribe, 2016). This generation clash requires respect from both sides, adequate coexistence, and new ways to work. When choosing an organization to work for, they pay close attention to the challenges they are going to face in their jobs, because that is an important feature for them. To retain such workers is not easy. However, it is necessary to find ways to do so. It is essential that they get involved in collaborative processes in which they feel that their input, creativity, and originality are required and that they are needed to have a better world. Like this, it is expected that the social dimension has an impact and adds value to their society, their community, their region, their country, and the world.

The Economic Dimension, from Latin "economics meaning related to the economy, efficient and reasonable administration of resources, science that studies the most efficient ways to satisfy human needs." A win-win situation must exist in order to create an economic impact in the society, and it is then when the economic dimension plays an important role in an enterprise. Traditionally, returns were thought to be made to increase the shareholders' wealth; the new thought, based on the economic dimension, is that such wealth must benefit all stakeholders if the enterprise wants to continue operating through time. It is the dimension that must make evident the investments that enterprises make every year in order to benefit their stakeholders. Value creation for people will be reflected in the benefits that the enterprise has established (Porter, 1991; Porter & Kramer, 2002).

Traditionally, value creation was a set of activities that lead the owner or shareholder to obtain a positive and superior benefit than what he/she would obtain with his/her second-best choice. Nowadays, enterprises that follow that approach will have no employees in the future because new generations do not want to work in an enterprise only to enrich others. New generations want to work in enterprises in which benefits and recognition are for all workers who give their best efforts to the enterprises they work for.

The financial model called the circular economy is born to catch the interest from new stakeholders and with the aim to restore what is being harmed in the environment—the concept cradle to cradle consist of promoting the production of goods and services considering sustainability by reducing consumption, time, energy, and waste. This model is based on the rule of reducing, reusing, repairing, and recycling in a continuous circle. The business model for a circular economy wants enterprises to develop new goods and services generating the minimum possible negative impact, following standards that keep its value through time (Leitão, 2015; McDonough & Braungart, 2010; Polo, 2018).

To value the work performed by workers is part of the economic dimension. An adequate and diverse way to recognize jobs assigned, whether in kind or with financial resources, will bring easier retention and better motivation for workers, resulting in more efficiency at work. A worker with low recognition will be as productive as he/she could at his/her best (Jiménez-Rodríguez & Gamboa-Suárez, 2017). Since an enterprise can be more efficient when such strategic decisions are taken, it is of prime importance to review the annual action plan in order to look for strategies that maximize the enterprise's profits, providing that human capital has had the best possible stimuli and that there is high social investment to improve the situation in the communities located nearby the enterprise. On the other side, managers have found a new way to generate value from a collaboration called *corporative voluntary work*, which consists of getting workers involved into supporting others who need their help (Santos & Fernández, 2017; Villar-Gómez, 2015). This is similar to what is practiced in churches; if I have, I can give to others in need.

To summarize, the financial dimension is as important to shareholders as it is to all stakeholders; having a clear strategy in commercial matters, surrounding improvement, technological investment for innovation, and social investment will result in the enterprise's survival, as well as in better liquidity, turnover, and profitability indicators. It is not just about selling to earn a profit; it is also about knowing that the enterprise's actions are causing a positive impact on the society with a good or service that is friendly and healthy; it is not just about selling products to become rich but is also about knowing that the enterprise is collaborating with the country's economy; that is what will make the enterprise different from others and will make it stand out in the industry, resulting in financial indicators that increase in the correct way, which is an example for stakeholders and future generations (Listerri et al., 2002).

Finally, the RISE model includes the **Managerial Dimension**—*managerial*[6] is about administering something. In the RISE model context, the managerial dimension deals with the way of managing or administering the enterprise, aimed at reaching the objectives related to innovation and corporate sustainability. This is why considering the different types of innovation is part of this dimension. According to the Oslo Manual, there are six types of innovation:

1. Product innovation: it refers to the launch of a new or significate product, in which its characteristics are improved.
2. Service innovation: that is, the launch of a new or significantly improved service.
3. Organizational innovation: which refers to the implementation of a new commercial method or in the organization of the workplace, the external relations, or in the internal processes.
4. Innovation of the system: which refers to the interconnected innovations.
5. The innovation of governance: which includes new ways of citizen participation.
6. Social innovation: which refers to the new solutions that satisfy a social need (Casipedia, 2016).

Any innovation chosen by the manager must always go together with the application of best practices in the area and the best possible technology available for the industry. That is the reason why since the 1990s, business certifications/standards started to appear. The objective of such certifications/standards in sustainability and business innovation matters is that managers manage their enterprises in a more qualified way. Table 1 shows the most demanded certifications/standards as well as a brief description of each one of them.

In their daily operations, it is valuable for enterprises to incorporate practices that arise from guidelines suggested by whatever standards they decide to implement. Therefore, adequate knowledge management must be ensured; besides, processes and procedures must be documented, formalized, and open to being monitored (Canals, Boisot, & Cornella, 2003). Whenever a merger or acquisition occurs, a better adaptation, better knowledge transfer, and faster adaptation and integration will take place.

Every enterprise must have clear corporate governance, strategies, principles, norms, and procedures that lead to a healthy organization: an organization that is motivated by good leadership, in which employees, suppliers, customers, the community, and the industry feel proud to be part of it and that stands out because of its world-class social, environmental, economic, and managerial practices (Lefort, 2003).

[6]"Managerial means relating to the work of a manager" according to Collins Dictionary.

Table 1 Standards that improve social, environmental, economic, and managerial practices

Standard	Description
ISO 26000	Set of guides that provide standardized regulations in social responsibility according to what is determined by ISO
AA 1000 Standards	Standard to ensure the quality of sustainability reports in order to comply with the law, the commitment with the regulatory policy, reputation, risk management, and the perception that the enterprise has about its ethics and morals
Global Reporting Initiative (GRI)	It provides specific economic, environmental, and social guidelines that have an important influence on stakeholders when they make decisions
SGE 21: 2008, Sistema de Gestión Ética y Socialmente Responsable	It is centered on fulfilling legislation and norms, Policy of Ethics Management and Social Responsibility, Code of Conduct, Ethics Management and Social Responsibility Committee, dialogue with evaluation groups, review by management, continuous improvement, and Report on Social Responsibility and Communication
Ethos Corporate Social Responsibility Indicators	Indicators that allow enterprises to evaluate the development of strategies, policies, and practices in matters of social responsibility. These indicators comprehensively evaluate CSR, including enterprises' policies and actions from seven dimensions
SA 8000	It actively involves top management. It includes CSR matters in the enterprises' policies. Previously, it is essential to have a management system, usually ISO 9001. It does not involve systematical joint work with external stakeholders
Global Pact	Guidelines that are part of the management, strategy, culture, and daily operations of enterprises. It covers the following four topics: human rights, labor conditions, environment, and anti-corruption
LEED (Leadership in Energy and Environmental Design)	It is based on aspects related to energy efficiency, use of alternative energies, improvement of interior spaces quality, water consumption efficiency, sustainable development of spaces, and material selection
OHSAS 18001	The system of safety and health management in the workplace. The enterprise is certified as one that has developed policies and strategies to guarantee workers safety and health
B Corporation Certification	A B corporation redefines success and gives importance to its financial results as well as to its social and environmental impact on the society

Source: Authors' own table, adapted from Orozco, Acevedo, and Acevedo (2013)

3 Methodology

Based on Hernández-Sampieri, Fernández, and Baptista (2010), this research is descriptive and transversal since data is collected in a single period, and variables are analyzed and correlated in a specific time. The instrument used is the RISE model, which currently is being applied to the whole group of experts.[7] The RISE model matrix includes 4 dimensions and 11 factors, each one with its corresponding descriptors. Each descriptor has five maturity levels:

Level 1: **incipient level**, in which there is a nonexisting or very low relation with the descriptor of the evaluated factor;
Level 2: **developing level**, a basic stage in which there is a partial and/or informal relation with the descriptor of the evaluated factor;
Level 3: **intermediate level**, in which there is evidence that there is an initial, formal, planned way to work toward the descriptor of the evaluated factor;
Level 4: **maturity level**, in which the owner considers important to keep working toward reaching the highest level in order to have his/her enterprise positioned in the industry as innovative and sustainable; and
Level 5: **excellence level**, in which the enterprise stands above other enterprises due to its good practices in innovation and sustainability in national and international scenarios (Pérez-Uribe & Ramirez Salazar, 2018).

The enterprise's assessment is performed using the Matrix.[8] The Matrix must be answered by the general manager (CEO) along with its strategic management team. They must determine the level for each factor by analyzing the general situation regarding each one of the descriptors. The score goes from 1 to 5 according to the description provided in the scoring column.

Currently, there are five diving enterprises; only three of them have a similar process; therefore, they become the sample for this research.

3.1 Enterprise 1 Description: Sonny Dive Shop

Started operations in 1990. It offers Open Water, Advance, Rescue, and Dive Master services (Table 2).[9]

---

[7]Coordinating team: five members—four holding a Ph.D. degree and one holding a master's degree. Collaborator team: 12 professors with expertise and research background in all 11 factors.

[8]By August 2018, using an Excel matrix. In a later stage, a matrix in a Web questionnaire and an APP that automatically calculate results are going to be sent to participating managers.

[9]Categories are those levels in which a diver can get a certificate. This means that, first, it is necessary to get the Open Water certificate to be able to start the Advance certification and so on.

Table 2 Sonny Dive Shop financial indicators

ENTERPRISE: Sonny Dive Shop				FINANCIAL PROFILE			
Financial data on Dec 31 (thousands of COP)	2015	2016	2017	Data in thousands of COP($000,00)	2015	2016	2017
				DATA AND INDICATORS			
TOTAL ASSETS	380	395	410	RETURN ON ASSETS	47,37	16,20	47,80
EQUITY	320	340	385	RETURN ON INVESTMENT (ROI)(ROE-RETURN ON EQUITY)	10,31	10,59	7,79
OPERATING INCOME	280	250	295	NET MARGIN	11,79	14,40	10,17
GROSS PROFIT	150	170	70	GROSS MARGIN	53,57	68,00	23,73
OPERTING PROFIT	180	64	196	OPERATING MARGIN	64,29	25,60	66,44
PROFIT AND LOSS	33	36	30				

Source: Authors' own table

3.2 *Enterprise 2 Description: Ocean Paradise Scuba Dive*

Was founded in 2017 and has a strategic alliance with Hotel Deep Blue. It offers Open Water, Advance, Rescue, and Dive Master services (Table 3).

3.3 *Enterprise 3 Description: Sirius Dive Center*

Founded in 2011, the Hotel Sirius is strategically located. It offers services of Open Water, Advance, Rescue, and Dive Master (Table 4).

Table 3 Financial data for Ocean Paradise Scuba Dive[a]

ENTERPRISE: Ocean Paradise Scuba Dive				FINANCIAL PROFILE			
Financial data on Dec 31 (thousands of COP)	2015	2016	2017	Data in thousands of COP($000,00)	2015	2016	2017
				DATA AND INDICATORS			
TOTAL ASSETS			16	RETURN ON ASSETS			256,25
EQUITY			15	RETURN ON INVESTMENT (ROI)(ROE-RETURN ON EQUITY)			60,00
OPERATING INCOME			56	NET MARGIN			16,07
GROSS PROFIT			13	GROSS MARGIN			23,21
OPERTING PROFIT			41	OPERATING MARGIN			73,21
PROFIT AND LOSS			9				

Source: Authors' own table

[a]Data only for 2017, considering that has been operating for just 1 year so far

Table 4 Financial data for Sirius Dive Center

ENTERPRISE: SIRIUS DIVE CENTER				FINANCIAL PROFILE			
Financial data on Dec 31 (thousands of COP)	2015	2016	2017	Data in thousands of COP($000,00)	2015	2016	2017
				DATA AND INDICATORS			
TOTAL ASSETS	254	267	315	RETURN ON ASSETS	24,80	23,97	41,27
EQUITY	210	233	281	RETURN ON INVESTMENT (ROI)(ROE-RETURN ON EQUITY)	16,67	9,01	12,46
OPERATING INCOME	179	98	199	NET MARGIN	19,55	21,43	17,59
GROSS PROFIT	114	35	70	GROSS MARGIN	63,69	35,71	35,18
OPERTING PROFIT	63	64	130	OPERATING MARGIN	35,20	65,31	65,33
PROFIT AND LOSS	35	21	35				

Source: Authors' own table

4 Results Analysis

The EAN-RISE model (a scientific EAN model of business evaluation) was applied, providing data that shows the current situation in which diving schools from Providencia y Santa Catalina operate. The model considered the 4 sustainability dimensions and 11 factors. The following table shows the results obtained (Table 5):

Then, each one of the 4 dimensions and 11 factors is analyzed to assess the diving enterprises and to evaluate the results, following the corresponding methodology (Fig. 1). Ocean Paradise excels at the sustainable production factor with a score of 100%. The other two enterprises scored less than 60%. For the new markets factor, Sonny Dive Shop and Sirius Dive Center obtained an 80% score. However, 6 out of 11 factors scored 20% in all three enterprises. These factors are strategic direction, organizational culture, recognition, collaborative processes, technology, and financial indicators. Overall, the average for the dimension for each enterprise is Ocean Paradise Scuba Dive (35%), Sonny Dive Shop (38%), and Sirius Dive Center (38%). All enterprises scored low in the social dimension; therefore, they require a priority intervention.

Table 5 Comparative table among enterprises (dimensions and factors of the EAN-RISE model)

FINAL REPORT. EAN RISE DIMENSIONS AND FACTORS	ENTERPRISE	INNOVATION	SUSTAINABLE PRODUCTION	LEADERSHIP	STRATEGIC DIRECTION	ORGANIZATIONAL CULTURE	RECOGNITION	COLLABORATIVE PROCESSES	GOVERNANCE	NEW MARKETS	TECHNOLOGY	FINANCIAL INDICATORS	AVERAGE BY DIMENSION
Social	Ocean Paradise Scuba Dive	60	100	40	20	20	20	20	20	20	20	20	35%
	Sonny Dive Shop	60	60	40	20	20	20	20	60	80	20	20	38%
	Sirius Dive Center	60	60	40	20	20	20	20	60	80	20	20	38%
Environmental	Ocean Paradise Scuba Dive	40	28	20	80	80	80	80	20	20	80	20	60%
	Sonny Dive Shop	70	24	40	80	80	80	80	40	60	80	20	59%
	Sirius Dive Center	70	24	40	80	80	80	80	40	60	80	20	59%
Managerial	Ocean Paradise Scuba Dive	40	20	20	60	60	60	60	60	20	60	20	52%
	Sonny Dive Shop	80	60	40	60	60	60	60	60	80	60	20	58%
	Sirius Dive Center	80	60	40	60	60	60	60	60	80	60	20	58%
Economic	Ocean Paradise Scuba Dive	40	20	20	40	40	40	40	20	20	40	20	37%
	Sonny Dive Shop	80	20	40	40	40	40	40	60	80	40	20	45%
	Sirius Dive Center	80	20	40	40	40	40	40	60	80	40	20	45%
AVERAGE BY FACTOR		63	41	35	72	50	50%	50%	47%	57%	50%	20%	

Source: Authors' own table

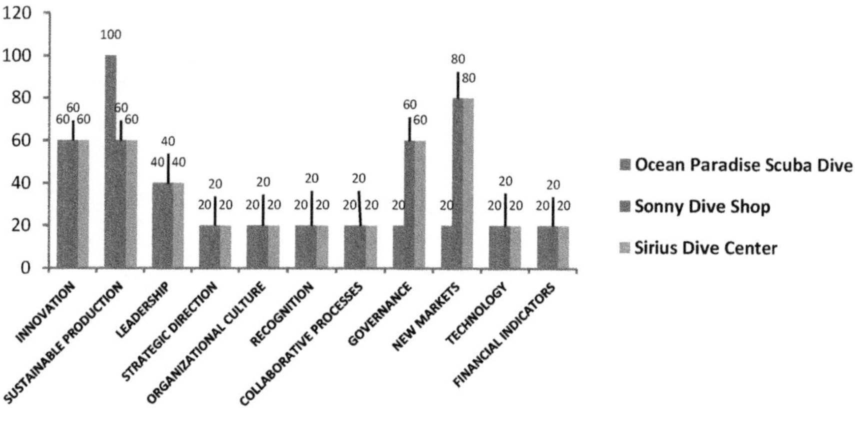

Fig. 1 Consolidated data for social dimension. Source: Authors' own figure

For the environmental dimension (Fig. 2), all enterprises scored high, with 80% in strategic direction, organizational culture, recognition, collaborative processes, and technology. Factors with low scores and therefore at risk are sustainable production (20–28%) and financial indicators (20%).

Overall, the average for the dimension for each enterprise is Ocean Paradise Scuba Dive (60%), Sonny Dive Shop (59%), and Sirius Dive Center (59%). In this dimension, enterprises require a medium priority, being necessary to correct the factors that affect the competitiveness of such dimension.

Sonny Dive Shop and Sirius Dive Center scored 80% in innovation and new markets, being those the highest scores. Riskiest factors for all three enterprises are financial indicators (20%) and leadership (20% and 40%). Overall, three enterprises got a fair average, scoring as follows: Ocean Paradise Scuba Dive (52%), Sonny Dive Shop (58%), and Sirius Dive Center (58%) (Fig. 3).

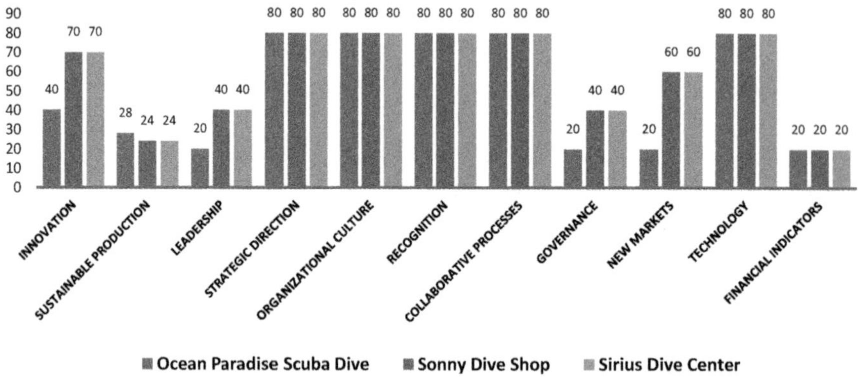

Fig. 2 Consolidated data for environmental dimension. Source: Authors' own figure

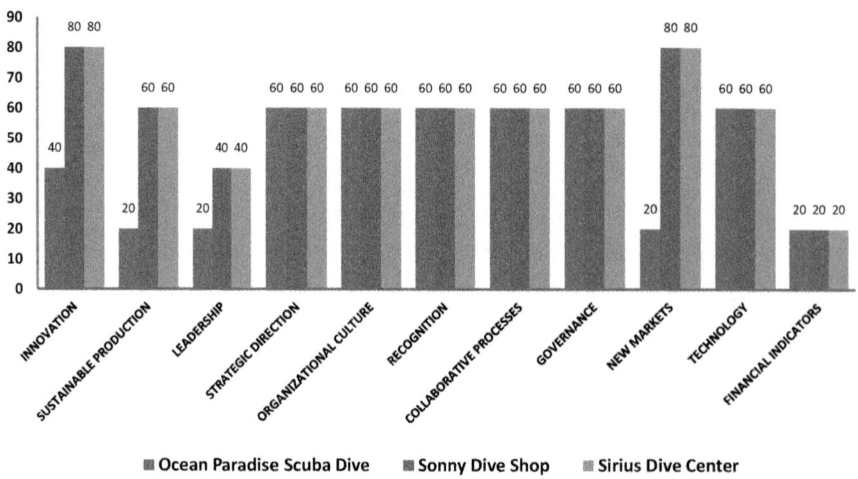

Fig. 3 Consolidated data for managerial dimension. Source: Authors' own figure

Seven factors with incipient level in all dimensions were found, being those are sustainable production (20%), financial indicators (20%), leadership (20% and 40%), strategic direction (40%), organizational culture (40%), recognition (40%), collaborative processes (40%), and technology (40%). The average of all three enterprises for the economic dimension is very low (Ocean Paradise Scuba Dive 37%, Sonny Dive Shop 45%, and Sirius Dive Center 45%), meaning that an intervention as soon as possible is needed (Fig. 4).

As Fig. 5 shows, social and economic dimensions are the first to intervene, given the fact that all three enterprises obtained scores lower than 50%, what locates them between the second and third maturity levels. The other must be consolidated so enterprises of San Andres, Providencia y Santa Catalina can stand out in the region and become an example for all diving enterprises in the Caribbean. Ocean Paradise obtained the lowest score, 46%, while the other two enterprises scored 50%.

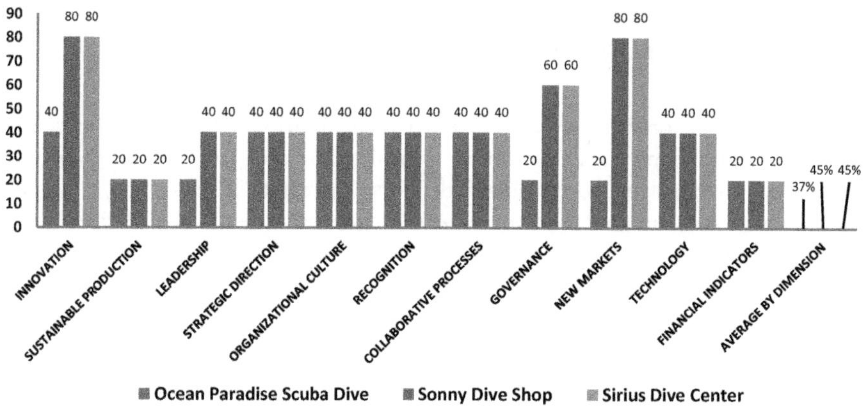

Fig. 4 Consolidated data for economic dimension. Source: Authors' own figure

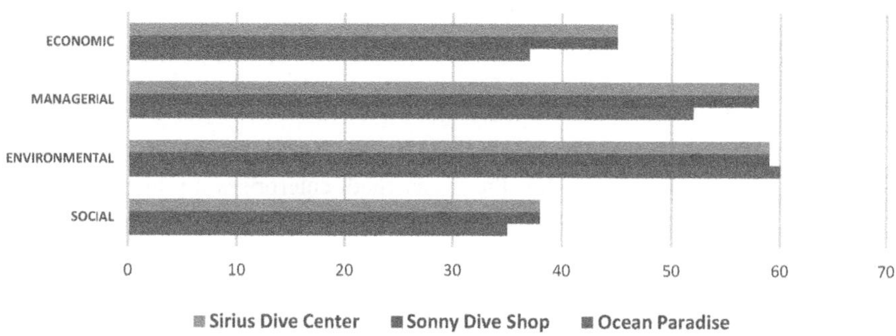

Fig. 5 General comparison of dimensions per enterprise. Source: Authors' own figure

Table 6 Factor prioritization matrix

Consolidated report of the EAN-RISE model	Factors (average)	Priority
Innovation	63%	Medium
Sustainable production	41%	Top
Leadership	35%	Top
Strategic direction	72%	Low
Organizational culture	50%	Medium
Recognition	50%	Medium
Collaborative processes	50%	Medium
Governance	47%	Top
New markets	57%	Medium
Technology	50%	Medium
Financial indicators	20%	Top

Source: Authors' own table

4.1 *Best Practices Manual Proposal*

Each of the 11 factors was analyzed to evaluate the priority in the interventions. The following figure shows four factors in critical condition: sustainable production, leadership, governance, and financial indicators. Therefore, it is necessary to implement an improvement plan to increase the scores to move them to the desired levels 4 and 5 (Table 6).

4.2 *Best Practices Plan*

The innovation and sustainability route suggested to companies is presented below (Table 7).

5 Conclusions

This study provides benefits for the researched enterprises in all dimensions covered by this project. There are environmental benefits such as preservation of nonrenewable resources, a decrease in operational expenses, reduction of raw material consumption, preservation of fauna and flora, and commitment and empowerment of all those involved in adopting better sustainable practices. Regarding managerial benefits, there will be clear policies and guidelines that will lead operations toward sustainable development. Benefits in the economic dimension include the evidence of the added value generated by the enterprise's investment in projects that have a positive impact in the community. Finally, there are social benefits such as

Table 7 Consolidated table of activities and indicators of success

Dimension	Descriptor	Activities to move to levels 4 and 5	Indicators of success
Sustainable production factor			
Social	Suppliers	To implement a supplier policy that considers eco-efficient, eco-innovative, environment-friendly purchases	Total number of purchases done under the eco-efficient suppliers' policies
Environmental	Water-electricity-air-solid waste	(1) Water and electricity. Water and electricity saving campaigns. Water storage during rainy seasons. Implementation of a monitoring system of water and electricity consumption. Implementation of clean techs. Incentives to reduce consumption. (2) Air. Use of environmental-friendly bio-oils to fight pollution caused by boats. (3) Solid waste. Reuse, reduction, and recycling of waste generated by diving schools	Total value paid for electricity and water in 2018 compared to the same value in 2017
Managerial	Planning, paperwork, certifications	To adopt the RNT (National Tourism Registration) standard and get certified on NTS, Technical Industry Norms for the industry. Try to become a B corporation	The number of certifications compared to the number of certifications of the competitors
Economic	Environmental management Budget	To assign 15% of the annual budget to restore the ecosystem where diving enterprises operate	Percentage assigned to environmental management in 2018 from the 2018 budget
Leadership factor			
Social	Mobilizing capacity	To implement the annual program of intrapreneurship and innovation	Number of intrapreneurships 2018/number of intrapreneurships 2017
Environmental	Sustainability	Incentives plan for achievements in sustainability matters	Total number of incentives given for sustainability/total number of incentives given in all matters
Managerial	Knowledge management	To train workers in management, monitoring, and surveillance of the enterprise's information	Total number of workers trained/total number of workers
Economic	Decision-making/clear path to follow	Balance score card implementation to evaluate each objective regarding the expected result and assigned budget	The total number of goals fulfilled in 2018/total number of goals expected to be fulfilled in 2018

(continued)

Table 7 (continued)

Dimension	Descriptor	Activities to move to levels 4 and 5	Indicators of success
Governance factor			
Social	Ethics, values and anti-corruption policies	To create a system to promote and educate workers, customers, and suppliers	Number of people trained in anti-corruption matters/total number of people in the enterprise
Environmental	Environmental management plan	To design the enterprise's Environmental Management Plan	Annual Results Report compared to the objectives proposed in the PMA
Managerial	Corporate governance	To structure principles and norms collaboratively	Number of workers who know the enterprise's principles compared to the total number of workers
Economic	Shared value	To design a program to evidence the social investment in the enterprise's workers; workers give back with knowledge and new projects	Total investment in shared value compared to total investments
Financial indicators			
Social	Impact on the society	To create a committee with the community to evidence how the enterprise has made an impact on it	Total number of meetings/ total number of people nonconformist
Environmental	Environment protection and restoration	To measure the investment in environmental programs.	2018 budget for the environmental programs/2017 budget
Managerial	Economic Value Added (EVA)	To measure the added value generated by the enterprise's activities	Total number of objectives that generate value/total number of objectives
Economic	Financial performance	To measure last year's financial performance 1. Debt 2. Liquidity 3. Profitability	Percentage of last year's financial performance compared to the previous year's financial performance

Source: Authors' own table

the contribution to the progress of the community, the preservation of local customs and traditions, a boost to consumption of local goods and services, and therefore the improvement of the quality of life of people in the San Andres Archipelago.

The RISE model is successfully validated in tourism enterprises, and it becomes a guide so consultants can evaluate enterprises and propose improvement paths. All three diving enterprises analyzed show low levels of maturity in most dimensions, being the social and economic dimensions the most critical situation. This proves the need to prepare managers in corporate finances, strategic direction, and human talent management so that they can move their enterprises to higher levels of business practices.

References

Aguilar, L. (2014). *Las dimensiones y los niveles de la gobernanza*. Retrieved from https://revistas.ucm.es/index.php/CGAP/article/viewFile/45156/42518

Alba Torres, S. (2015). *Cinco lugares para bucear en Colombia – Revista Diners*. Retrieved from https://revistadiners.com.co/ocio/31031_cinco-lugares-bucear-colombia/

Álvarez, M. J., Fernández, R. I., & Romera, R. (2014). ¿Es la eco-innovación una estrategia inteligente de especialización para Andalucía? Una aproximación desde el análisis multivariante. *Revista de Estudios Regionales, 100*, 171–195.

Aranda, L. E. (2016). *La gerencia de la felicidad: Un nuevo modelo para la gestión de las organizaciones. Trabajo de grado presentado como requisito para optar al título de: Especialista en Alta Gerencia*. Universidad Militar Nueva Granada (Colombia). Retrieved from https://repository.unimilitar.edu.co/bitstream/handle/10654/15964/ArandaLeytonEdgar2016.pdf;jsessionid=CEAA9D4A9DE106C2D86C865842514900?sequence=1

Berrone, P. (2016, September 15). *How to succeed at sustainability (and why greenwashing doesn't work)*. Retrieved from https://www.forbes.com/sites/iese/2016/09/15/how-to-succeed-at-sustainability-and-why-greenwashing-doesnt-work/#70b05670124e

Blázquez, F., Dorta, J. A., & Verona, M. C. (2006). Factores del crecimiento empresarial. Especial referencia a las pequeñas y medianas empresas. *Innovar, 16*(28), 43–56.

Canals, A., Boisot, M., & Cornella, A. (2003). *Gestión del conocimiento*. Madrid: Gestión.

Casipedia. (2016). *A data base with over 500 sustainable innovation cases*. Retrieved from http://www.casi2020.eu/casipedia/cases

Cerdá, E., & Khalilova, A. (2016). *Economía circular*. Retrieved from http://www.minetad.gob.es/Publicaciones/Publicacionesperiodicas/EconomiaIndustrial/RevistaEconomiaIndustrial/401/CERD%C3%81%20y%20KHALILOVA.pdf

CITUR – Centro de Información Turística. (2018). *Estadísticas Nacionales-Flujo de Turistas -Turismo Receptor*. Retrieved from http://citur.linktic.com/estadisticas/df_viajeros_ciudad_destino/all/2

Concha Velásquez, J. R., & Solikova, A. (2000). Relaciones a largo plazo entre compradores y proveedores: La importancia de la tecnología en el desarrollo de la confianza. *Estudios gerenciales, 16*(76), 13–25.

Coppola, M. (2016). *7 Tendencias de viaje para el 2017 que impactaran en la industria turística global*. Retrieved from https://www.trekksoft.com/es/blog/7-tendencias-viaje-2017-industria-turistica-global

Diario El Heraldo. (2016). *Turismo aportó 5.200 millones de dólares al PIB*. Retrieved from https://www.elheraldo.co/economia/turismo-aporto-5200-millones-de-dolares-al-pib-245250

Eizenberg, E., & Jabareen, Y. (2017). Social sustainability: A new conceptual framework. *Sustainability, 9*, 68. Retrieved from https://www.mdpi.com/2071-1050/9/1/68/pdf. https://doi.org/10.3390/su9010068

El Clima. (2018). *El buceo*. Retrieved from http://www.elclima.com.mx/el_buceo.htm

Entorno Turístico. (2018). *¿Qué es el turismo de aventura?* Retrieved from https://www.entornoturistico.com/que-es-el-turismo-de-aventura/

Epstein, M., & Mantilla, S. (2009). *Sostenibilidad empresarial: Administración y medición de los impactos sociales, ambientes y economía*. ProQuest Ebook Central. Retrieved from http://ebookcentral.proquest.com/lib/bibliotecaeansp/detail.action?docID=3198202

Ferruz, L., Marco, I., & Acero, I. (2010). *Códigos de buen gobierno: Un análisis comparativo. Especial incidencia en el caso español*. Retrieved from http://www.redalyc.org/pdf/4959/495950242001.pdf

García Álvarez, C. M. (2006). Una aproximación al concepto de cultura organizacional. *Universitas Psychologica, 5*(1), 163–174.

Gobernación de San Andrés, Providencia y Santa Catalina. (2016). *Plan Departamental de Gestión del Riesgo-Archipiélago de San Andrés, Providencia y Santa Catalina*. Retrieved from http://repositorio.gestiondelriesgo.gov.co/handle/20.500.11762/383

Hernández-Sampieri, R., Fernández, C., & Baptista, M. (2010). *Metodología de la Investigación* (5th ed.). Retrieved from https://www.esup.edu.pe/descargas/dep_investigacion/Metodologia%20de%20la%20investigaci%C3%B3n%205ta%20Edici%C3%B3n.pdf

Hosteltur. (2015). *Turismo de aventura: crecimiento a la vista y tendencias*. Retrieved from https://www.hosteltur.com/110225_turismo-aventura-crecimiento-vista-tendencias.html

ILO. (2012). *World of Work Report 2012 Better jobs for a better economy*. Retrieved from https://www.ilo.org/wcmsp5/groups/public/@dgreports/@dcomm/@publ/documents/publication/wcms_179453.pdf

James Cruz, J. L., & Márquez Calle, G. (2011). Valoración económica del buceo como estrategia de uso sostenible de la biodiversidad marina, Archipiélago de San Andrés y Providencia, Caribe Colombiano. *Gestión y Ambiente, 14*(1), 37–54.

Jiménez Rodríguez, L. A., & Gamboa Suárez, R. (2017). Gestión de valoración como estrategia de reconocimiento laboral del talento clave en empresas sociales del estado. *Desarrollo Gerencial, 9*(1), 144–159.

Lefort, F. (2003). Gobierno corporativo: ¿qué es? y ¿cómo andamos por casa? *Cuadernos de economía, 40*(120), 207–237.

Leitão, A. (2015). Economía circular: Uma nova filosofía de gestão para o séc. XXI. *Portuguese Journal of Finance, Management and Accounting, 1*(2), 149–171.

León, M. (2010). Reactivación económica para el Buen Vivir: Un acercamiento. *América Latina en movimiento, 452*, 23–26.

Listerri, J., Angelelli, P., Painter, F., Chrisney, M., Nieder, F., Micro, A., & Wilson, S. (2002). *Guía operativa para programas de competitividad para la pequeña y mediana empresa. Informe de trabajo*. Washington: Banco Interamericano de Desarrollo.

McCrindle, M., & Wolfinger, E. (2010). *The A, B, C of XYZ understanding the global generations* (237 pp.). ISBN 1742230350,9781742230351.

McDonough, W., & Braungart, M. (2010). *Cradle to cradle: Remaking the way we make things*. New York: North Point Press.

Naredo, J. M. (1990). La economía y su medio ambiente. *Ekonomiaz: Revista vasca de economía, 17*, 12–25.

Nelson, R. R., & Winter, S. G. (1982). The Schumpeterian tradeoff revisited. *The American Economic Review, 72*(1), 114–132.

Orozco, Y. D., Acevedo, M. C., & Acevedo, J. R. (2013). Responsabilidad social empresarial: Teorías, índices, estándares y certificaciones. *Cuadernos De Administración, 29*(50), 196–206.

PADI. (2018). *10 propósitos de buceo para 2018*. Retrieved from https://www2.padi.com/blog/es/2018/01/11/10-propositos-de-buceo-para-2018/

Pérez, E. H. (2006). *Desarrollo de alternativas de tratamiento de aguas residuales industriales mediante el uso de tecnologías limpias dirigidas al reciclaje y/o valoración de contaminantes*. Ph.D. dissertation, Universitat de València. Retrieved from http://roderic.uv.es/handle/10550/15133

Pérez-Uribe, R. (2012). *El ambiente laboral y su incidencia en el desempeño de las organizaciones: Estudio de las mejores empresas para trabajar en Colombia*. Bogota, Colombia: EAN University.

Pérez-Uribe, R. (2015). Componentes organizacionales que explican la sostenibilidad de la gestión humana en las pymes bogotanas. In D. Argüelles & J. M. Saiz-Alvarez (Eds.), *Gestión de la sostenibilidad en el marco de las organizaciones* (pp. 130–162). Bogota, Colombia: EAN University.

Pérez-Uribe, R., & Ramirez Salazar, M. P. (2018). *Organizational components that explain the management of innovation and knowledge in Colombian Smes* (pp. 1–27). IGI Global. https://doi.org/10.4018/978-1-5225-3543-0.ch001.

Polo, D. (2018). *¿Qué es la economía circular?* Retrieved from https://www.gestionar-facil.com/enconomia-circular-28-ejemplos/

Porter, M. E. (1991). *La ventaja competitiva de las naciones* (Vol. 1025). Buenos Aires: Vergara.

Porter, M. E., & Kramer, M. R. (2002). The competitive advantage of corporate philanthropy. *Harvard Business Review, 80*(12), 56–68.

Prato, J., & Newball, R. (2015). *Aproximación a la Valoración Económica Ambiental del departamento archipiélago de San Andrés, Providencia y Santa Catalina Reserva de Biósfera de Seaflower.* Retrieved from www.cco.gov.co/docs/publicaciones/valoracion-seaflower.pdf

Ramírez-Salazar, M. P., & Pérez-Uribe, R. (2016). Open collaborative innovation: Booster of solutions for the challenges of a global world – Collaborative processes and innovation networks create value. In I. Hosu & I. Iancu (Eds.), *Digital entrepreneurship and global innovation* (pp. 18–36). Hershey, PA: IGI Global.

Redclift, M. (1987). The production of nature and the reproduction of the species. *Antipode, 19*(2), 222–230.

Revista Dinero. (2018). *Colombia: Récord en visitas de turistas en 2017.* Retrieved from https://www.dinero.com/pais/articulo/record-de-turistas-en-colombia-2017/255180

Rieradevall, J., Gabarrell, X., & Garcia, R. (2009). *Guía Práctica de introducción ecodiseño* (p. 64). Generalitat Valenciana.

Salvo, S., & Kitsos, E. (2016). *Programa internacional de voluntariado ambiental "Ocean Initiatives".* Centro Nacional de Educación Ambiental CENEAM. Retrieved from https://www.mapama.gob.es/es/ceneam/quienes-somos/

Sánchez-Jabba, A. (2012). *Manejo Ambiental en Seaflower: Reserva de Biosfera en el Archipiélago de San Andrés, Providencia y Santa Catalina.* San Andrés, Colombia: Adolfo Meisel Roca.

Santos, P. G., & Fernández, J. F. (2017). Strategies for corporate volunteer programs. *Universia Business Review, 55*, 34–63.

Shiva, V., & Bandyopadhyay, J. (1989). Development, poverty and the growth of the green movement in India. *Ecologist, 19*, 111–117.

Trekksoft. (2016). *Tendencias de viaje para el 2017 que impactaran en la industria turística global.* Retrieved from https://www.trekksoft.com/es/blog/7-tendencias-viaje-2017-industria-turistica-global

UNESCO. (2000). The MAB programe. *Biosphere Reserves Directory.* Accessed March 27, 2011, from http://www.unesco.org/mabdb/br/brdir/directory/biores.asp?mode=all&code=COL+05

UNESCO. (2006, September 27). *Our common future.* Brundtland Report. Retrieved from https://desarrollosostenible.wordpress.com/2006/09/27/informe-brundtland/http://www.unesco.org/new/fileadmin/MULTIMEDIA/FIELD/Havana/pdf/Cap3.pdf

United Nations. (1994). *United Nations terms. Definition of sustainable consumption.* Retrieved from https://uterm.un.org/UNTERM/Display/record/UNHQ/sustainable_consumption/925E0D371E6561D185256EA8005651D6

UNWTO. (2016). *UNWTO Annual Report 2015.* Retrieved from http://www2.unwto.org/publication/unwto-annual-report-2015

Villar Gómez, R. (2015). *Recursos privados para la transformación social: filantropía e inversión social privada en América Latina hoy.* Argentina – Brasil – Colombia – México. Bogota, Colombia: Grupo de Fundaciones y Empresas, Asociación de Fundaciones Empresariales.

World Tourism Organization. (2017). *Panorama OMT del turismo internacional.* Retrieved from https://www.e-unwto.org/doi/pdf/10.18111/9789284419043

Zarate Torres, R. (2015). *Liderazgo como factor clave en la sostenibilidad empresarial. Gestión De La Sostenibilidad en el Marco de las Organizaciones* (pp. 107–128). Bogota, Colombia: Publicaciones EAN.

Printed by Printforce, the Netherlands